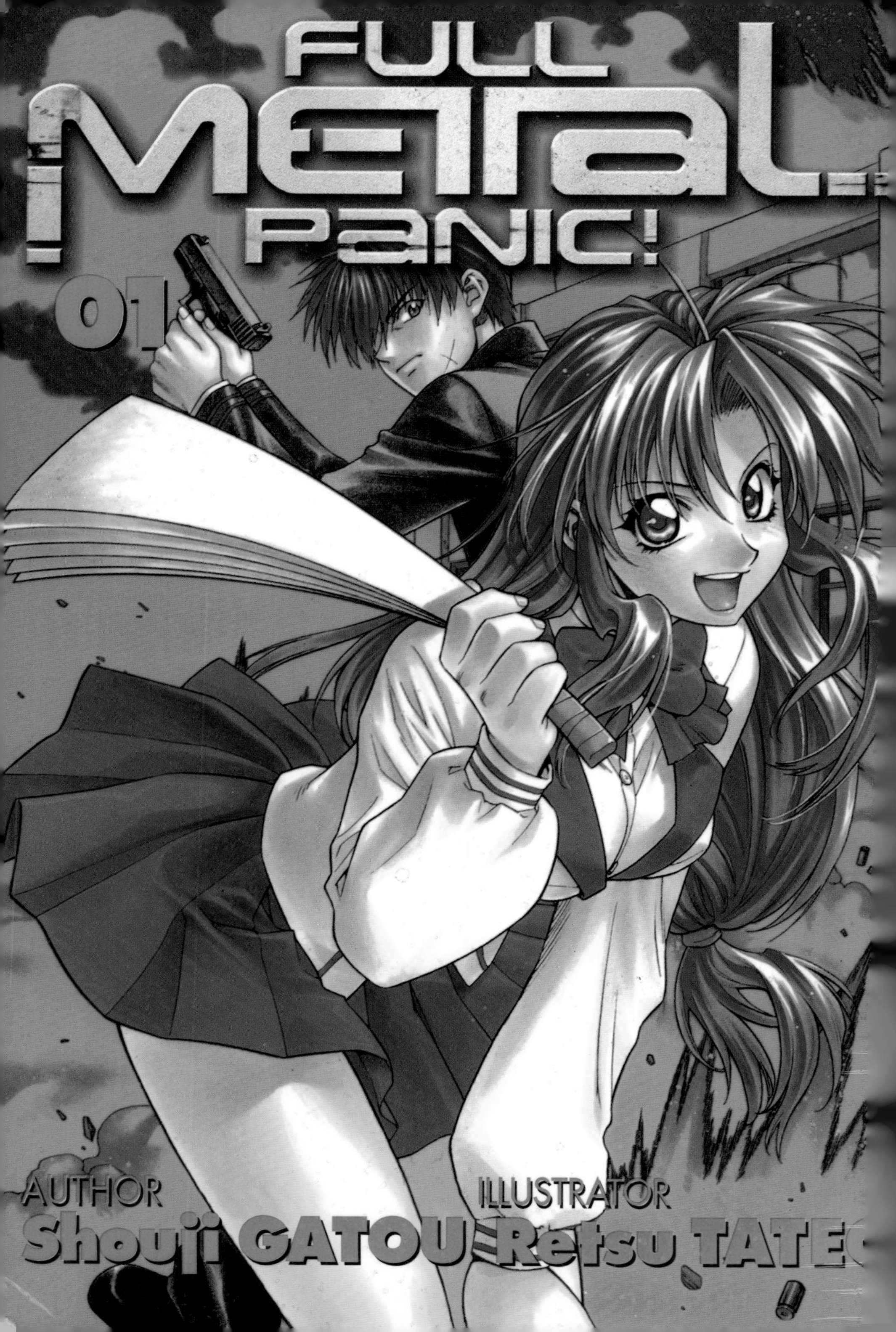
FULL
METAL
PANIC!
01
AUTHOR
Shouji GATOU
ILLUSTRATOR
Retsu TATE

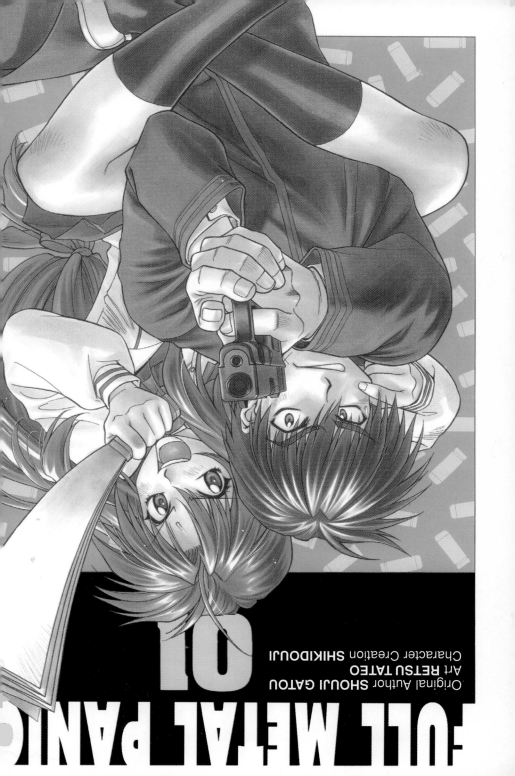

FULL METAL PANIC!

01

Original Author **SHOUJI GATOU**
Art **RETSU TATEO**
Character Creation **SHIKIDOUJI**

FULL METAL PANIC!

CONTENTS

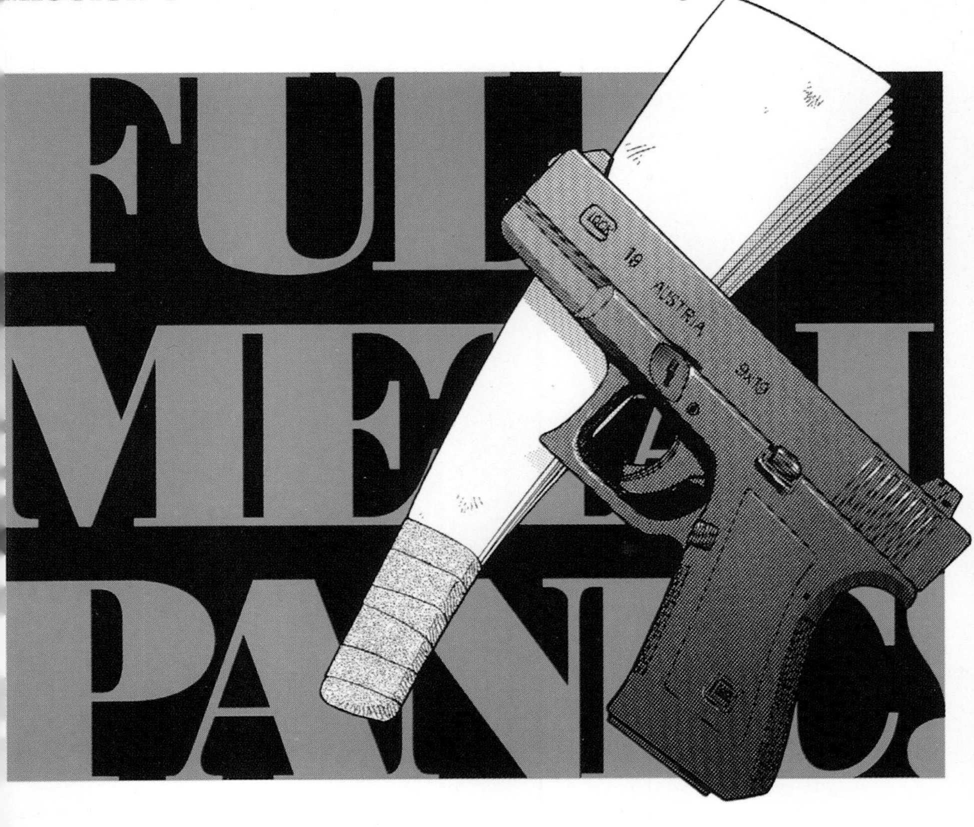

FULL METAL PANIC!
19
AUSTRIA
9x19

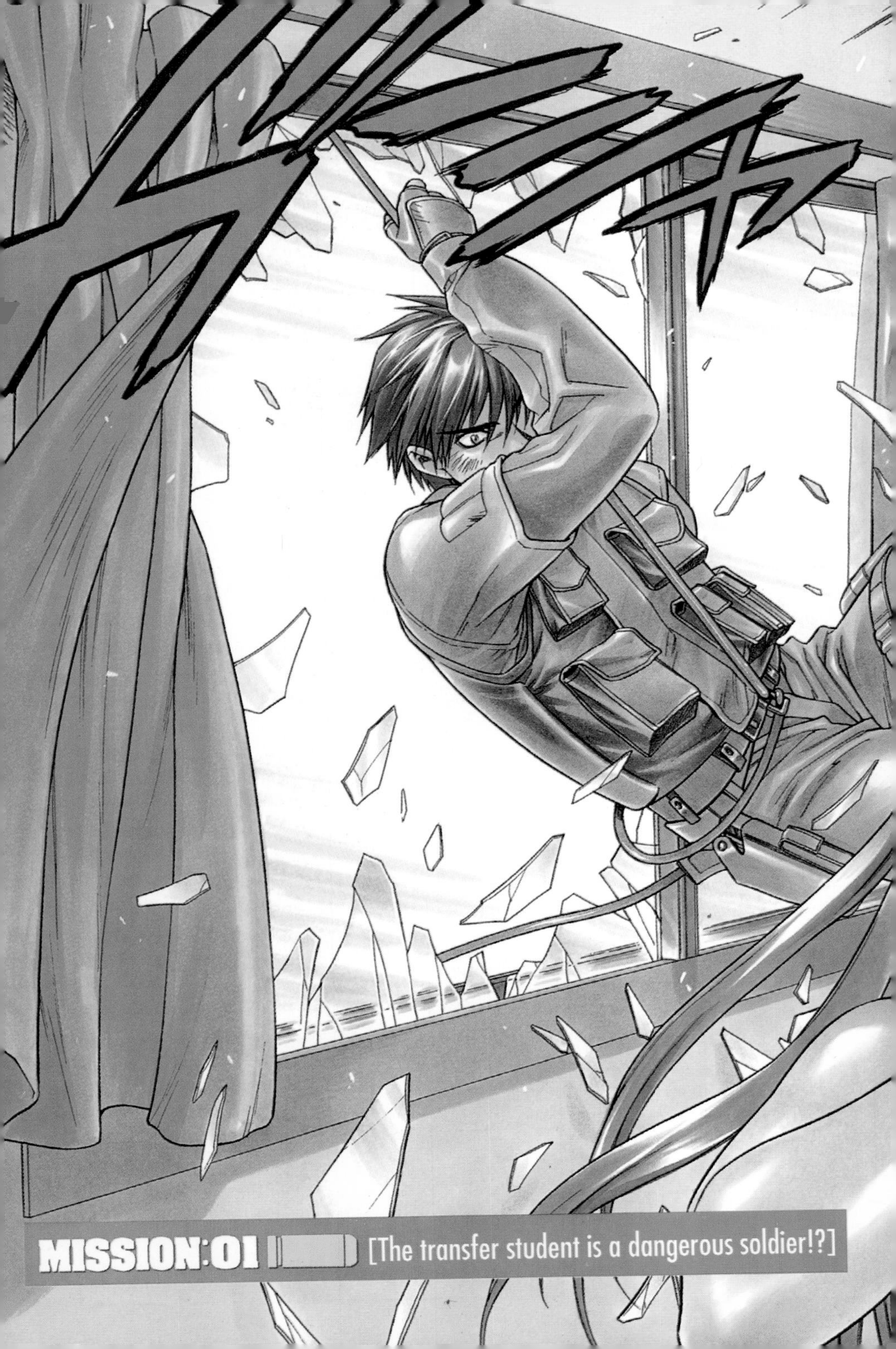
MISSION:01
[The transfer student is a dangerous soldier!?]

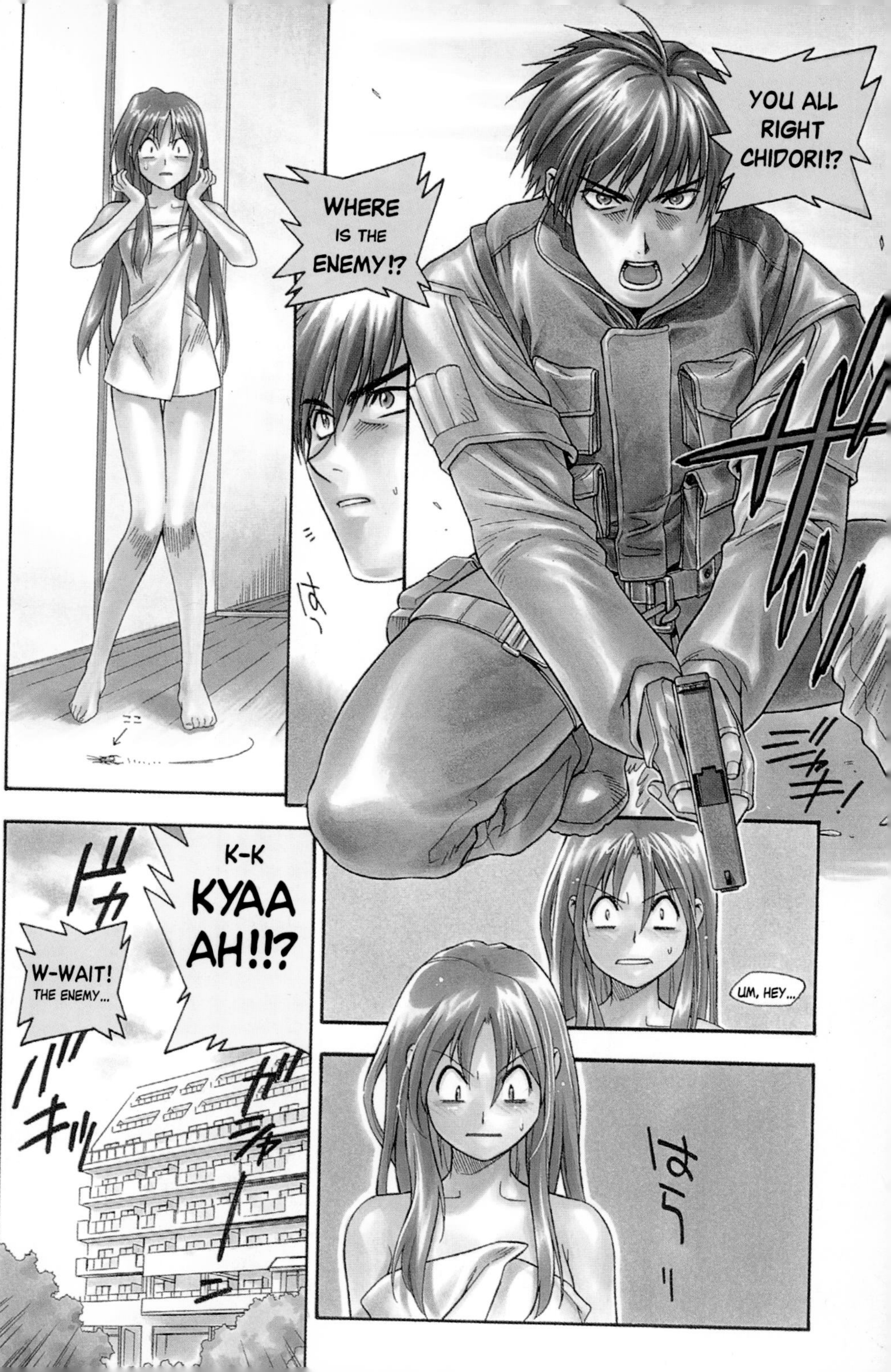
YOU ALL RIGHT CHIDORI!?
WHERE IS THE ENEMY!?
UM, HEY...
K-K KYAA AH!!?
W-WAIT! THE ENEMY...

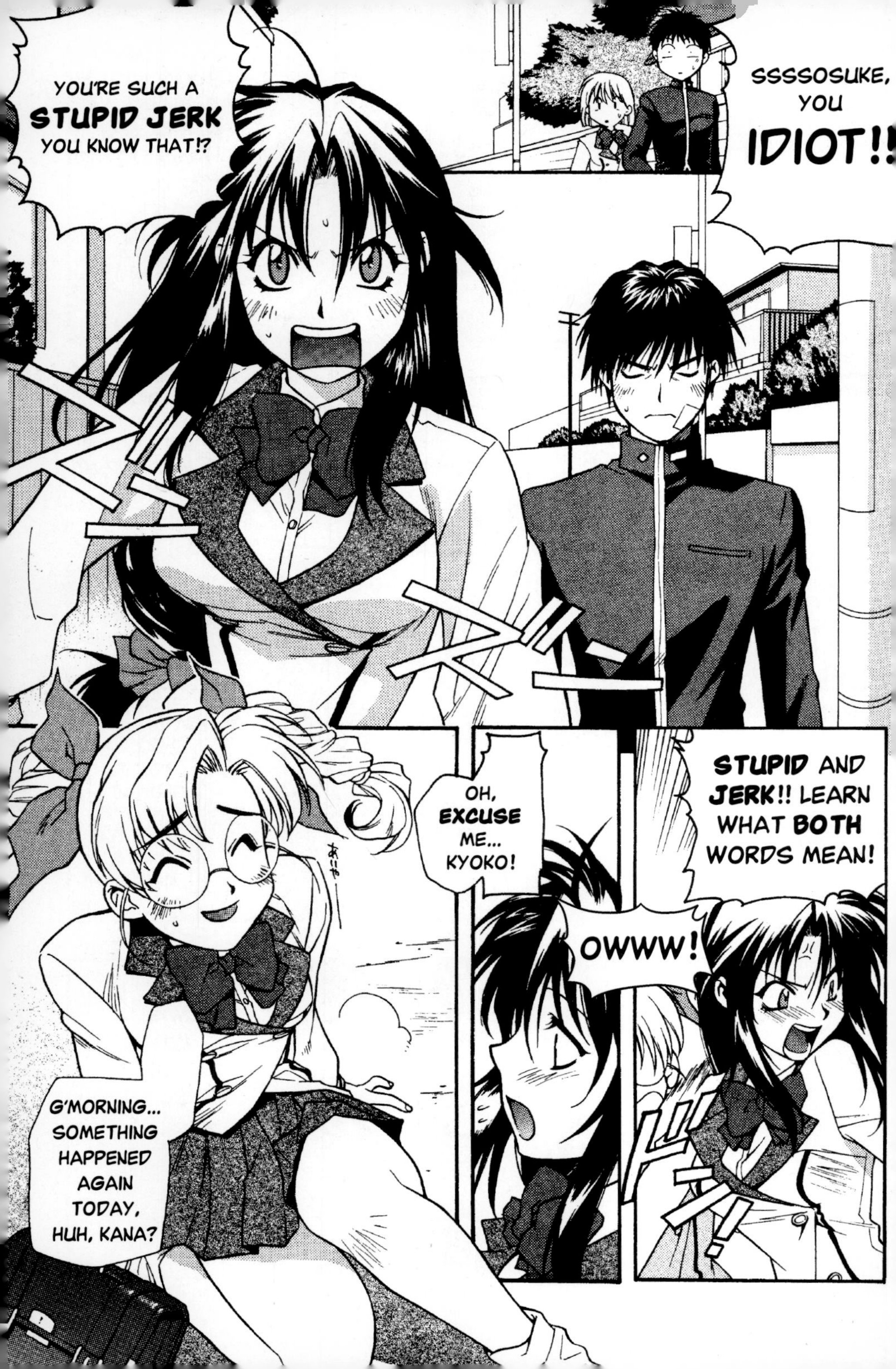
SSSSOSUKE, YOU IDIOT!!
YOU'RE SUCH A STUPID JERK YOU KNOW THAT!?
STUPID AND JERK!! LEARN WHAT BOTH WORDS MEAN!
OWWW!
OH, EXCUSE ME... KYOKO!
G'MORNING... SOMETHING HAPPENED AGAIN TODAY, HUH, KANA?

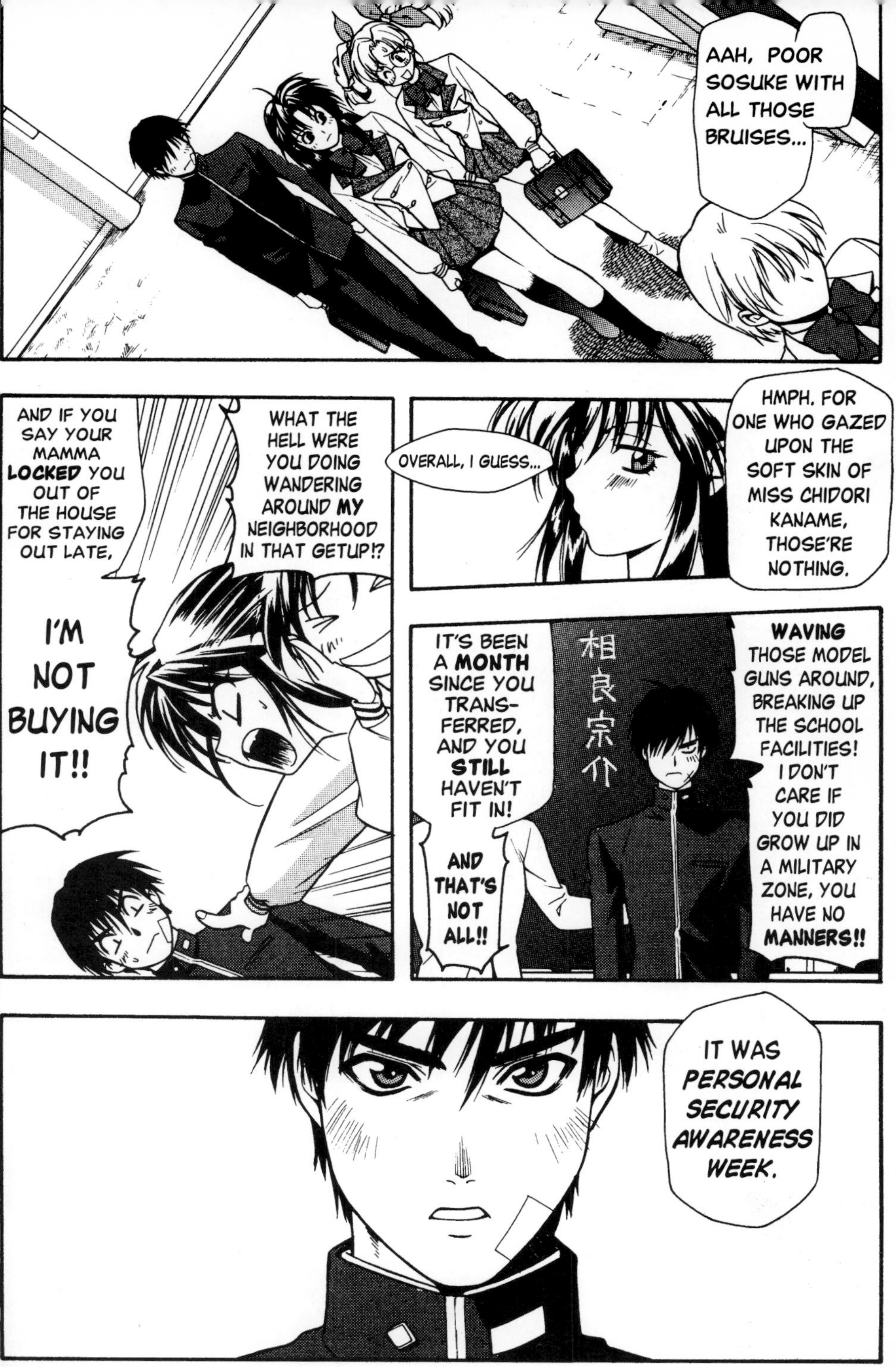
AAH, POOR SOSUKE WITH ALL THOSE BRUISES...
HMPH. FOR ONE WHO GAZED UPON THE SOFT SKIN OF MISS CHIDORI KANAME, THOSE'RE NOTHING.
OVERALL, I GUESS...
WAVING THOSE MODEL GUNS AROUND, BREAKING UP THE SCHOOL FACILITIES! I DON'T CARE IF YOU DID GROW UP IN A MILITARY ZONE, YOU HAVE NO MANNERS!!
相良宗介
IT'S BEEN A MONTH SINCE YOU TRANSFERRED, AND YOU STILL HAVEN'T FIT IN!
AND THAT'S NOT ALL!!
WHAT THE HELL WERE YOU DOING WANDERING AROUND MY NEIGHBORHOOD IN THAT GETUP!?
AND IF YOU SAY YOUR MAMMA LOCKED YOU OUT OF THE HOUSE FOR STAYING OUT LATE,
I'M NOT BUYING IT!!
IT WAS PERSONAL SECURITY AWARENESS WEEK.

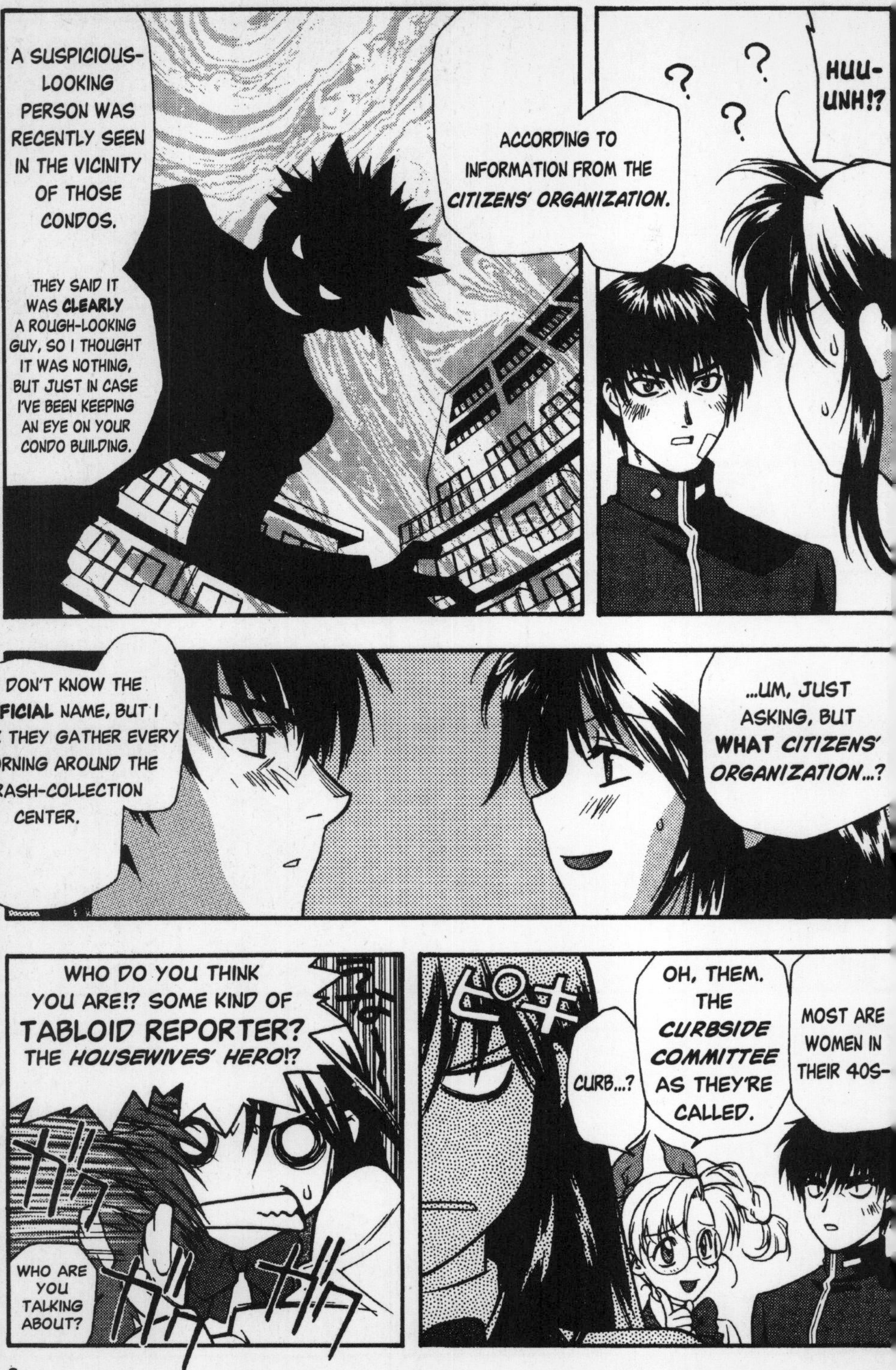

HUU-UNH!?
ACCORDING TO INFORMATION FROM THE CITIZENS' ORGANIZATION.
A SUSPICIOUS-LOOKING PERSON WAS RECENTLY SEEN IN THE VICINITY OF THOSE CONDOS.
THEY SAID IT WAS CLEARLY A ROUGH-LOOKING GUY, SO I THOUGHT IT WAS NOTHING, BUT JUST IN CASE I'VE BEEN KEEPING AN EYE ON YOUR CONDO BUILDING.
...UM, JUST ASKING, BUT WHAT CITIZENS' ORGANIZATION...?
I DON'T KNOW THE OFFICIAL NAME, BUT I THINK THEY GATHER EVERY MORNING AROUND THE TRASH-COLLECTION CENTER.
OH, THEM. THE CURBSIDE COMMITTEE AS THEY'RE CALLED.
CURB...?
MOST ARE WOMEN IN THEIR 40S-
WHO DO YOU THINK YOU ARE!? SOME KIND OF TABLOID REPORTER? THE HOUSEWIVES' HERO!?
WHO ARE YOU TALKING ABOUT?

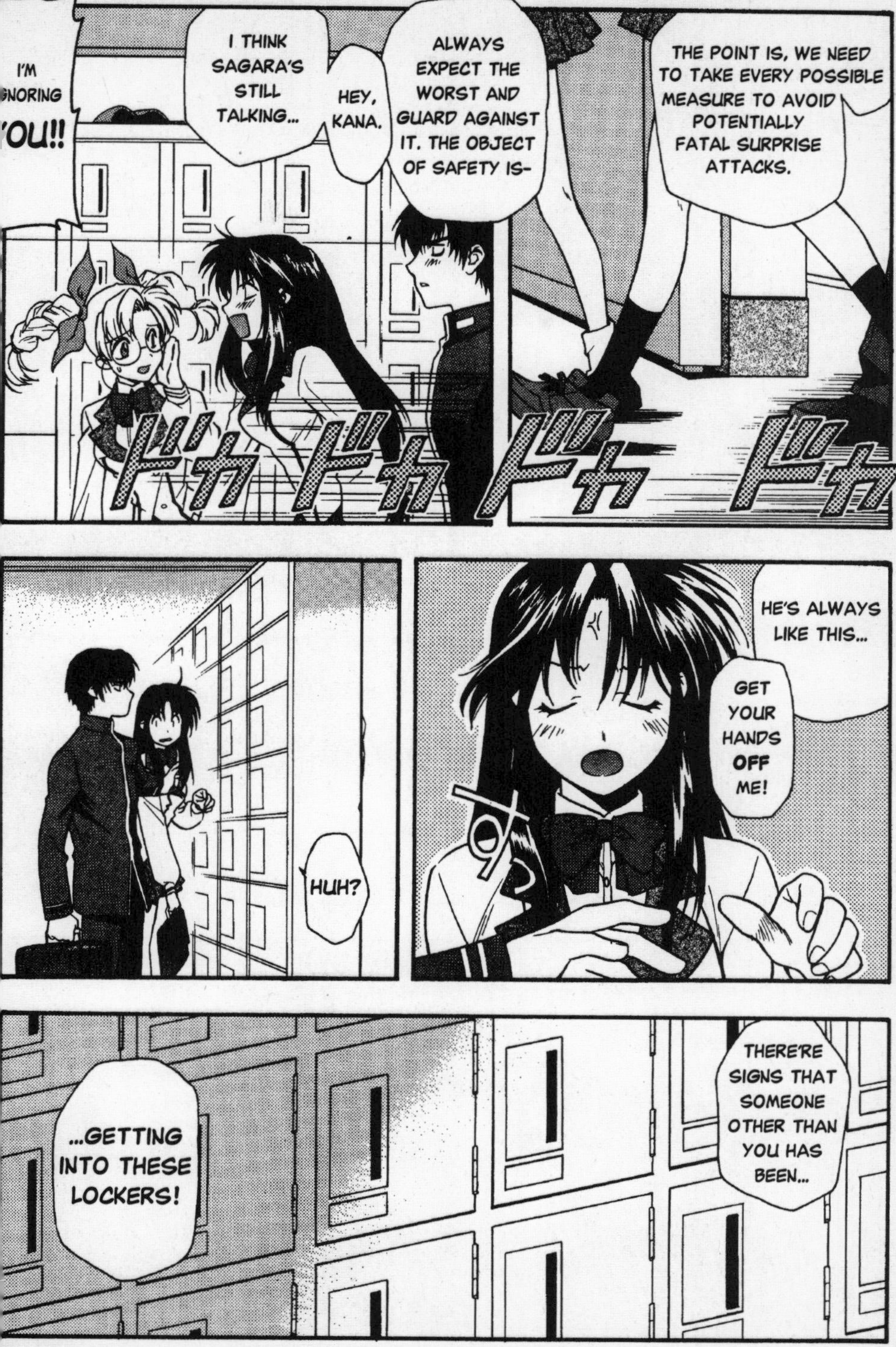

THE POINT IS, WE NEED TO TAKE EVERY POSSIBLE MEASURE TO AVOID POTENTIALLY FATAL SURPRISE ATTACKS.
ドカ
ALWAYS EXPECT THE WORST AND GUARD AGAINST IT. THE OBJECT OF SAFETY IS-
HEY, KANA.
I THINK SAGARA'S STILL TALKING...
I'M GNORING OU!!
ドカ ドカ ドカ
HE'S ALWAYS LIKE THIS...
GET YOUR HANDS OFF ME!
すっ
HUH?
THERE'RE SIGNS THAT SOMEONE OTHER THAN YOU HAS BEEN...
...GETTING INTO THESE LOCKERS!

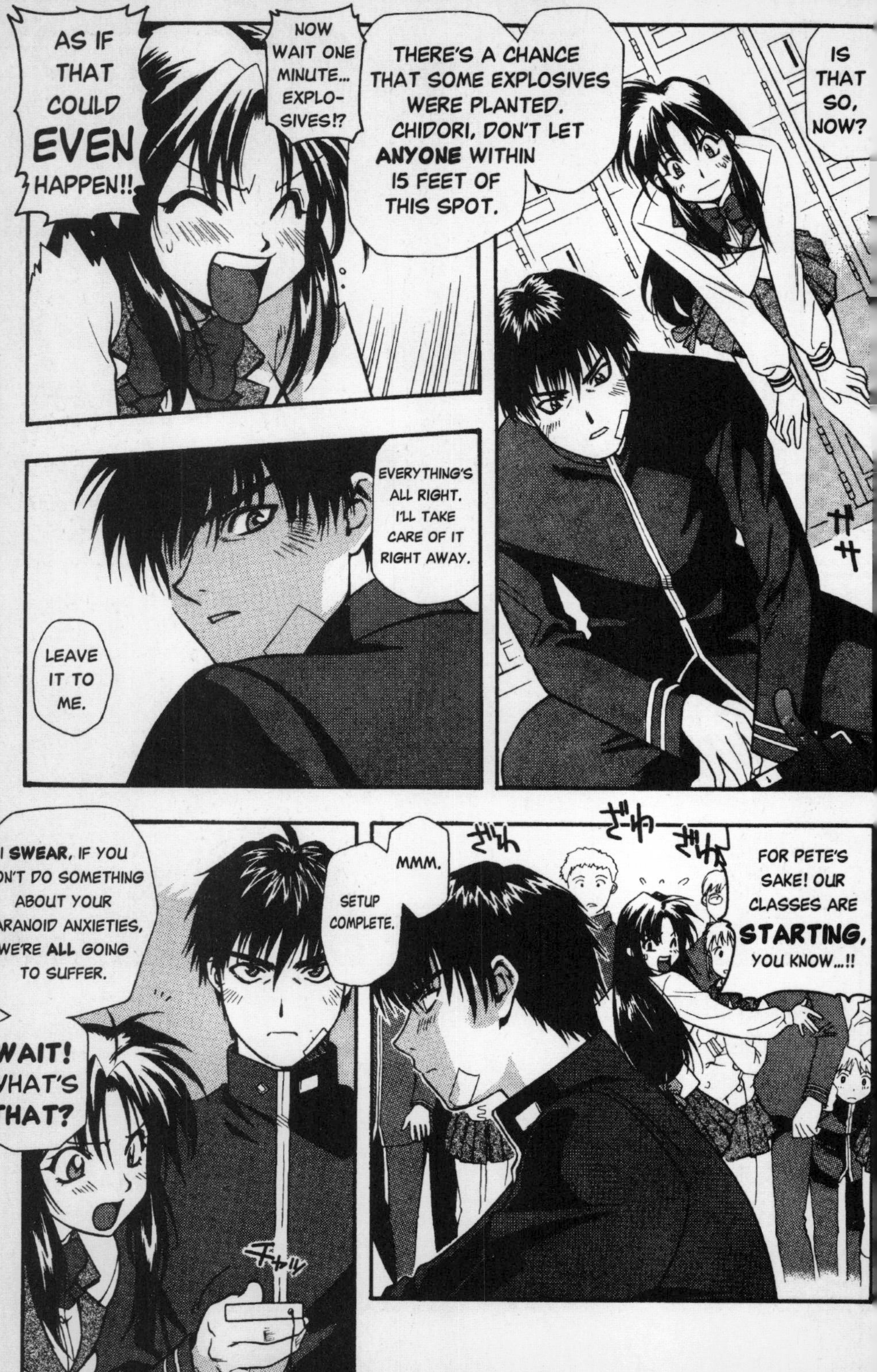
IS THAT SO, NOW?
THERE'S A CHANCE THAT SOME EXPLOSIVES WERE PLANTED. CHIDORI, DON'T LET ANYONE WITHIN 15 FEET OF THIS SPOT.
NOW WAIT ONE MINUTE... EXPLOSIVES!?
AS IF THAT COULD EVEN HAPPEN!!
EVERYTHING'S ALL RIGHT. I'LL TAKE CARE OF IT RIGHT AWAY.
LEAVE IT TO ME.
FOR PETE'S SAKE! OUR CLASSES ARE STARTING, YOU KNOW...!!
MMM.
SETUP COMPLETE.
I SWEAR, IF YOU DON'T DO SOMETHING ABOUT YOUR PARANOID ANXIETIES, WE'RE ALL GOING TO SUFFER.
WAIT! WHAT'S THAT?

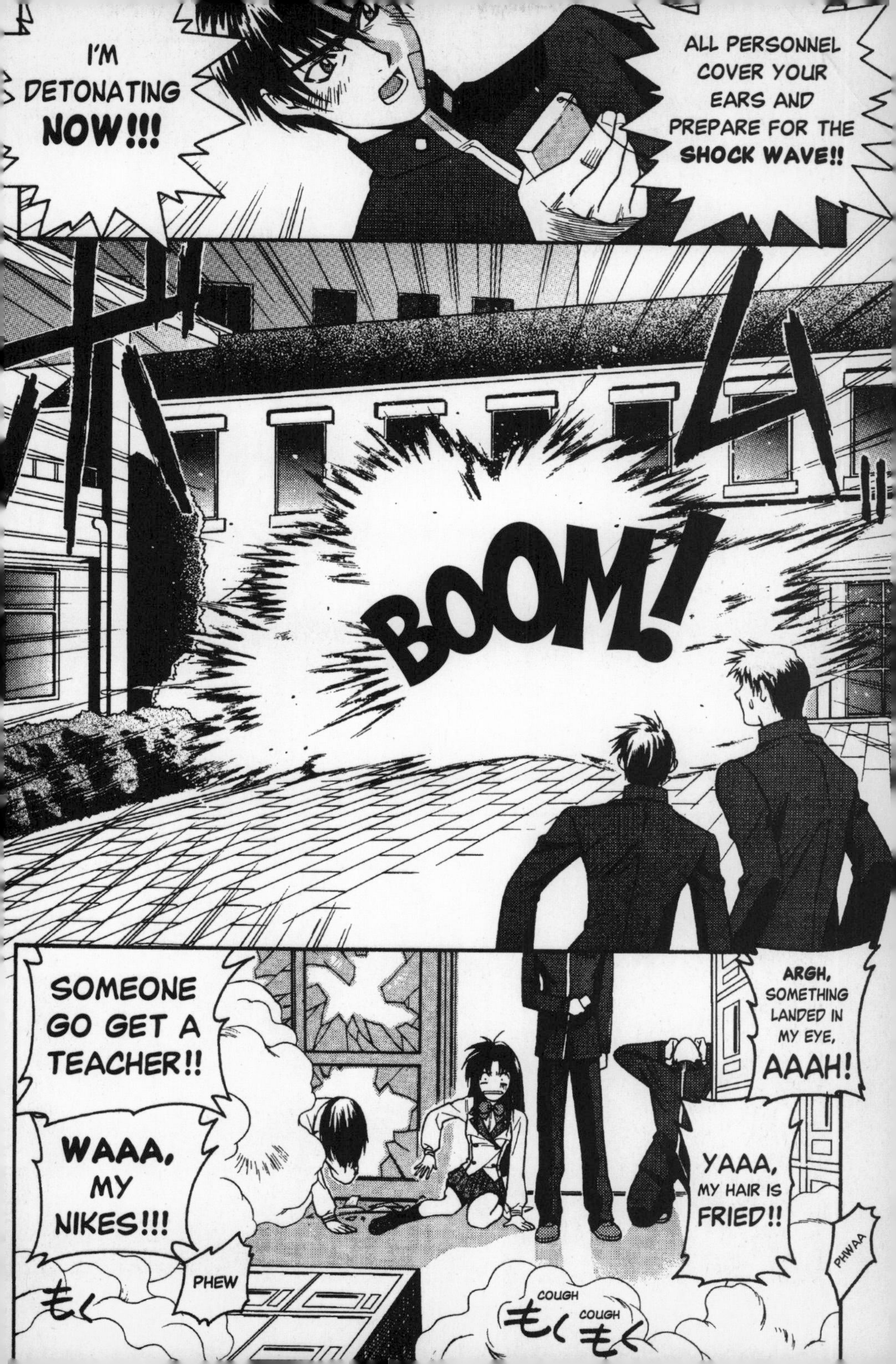

ALL PERSONNEL COVER YOUR EARS AND PREPARE FOR THE SHOCK WAVE!!
I'M DETONATING NOW!!!
BOOM!
ARGH, SOMETHING LANDED IN MY EYE, AAAH!
YAAA, MY HAIR IS FRIED!!
PHWAA
SOMEONE GO GET A TEACHER!!
WAAA, MY NIKES!!!
COUGH
もく
COUGH
もく
PHEW
もく

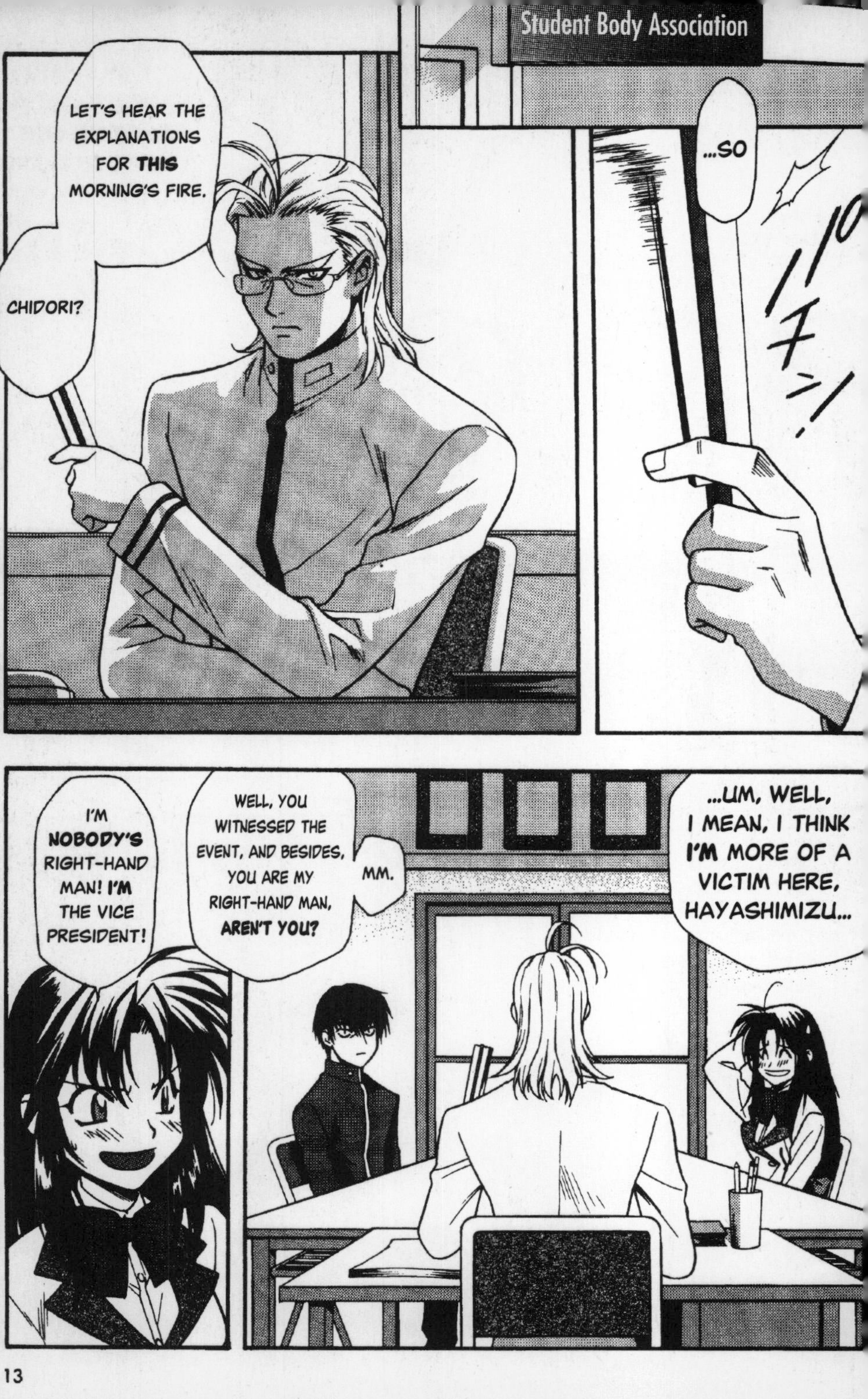
Student Body Association
...SO
LET'S HEAR THE EXPLANATIONS FOR THIS MORNING'S FIRE.
CHIDORI?
...UM, WELL, I MEAN, I THINK I'M MORE OF A VICTIM HERE, HAYASHIMIZU...
MM.
WELL, YOU WITNESSED THE EVENT, AND BESIDES, YOU ARE MY RIGHT-HAND MAN, AREN'T YOU?
I'M NOBODY'S RIGHT-HAND MAN! I'M THE VICE PRESIDENT!

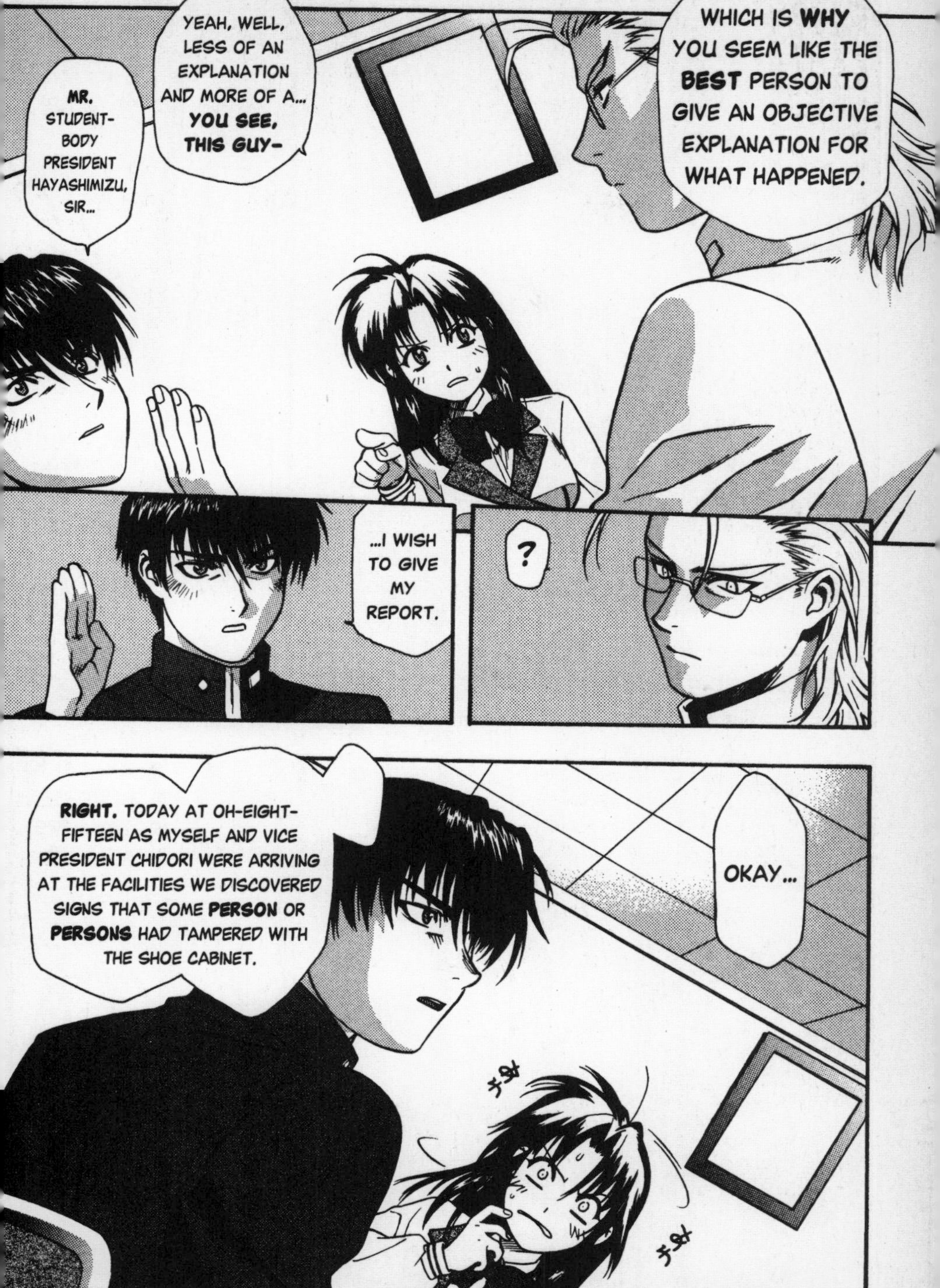
WHICH IS WHY YOU SEEM LIKE THE BEST PERSON TO GIVE AN OBJECTIVE EXPLANATION FOR WHAT HAPPENED.
YEAH, WELL, LESS OF AN EXPLANATION AND MORE OF A... YOU SEE, THIS GUY-
MR. STUDENT-BODY PRESIDENT HAYASHIMIZU, SIR...
?
...I WISH TO GIVE MY REPORT.
OKAY...
RIGHT. TODAY AT OH-EIGHT-FIFTEEN AS MYSELF AND VICE PRESIDENT CHIDORI WERE ARRIVING AT THE FACILITIES WE DISCOVERED SIGNS THAT SOME PERSON OR PERSONS HAD TAMPERED WITH THE SHOE CABINET.

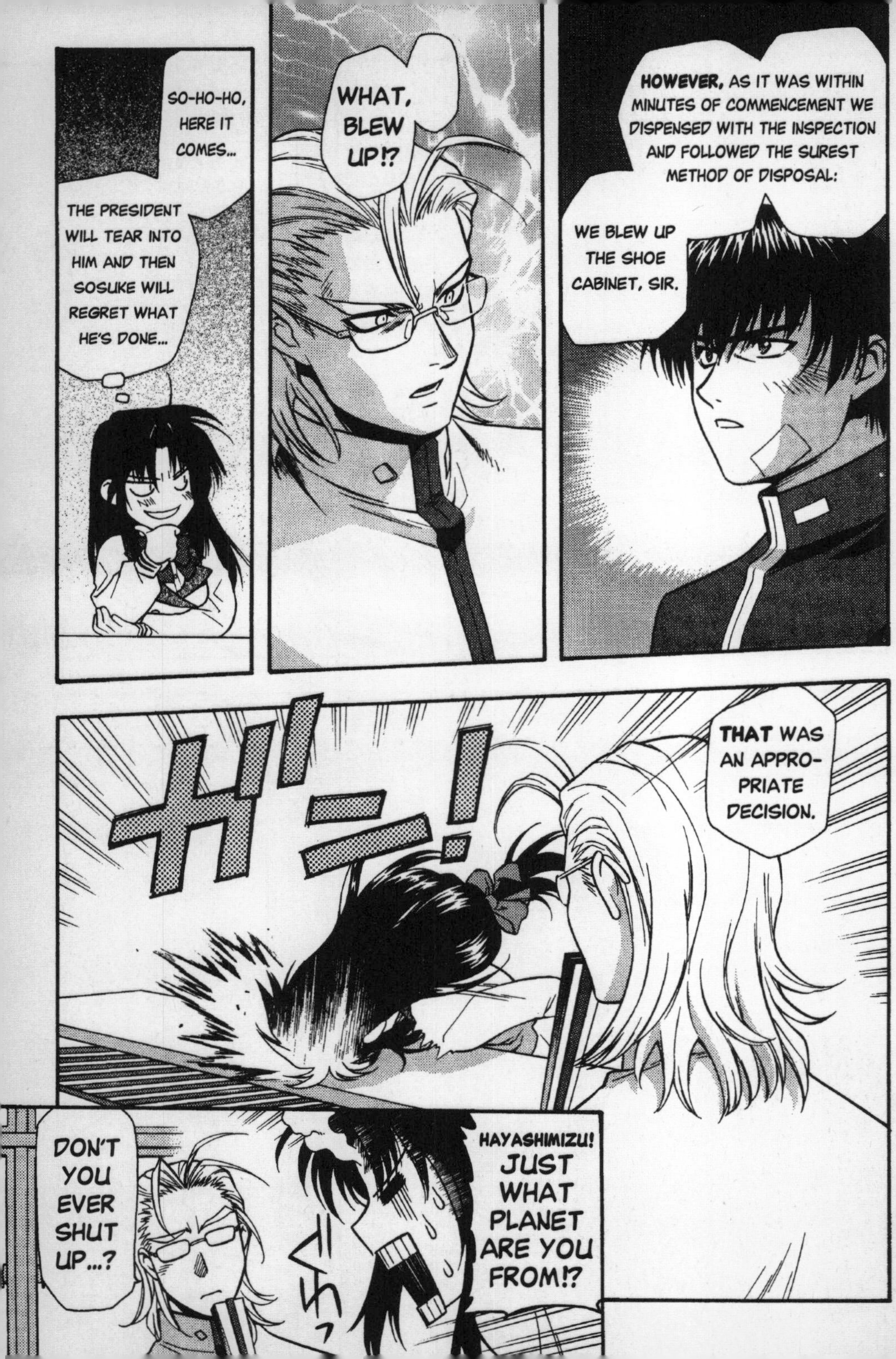
HOWEVER, AS IT WAS WITHIN MINUTES OF COMMENCEMENT WE DISPENSED WITH THE INSPECTION AND FOLLOWED THE SUREST METHOD OF DISPOSAL:
WE BLEW UP THE SHOE CABINET, SIR.
WHAT, BLEW UP!?
SO-HO-HO, HERE IT COMES...
THE PRESIDENT WILL TEAR INTO HIM AND THEN SOSUKE WILL REGRET WHAT HE'S DONE...
THAT WAS AN APPRO-PRIATE DECISION.
HAYASHIMIZU! JUST WHAT PLANET ARE YOU FROM!?
DON'T YOU EVER SHUT UP...?

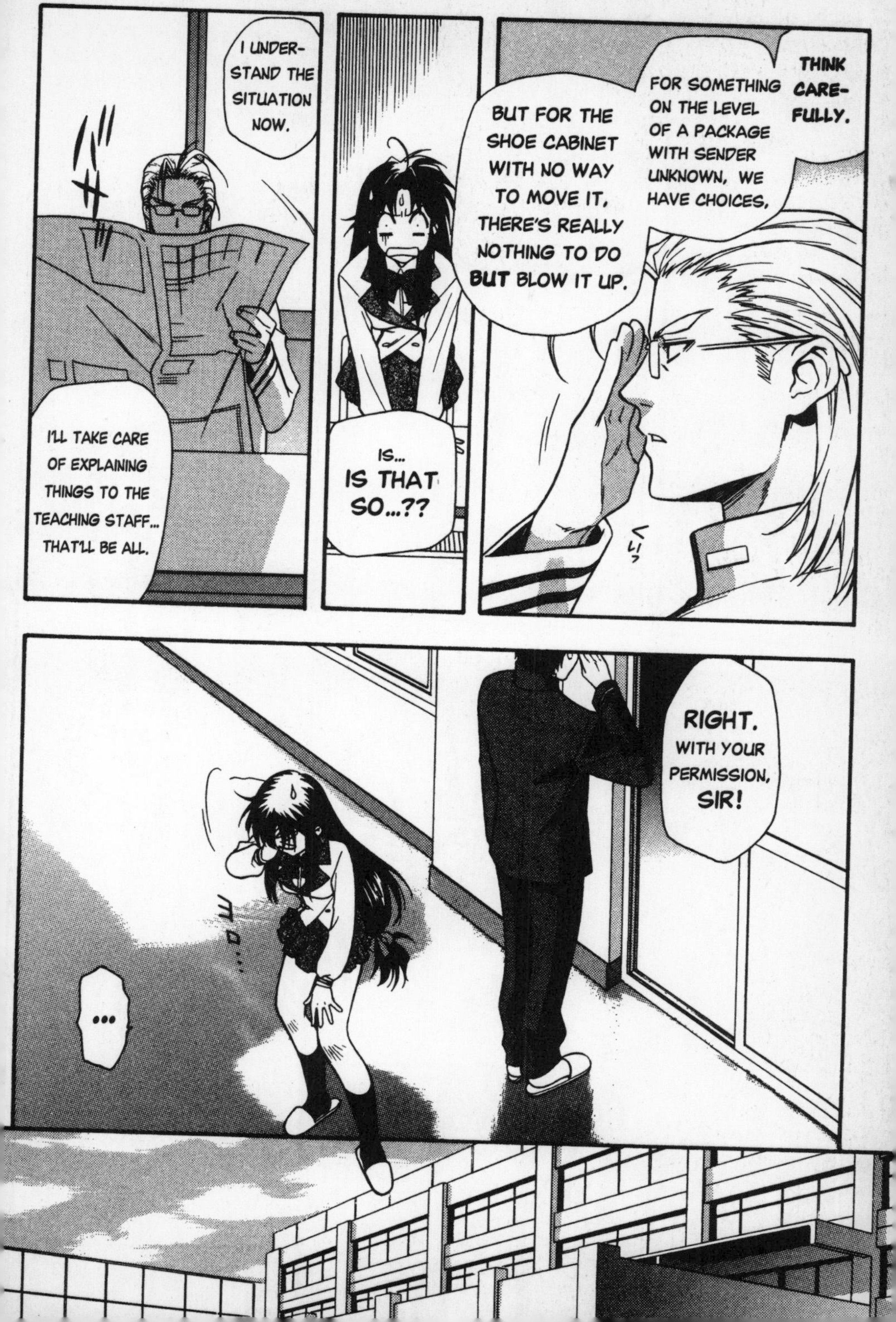
THINK CAREFULLY.
FOR SOMETHING ON THE LEVEL OF A PACKAGE WITH SENDER UNKNOWN, WE HAVE CHOICES,
BUT FOR THE SHOE CABINET WITH NO WAY TO MOVE IT, THERE'S REALLY NOTHING TO DO BUT BLOW IT UP.
IS... IS THAT SO...??
I UNDERSTAND THE SITUATION NOW.
I'LL TAKE CARE OF EXPLAINING THINGS TO THE TEACHING STAFF... THAT'LL BE ALL.
RIGHT. WITH YOUR PERMISSION, SIR!
...

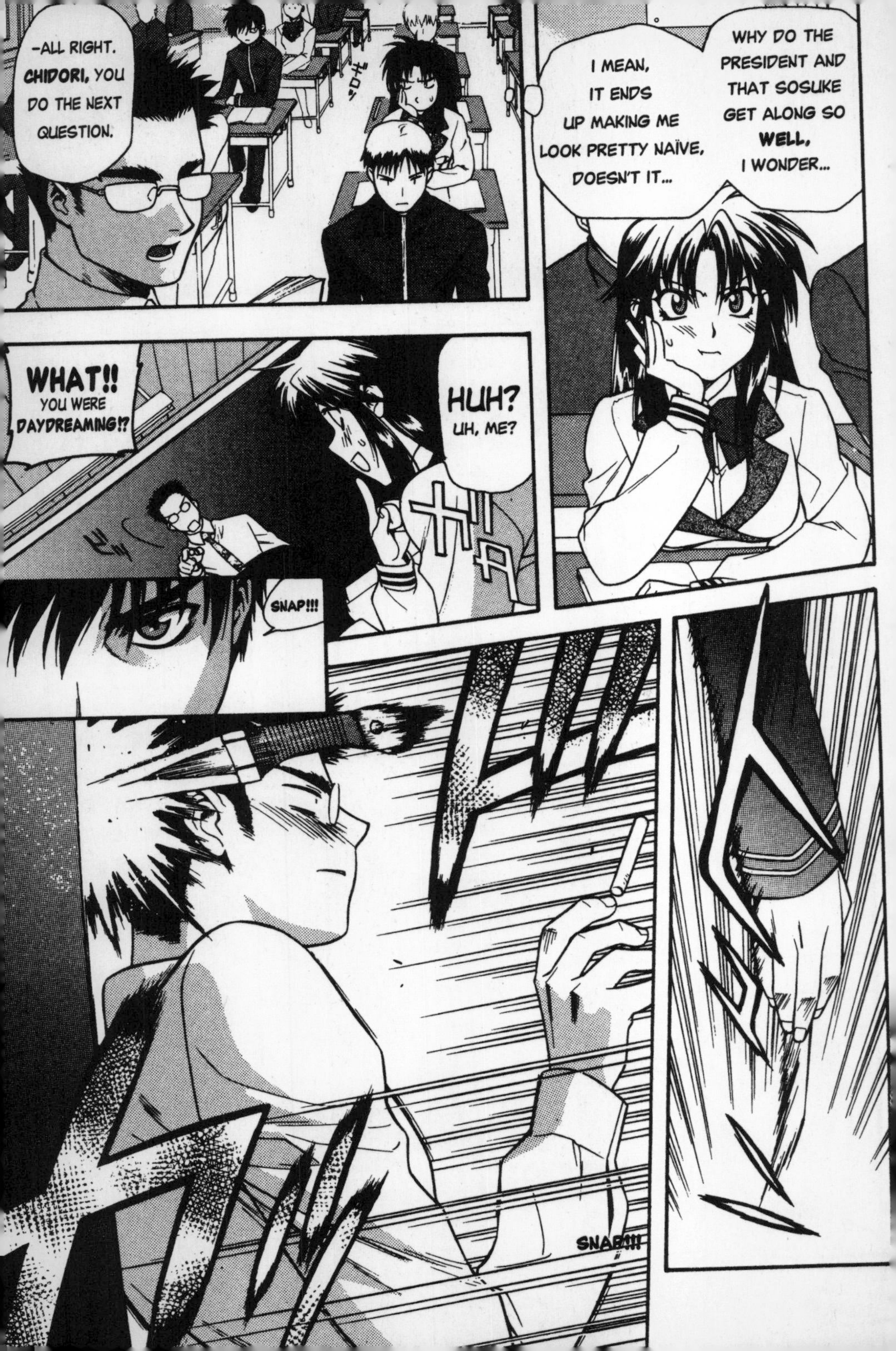
WHY DO THE PRESIDENT AND THAT SOSUKE GET ALONG SO WELL, I WONDER...
I MEAN, IT ENDS UP MAKING ME LOOK PRETTY NAÏVE, DOESN'T IT...
-ALL RIGHT. CHIDORI, YOU DO THE NEXT QUESTION.
HUH? UH, ME?
WHAT!! YOU WERE DAYDREAMING!?
SNAP!!!
SNAP!!!

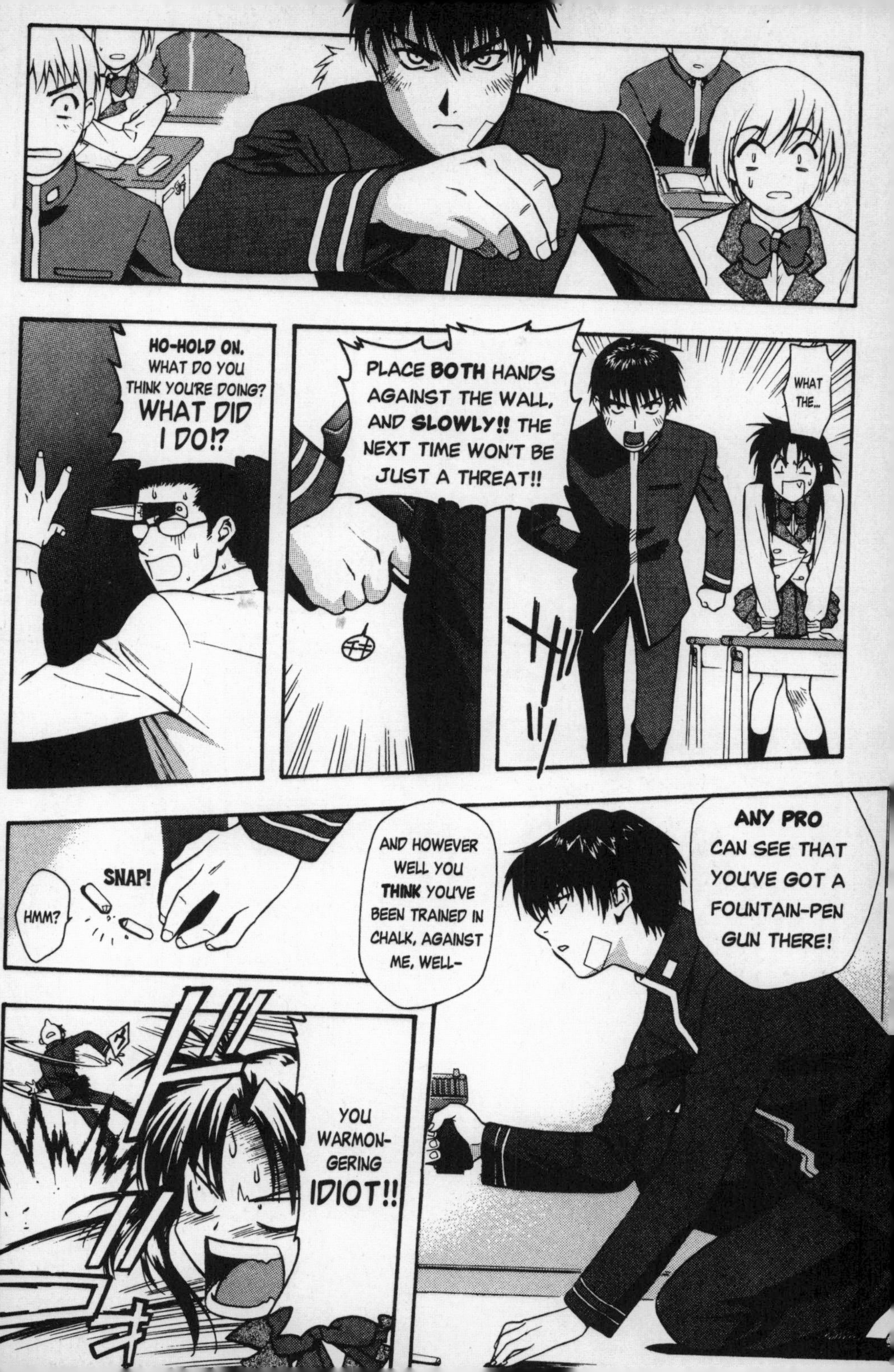
WHAT THE...
PLACE BOTH HANDS AGAINST THE WALL, AND SLOWLY!! THE NEXT TIME WON'T BE JUST A THREAT!!
HO-HOLD ON. WHAT DO YOU THINK YOU'RE DOING? WHAT DID I DO!?
ANY PRO CAN SEE THAT YOU'VE GOT A FOUNTAIN-PEN GUN THERE!
AND HOWEVER WELL YOU THINK YOU'VE BEEN TRAINED IN CHALK, AGAINST ME, WELL-
SNAP!
HMM?
YOU WARMON-GERING IDIOT!!

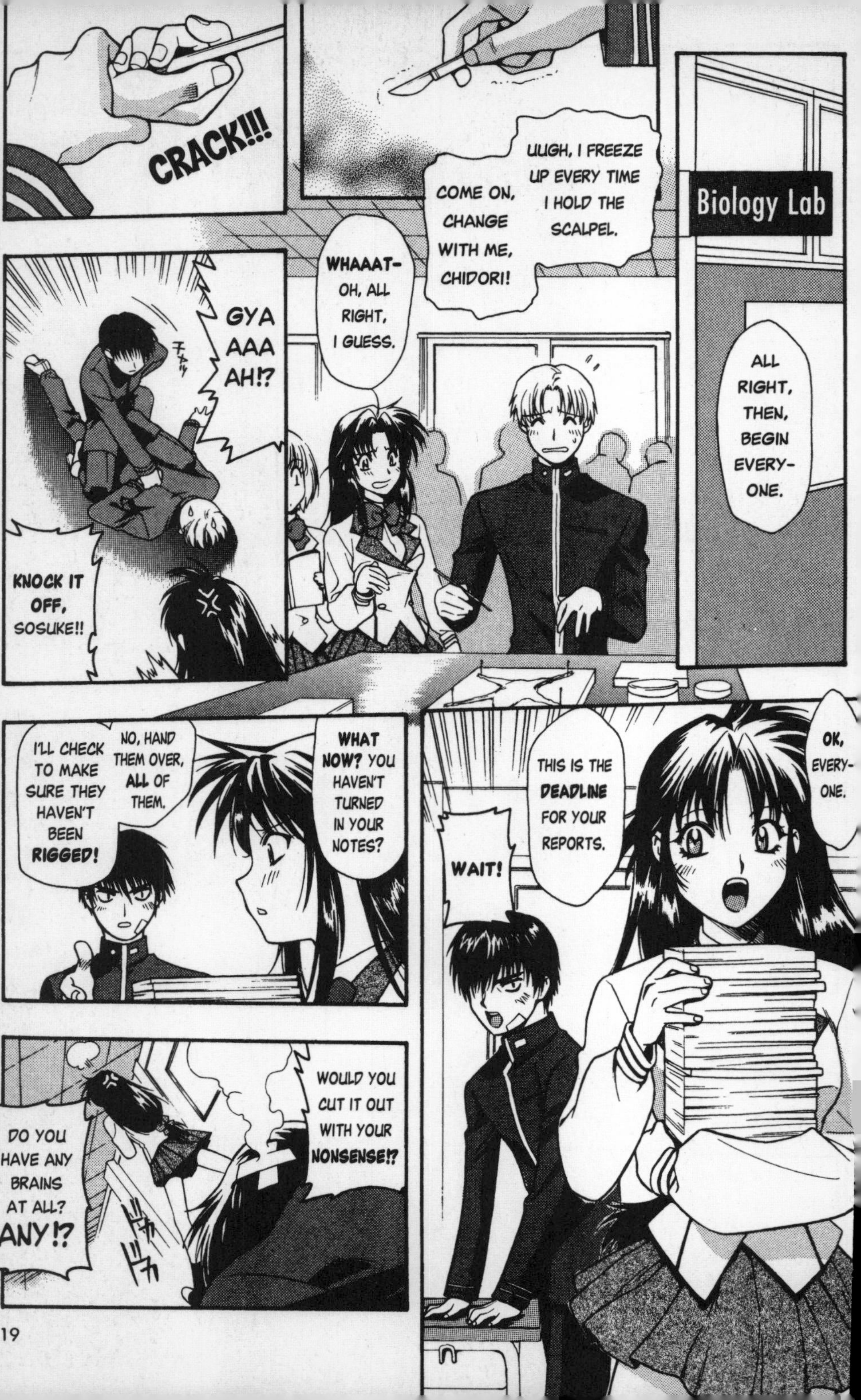
Biology Lab
ALL RIGHT, THEN, BEGIN EVERY-ONE.
UUGH, I FREEZE UP EVERY TIME I HOLD THE SCALPEL.
COME ON, CHANGE WITH ME, CHIDORI!
WHAAAT- OH, ALL RIGHT, I GUESS.
CRACK!!!
GYA AAA AH!?
KNOCK IT OFF, SOSUKE!!
OK, EVERY-ONE.
THIS IS THE DEADLINE FOR YOUR REPORTS.
WAIT!
WHAT NOW? YOU HAVEN'T TURNED IN YOUR NOTES?
NO, HAND THEM OVER, ALL OF THEM.
I'LL CHECK TO MAKE SURE THEY HAVEN'T BEEN RIGGED!
WOULD YOU CUT IT OUT WITH YOUR NONSENSE!?
DO YOU HAVE ANY BRAINS AT ALL? ANY!?

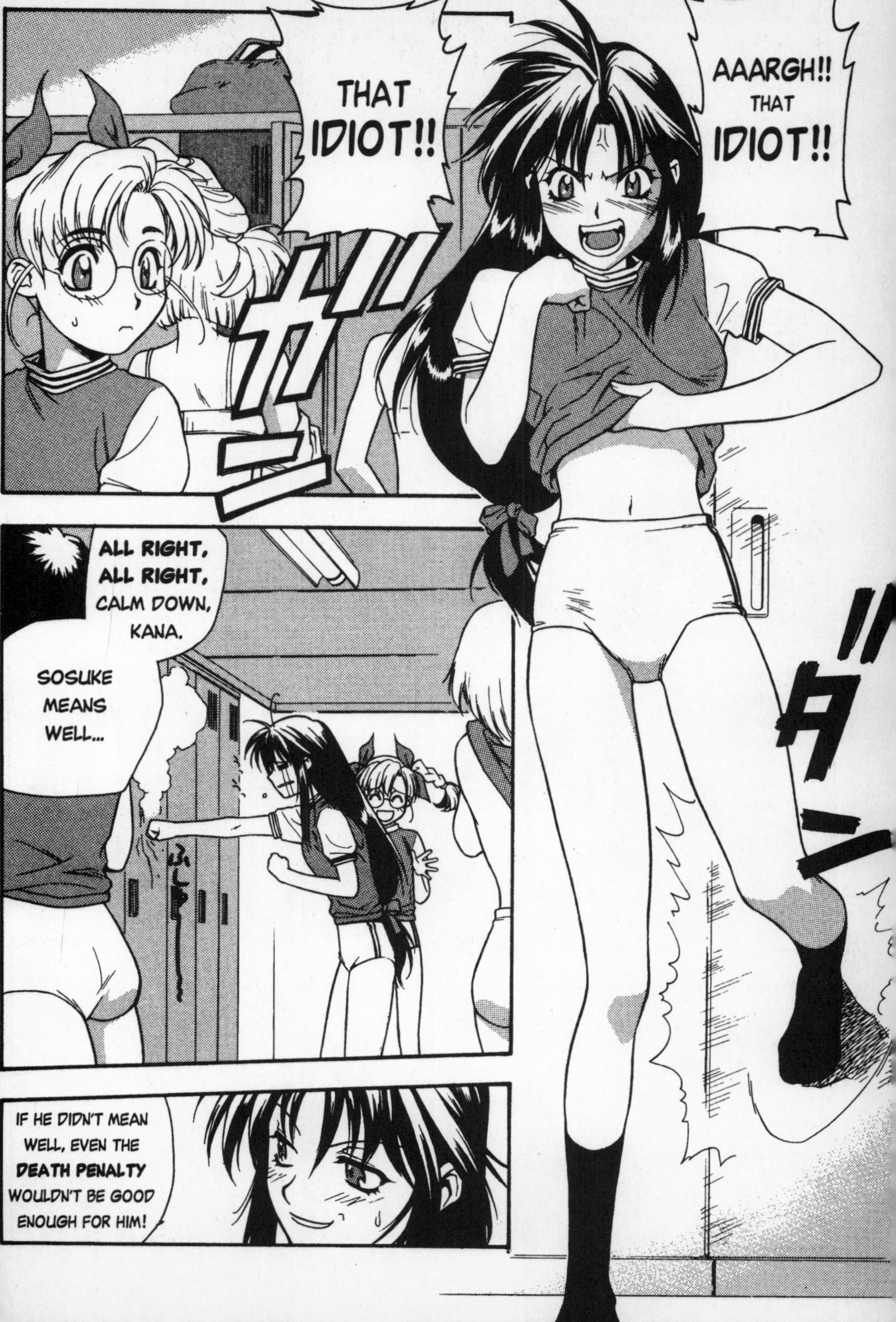
AAARGH!! THAT IDIOT!!
THAT IDIOT!!
ALL RIGHT, ALL RIGHT, CALM DOWN, KANA.
SOSUKE MEANS WELL...
IF HE DIDN'T MEAN WELL, EVEN THE DEATH PENALTY WOULDN'T BE GOOD ENOUGH FOR HIM!

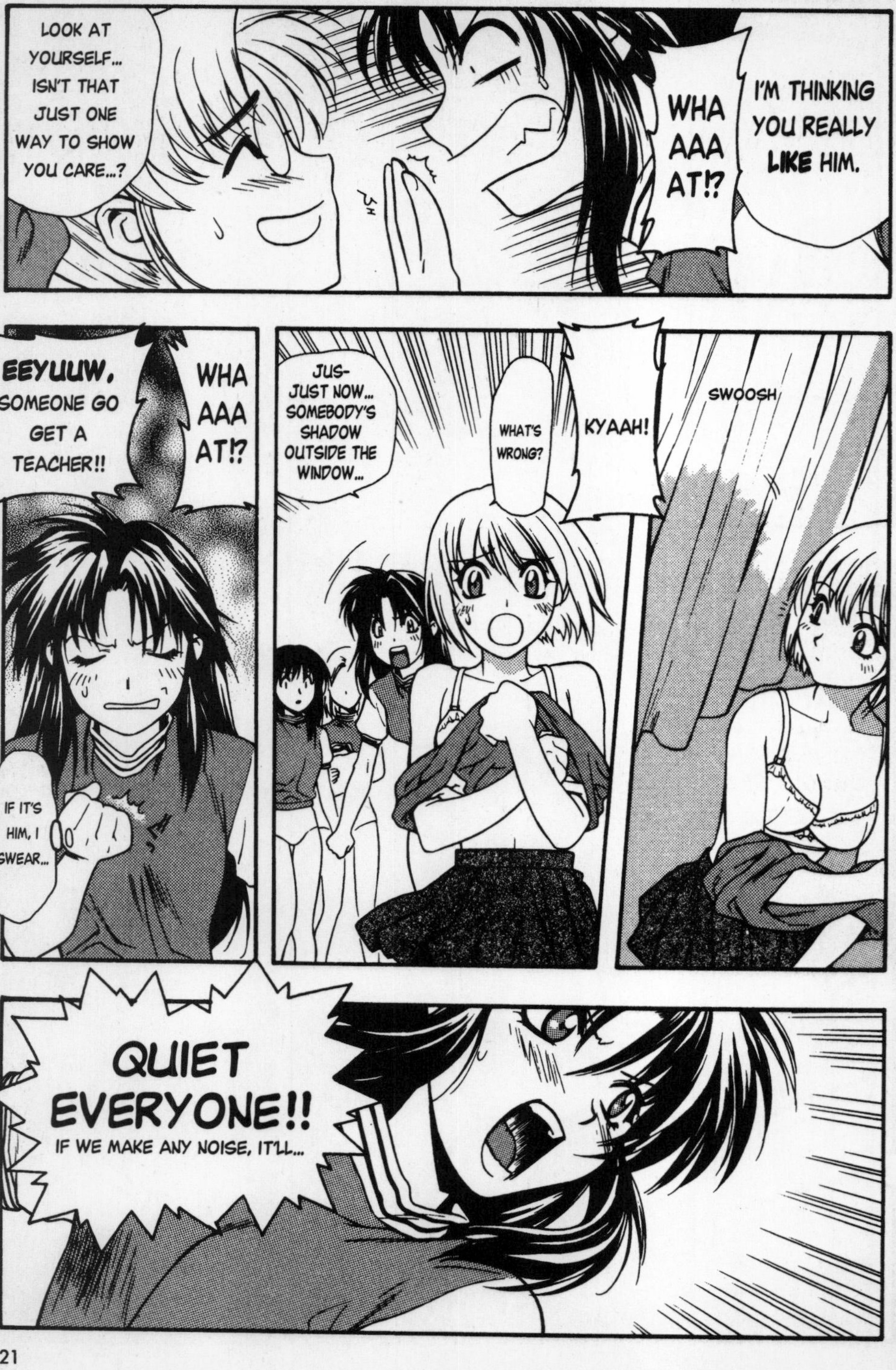
I'M THINKING YOU REALLY LIKE HIM.
WHA AAA AT!?
LOOK AT YOURSELF... ISN'T THAT JUST ONE WAY TO SHOW YOU CARE...?
SWOOSH
KYAAH!
WHAT'S WRONG?
JUS- JUST NOW... SOMEBODY'S SHADOW OUTSIDE THE WINDOW...
WHA AAA AT!?
EEYUUW, SOMEONE GO GET A TEACHER!!
IF IT'S HIM, I SWEAR...
QUIET EVERYONE!!
IF WE MAKE ANY NOISE, IT'LL...

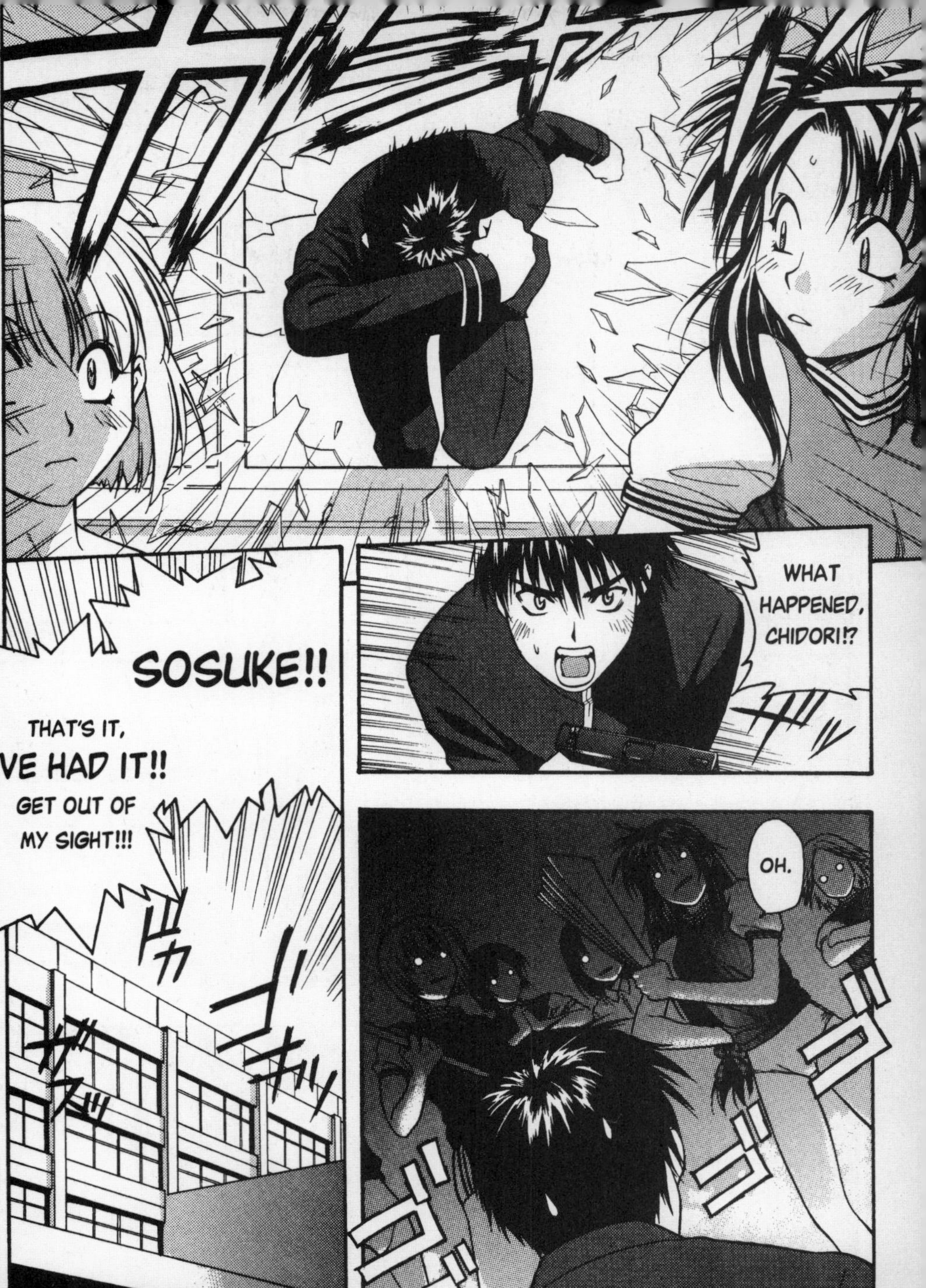
WHAT HAPPENED, CHIDORI!?
SOSUKE!!
THAT'S IT, I'VE HAD IT!! GET OUT OF MY SIGHT!!!
OH.

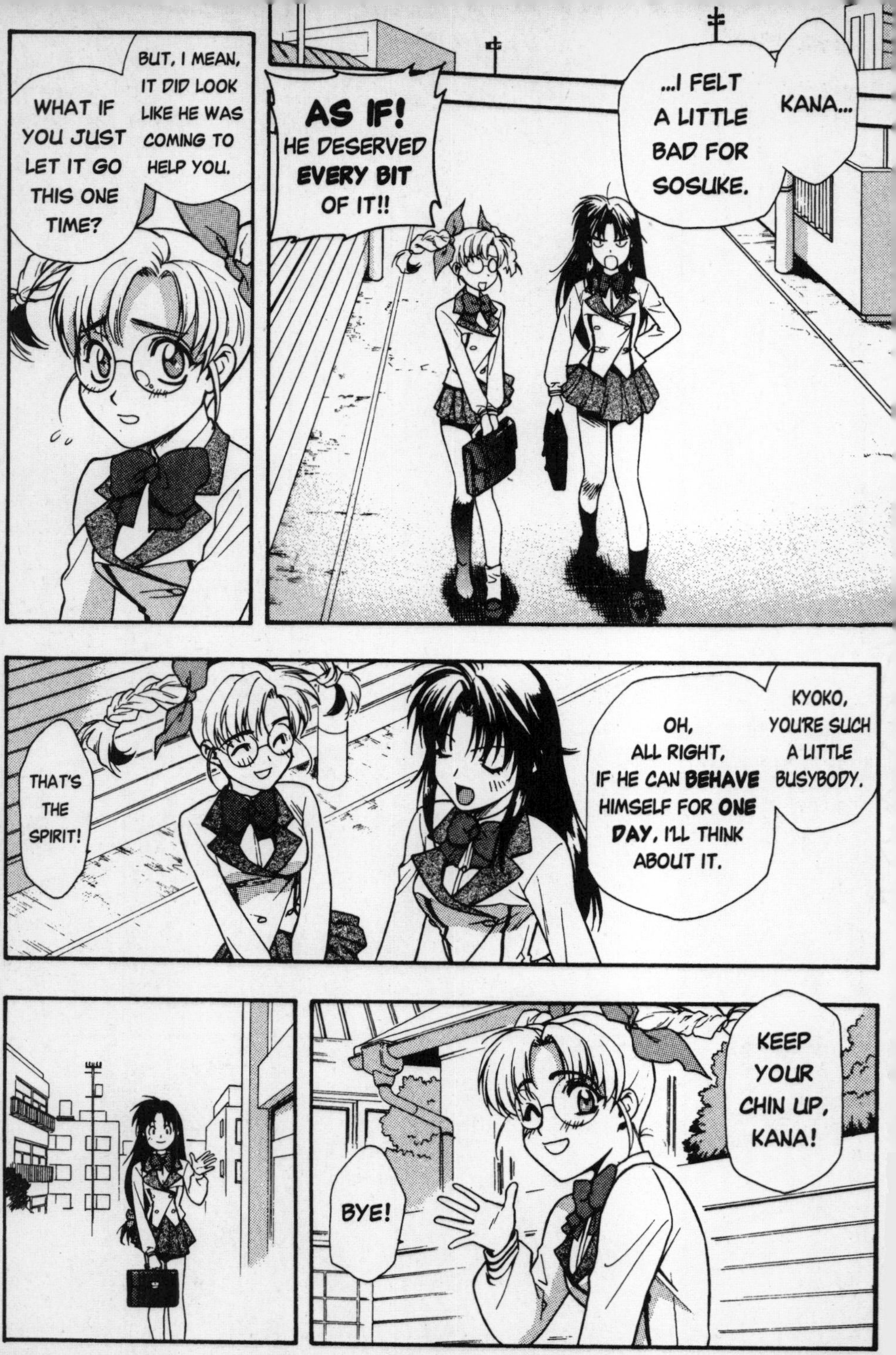

KANA...
...I FELT A LITTLE BAD FOR SOSUKE.
AS IF! HE DESERVED EVERY BIT OF IT!!
BUT, I MEAN, IT DID LOOK LIKE HE WAS COMING TO HELP YOU.
WHAT IF YOU JUST LET IT GO THIS ONE TIME?
KYOKO, YOU'RE SUCH A LITTLE BUSYBODY.
OH, ALL RIGHT, IF HE CAN BEHAVE HIMSELF FOR ONE DAY, I'LL THINK ABOUT IT.
THAT'S THE SPIRIT!
KEEP YOUR CHIN UP, KANA!
BYE!

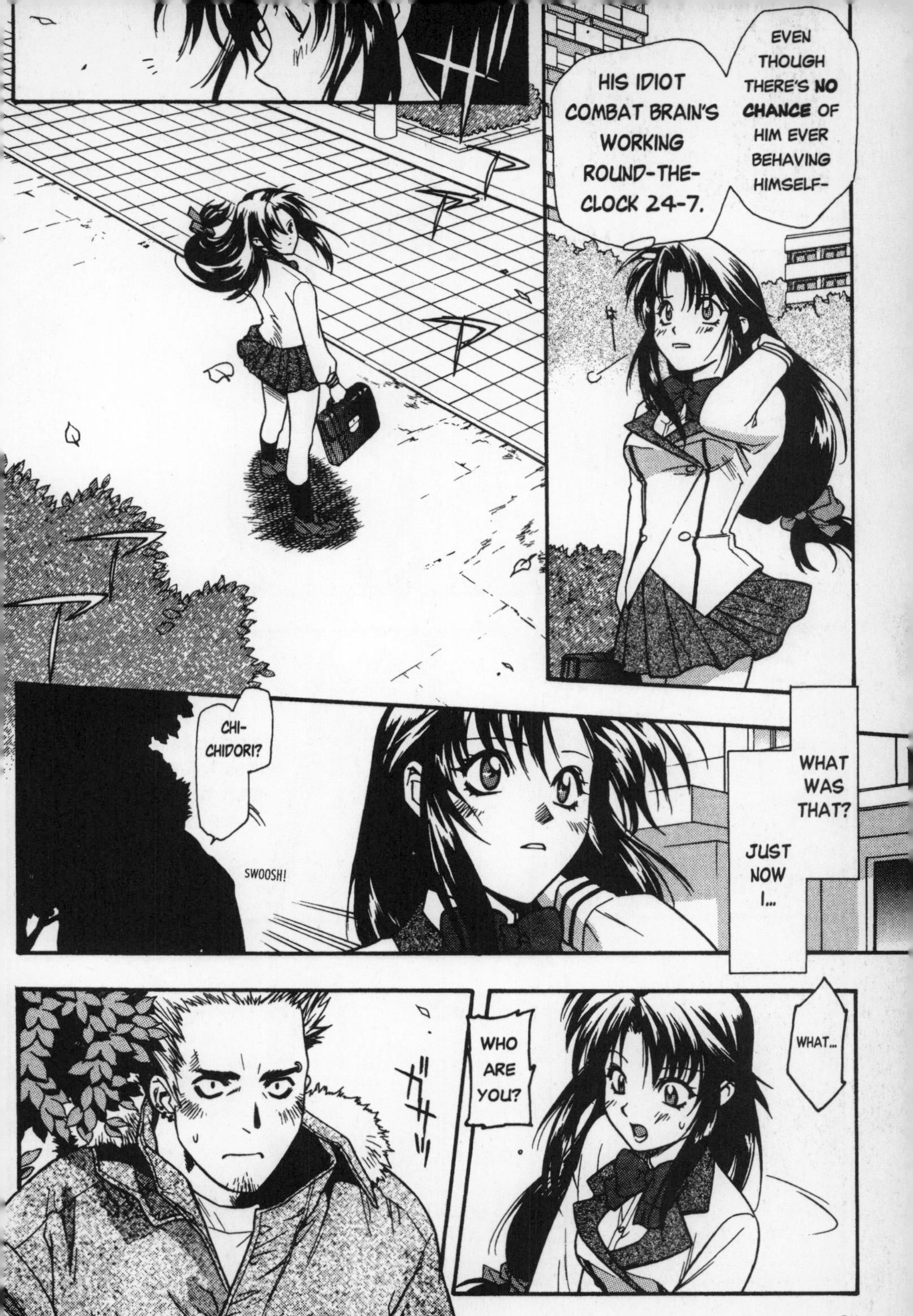
EVEN THOUGH THERE'S **NO CHANCE** OF HIM EVER BEHAVING HIMSELF-
HIS IDIOT COMBAT BRAIN'S WORKING ROUND-THE-CLOCK 24-7.
WHAT WAS THAT?
JUST NOW I...
CHI-CHIDORI?
SWOOSH!
WHAT...
WHO ARE YOU?

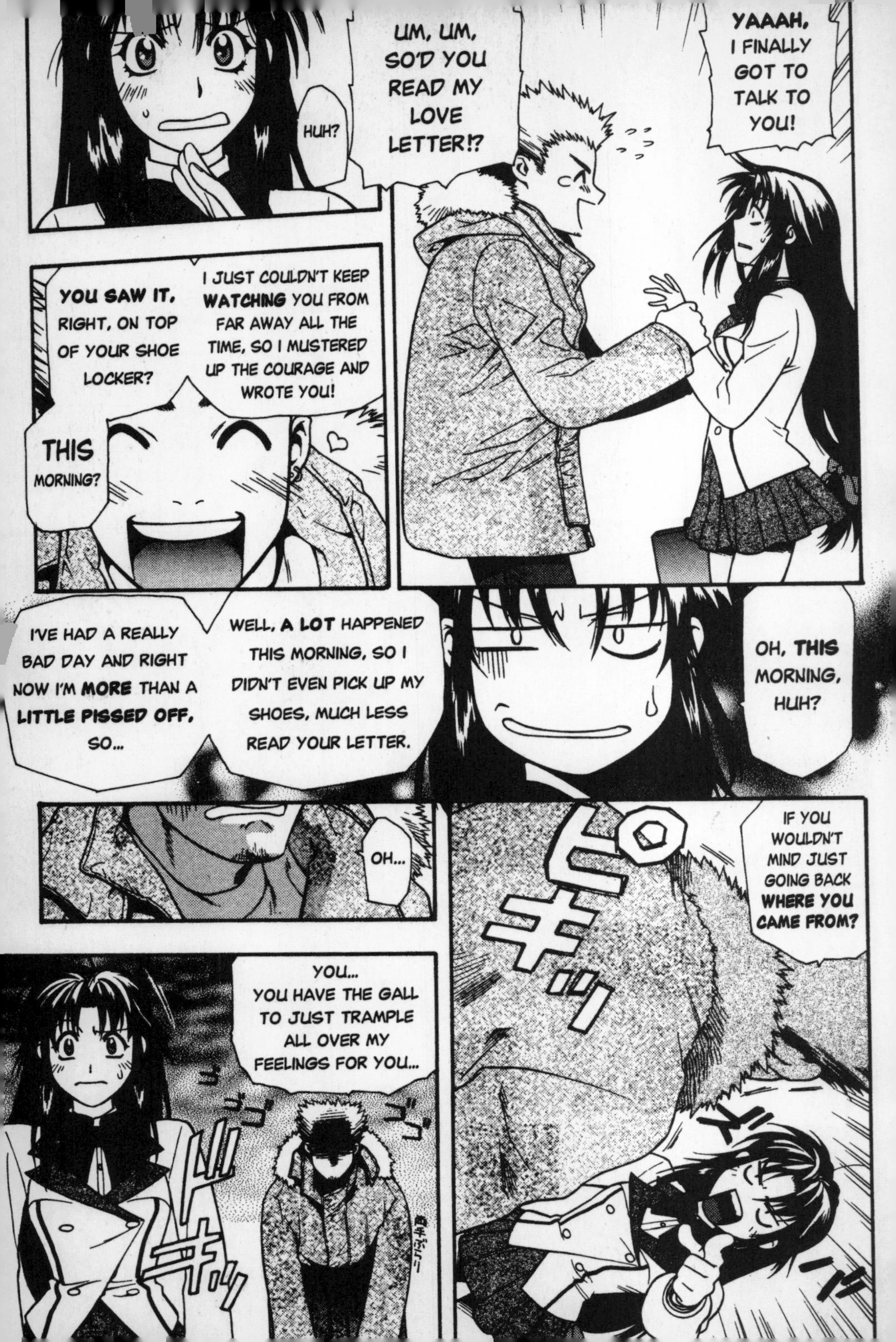
YAAAH, I FINALLY GOT TO TALK TO YOU!
UM, UM, SO'D YOU READ MY LOVE LETTER!?
HUH?
I JUST COULDN'T KEEP WATCHING YOU FROM FAR AWAY ALL THE TIME, SO I MUSTERED UP THE COURAGE AND WROTE YOU!
YOU SAW IT, RIGHT, ON TOP OF YOUR SHOE LOCKER?
THIS MORNING?
OH, THIS MORNING, HUH?
WELL, A LOT HAPPENED THIS MORNING, SO I DIDN'T EVEN PICK UP MY SHOES, MUCH LESS READ YOUR LETTER.
I'VE HAD A REALLY BAD DAY AND RIGHT NOW I'M MORE THAN A LITTLE PISSED OFF, SO...
IF YOU WOULDN'T MIND JUST GOING BACK WHERE YOU CAME FROM?
OH...
YOU... YOU HAVE THE GALL TO JUST TRAMPLE ALL OVER MY FEELINGS FOR YOU...

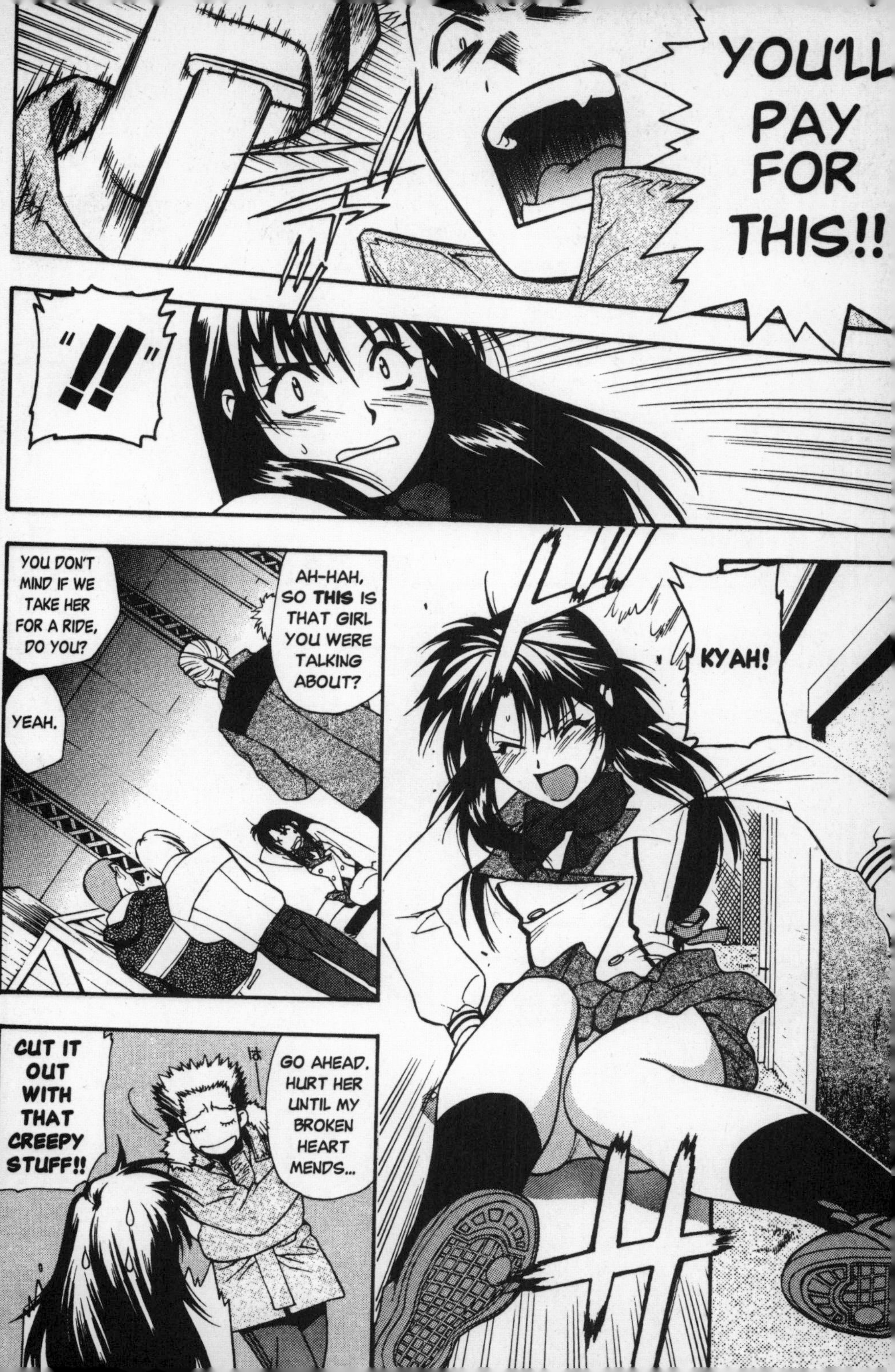
YOU'LL PAY FOR THIS!!
"!!"
KYAH!
AH-HAH, SO THIS IS THAT GIRL YOU WERE TALKING ABOUT?
YOU DON'T MIND IF WE TAKE HER FOR A RIDE, DO YOU?
YEAH.
GO AHEAD. HURT HER UNTIL MY BROKEN HEART MENDS...
CUT IT OUT WITH THAT CREEPY STUFF!!

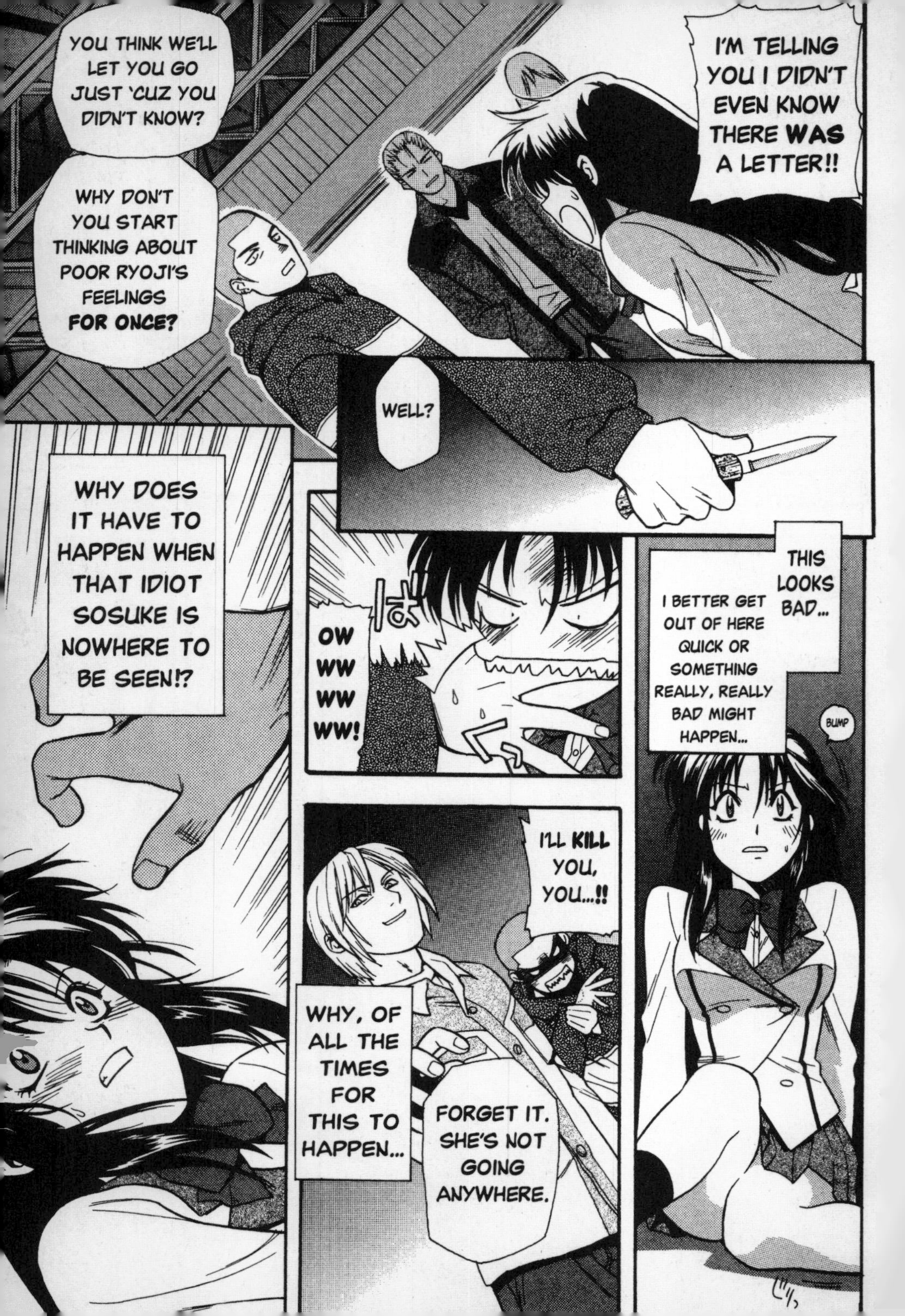
I'M TELLING YOU I DIDN'T EVEN KNOW THERE **WAS** A LETTER!!
YOU THINK WE'LL LET YOU GO JUST 'CUZ YOU DIDN'T KNOW?
WHY DON'T YOU START THINKING ABOUT POOR RYOJI'S FEELINGS **FOR ONCE?**
WELL?
THIS LOOKS BAD...
I BETTER GET OUT OF HERE QUICK OR SOMETHING REALLY, REALLY BAD MIGHT HAPPEN...
BUMP
じり
は
OW WW WW WW!
I'LL **KILL** YOU, YOU...!!
WHY, OF ALL THE TIMES FOR THIS TO HAPPEN...
FORGET IT. SHE'S NOT GOING ANYWHERE.
WHY DOES IT HAVE TO HAPPEN WHEN THAT IDIOT SOSUKE IS NOWHERE TO BE SEEN!?

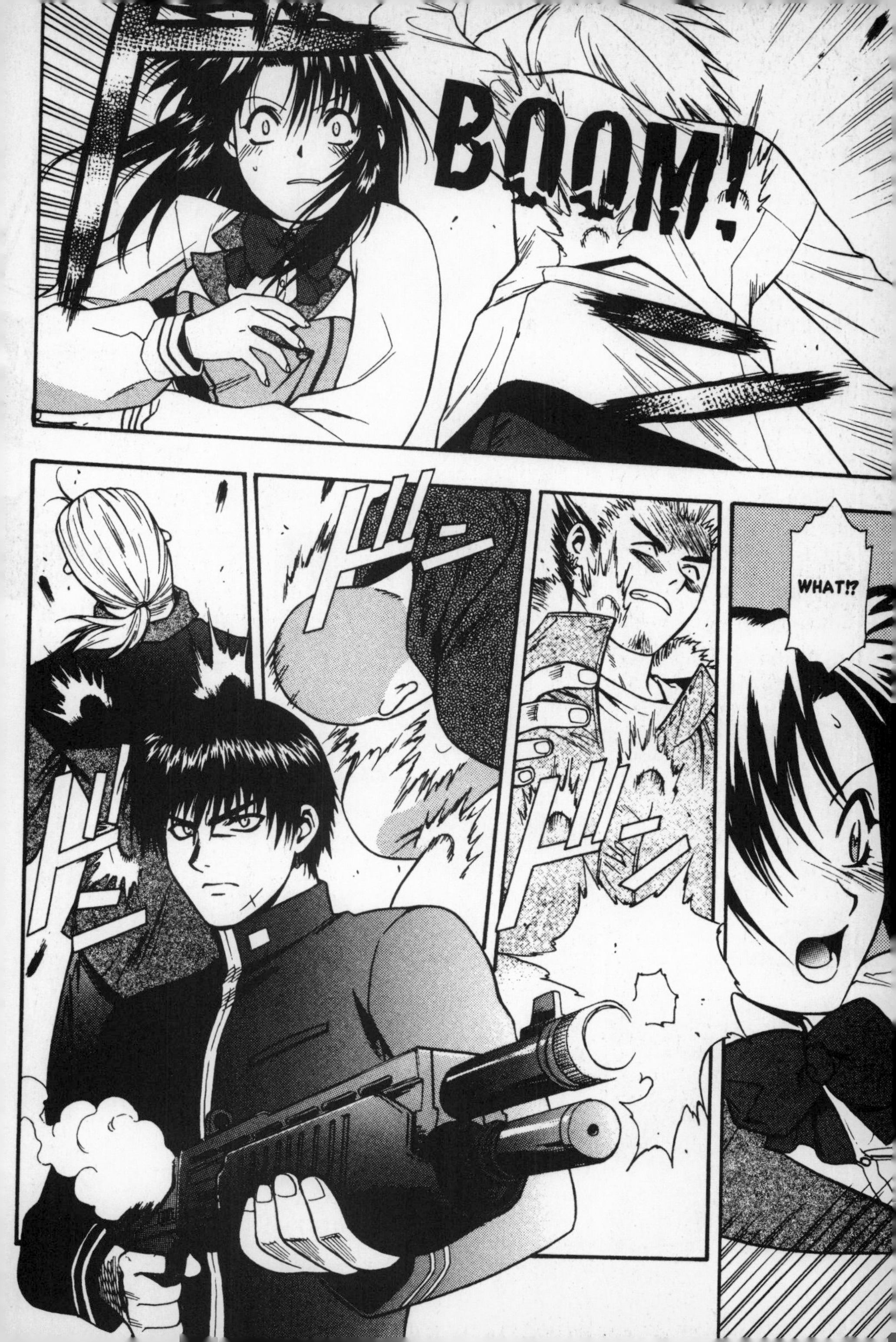
BOOM!
WHAT!?

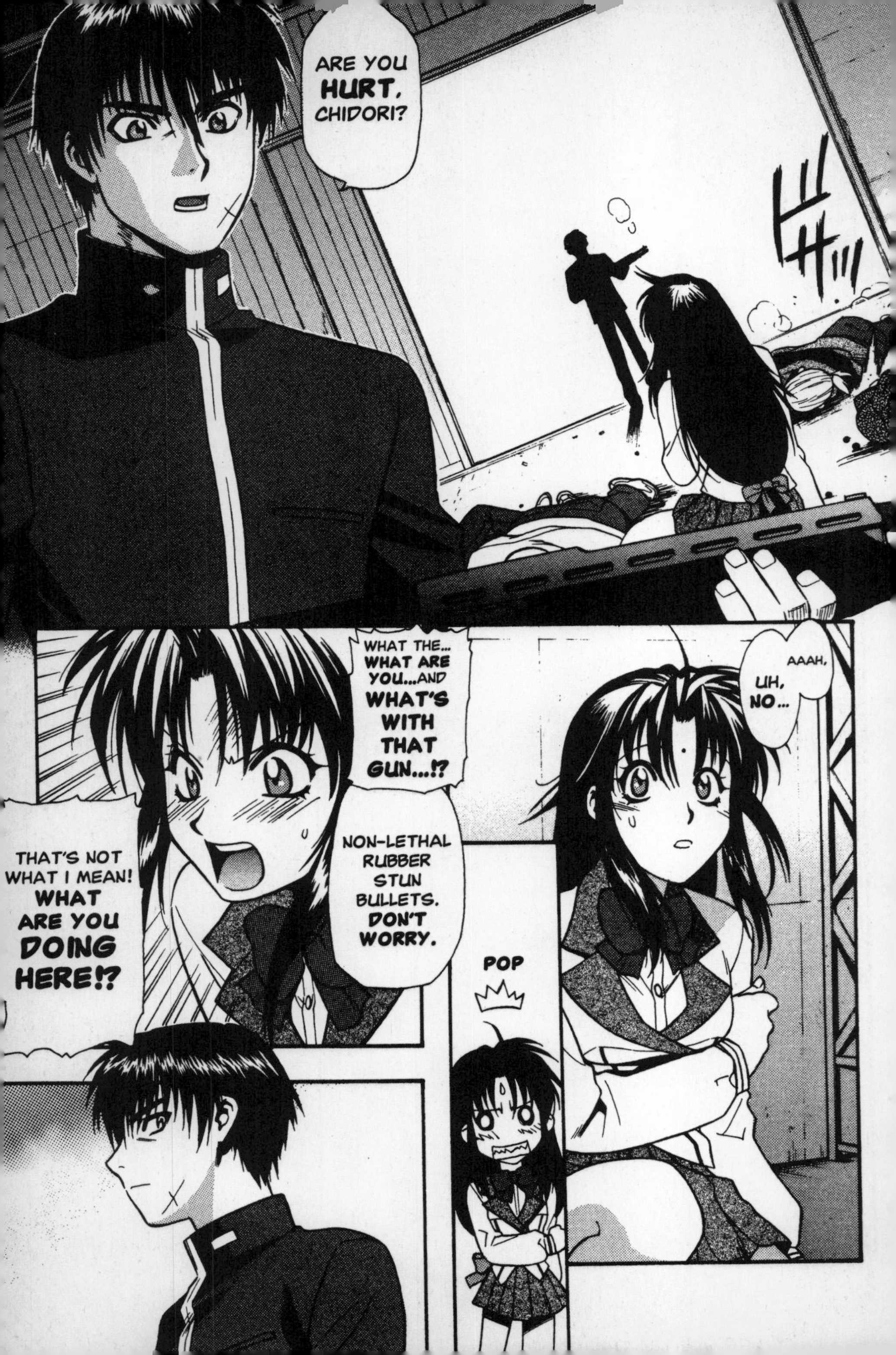
ARE YOU **HURT**, CHIDORI?
AAAH, UH, NO...
WHAT THE... **WHAT ARE YOU...**AND **WHAT'S WITH THAT GUN...!?**
NON-LETHAL RUBBER STUN BULLETS. **DON'T WORRY.**
POP
THAT'S NOT WHAT I MEAN! **WHAT ARE YOU DOING HERE!?**

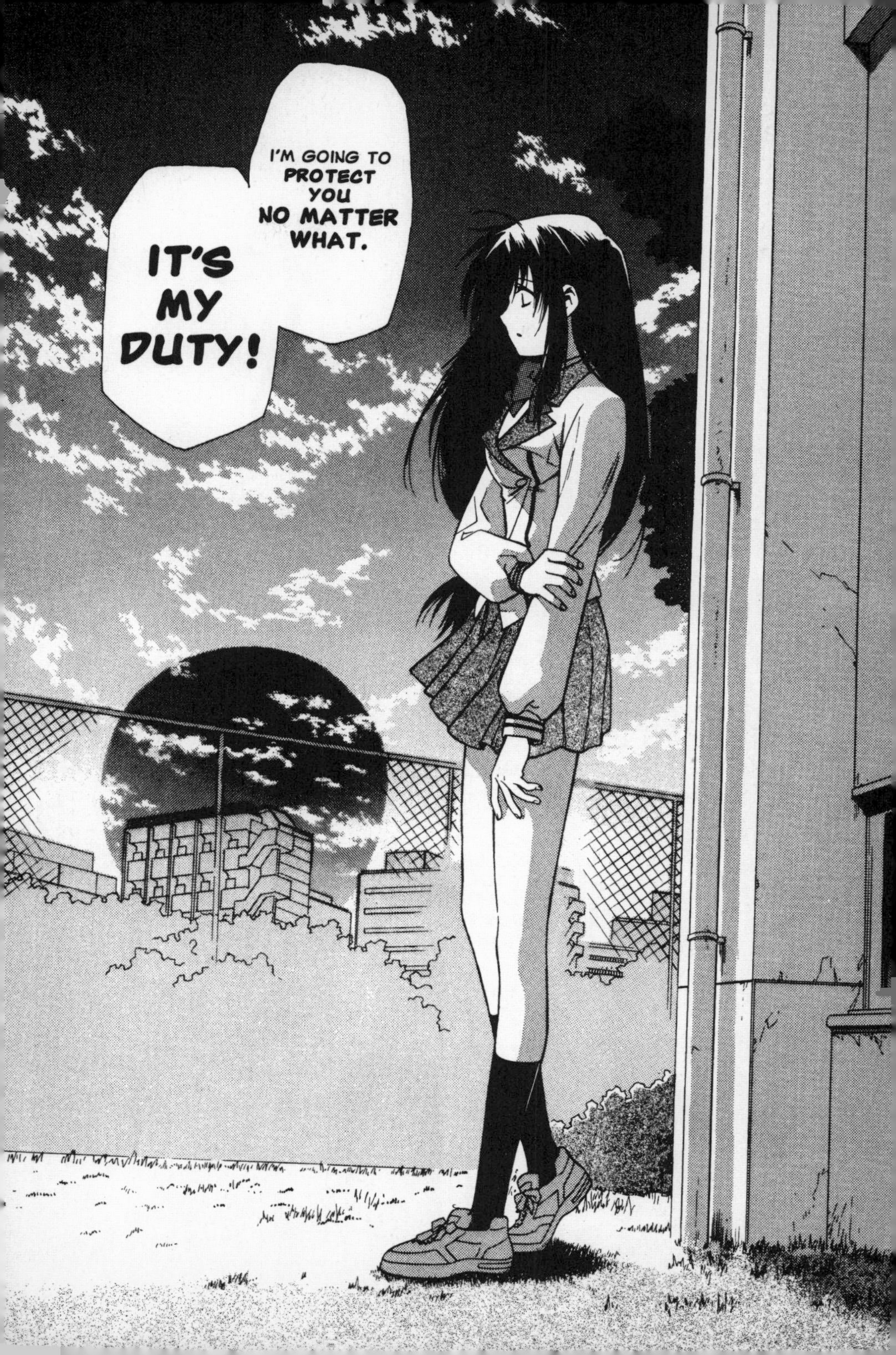
I'M GOING TO PROTECT YOU NO MATTER WHAT.
IT'S MY DUTY!

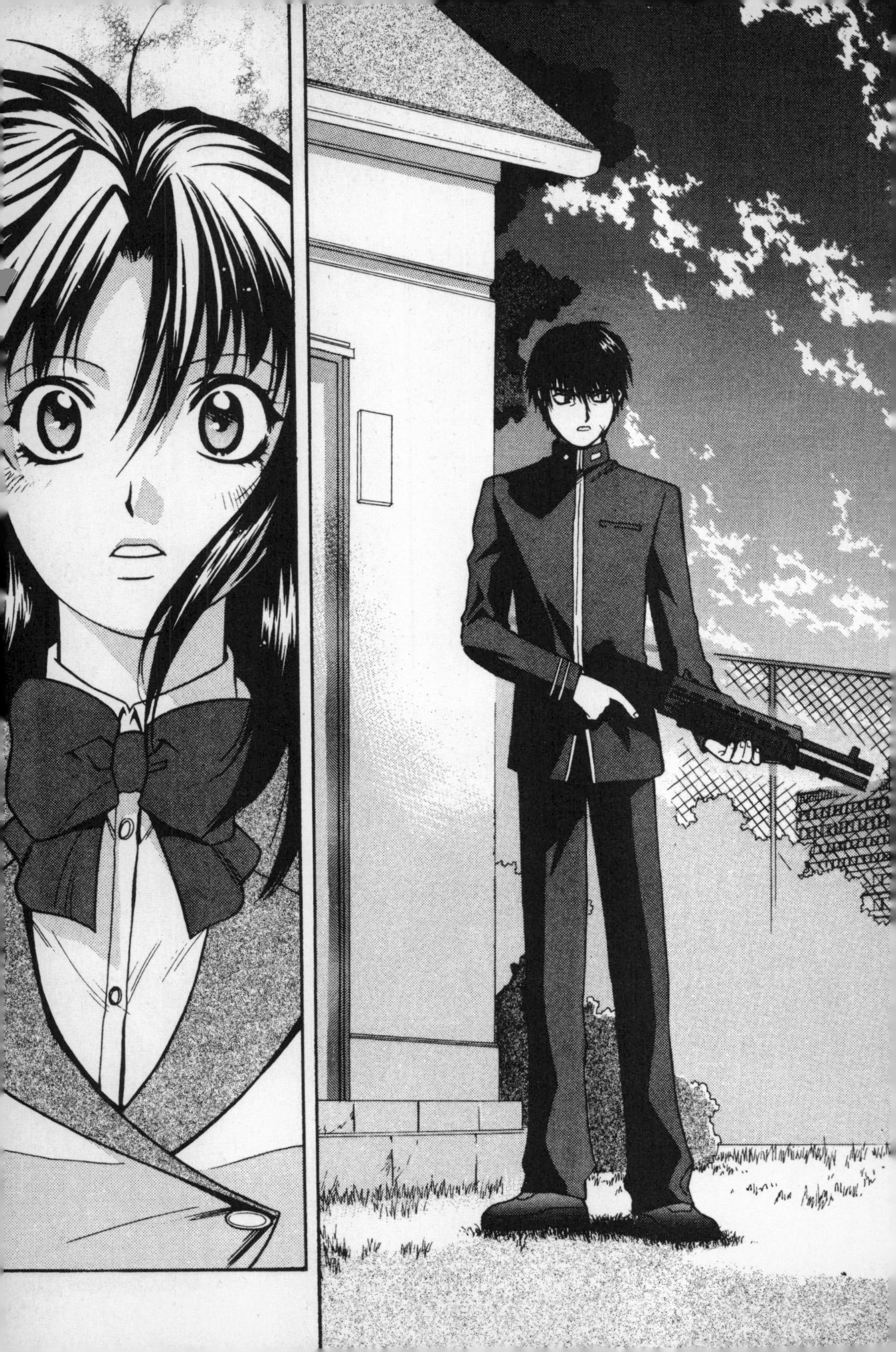

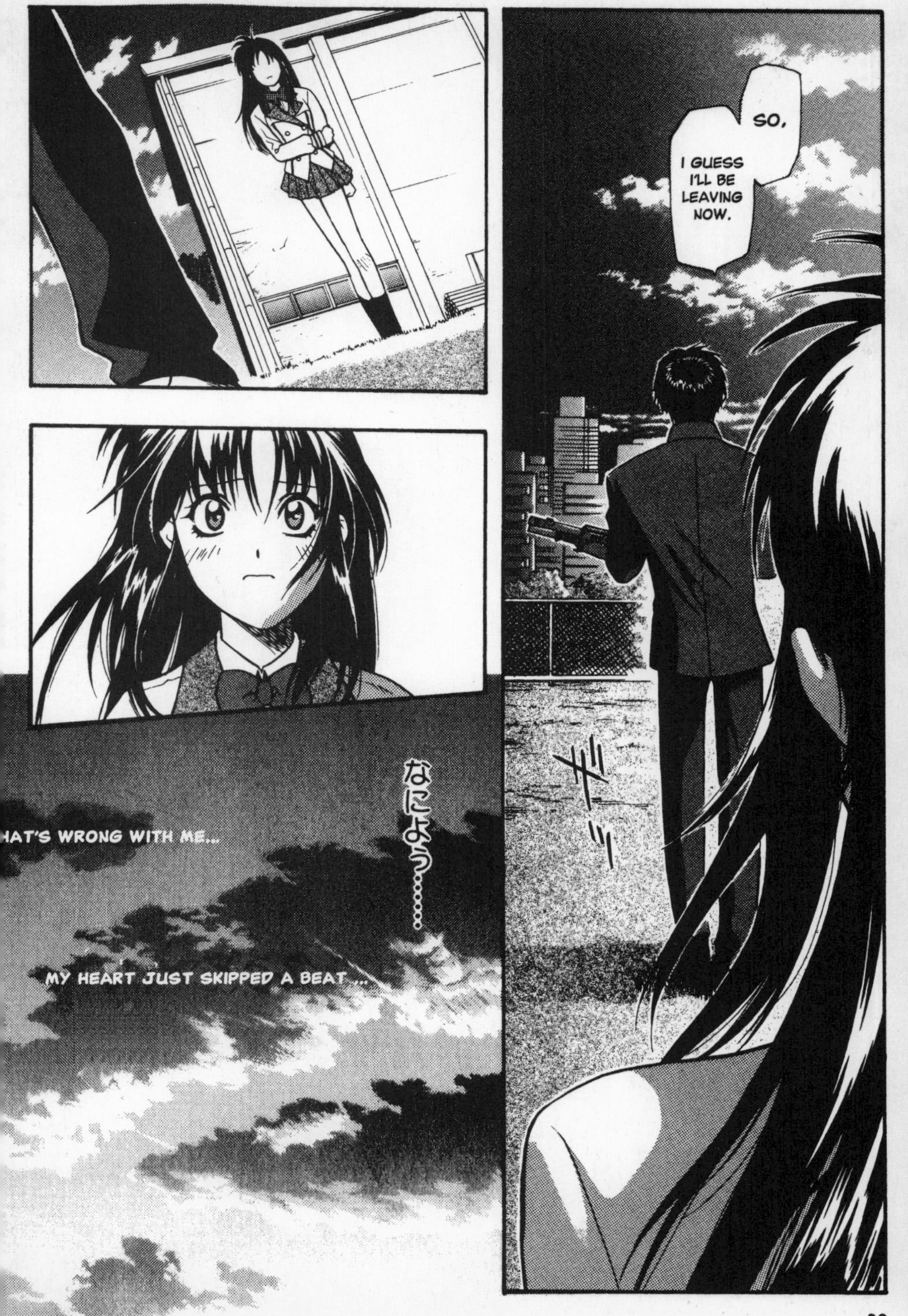
SO,
I GUESS I'LL BE LEAVING NOW.
ザッ
HAT'S WRONG WITH ME...
なによう……
MY HEART JUST SKIPPED A BEAT ...

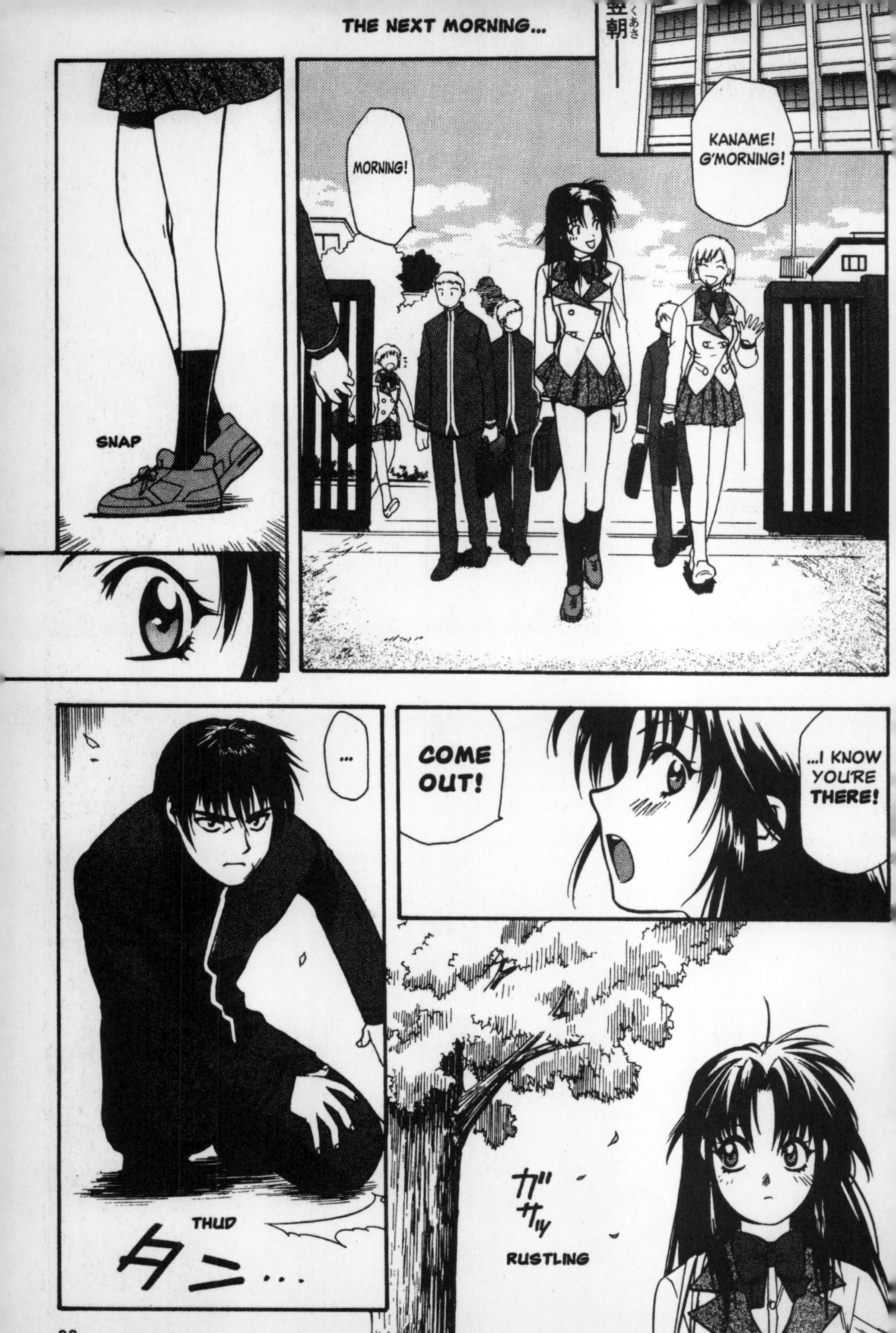
THE NEXT MORNING...
翌朝——
KANAME! G'MORNING!
MORNING!
SNAP
...I KNOW YOU'RE THERE!
COME OUT!
ガサッ
RUSTLING
...
THUD
タン...

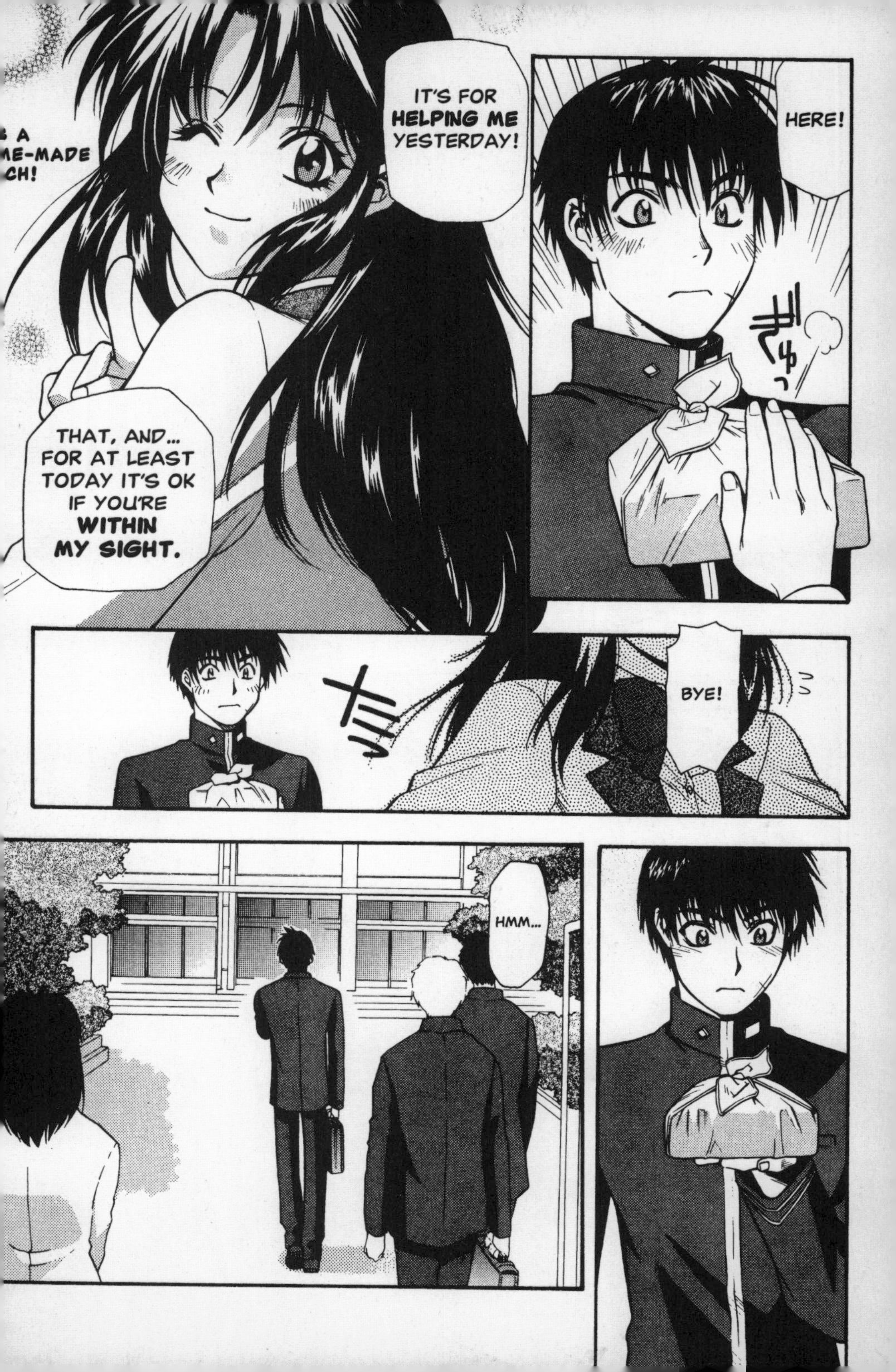
HERE!
ぎゅっ
IT'S FOR HELPING ME YESTERDAY!
THAT, AND... FOR AT LEAST TODAY IT'S OK IF YOU'RE WITHIN MY SIGHT.
BYE!
タ
HMM...

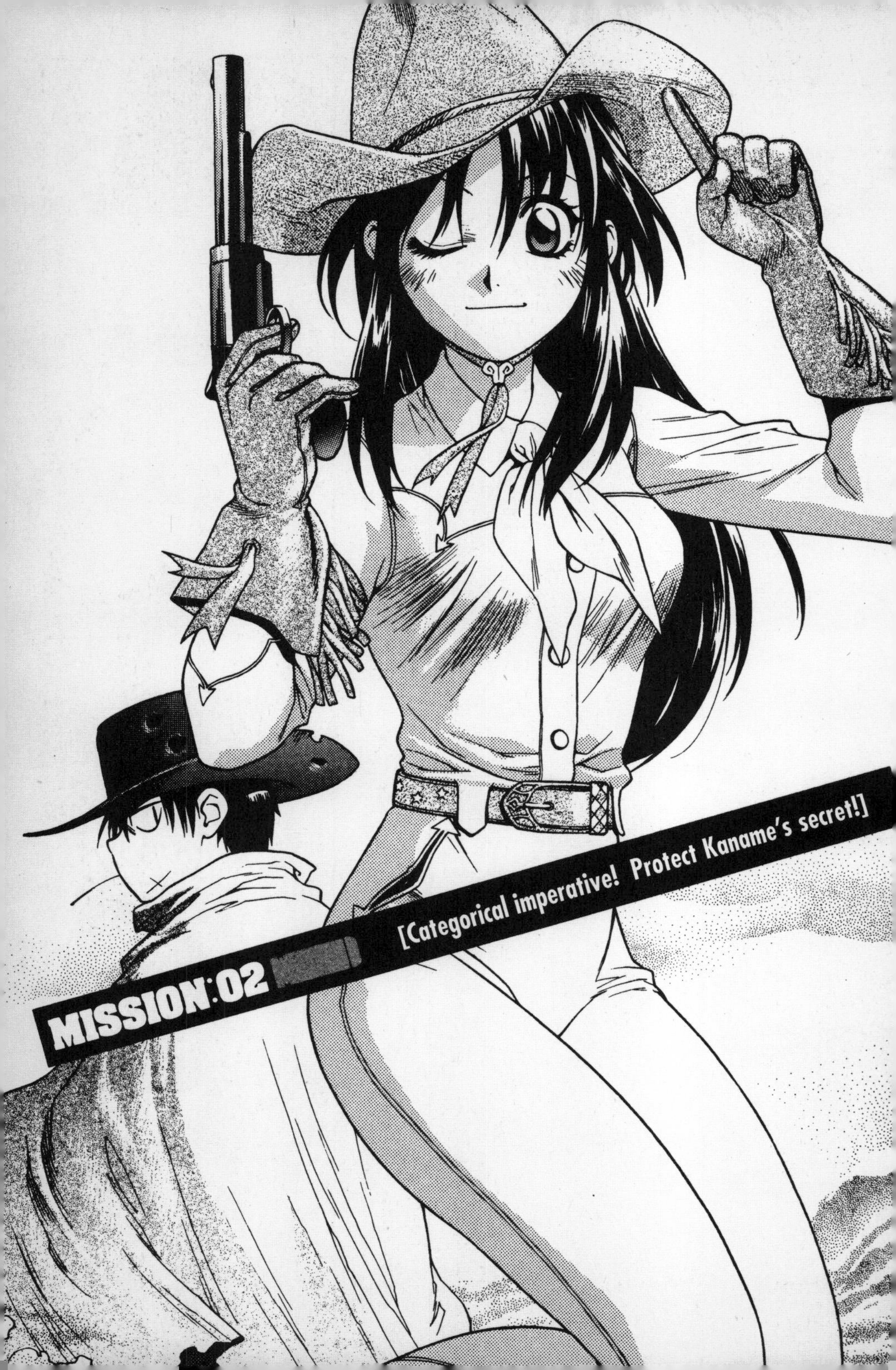
MISSION:02
[Categorical imperative! Protect Kaname's secret!]

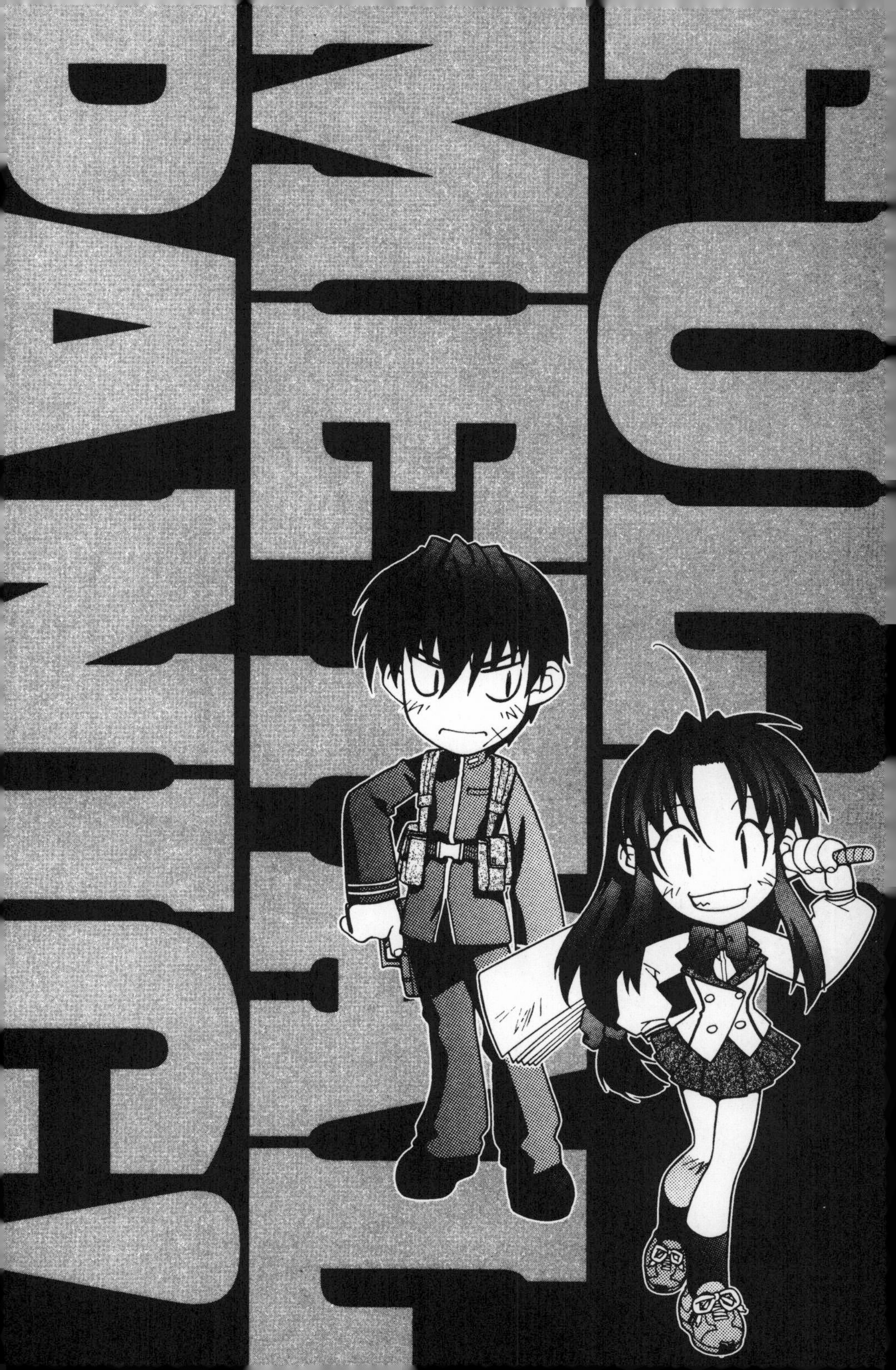
FULL
METAL
PANIC

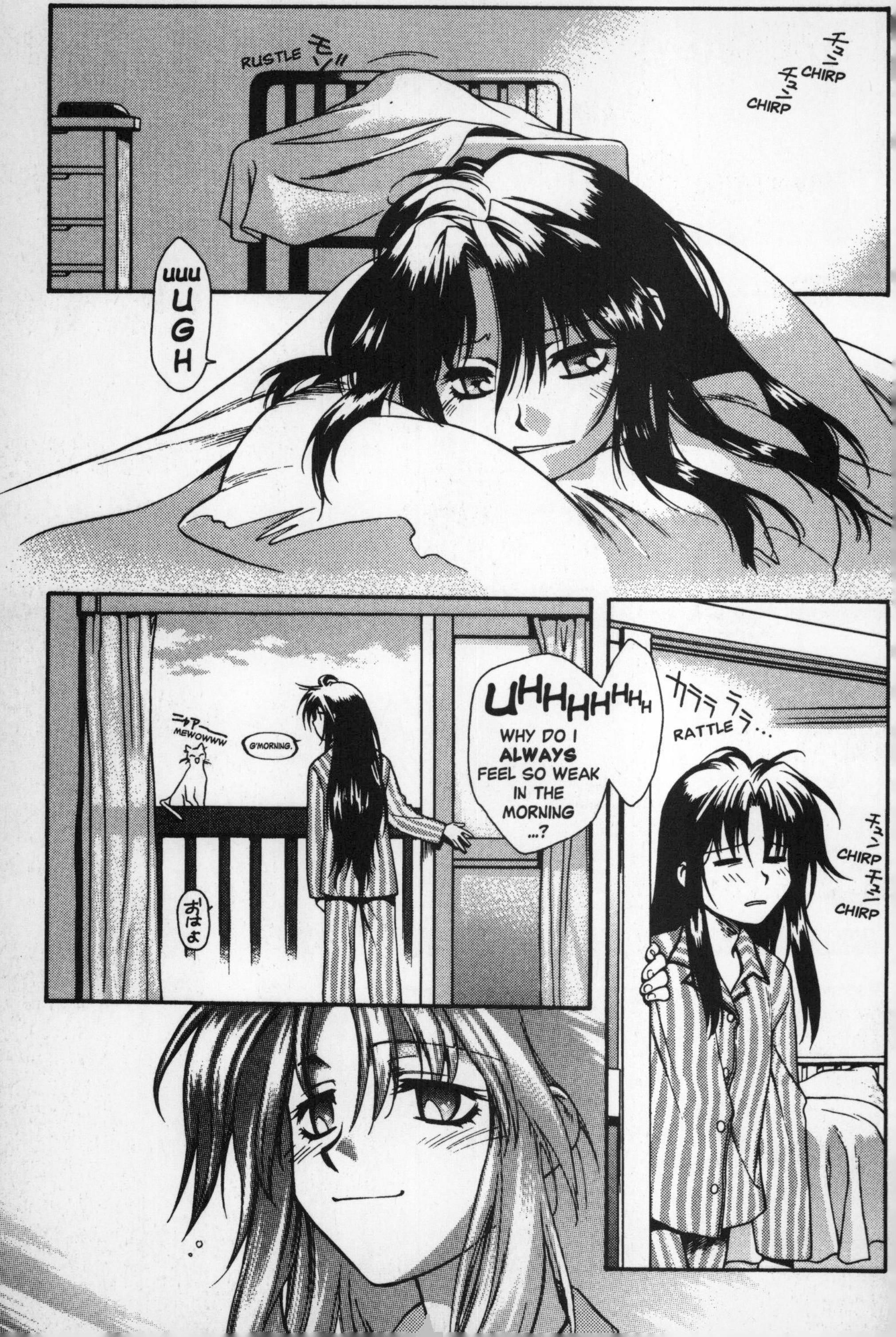

CHIRP
CHIRP
RUSTLE
uuu UGH
UHHHHHHH WHY DO I ALWAYS FEEL SO WEAK IN THE MORNING ...?
RATTLE
CHIRP
CHIRP
G'MORNING.
MEWOWWW
おはよ

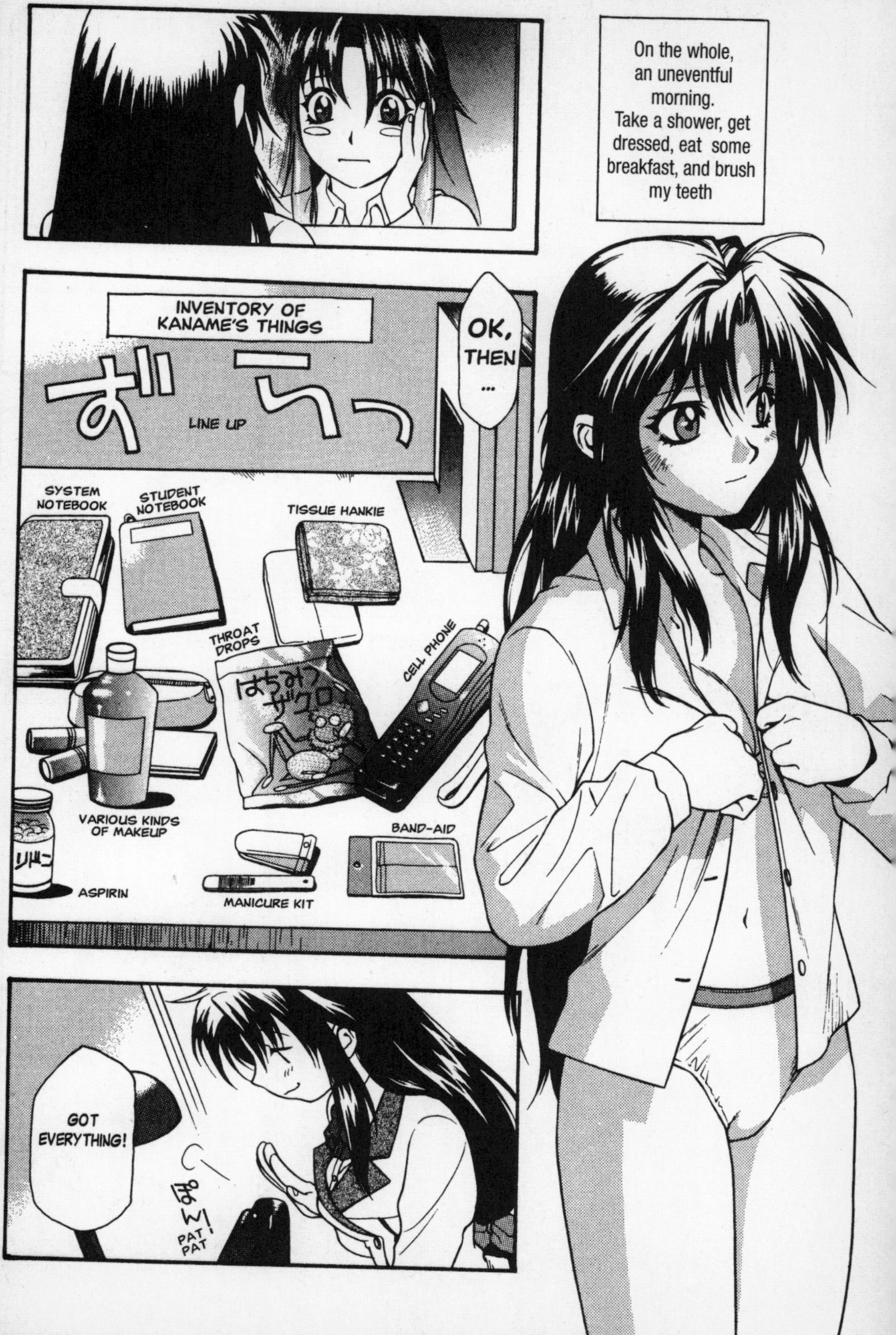
On the whole, an uneventful morning. Take a shower, get dressed, eat some breakfast, and brush my teeth
OK, THEN ...
INVENTORY OF KANAME'S THINGS
ずらっ
LINE UP
SYSTEM NOTEBOOK
STUDENT NOTEBOOK
TISSUE HANKIE
THROAT DROPS
はちみつザクロ
CELL PHONE
VARIOUS KINDS OF MAKEUP
BAND-AID
ASPIRIN
MANICURE KIT
GOT EVERYTHING!
ぽん!
PAT PAT

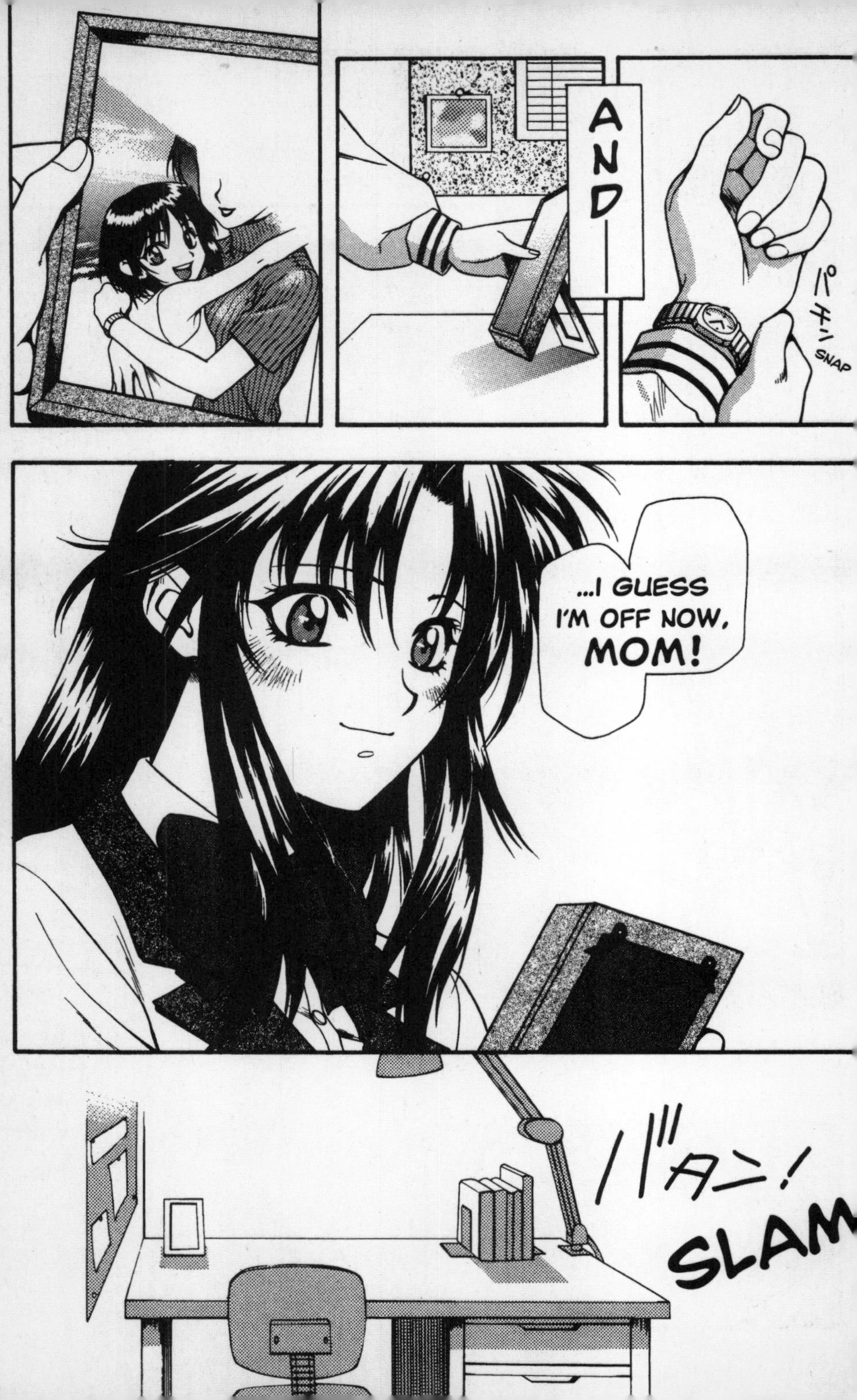
パキン
SNAP
AND—
...I GUESS I'M OFF NOW, MOM!
バタン!
SLAM

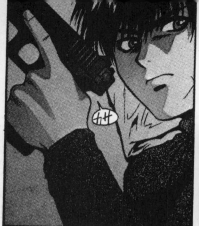

CHIRP CHIRP...

Meanwhile——

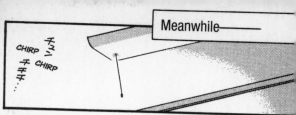

RATTLE

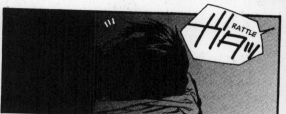

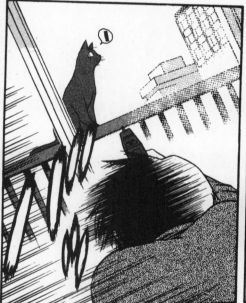

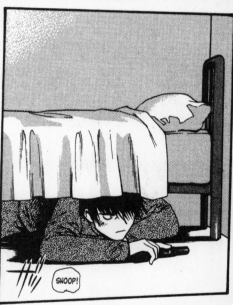

SNOOP!

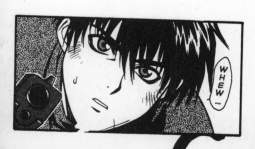

WHEW...

MEOW WWWW WWW WW~?

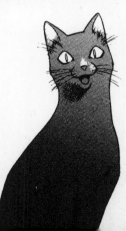

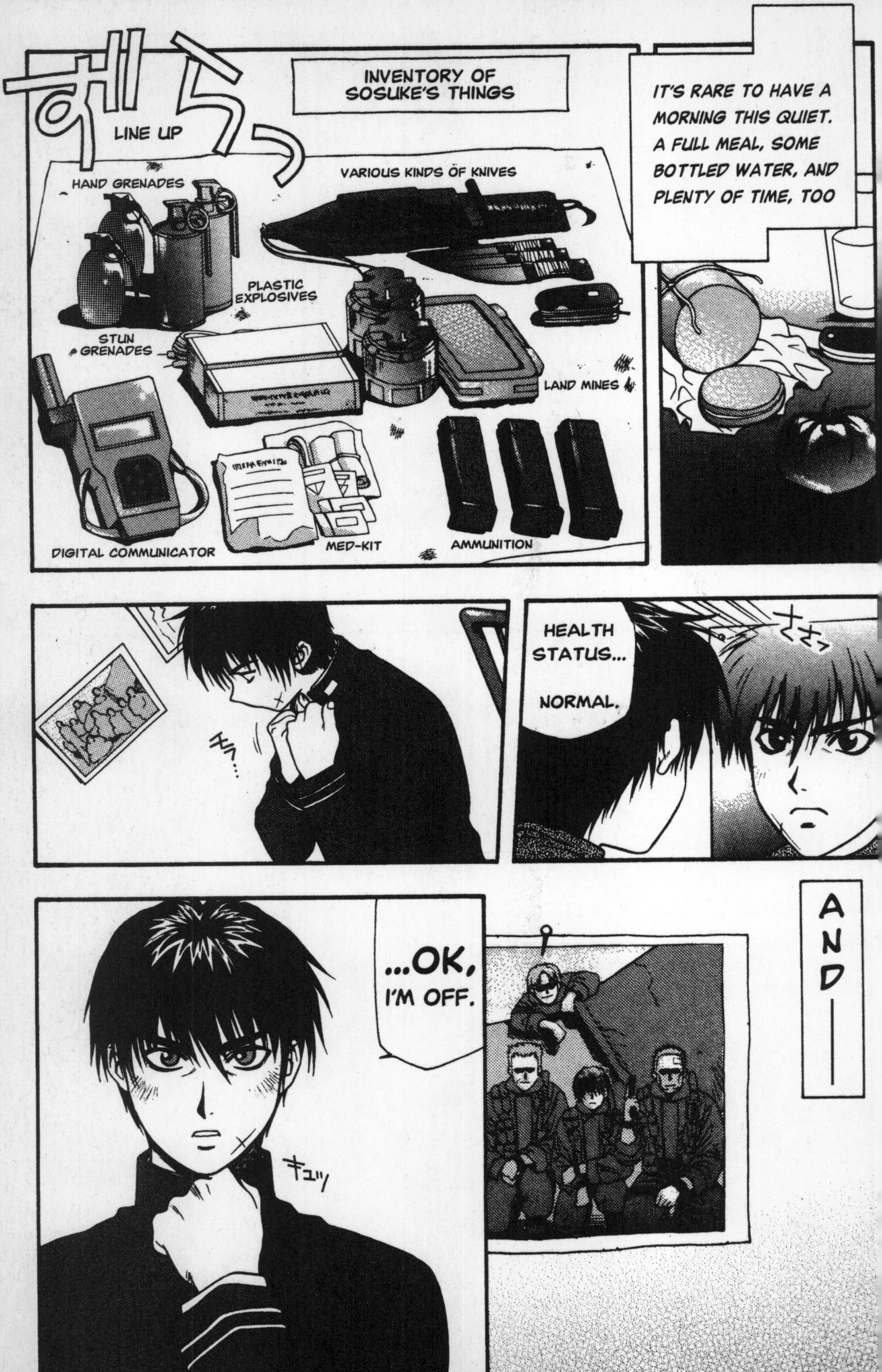
IT'S RARE TO HAVE A MORNING THIS QUIET. A FULL MEAL, SOME BOTTLED WATER, AND PLENTY OF TIME, TOO
ずらっ
LINE UP
INVENTORY OF SOSUKE'S THINGS
VARIOUS KINDS OF KNIVES
HAND GRENADES
PLASTIC EXPLOSIVES
STUN GRENADES
LAND MINES
DIGITAL COMMUNICATOR
MED-KIT
AMMUNITION
さっ
HEALTH STATUS...
NORMAL.
AND—
...OK, I'M OFF.
キュッ

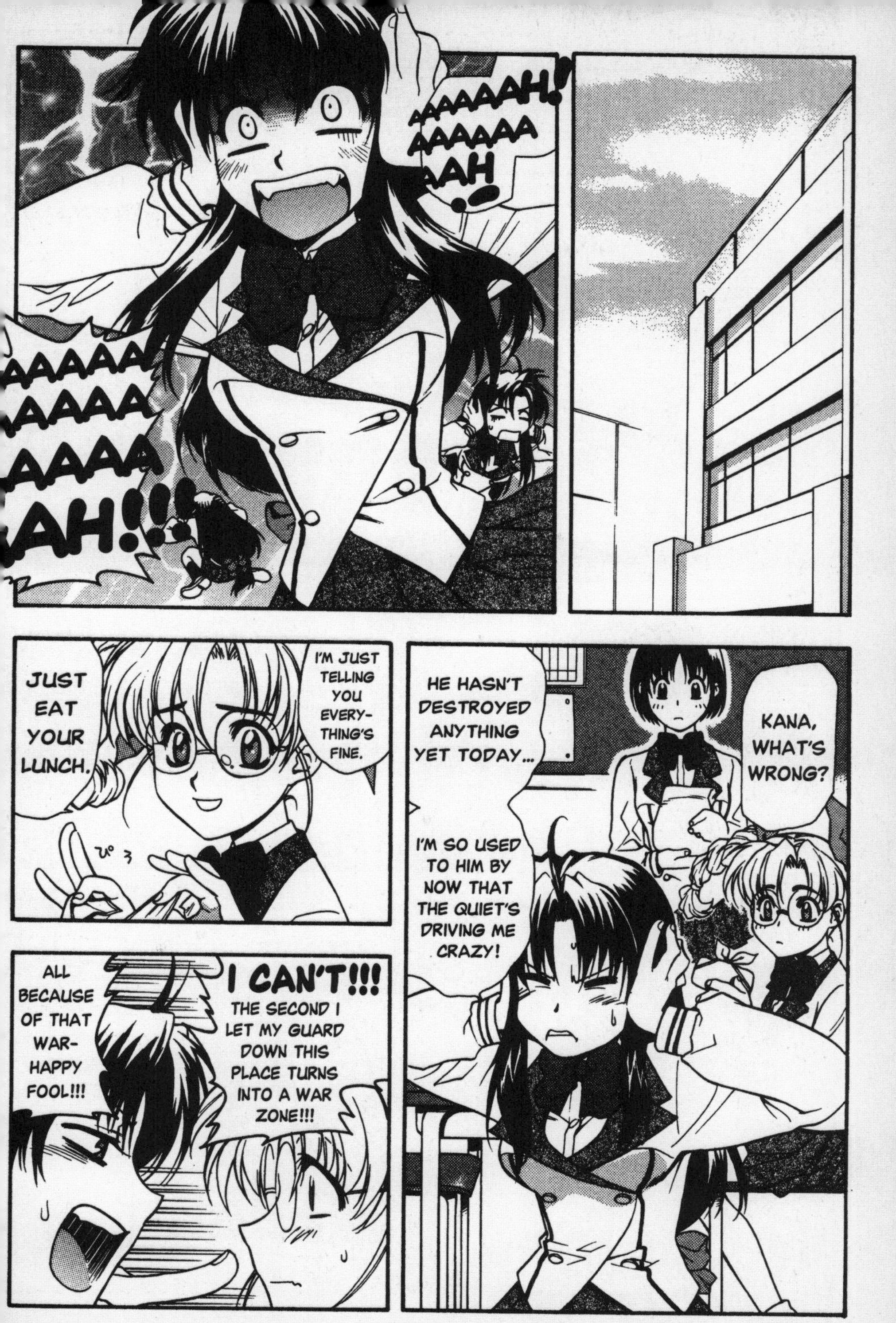
AAAAAAH!!
AAAAAA
AAH..!
AAAAAA
AAAAA
AAAAA
AH!!!
KANA, WHAT'S WRONG?
HE HASN'T DESTROYED ANYTHING YET TODAY...
I'M SO USED TO HIM BY NOW THAT THE QUIET'S DRIVING ME CRAZY!
I'M JUST TELLING YOU EVERY-THING'S FINE.
JUST EAT YOUR LUNCH.
ぴろ
I CAN'T!!!
THE SECOND I LET MY GUARD DOWN THIS PLACE TURNS INTO A WAR ZONE!!!
ALL BECAUSE OF THAT WAR-HAPPY FOOL!!!

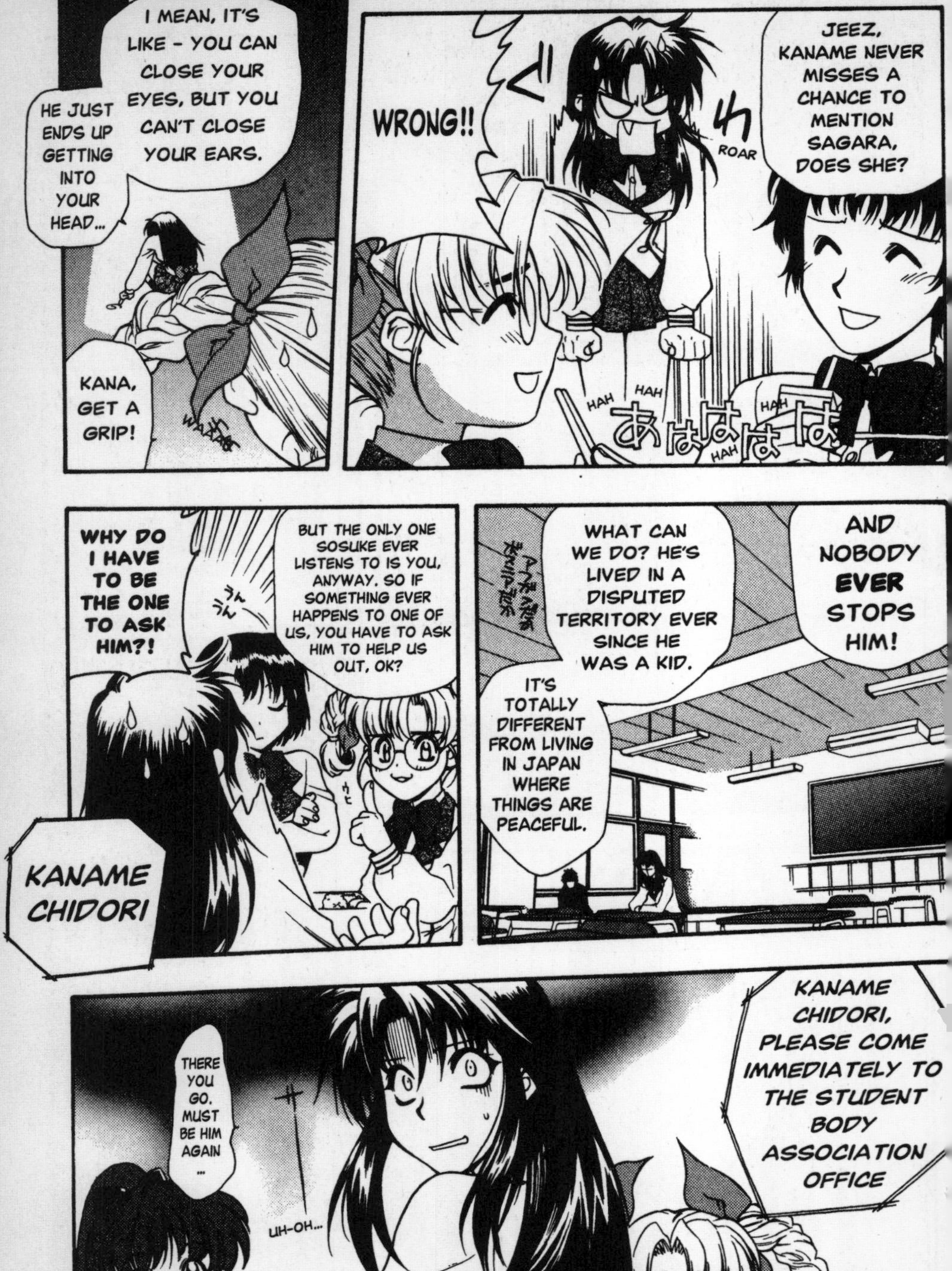
JEEZ, KANAME NEVER MISSES A CHANCE TO MENTION SAGARA, DOES SHE?
ROAR
WRONG!!
HAH HAH HAH HAH
I MEAN, IT'S LIKE - YOU CAN CLOSE YOUR EYES, BUT YOU CAN'T CLOSE YOUR EARS.
HE JUST ENDS UP GETTING INTO YOUR HEAD...
KANA, GET A GRIP!
AND NOBODY EVER STOPS HIM!
WHAT CAN WE DO? HE'S LIVED IN A DISPUTED TERRITORY EVER SINCE HE WAS A KID.
IT'S TOTALLY DIFFERENT FROM LIVING IN JAPAN WHERE THINGS ARE PEACEFUL.
BUT THE ONLY ONE SOSUKE EVER LISTENS TO IS YOU, ANYWAY. SO IF SOMETHING EVER HAPPENS TO ONE OF US, YOU HAVE TO ASK HIM TO HELP US OUT, OK?
WHY DO I HAVE TO BE THE ONE TO ASK HIM?!
KANAME CHIDORI
KANAME CHIDORI, PLEASE COME IMMEDIATELY TO THE STUDENT BODY ASSOCIATION OFFICE
UH-OH...
THERE YOU GO. MUST BE HIM AGAIN ...

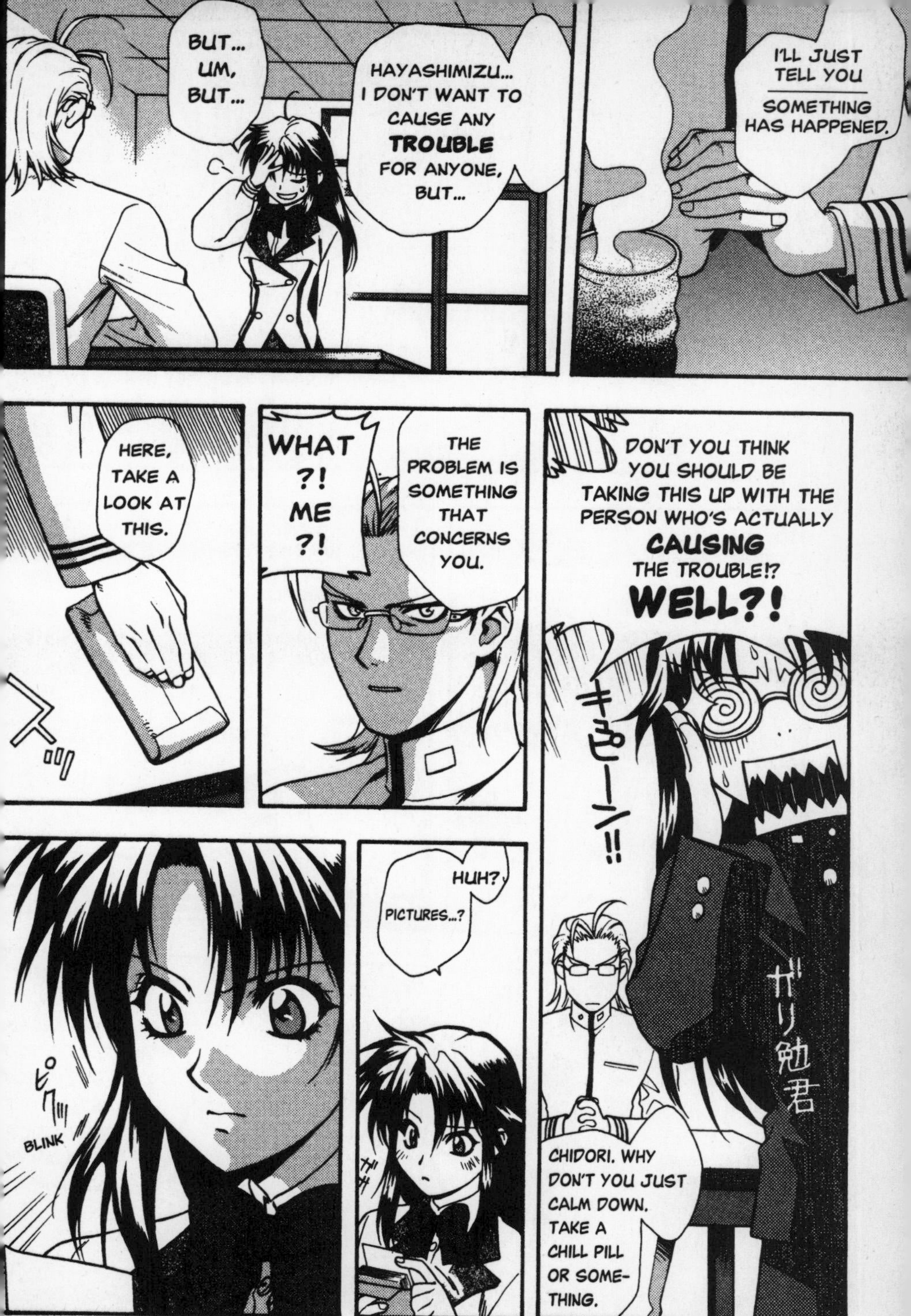
I'LL JUST TELL YOU
SOMETHING HAS HAPPENED.
HAYASHIMIZU... I DON'T WANT TO CAUSE ANY TROUBLE FOR ANYONE, BUT...
BUT... UM, BUT...
DON'T YOU THINK YOU SHOULD BE TAKING THIS UP WITH THE PERSON WHO'S ACTUALLY CAUSING THE TROUBLE!? WELL?!
キュピーン!!
ガリ勉君
CHIDORI. WHY DON'T YOU JUST CALM DOWN. TAKE A CHILL PILL OR SOME-THING.
THE PROBLEM IS SOMETHING THAT CONCERNS YOU.
WHAT?! ME?!
HERE, TAKE A LOOK AT THIS.
スッ
HUH?
PICTURES...?
ピク
BLINK

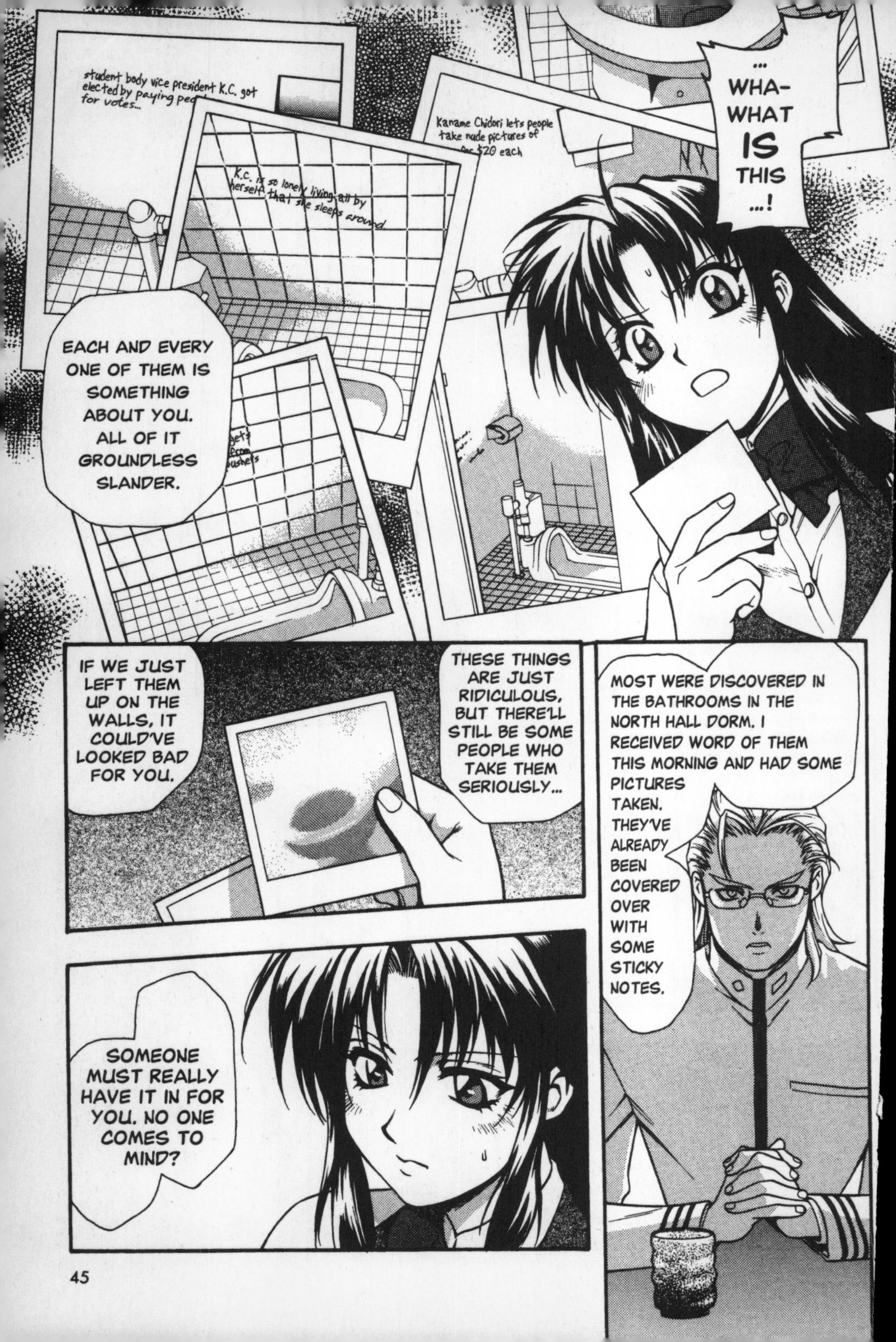
...WHA-WHAT IS THIS...!
Kaname Chidori lets people take nude pictures of
for $20 each
student body vice president K.C. got elected by paying peo
for votes...
K.C. is so lonely living all by herself that she sleeps around.
EACH AND EVERY ONE OF THEM IS SOMETHING ABOUT YOU. ALL OF IT GROUNDLESS SLANDER.
MOST WERE DISCOVERED IN THE BATHROOMS IN THE NORTH HALL DORM. I RECEIVED WORD OF THEM THIS MORNING AND HAD SOME PICTURES TAKEN. THEY'VE ALREADY BEEN COVERED OVER WITH SOME STICKY NOTES.
THESE THINGS ARE JUST RIDICULOUS, BUT THERE'LL STILL BE SOME PEOPLE WHO TAKE THEM SERIOUSLY...
IF WE JUST LEFT THEM UP ON THE WALLS, IT COULD'VE LOOKED BAD FOR YOU.
SOMEONE MUST REALLY HAVE IT IN FOR YOU. NO ONE COMES TO MIND?

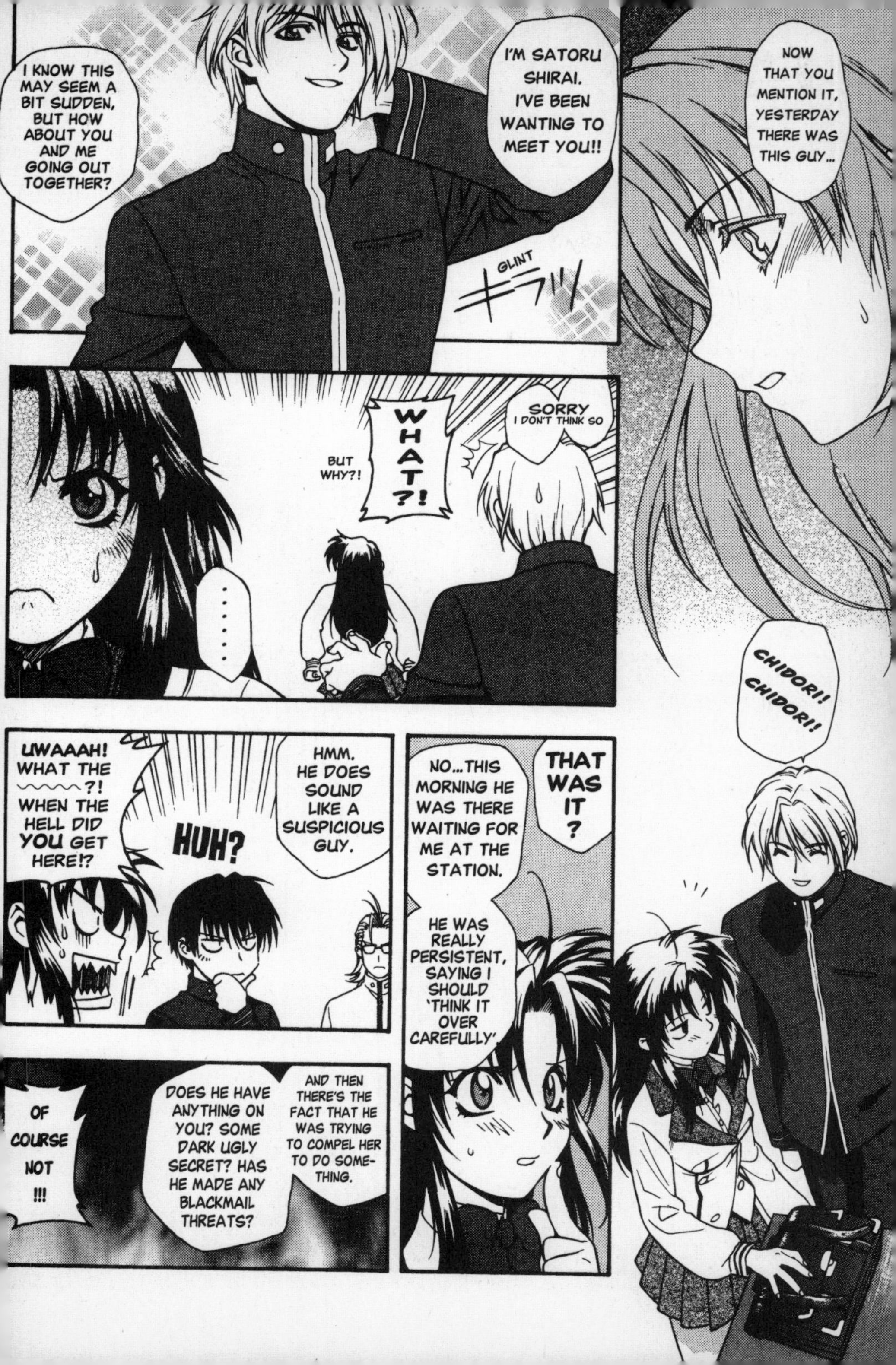
NOW THAT YOU MENTION IT, YESTERDAY THERE WAS THIS GUY...
I'M SATORU SHIRAI. I'VE BEEN WANTING TO MEET YOU!!
I KNOW THIS MAY SEEM A BIT SUDDEN, BUT HOW ABOUT YOU AND ME GOING OUT TOGETHER?
GLINT
SORRY I DON'T THINK SO
WHAT?!
BUT WHY?!
......
CHIDORI!! CHIDORI!!
THAT WAS IT?
NO...THIS MORNING HE WAS THERE WAITING FOR ME AT THE STATION.
HE WAS REALLY PERSISTENT, SAYING I SHOULD 'THINK IT OVER CAREFULLY'.
HMM. HE DOES SOUND LIKE A SUSPICIOUS GUY.
HUH?
UWAAAH! WHAT THE ~~~~?! WHEN THE HELL DID YOU GET HERE!?
AND THEN THERE'S THE FACT THAT HE WAS TRYING TO COMPEL HER TO DO SOME-THING.
DOES HE HAVE ANYTHING ON YOU? SOME DARK UGLY SECRET? HAS HE MADE ANY BLACKMAIL THREATS?
OF COURSE NOT !!!

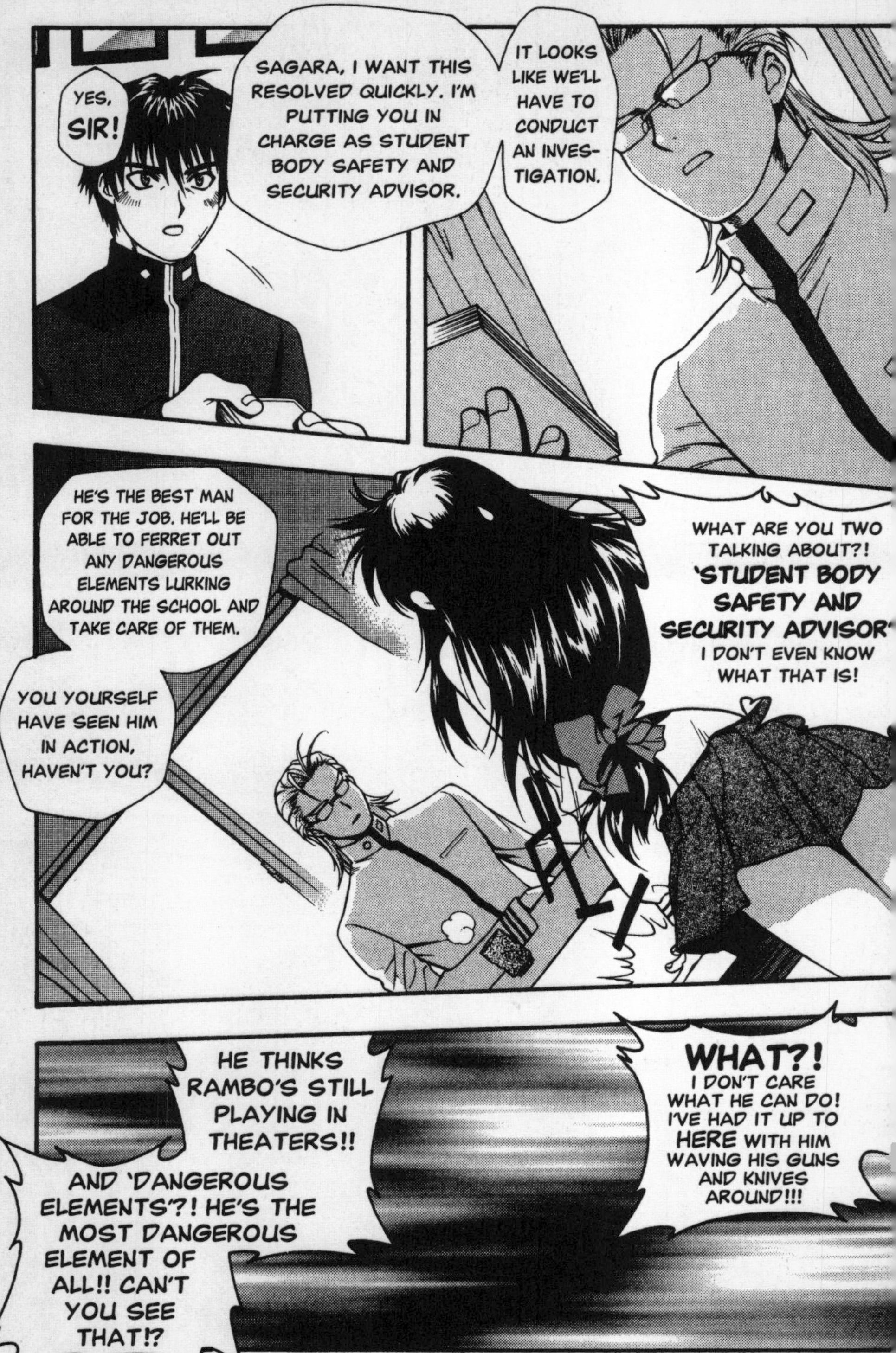
IT LOOKS LIKE WE'LL HAVE TO CONDUCT AN INVESTIGATION.
SAGARA, I WANT THIS RESOLVED QUICKLY. I'M PUTTING YOU IN CHARGE AS STUDENT BODY SAFETY AND SECURITY ADVISOR.
YES, SIR!
WHAT ARE YOU TWO TALKING ABOUT?! 'STUDENT BODY SAFETY AND SECURITY ADVISOR' I DON'T EVEN KNOW WHAT THAT IS!
HE'S THE BEST MAN FOR THE JOB. HE'LL BE ABLE TO FERRET OUT ANY DANGEROUS ELEMENTS LURKING AROUND THE SCHOOL AND TAKE CARE OF THEM.
YOU YOURSELF HAVE SEEN HIM IN ACTION, HAVEN'T YOU?
WHAT?! I DON'T CARE WHAT HE CAN DO! I'VE HAD IT UP TO HERE WITH HIM WAVING HIS GUNS AND KNIVES AROUND!!!
HE THINKS RAMBO'S STILL PLAYING IN THEATERS!!
AND 'DANGEROUS ELEMENTS'?! HE'S THE MOST DANGEROUS ELEMENT OF ALL!! CAN'T YOU SEE THAT!?

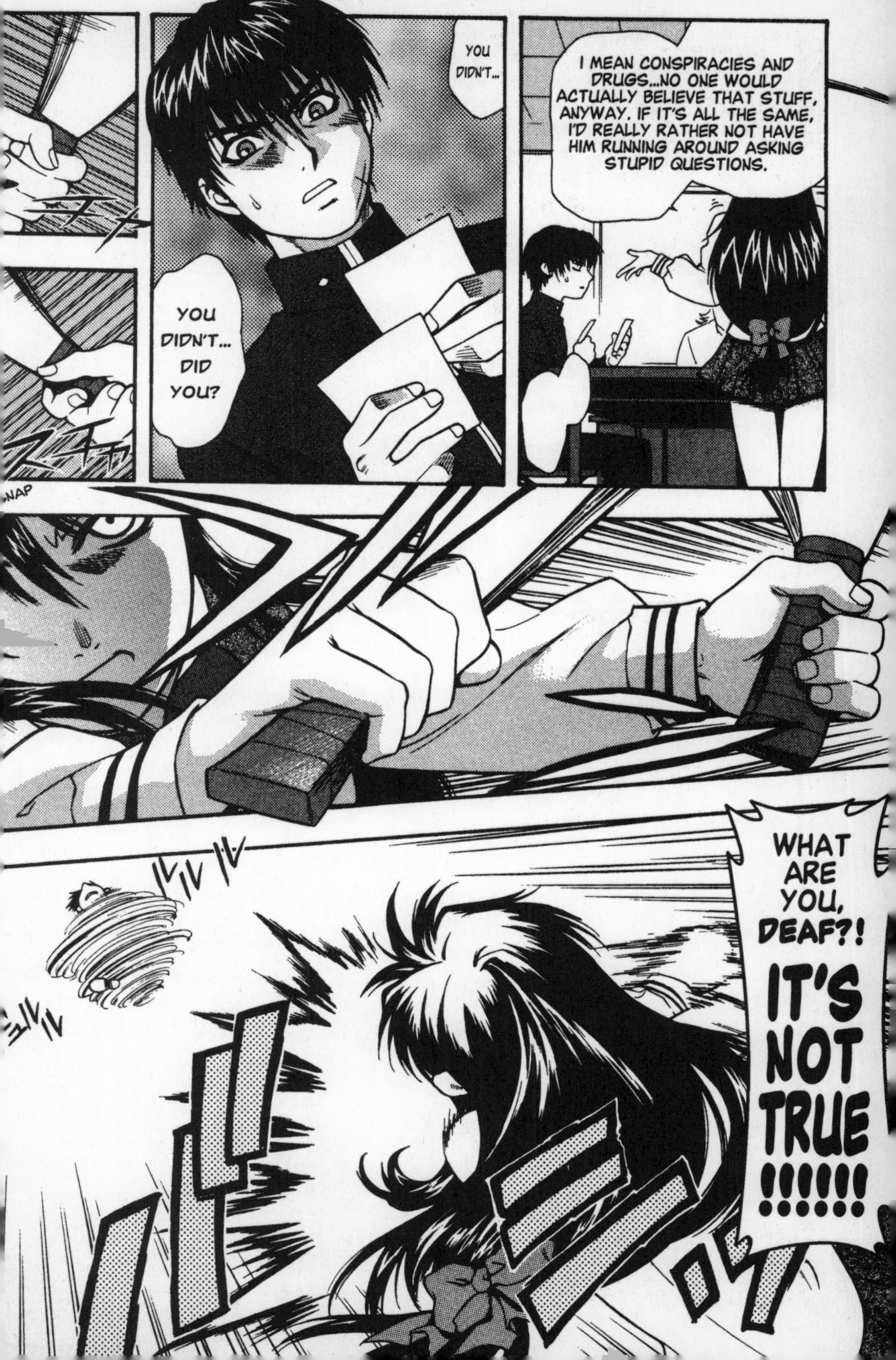
I MEAN CONSPIRACIES AND DRUGS...NO ONE WOULD ACTUALLY BELIEVE THAT STUFF, ANYWAY. IF IT'S ALL THE SAME, I'D REALLY RATHER NOT HAVE HIM RUNNING AROUND ASKING STUPID QUESTIONS.
YOU DIDN'T...
YOU DIDN'T... DID YOU?
WHAT ARE YOU, DEAF?!
IT'S NOT TRUE!!!!!!!

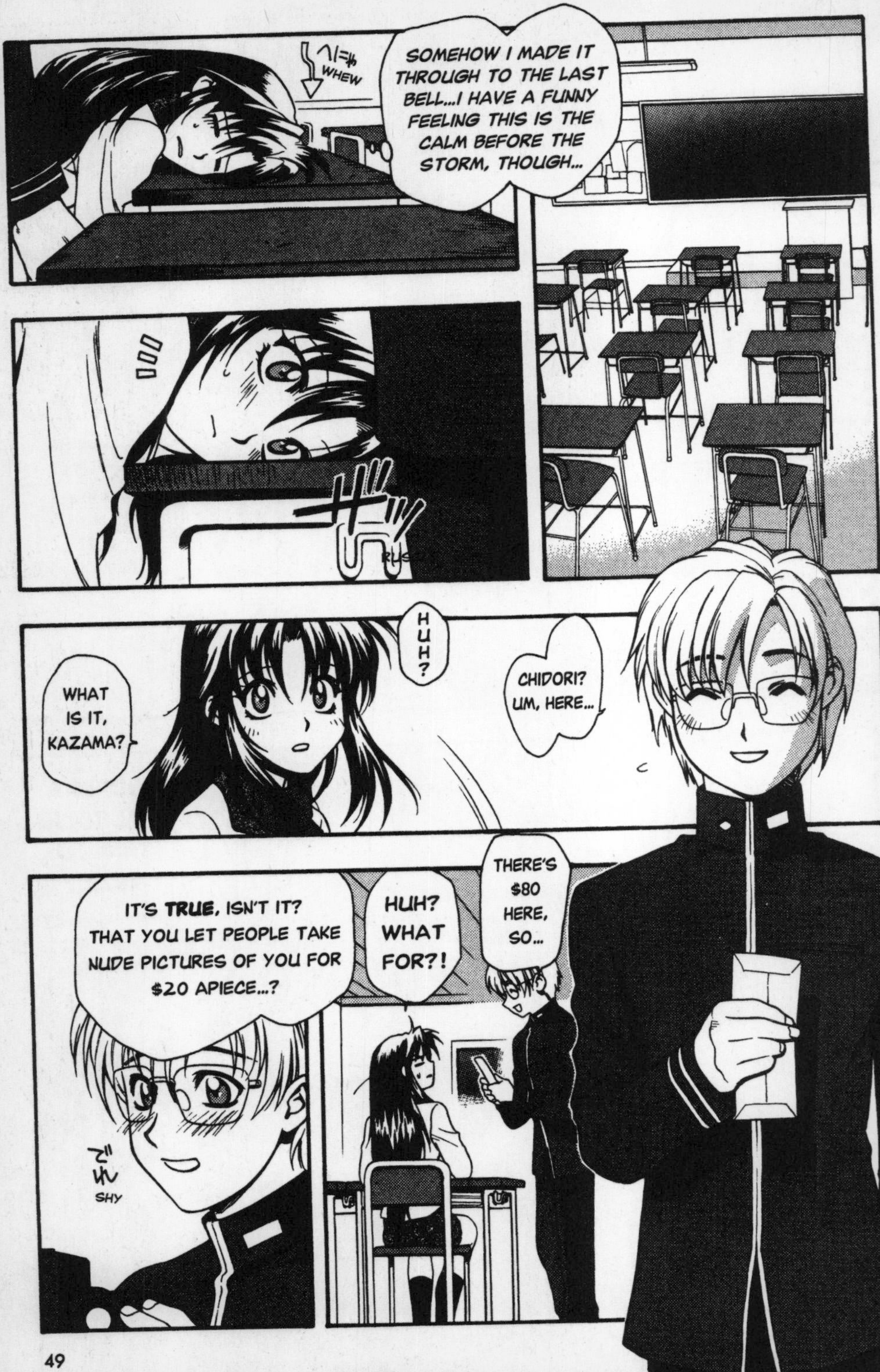
へにゅ
WHEW
SOMEHOW I MADE IT THROUGH TO THE LAST BELL...I HAVE A FUNNY FEELING THIS IS THE CALM BEFORE THE STORM, THOUGH...
ガッ
CHIDORI? UM, HERE...
HUH?
WHAT IS IT, KAZAMA?
THERE'S $80 HERE, SO...
HUH? WHAT FOR?!
IT'S **TRUE**, ISN'T IT? THAT YOU LET PEOPLE TAKE NUDE PICTURES OF YOU FOR $20 APIECE...?
ぞれ
SHY

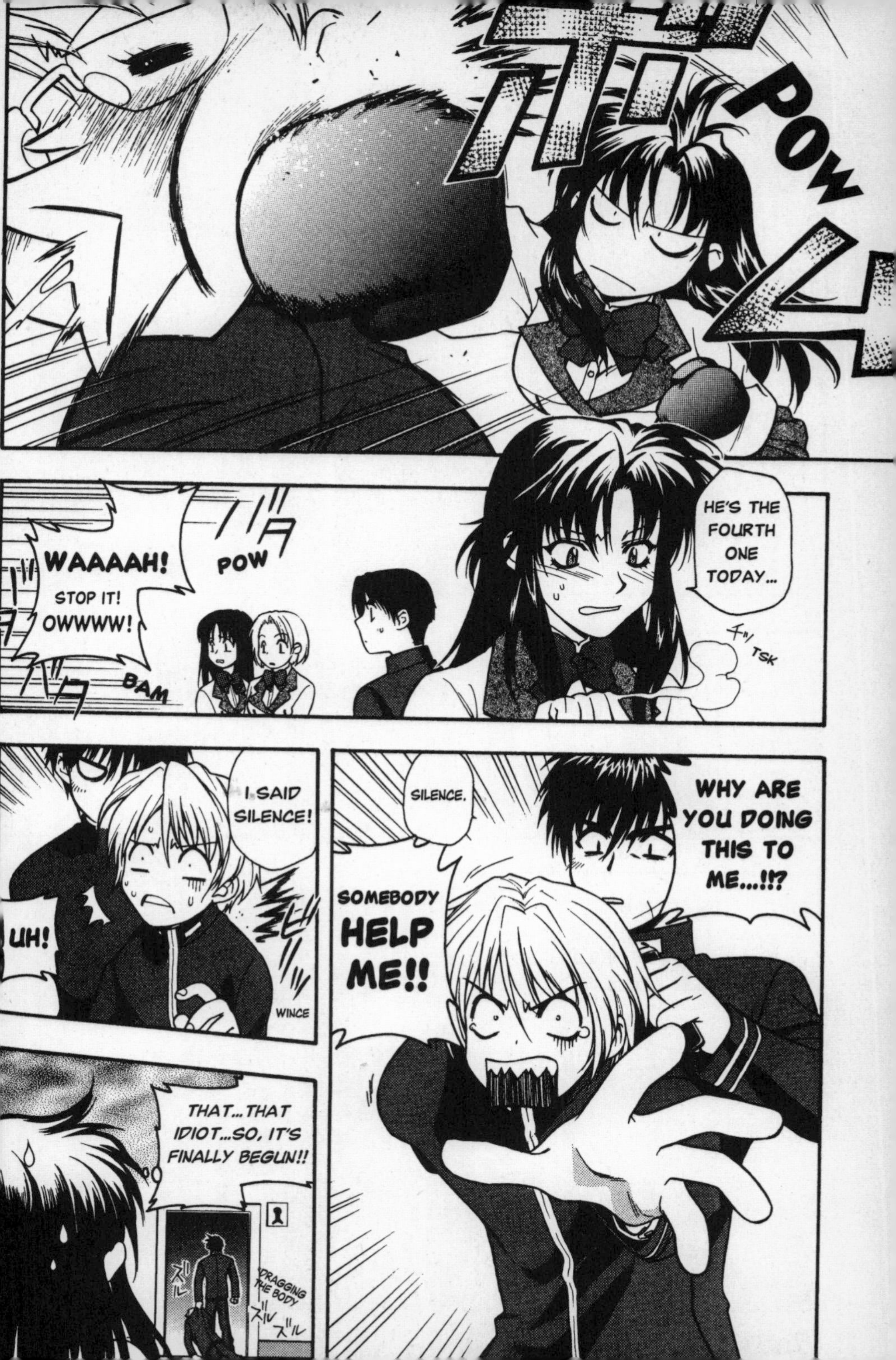
POW
HE'S THE FOURTH ONE TODAY...
TSK
POW
WAAAAH! STOP IT! OWWWW!
BAM
WHY ARE YOU DOING THIS TO ME...!!?
SILENCE.
SOMEBODY HELP ME!!
I SAID SILENCE!
UH!
WINCE
THAT...THAT IDIOT...SO, IT'S FINALLY BEGUN!!
DRAGGING THE BODY

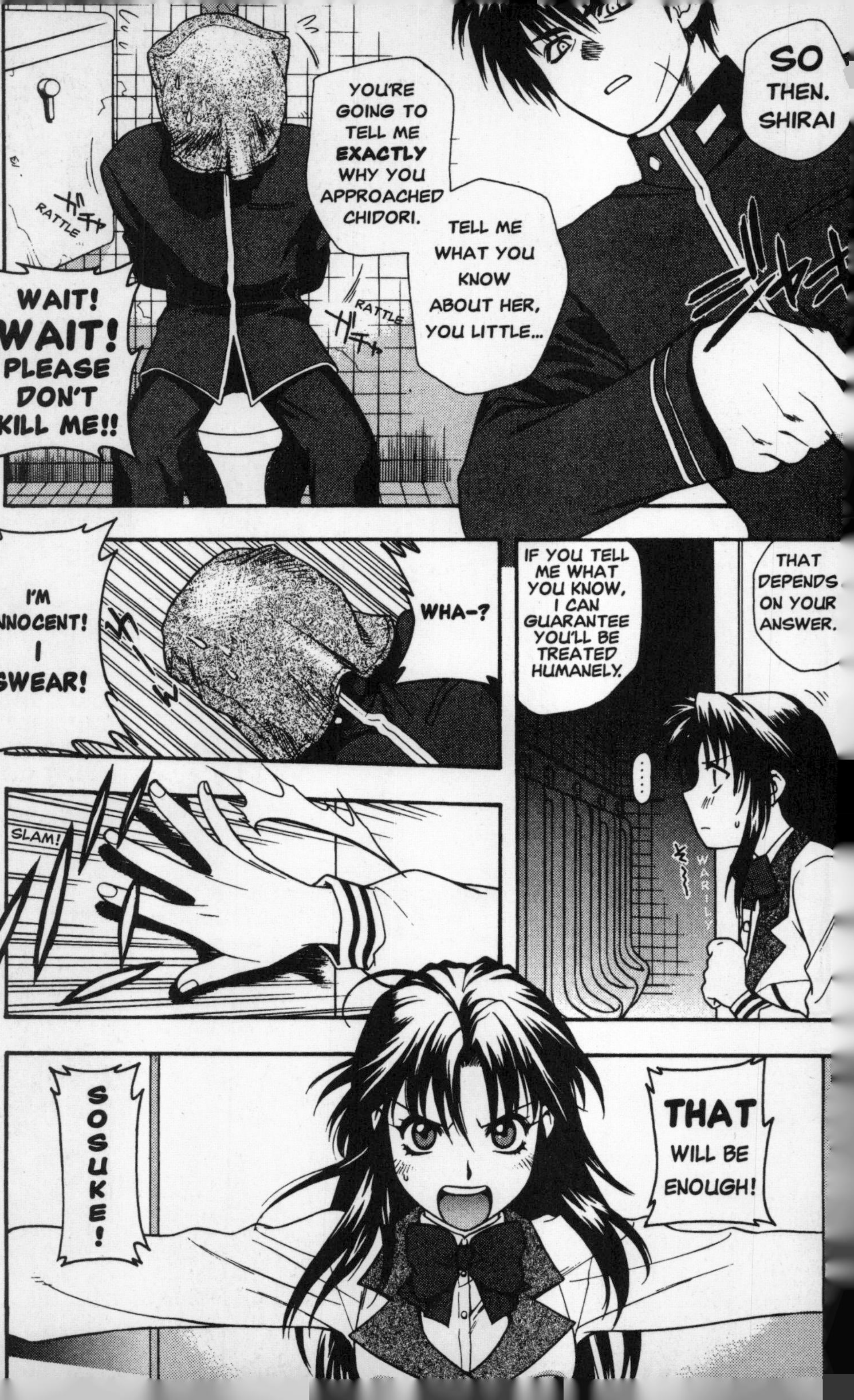
SO THEN. SHIRAI
YOU'RE GOING TO TELL ME EXACTLY WHY YOU APPROACHED CHIDORI.
TELL ME WHAT YOU KNOW ABOUT HER, YOU LITTLE...
RATTLE
WAIT! WAIT! PLEASE DON'T KILL ME!!
RATTLE
THAT DEPENDS ON YOUR ANSWER.
IF YOU TELL ME WHAT YOU KNOW, I CAN GUARANTEE YOU'LL BE TREATED HUMANELY.
...
WARILY
WHA-?
I'M INNOCENT! I SWEAR!
SLAM!
THAT WILL BE ENOUGH!
SOSUKE!

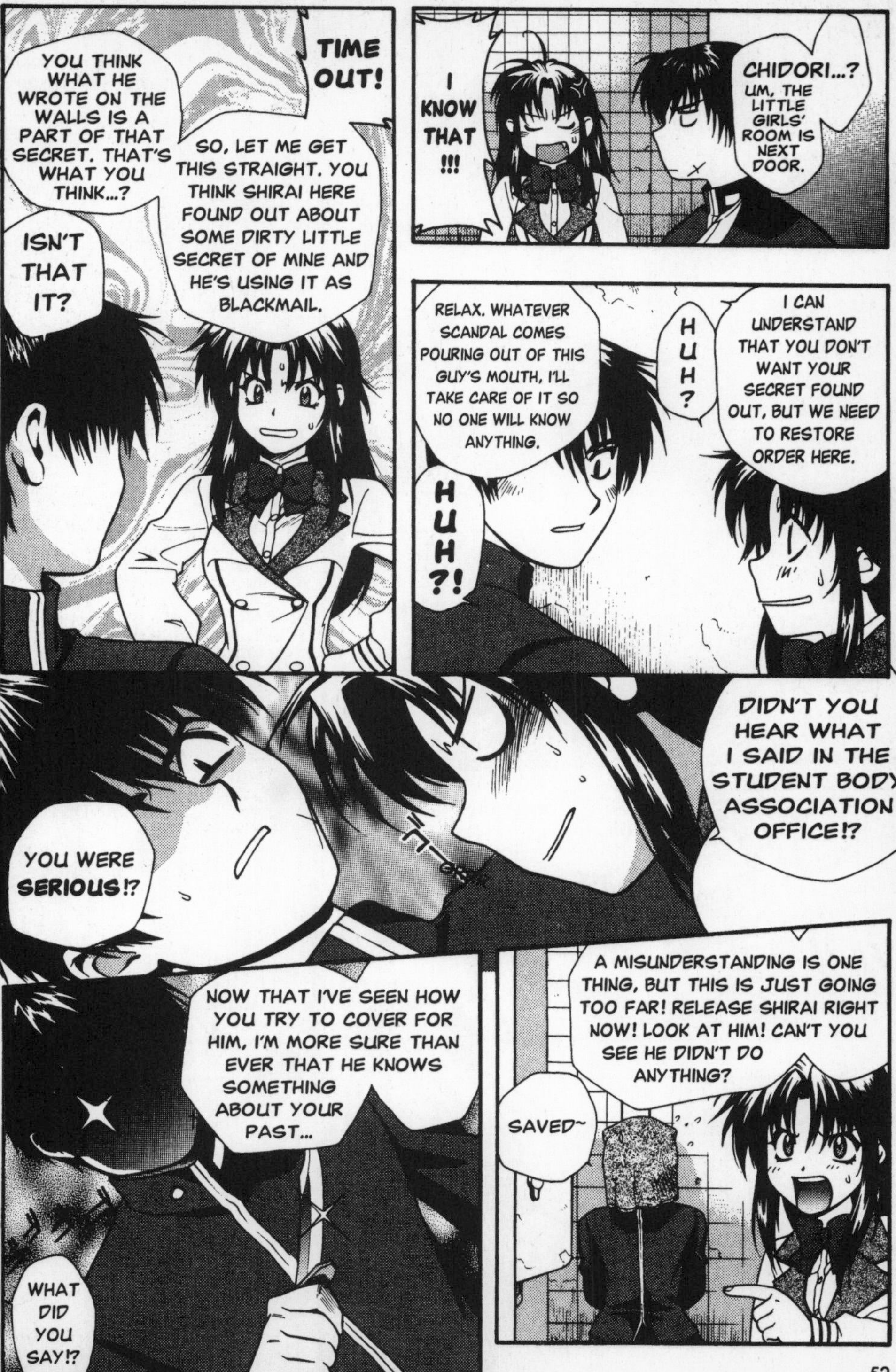

CHIDORI...? UM, THE LITTLE GIRLS' ROOM IS NEXT DOOR.
I KNOW THAT !!!
I CAN UNDERSTAND THAT YOU DON'T WANT YOUR SECRET FOUND OUT, BUT WE NEED TO RESTORE ORDER HERE.
HUH?
RELAX. WHATEVER SCANDAL COMES POURING OUT OF THIS GUY'S MOUTH, I'LL TAKE CARE OF IT SO NO ONE WILL KNOW ANYTHING.
HUH?!
TIME OUT!
SO, LET ME GET THIS STRAIGHT. YOU THINK SHIRAI HERE FOUND OUT ABOUT SOME DIRTY LITTLE SECRET OF MINE AND HE'S USING IT AS BLACKMAIL.
YOU THINK WHAT HE WROTE ON THE WALLS IS A PART OF THAT SECRET. THAT'S WHAT YOU THINK...?
ISN'T THAT IT?
DIDN'T YOU HEAR WHAT I SAID IN THE STUDENT BODY ASSOCIATION OFFICE!?
YOU WERE SERIOUS!?
A MISUNDERSTANDING IS ONE THING, BUT THIS IS JUST GOING TOO FAR! RELEASE SHIRAI RIGHT NOW! LOOK AT HIM! CAN'T YOU SEE HE DIDN'T DO ANYTHING?
SAVED~
NOW THAT I'VE SEEN HOW YOU TRY TO COVER FOR HIM, I'M MORE SURE THAN EVER THAT HE KNOWS SOMETHING ABOUT YOUR PAST...
WHAT DID YOU SAY!?

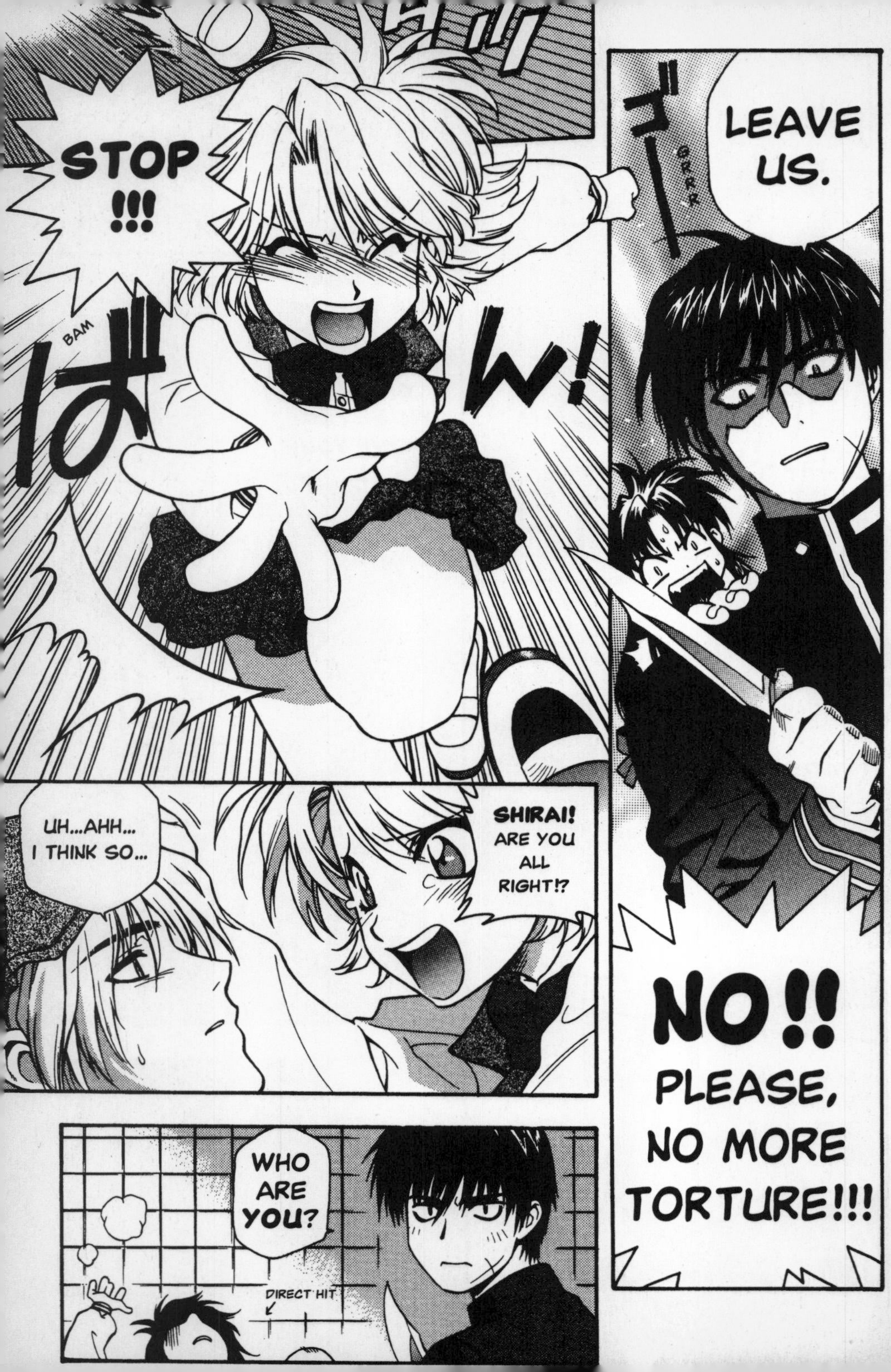
LEAVE US.
GRRRR
NO!! PLEASE, NO MORE TORTURE!!!
STOP !!!
BAM
SHIRAI! ARE YOU ALL RIGHT!?
UH...AHH... I THINK SO...
WHO ARE YOU?
DIRECT HIT

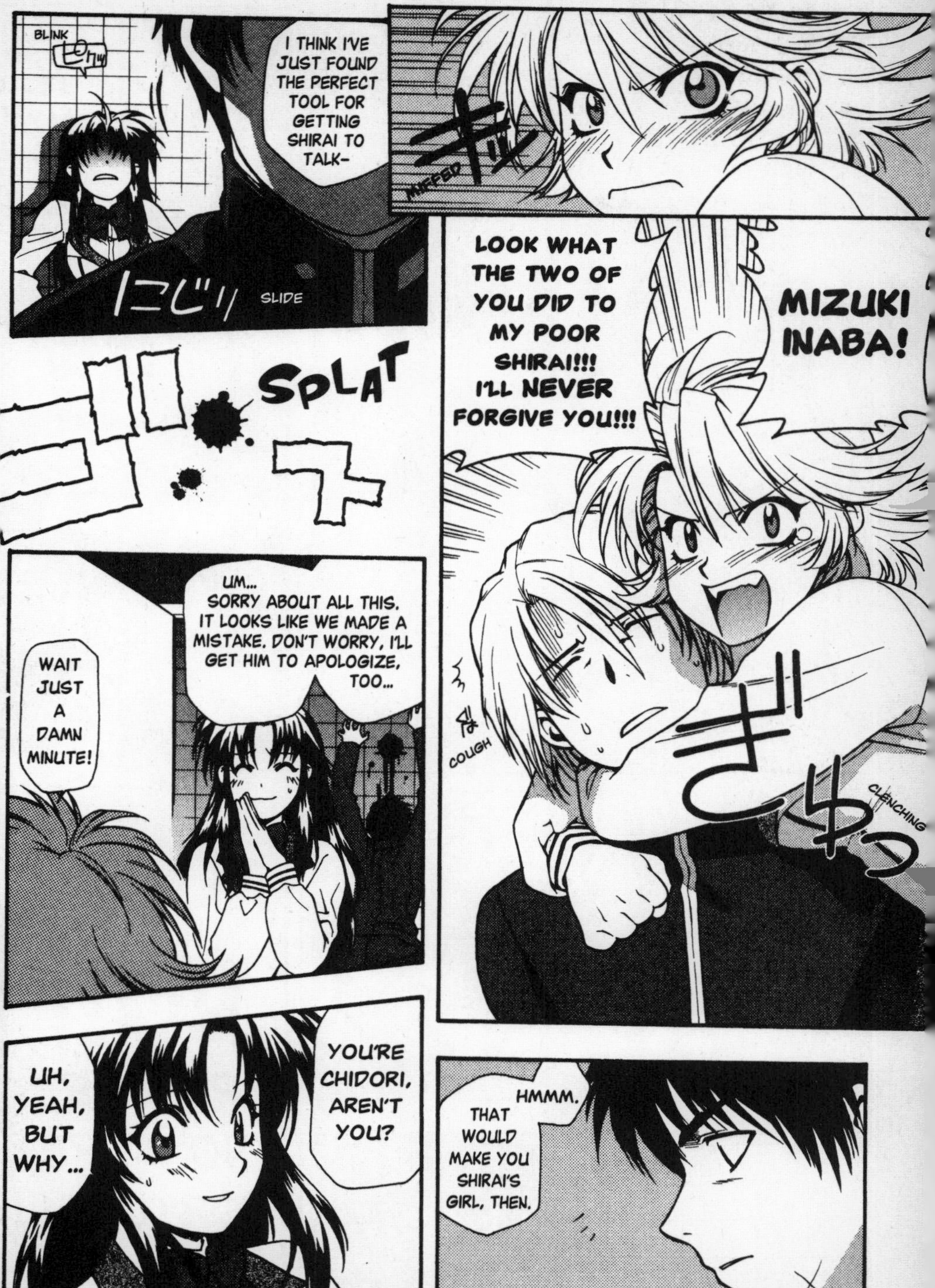
MIFFED
BLINK
I THINK I'VE JUST FOUND THE PERFECT TOOL FOR GETTING SHIRAI TO TALK-
SLIDE
MIZUKI INABA!
LOOK WHAT THE TWO OF YOU DID TO MY POOR SHIRAI!!! I'LL NEVER FORGIVE YOU!!!
COUGH
CLENCHING
SPLAT
UM... SORRY ABOUT ALL THIS. IT LOOKS LIKE WE MADE A MISTAKE. DON'T WORRY, I'LL GET HIM TO APOLOGIZE, TOO...
WAIT JUST A DAMN MINUTE!
HMMM.
THAT WOULD MAKE YOU SHIRAI'S GIRL, THEN.
YOU'RE CHIDORI, AREN'T YOU?
UH, YEAH, BUT WHY...

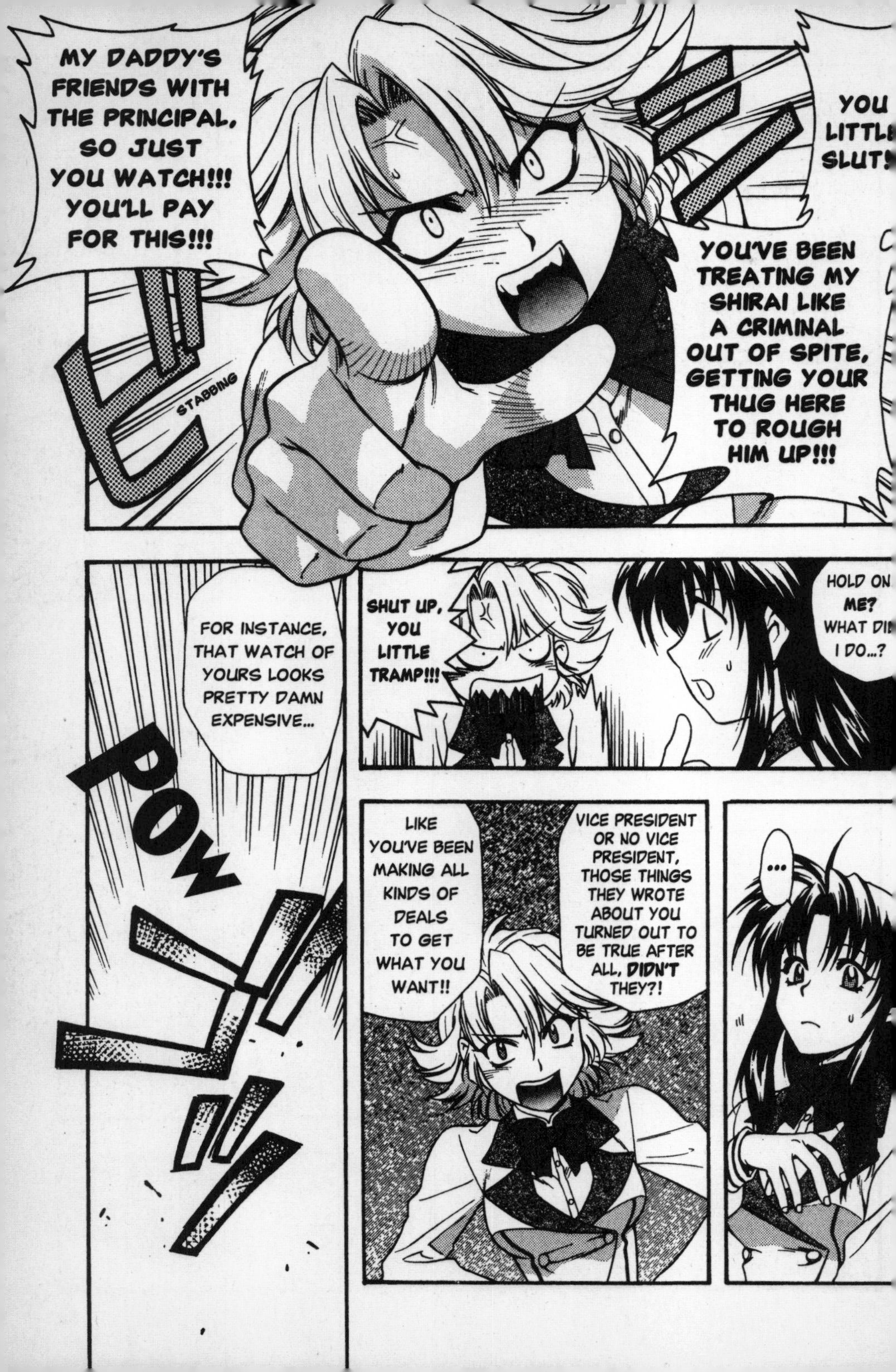
YOU LITTL SLUT!
YOU'VE BEEN TREATING MY SHIRAI LIKE A CRIMINAL OUT OF SPITE, GETTING YOUR THUG HERE TO ROUGH HIM UP!!!
MY DADDY'S FRIENDS WITH THE PRINCIPAL, SO JUST YOU WATCH!!! YOU'LL PAY FOR THIS!!!
STABBING
HOLD ON ME? WHAT DI I DO...?
SHUT UP, YOU LITTLE TRAMP!!!
...
VICE PRESIDENT OR NO VICE PRESIDENT, THOSE THINGS THEY WROTE ABOUT YOU TURNED OUT TO BE TRUE AFTER ALL, DIDN'T THEY?!
LIKE YOU'VE BEEN MAKING ALL KINDS OF DEALS TO GET WHAT YOU WANT!!
FOR INSTANCE, THAT WATCH OF YOURS LOOKS PRETTY DAMN EXPENSIVE...
POW

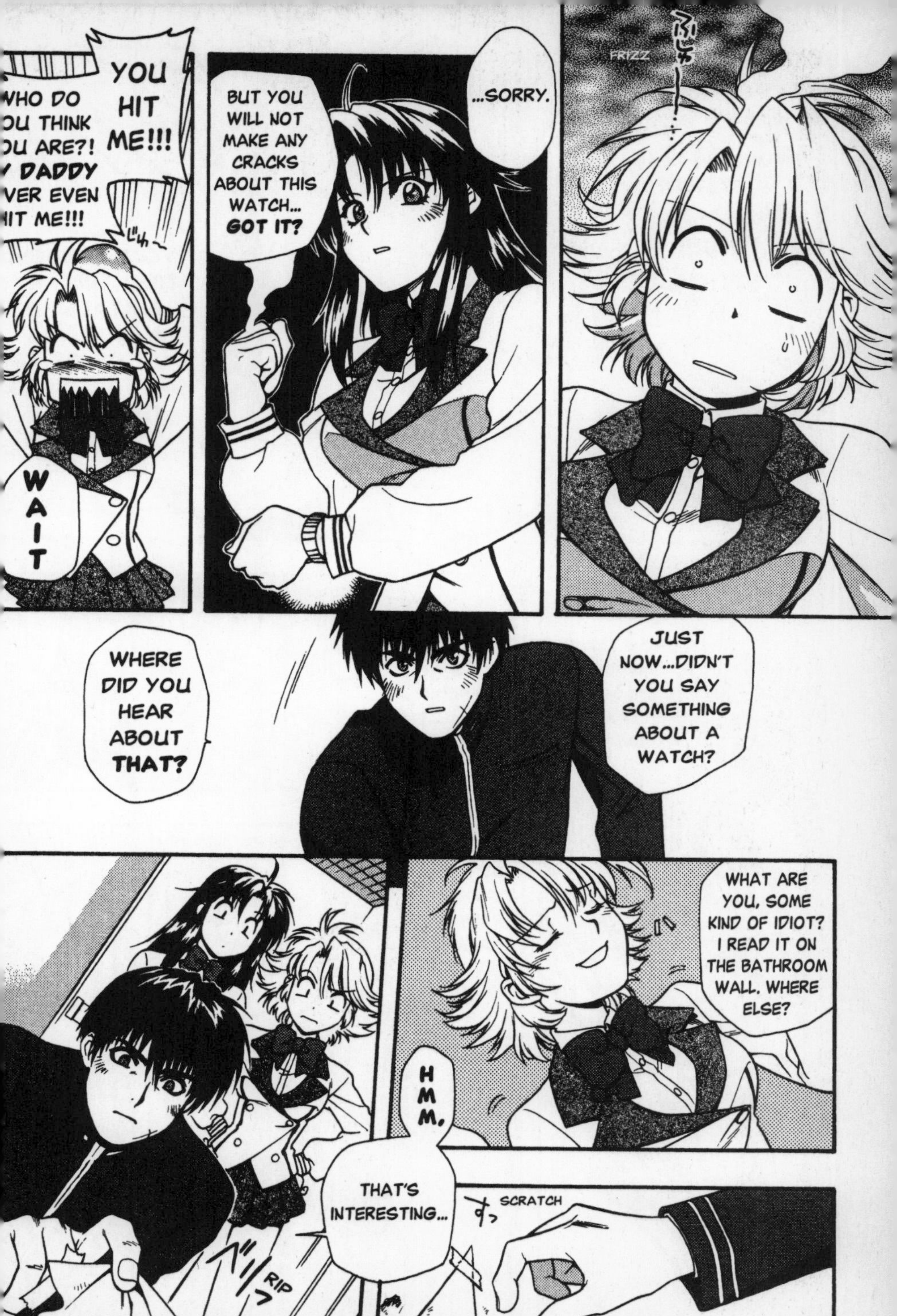
FRIZZ
...SORRY.
BUT YOU WILL NOT MAKE ANY CRACKS ABOUT THIS WATCH... GOT IT?
YOU HIT ME!!!
WHO DO OU THINK OU ARE?! Y DADDY VER EVEN IT ME!!!
WAIT
JUST NOW...DIDN'T YOU SAY SOMETHING ABOUT A WATCH?
WHERE DID YOU HEAR ABOUT THAT?
WHAT ARE YOU, SOME KIND OF IDIOT? I READ IT ON THE BATHROOM WALL. WHERE ELSE?
HMM,
THAT'S INTERESTING...
SCRATCH
RIP

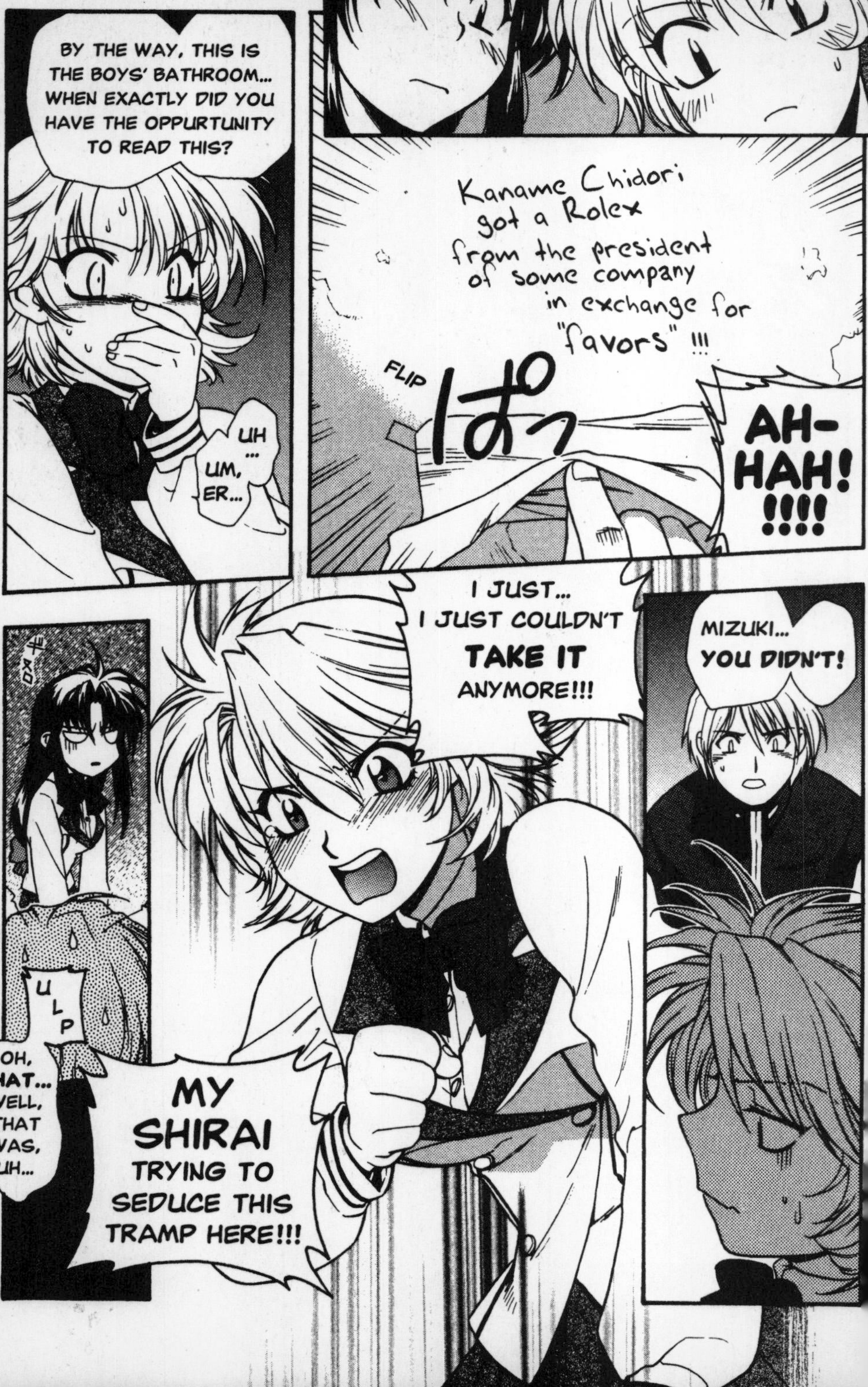

Kaname Chidori got a Rolex from the president of some company in exchange for "favors" !!!
FLIP
ぱっ
AH-HAH! !!!!
BY THE WAY, THIS IS THE BOYS' BATHROOM... WHEN EXACTLY DID YOU HAVE THE OPPURTUNITY TO READ THIS?
UH... UM, ER...
MIZUKI... YOU DIDN'T!
I JUST... I JUST COULDN'T TAKE IT ANYMORE!!!
MY SHIRAI TRYING TO SEDUCE THIS TRAMP HERE!!!
ULP
OH, THAT... WELL, THAT WAS, UH...

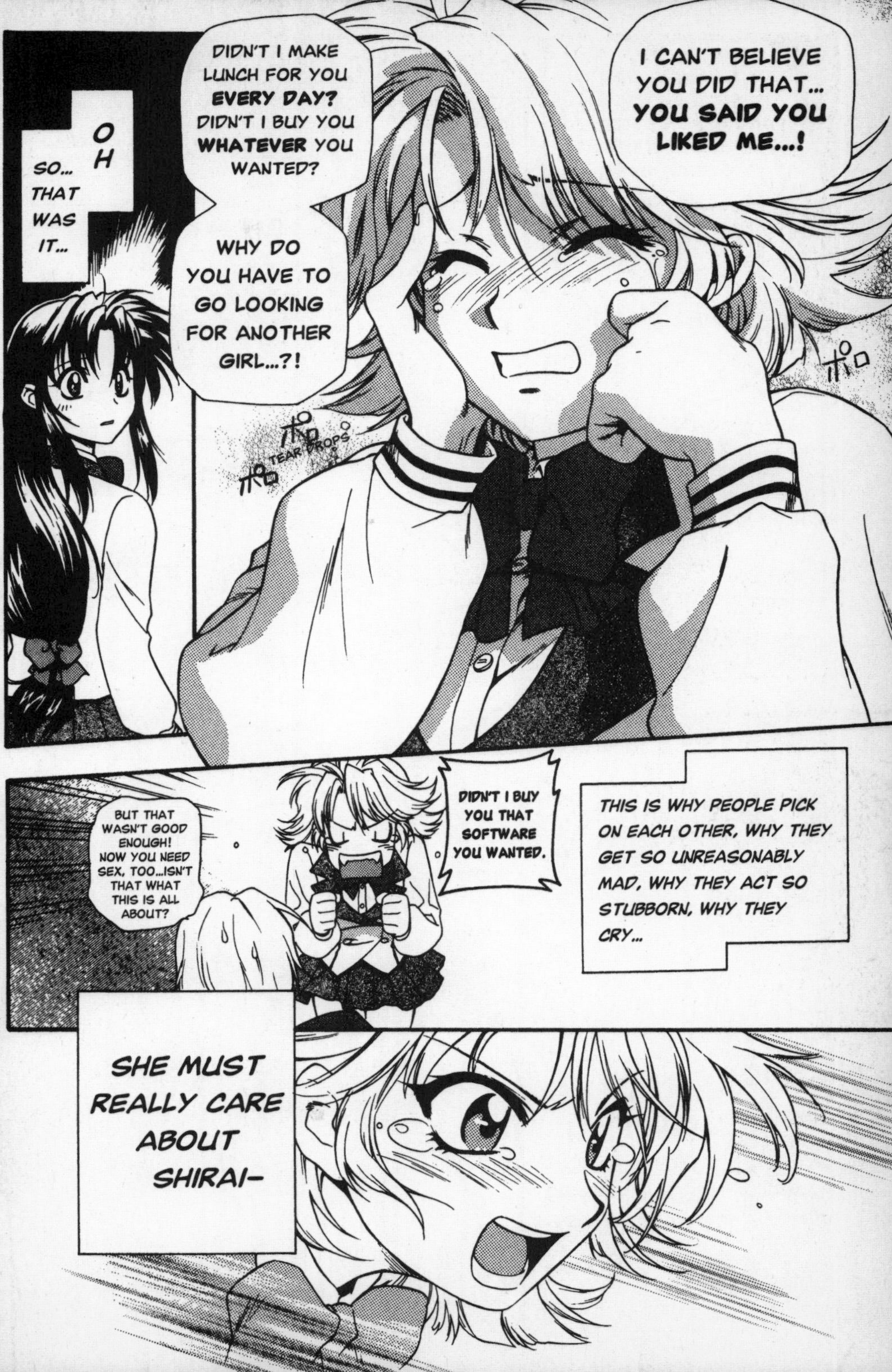
I CAN'T BELIEVE YOU DID THAT... YOU SAID YOU LIKED ME...!
DIDN'T I MAKE LUNCH FOR YOU EVERY DAY? DIDN'T I BUY YOU WHATEVER YOU WANTED?
WHY DO YOU HAVE TO GO LOOKING FOR ANOTHER GIRL...?!
ポロ
ポロ TEAR DROPS
ポロ
OH
SO... THAT WAS IT...
THIS IS WHY PEOPLE PICK ON EACH OTHER, WHY THEY GET SO UNREASONABLY MAD, WHY THEY ACT SO STUBBORN, WHY THEY CRY...
DIDN'T I BUY YOU THAT SOFTWARE YOU WANTED.
BUT THAT WASN'T GOOD ENOUGH! NOW YOU NEED SEX, TOO...ISN'T THAT WHAT THIS IS ALL ABOUT?
SHE MUST REALLY CARE ABOUT SHIRAI-

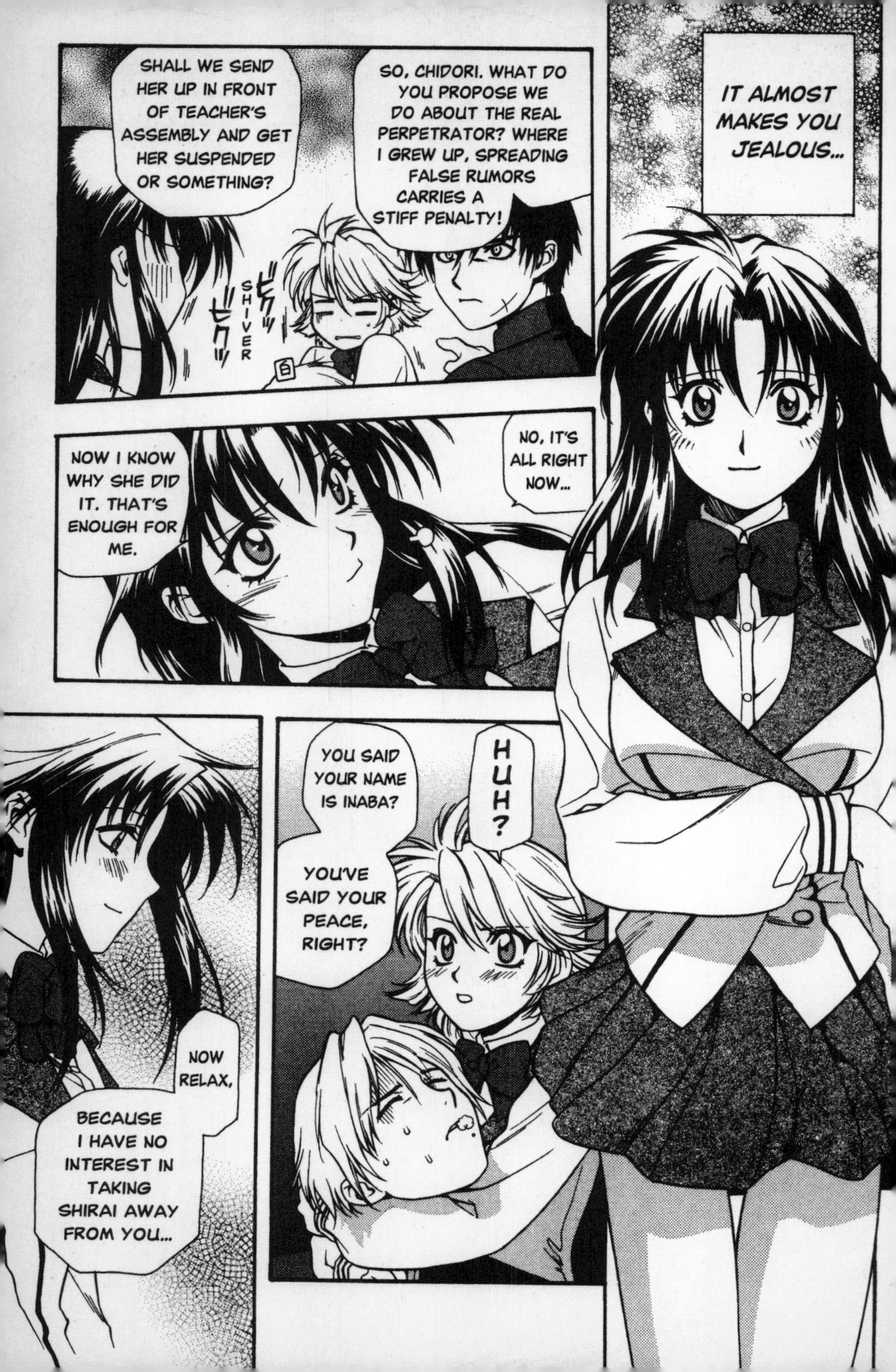
IT ALMOST MAKES YOU JEALOUS...
SO, CHIDORI. WHAT DO YOU PROPOSE WE DO ABOUT THE REAL PERPETRATOR? WHERE I GREW UP, SPREADING FALSE RUMORS CARRIES A STIFF PENALTY!
SHALL WE SEND HER UP IN FRONT OF TEACHER'S ASSEMBLY AND GET HER SUSPENDED OR SOMETHING?
SHIVER
NO, IT'S ALL RIGHT NOW...
NOW I KNOW WHY SHE DID IT. THAT'S ENOUGH FOR ME.
HUH?
YOU SAID YOUR NAME IS INABA?
YOU'VE SAID YOUR PEACE, RIGHT?
NOW RELAX,
BECAUSE I HAVE NO INTEREST IN TAKING SHIRAI AWAY FROM YOU...

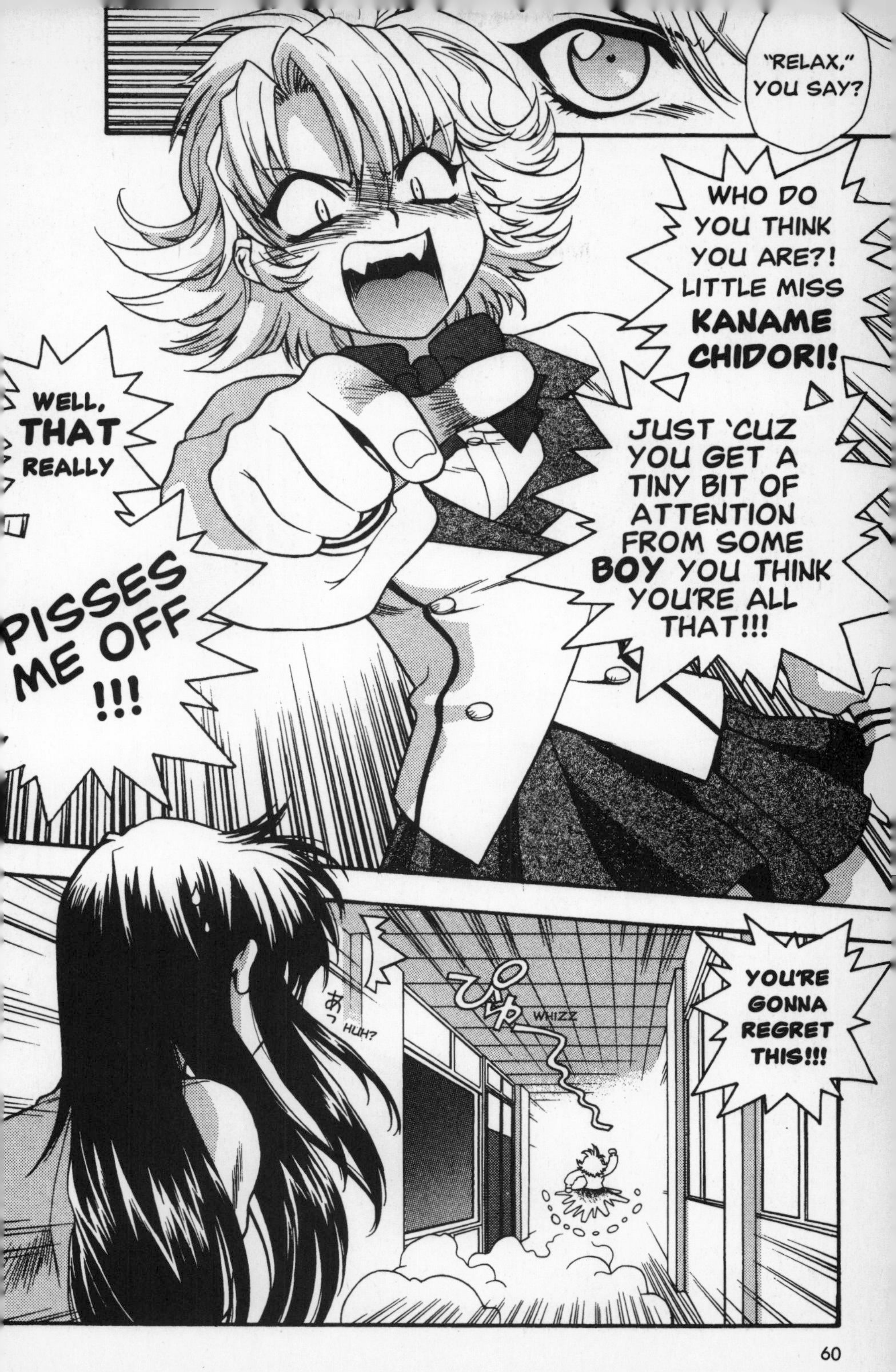
"RELAX," YOU SAY?
WHO DO YOU THINK YOU ARE?! LITTLE MISS KANAME CHIDORI!
JUST 'CUZ YOU GET A TINY BIT OF ATTENTION FROM SOME BOY YOU THINK YOU'RE ALL THAT!!!
WELL, THAT REALLY
PISSES ME OFF !!!
YOU'RE GONNA REGRET THIS!!!
ぴゅ〜
WHIZZ
あっ
HUH?

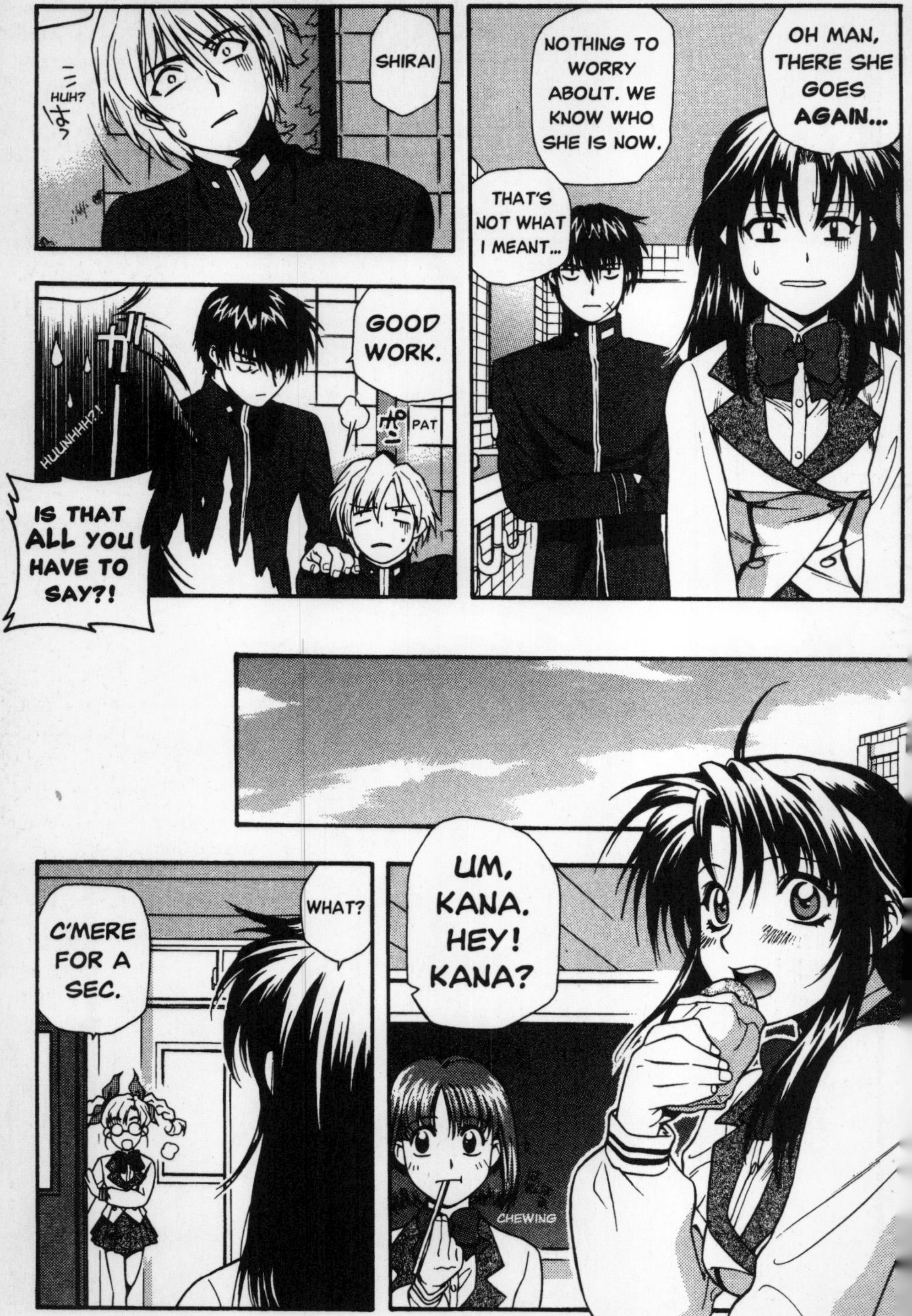
OH MAN, THERE SHE GOES AGAIN...
NOTHING TO WORRY ABOUT. WE KNOW WHO SHE IS NOW.
THAT'S NOT WHAT I MEANT...
SHIRAI
HUH?
GOOD WORK.
PAT
HUUNHHH?!
IS THAT ALL YOU HAVE TO SAY?!
UM, KANA. HEY! KANA?
CHEWING
WHAT?
C'MERE FOR A SEC.

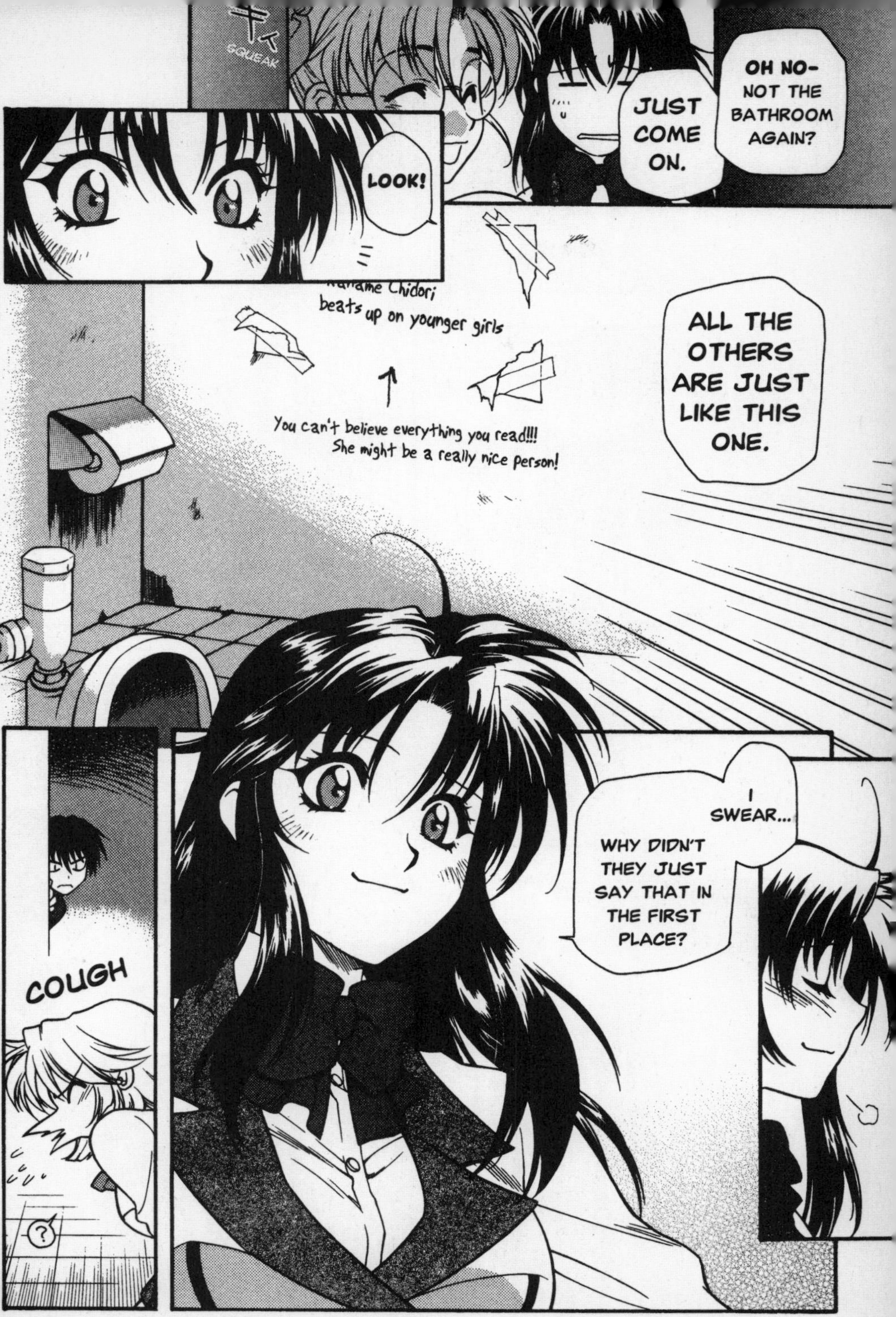
OH NO- NOT THE BATHROOM AGAIN?
JUST COME ON.
SQUEAK
LOOK!
ALL THE OTHERS ARE JUST LIKE THIS ONE.
Chidori beats up on younger girls
You can't believe everything you read!!! She might be a really nice person!
I SWEAR...
WHY DIDN'T THEY JUST SAY THAT IN THE FIRST PLACE?
COUGH

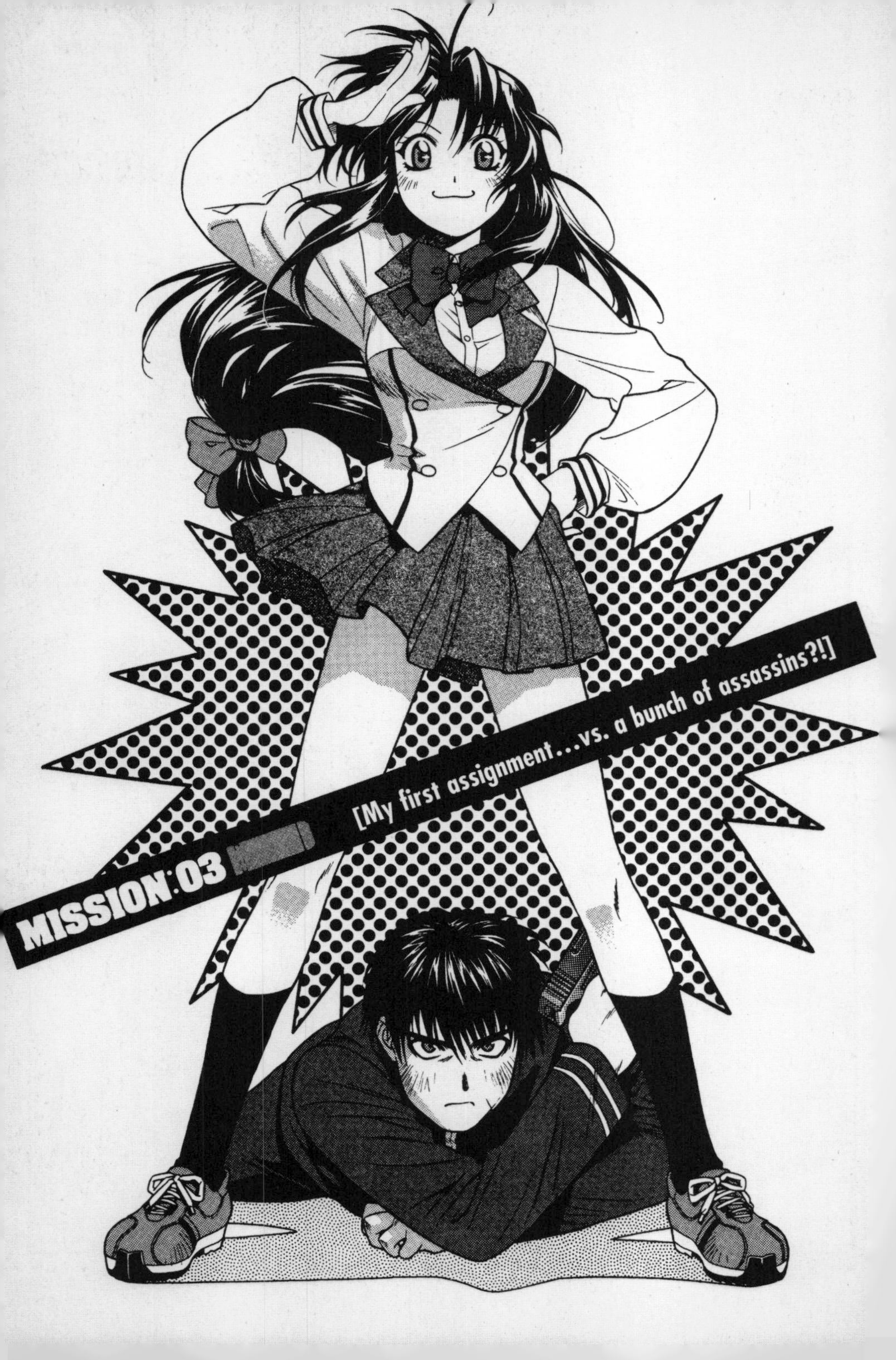
MISSION:03
[My first assignment...vs. a bunch of assassins?!]

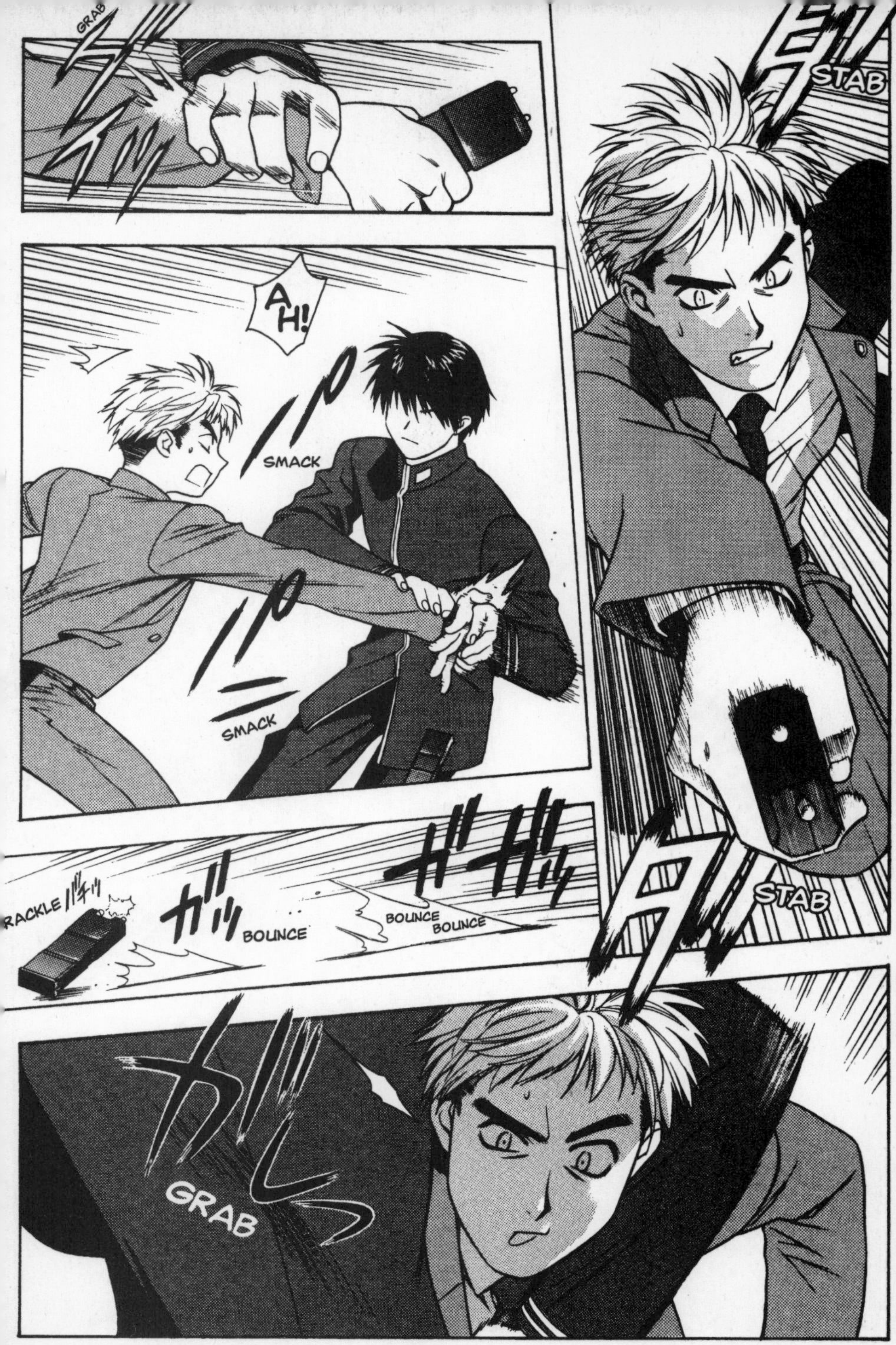
STAB
STAB
GRAB
AH!
SMACK
SMACK
RACKLE
BOUNCE
BOUNCE
BOUNCE
GRAB

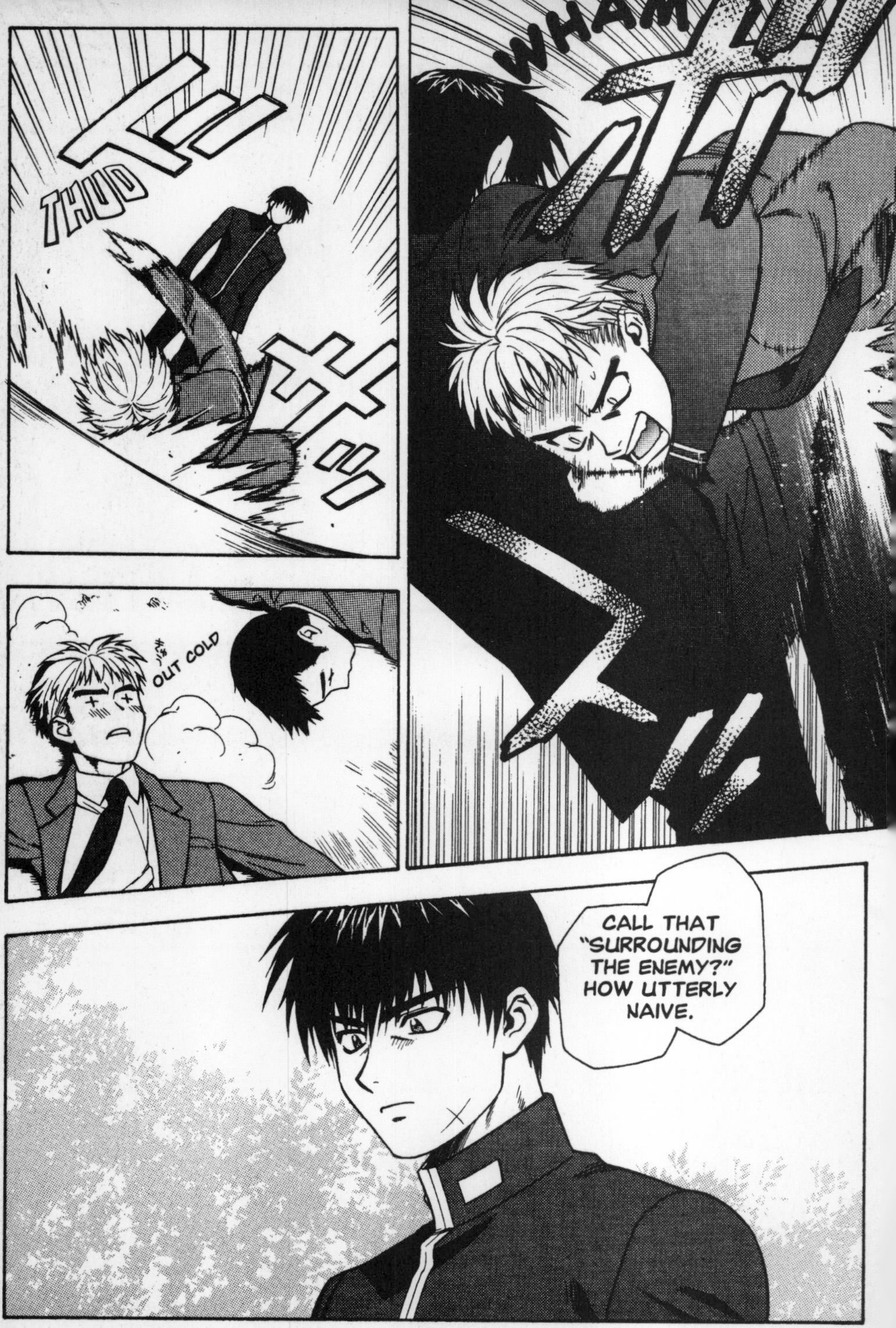
WHAM
THUD
OUT COLD
CALL THAT "SURROUNDING THE ENEMY?" HOW UTTERLY NAIVE.

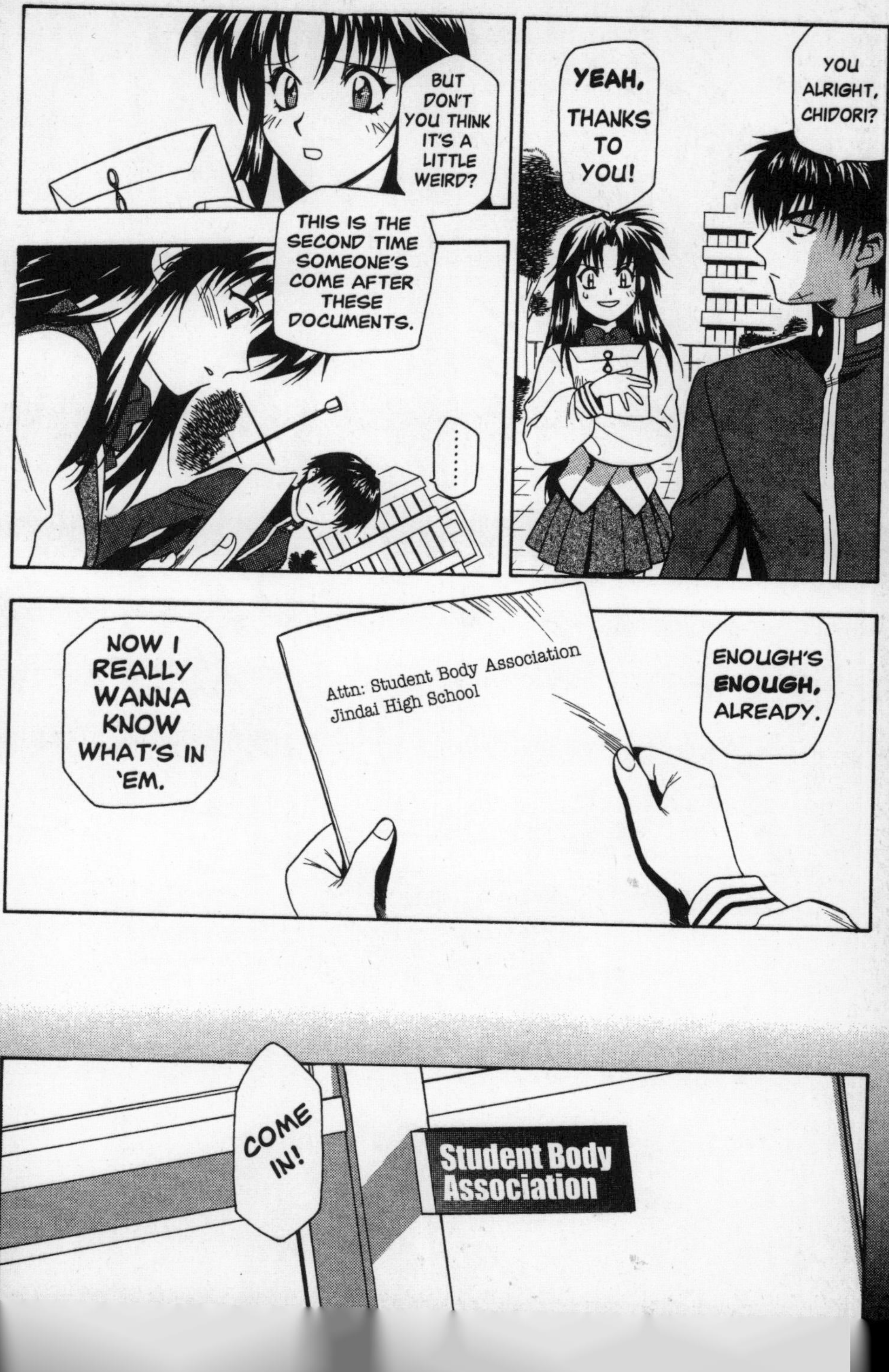
YOU ALRIGHT, CHIDORI?
YEAH, THANKS TO YOU!
BUT DON'T YOU THINK IT'S A LITTLE WEIRD?
THIS IS THE SECOND TIME SOMEONE'S COME AFTER THESE DOCUMENTS.
......
ENOUGH'S ENOUGH, ALREADY.
Attn: Student Body Association
Jindai High School
NOW I REALLY WANNA KNOW WHAT'S IN 'EM.
Student Body Association
COME IN!

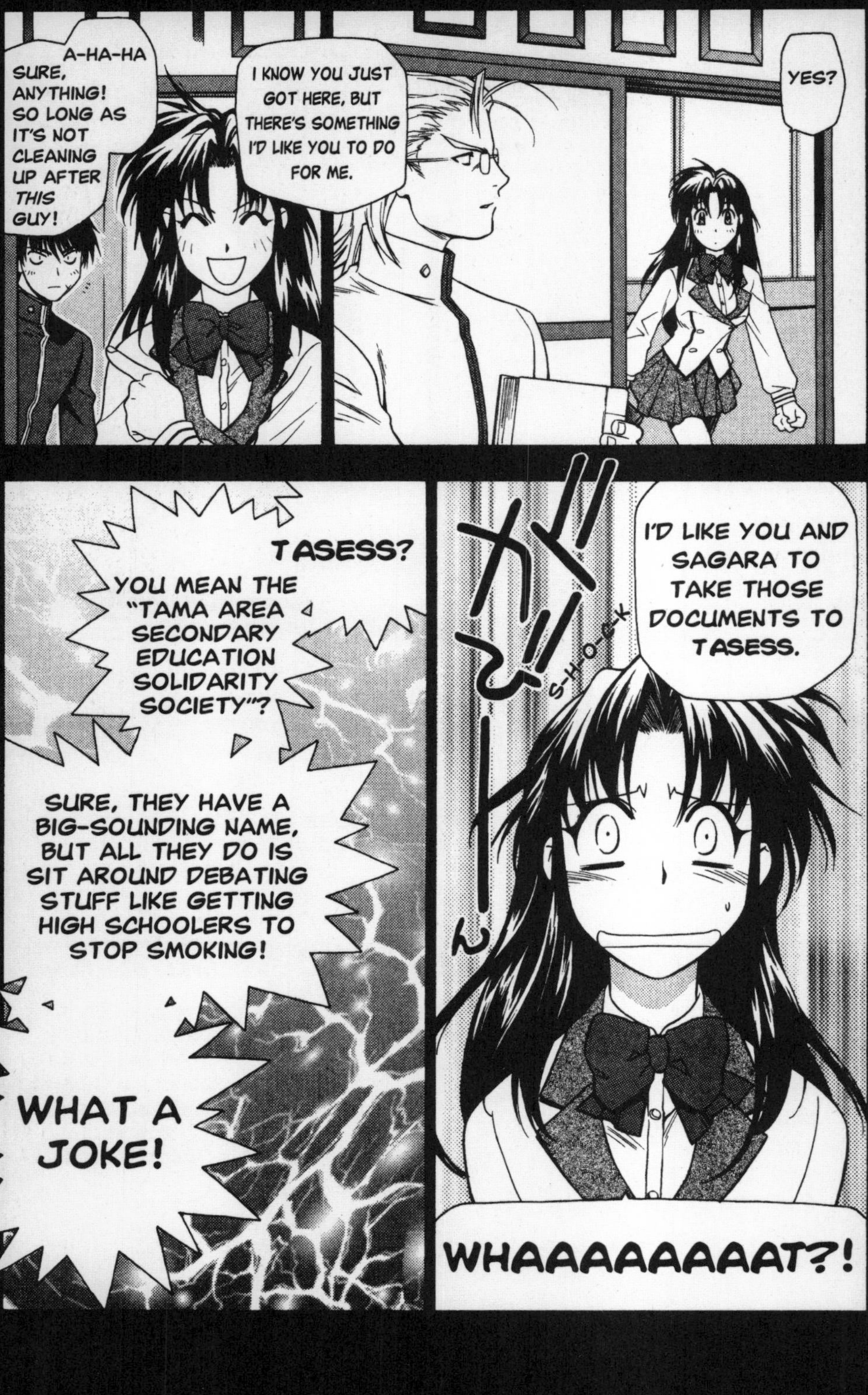
YES?
I KNOW YOU JUST GOT HERE, BUT THERE'S SOMETHING I'D LIKE YOU TO DO FOR ME.
A-HA-HA SURE, ANYTHING! SO LONG AS IT'S NOT CLEANING UP AFTER THIS GUY!
I'D LIKE YOU AND SAGARA TO TAKE THOSE DOCUMENTS TO TASESS.
S-H-O-C-K
WHAAAAAAAAAT?!
TASESS?
YOU MEAN THE "TAMA AREA SECONDARY EDUCATION SOLIDARITY SOCIETY"?
SURE, THEY HAVE A BIG-SOUNDING NAME, BUT ALL THEY DO IS SIT AROUND DEBATING STUFF LIKE GETTING HIGH SCHOOLERS TO STOP SMOKING!
WHAT A JOKE!

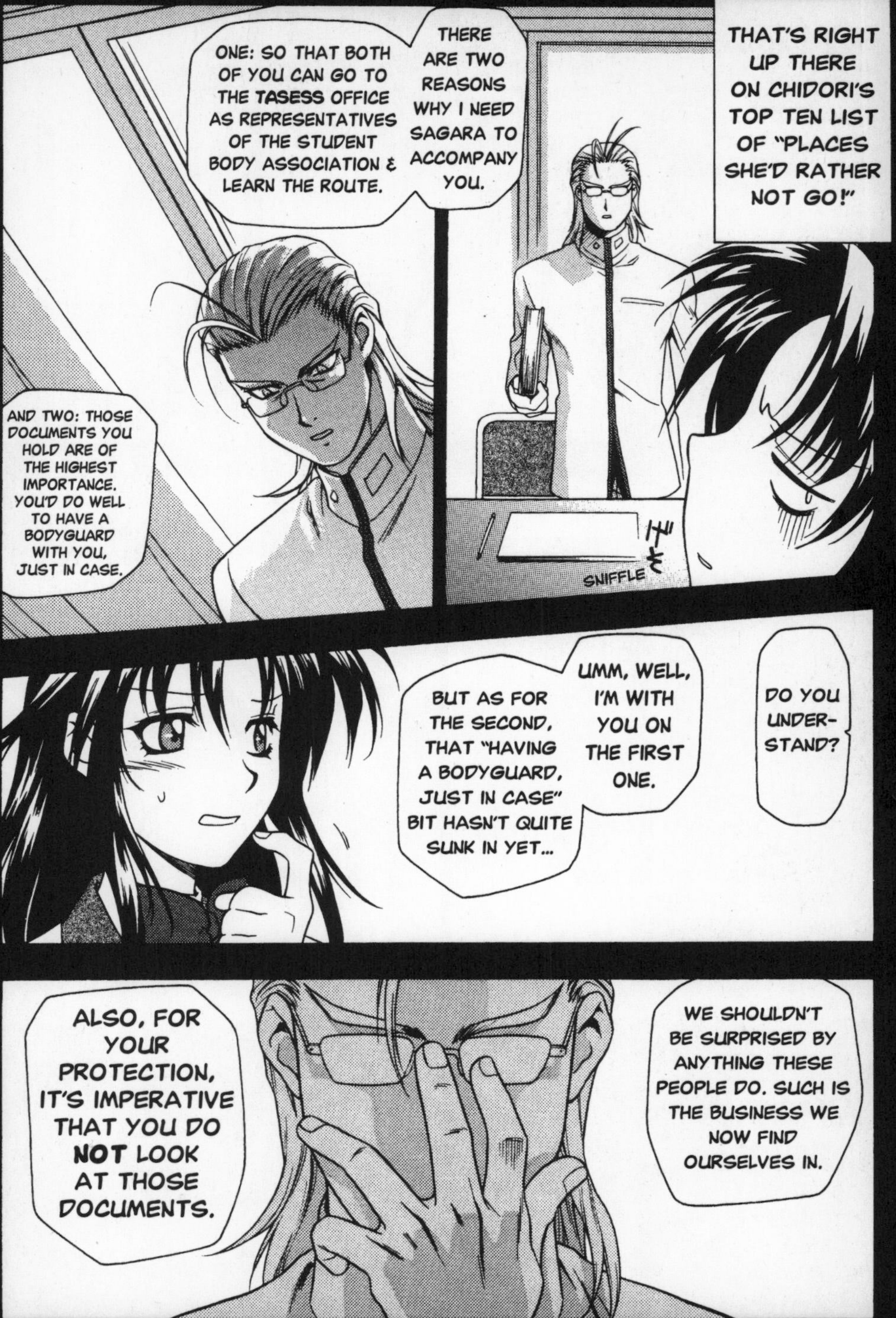
THAT'S RIGHT UP THERE ON CHIDORI'S TOP TEN LIST OF "PLACES SHE'D RATHER NOT GO!"
SNIFFLE
THERE ARE TWO REASONS WHY I NEED SAGARA TO ACCOMPANY YOU.
ONE: SO THAT BOTH OF YOU CAN GO TO THE TASESS OFFICE AS REPRESENTATIVES OF THE STUDENT BODY ASSOCIATION & LEARN THE ROUTE.
AND TWO: THOSE DOCUMENTS YOU HOLD ARE OF THE HIGHEST IMPORTANCE. YOU'D DO WELL TO HAVE A BODYGUARD WITH YOU, JUST IN CASE.
DO YOU UNDERSTAND?
UMM, WELL, I'M WITH YOU ON THE FIRST ONE.
BUT AS FOR THE SECOND, THAT "HAVING A BODYGUARD, JUST IN CASE" BIT HASN'T QUITE SUNK IN YET...
WE SHOULDN'T BE SURPRISED BY ANYTHING THESE PEOPLE DO. SUCH IS THE BUSINESS WE NOW FIND OURSELVES IN.
ALSO, FOR YOUR PROTECTION, IT'S IMPERATIVE THAT YOU DO **NOT** LOOK AT THOSE DOCUMENTS.

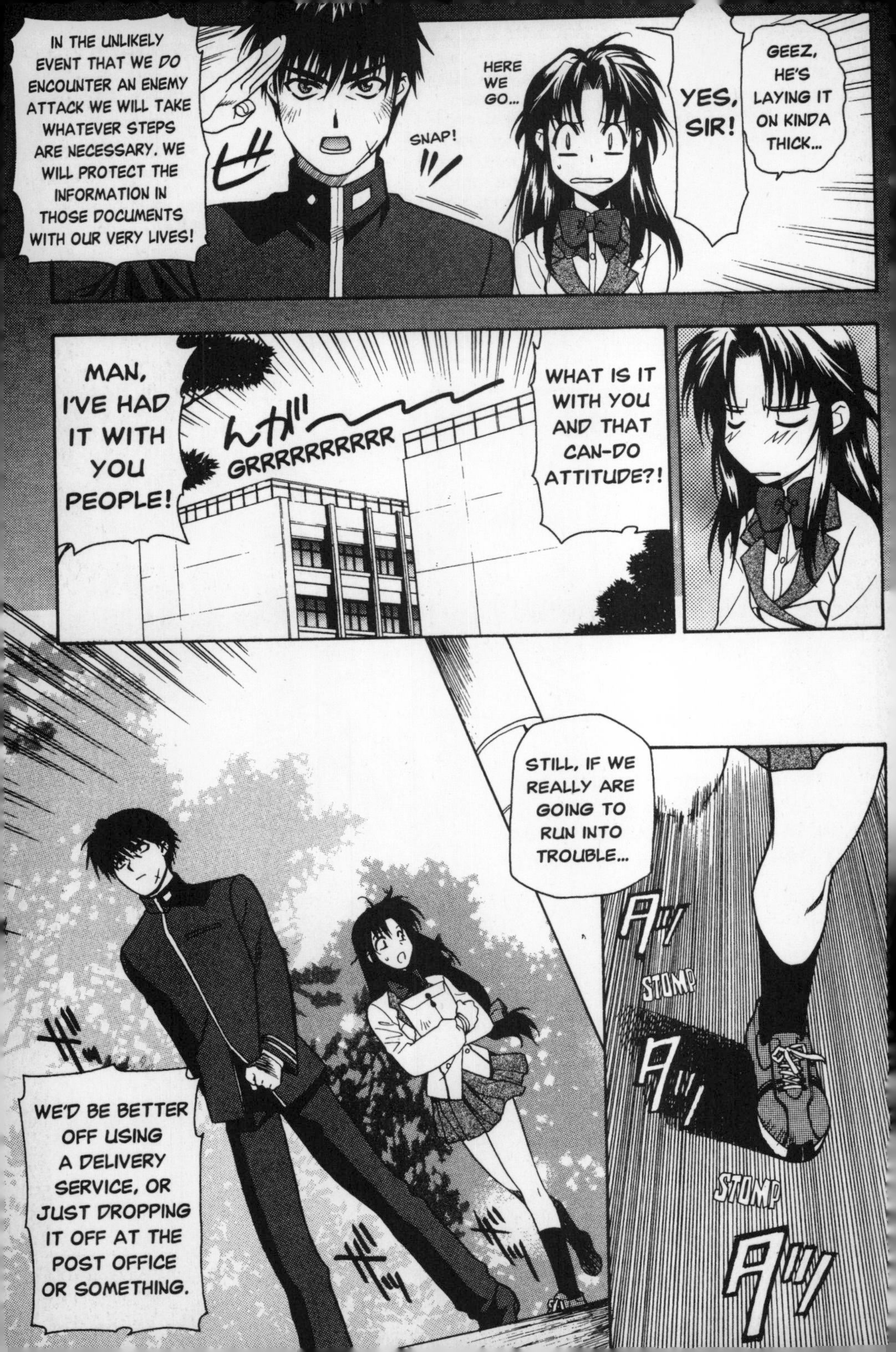
GEEZ, HE'S LAYING IT ON KINDA THICK...
YES, SIR!
HERE WE GO...
SNAP!
IN THE UNLIKELY EVENT THAT WE DO ENCOUNTER AN ENEMY ATTACK WE WILL TAKE WHATEVER STEPS ARE NECESSARY. WE WILL PROTECT THE INFORMATION IN THOSE DOCUMENTS WITH OUR VERY LIVES!
WHAT IS IT WITH YOU AND THAT CAN-DO ATTITUDE?!
んが
GRRRRRRRRR
MAN, I'VE HAD IT WITH YOU PEOPLE!
STILL, IF WE REALLY ARE GOING TO RUN INTO TROUBLE...
STOMP
STOMP
WE'D BE BETTER OFF USING A DELIVERY SERVICE, OR JUST DROPPING IT OFF AT THE POST OFFICE OR SOMETHING.

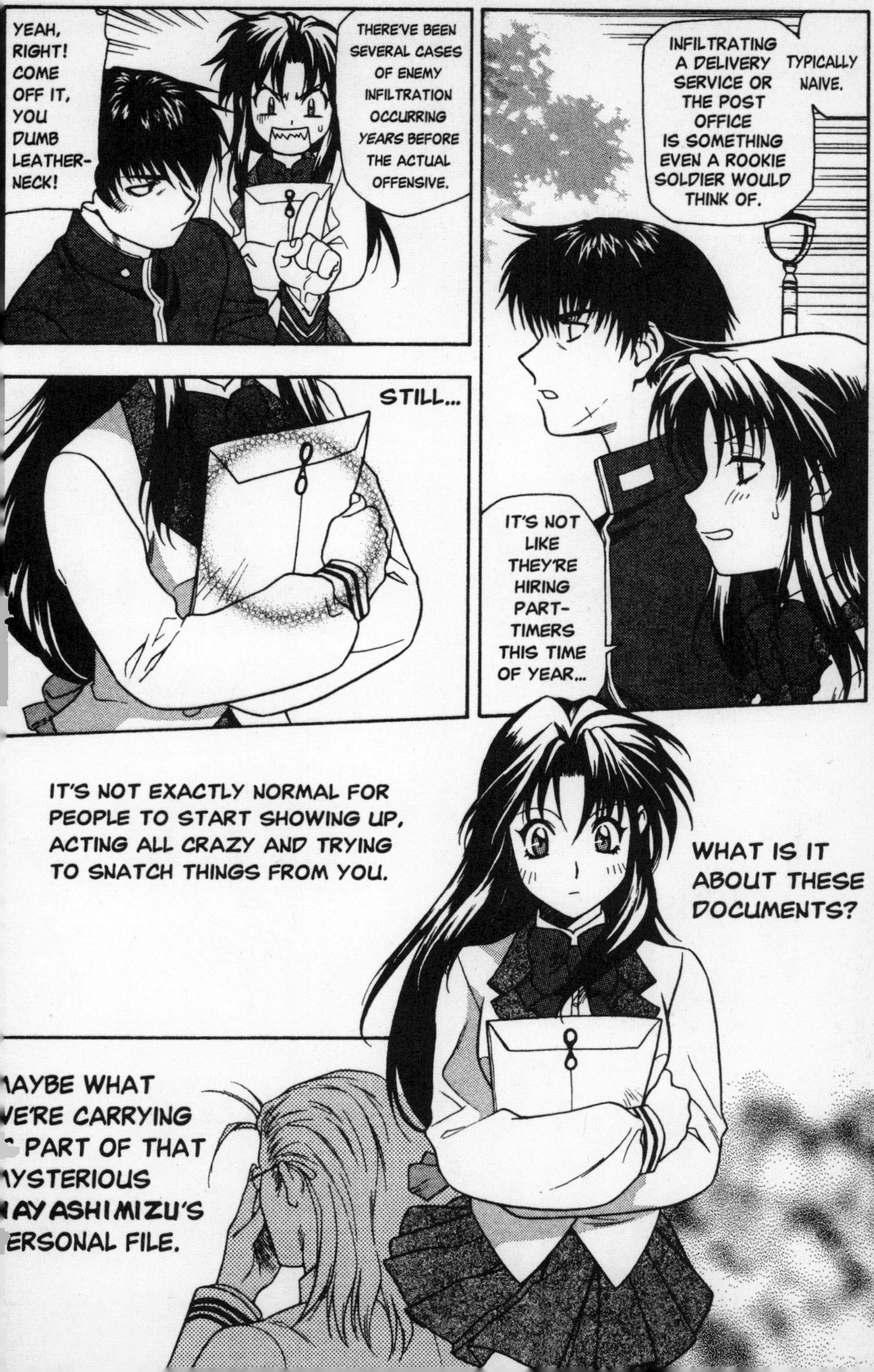
INFILTRATING A DELIVERY SERVICE OR THE POST OFFICE IS SOMETHING EVEN A ROOKIE SOLDIER WOULD THINK OF.
TYPICALLY NAIVE.
IT'S NOT LIKE THEY'RE HIRING PART-TIMERS THIS TIME OF YEAR...
THERE'VE BEEN SEVERAL CASES OF ENEMY INFILTRATION OCCURRING YEARS BEFORE THE ACTUAL OFFENSIVE.
YEAH, RIGHT! COME OFF IT, YOU DUMB LEATHER-NECK!
STILL...
IT'S NOT EXACTLY NORMAL FOR PEOPLE TO START SHOWING UP, ACTING ALL CRAZY AND TRYING TO SNATCH THINGS FROM YOU.
WHAT IS IT ABOUT THESE DOCUMENTS?
AYBE WHAT
E'RE CARRYING
PART OF THAT
YSTERIOUS
AYASHIMIZU'S
ERSONAL FILE.

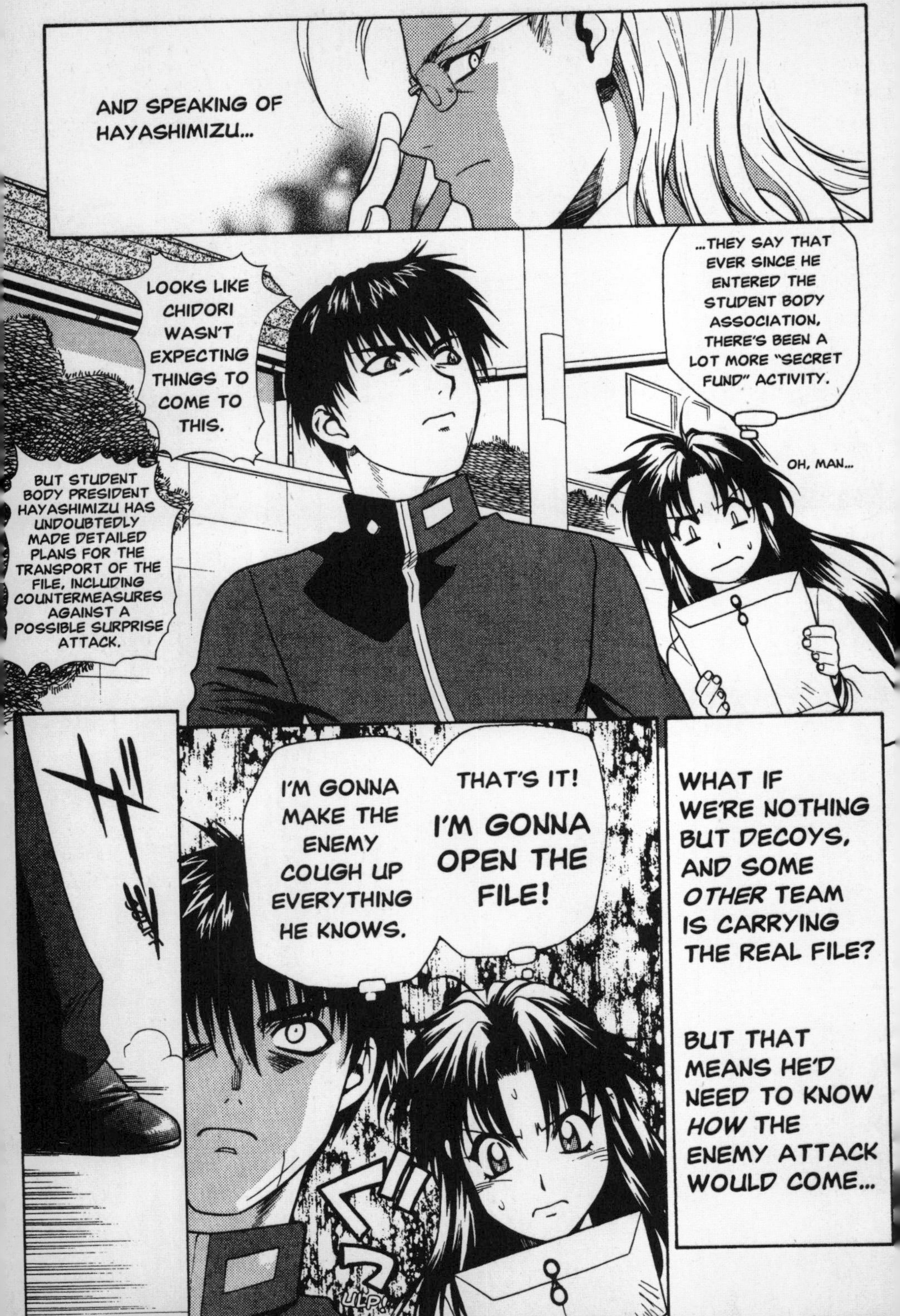
AND SPEAKING OF HAYASHIMIZU...
...THEY SAY THAT EVER SINCE HE ENTERED THE STUDENT BODY ASSOCIATION, THERE'S BEEN A LOT MORE "SECRET FUND" ACTIVITY.
OH, MAN...
LOOKS LIKE CHIDORI WASN'T EXPECTING THINGS TO COME TO THIS.
BUT STUDENT BODY PRESIDENT HAYASHIMIZU HAS UNDOUBTEDLY MADE DETAILED PLANS FOR THE TRANSPORT OF THE FILE, INCLUDING COUNTERMEASURES AGAINST A POSSIBLE SURPRISE ATTACK.
WHAT IF WE'RE NOTHING BUT DECOYS, AND SOME *OTHER* TEAM IS CARRYING THE REAL FILE?
BUT THAT MEANS HE'D NEED TO KNOW *HOW* THE ENEMY ATTACK WOULD COME...
THAT'S IT! I'M GONNA OPEN THE FILE!
I'M GONNA MAKE THE ENEMY COUGH UP EVERYTHING HE KNOWS.
ULP!

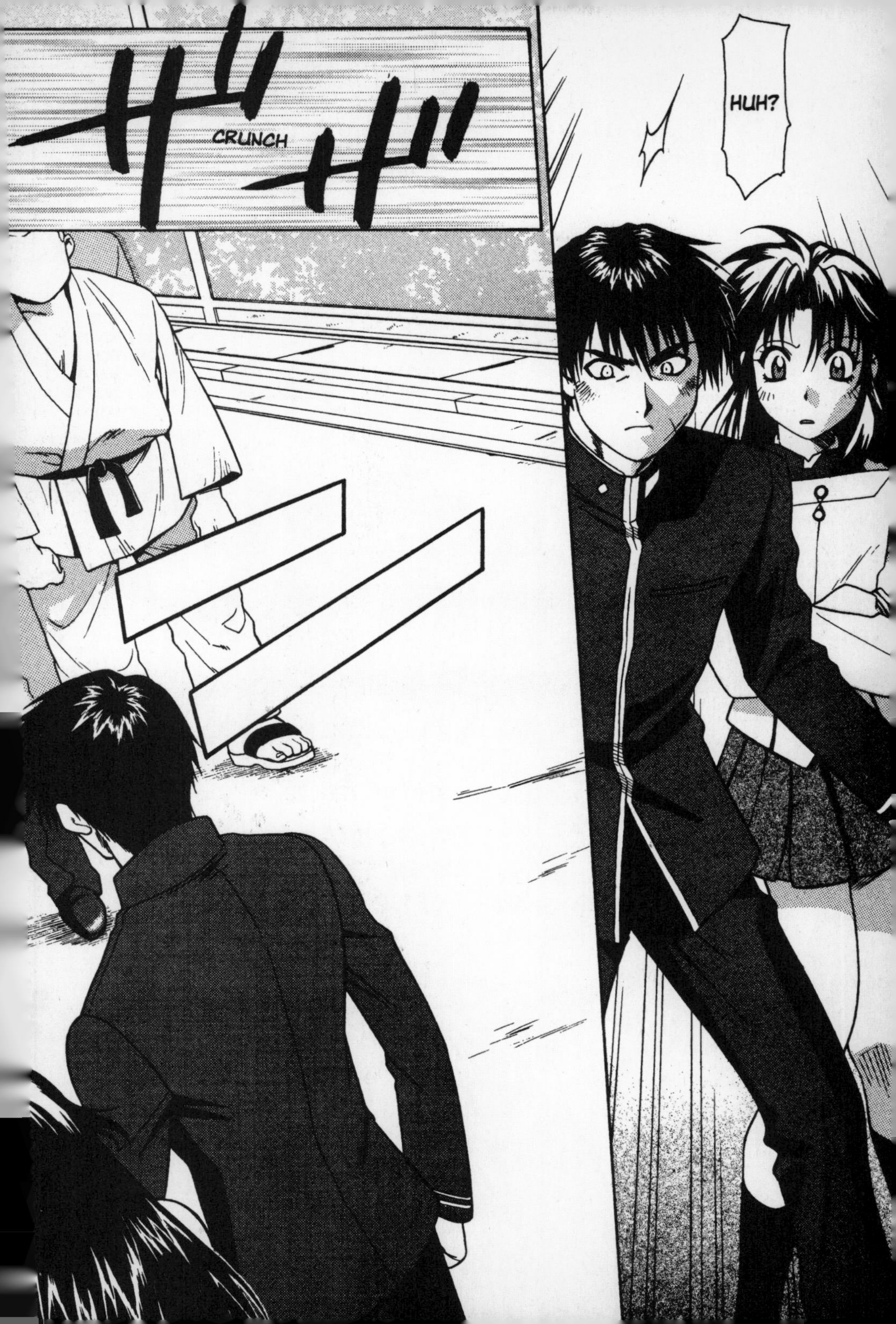
HUH?
CRUNCH

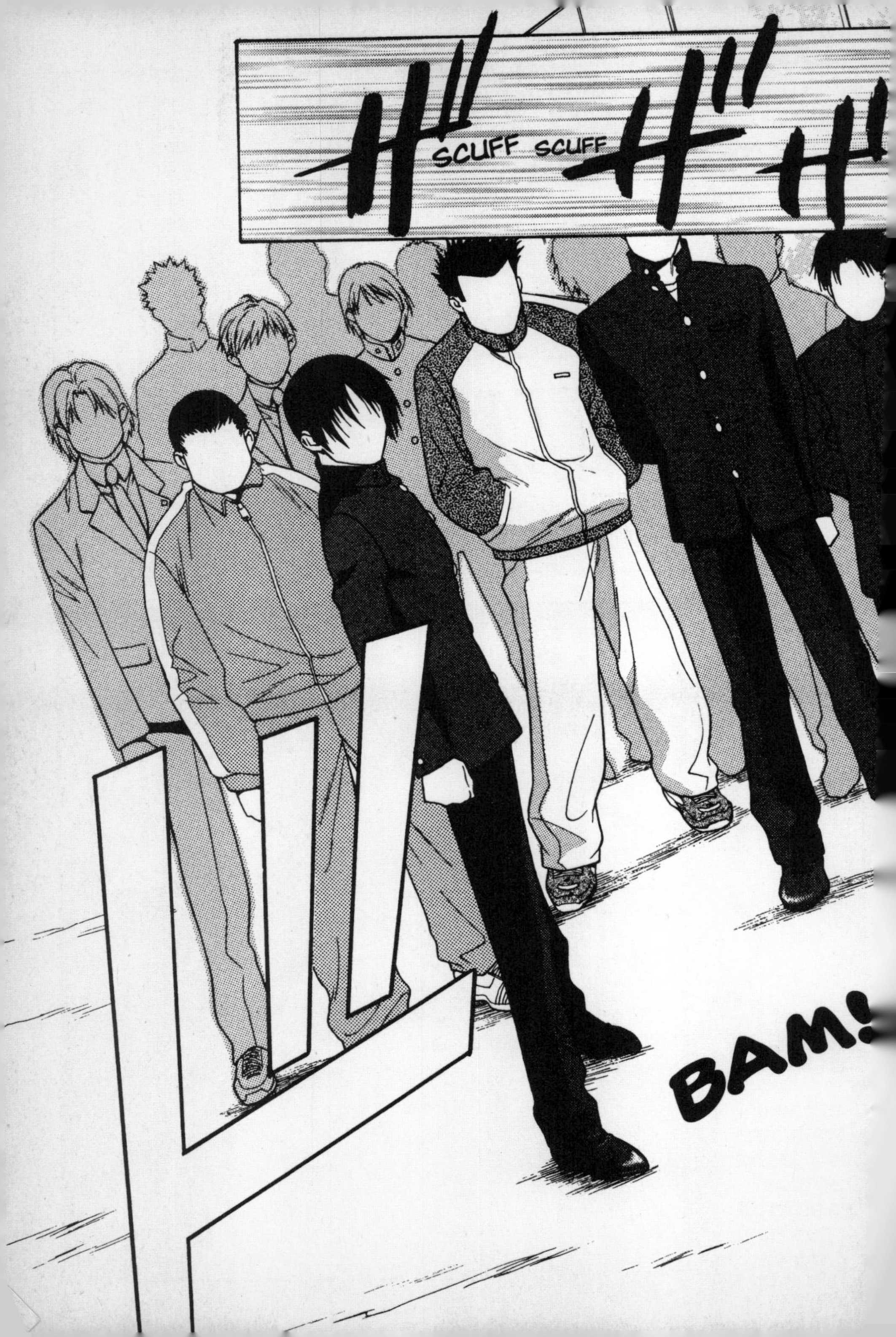
SCUFF SCUFF
BAM!

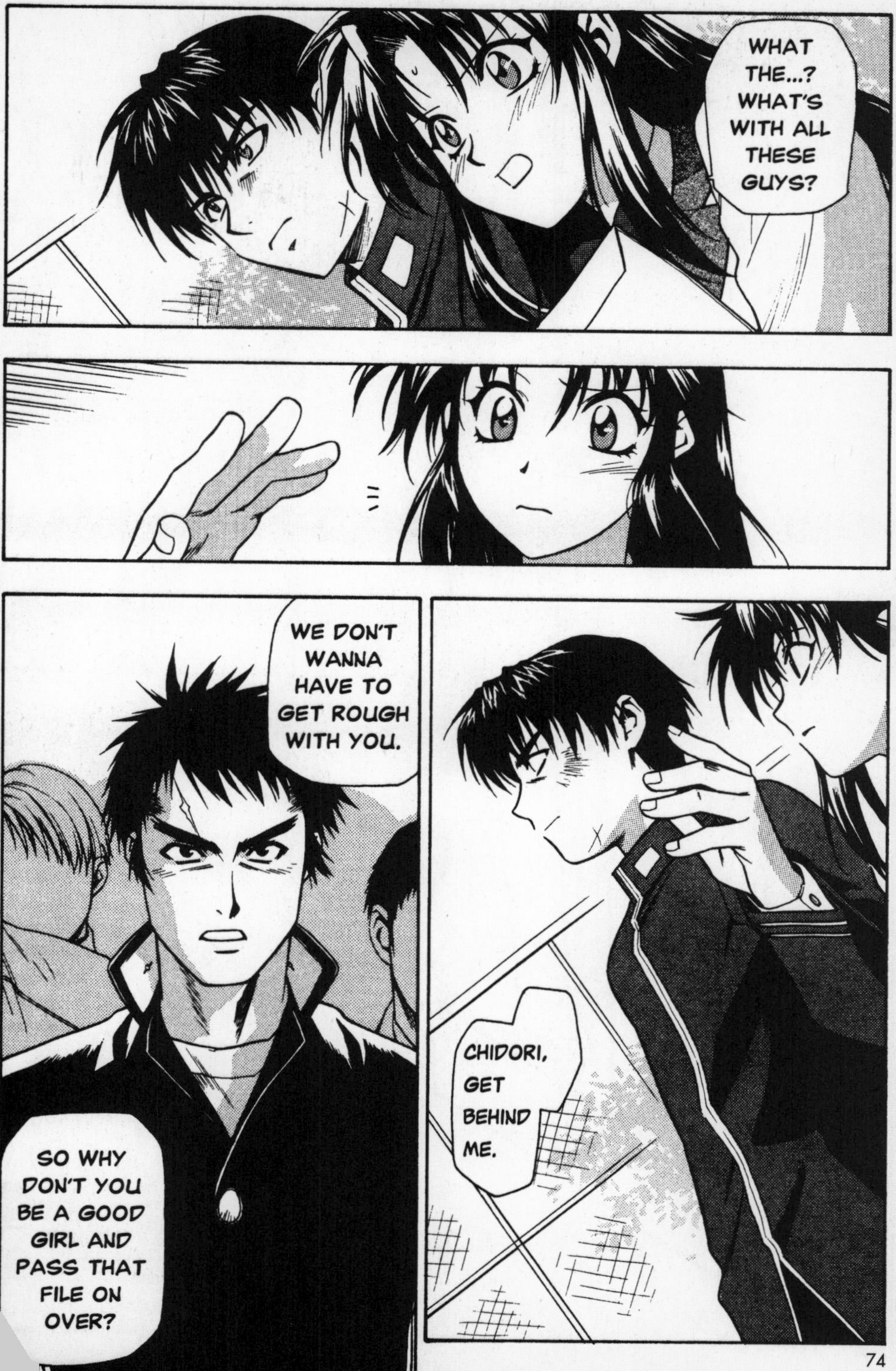
WHAT THE...? WHAT'S WITH ALL THESE GUYS?
CHIDORI, GET BEHIND ME.
WE DON'T WANNA HAVE TO GET ROUGH WITH YOU.
SO WHY DON'T YOU BE A GOOD GIRL AND PASS THAT FILE ON OVER?

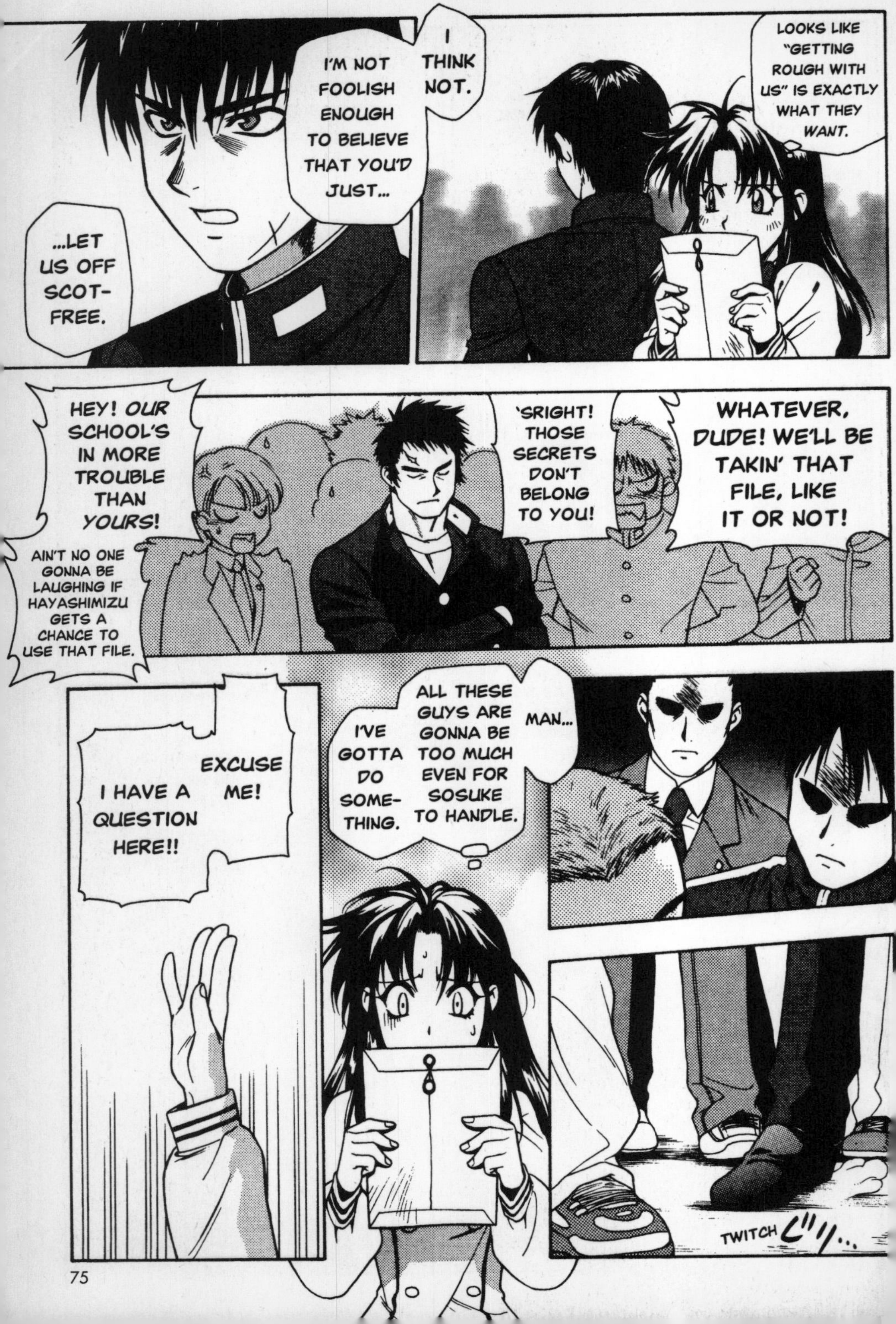
LOOKS LIKE "GETTING ROUGH WITH US" IS EXACTLY WHAT THEY *WANT.*
I THINK NOT.
I'M NOT FOOLISH ENOUGH TO BELIEVE THAT YOU'D JUST...
...LET US OFF SCOT-FREE.
WHATEVER, DUDE! WE'LL BE TAKIN' THAT FILE, LIKE IT OR NOT!
'SRIGHT! THOSE SECRETS DON'T BELONG TO YOU!
HEY! *OUR* SCHOOL'S IN MORE TROUBLE THAN *YOURS*!
AIN'T NO ONE GONNA BE LAUGHING IF HAYASHIMIZU GETS A CHANCE TO USE THAT FILE.
MAN...
ALL THESE GUYS ARE GONNA BE TOO MUCH EVEN FOR SOSUKE TO HANDLE.
I'VE GOTTA DO SOME-THING.
TWITCH
EXCUSE ME!
I HAVE A QUESTION HERE!!

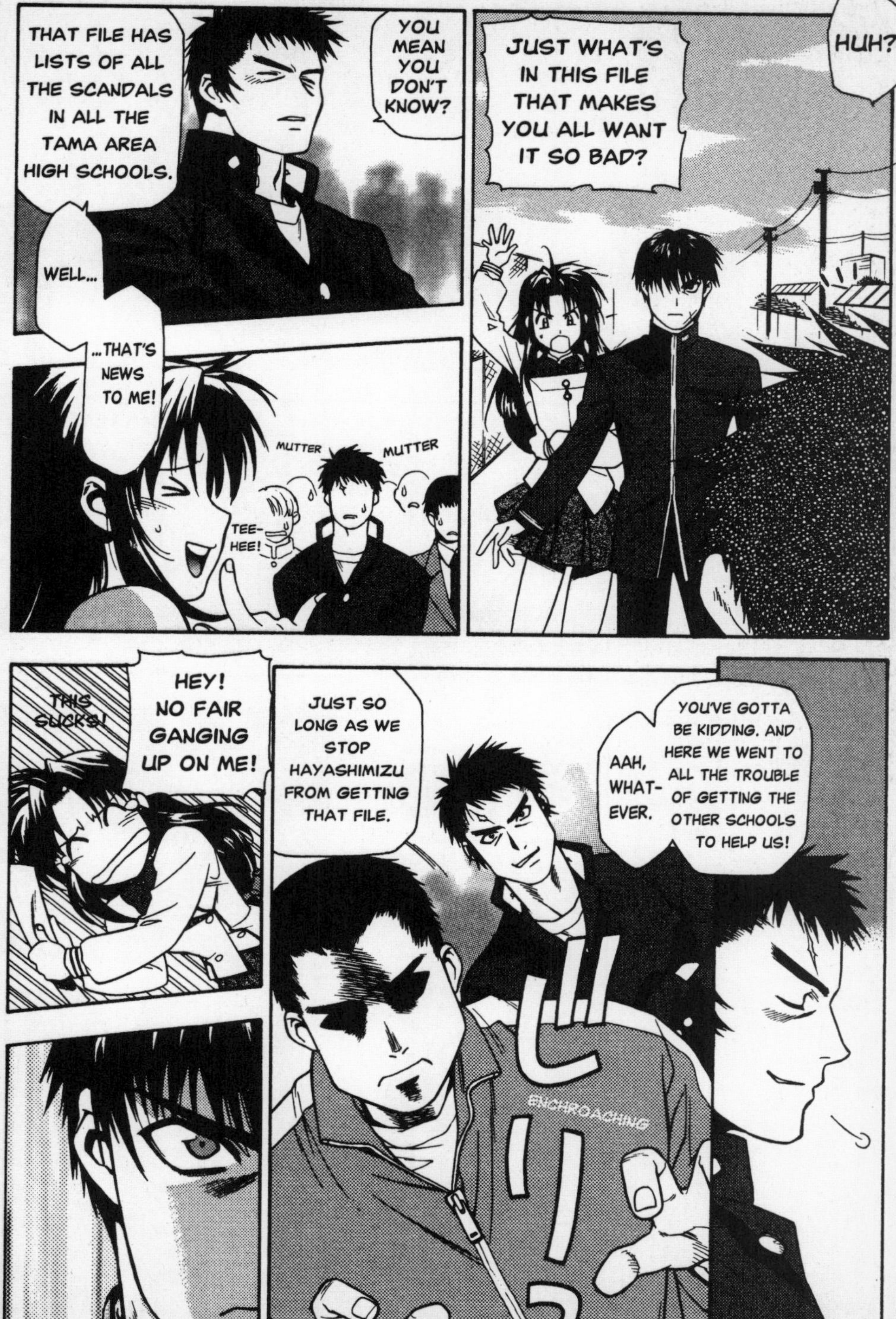
HUH?
JUST WHAT'S IN THIS FILE THAT MAKES YOU ALL WANT IT SO BAD?
YOU MEAN YOU DON'T KNOW?
THAT FILE HAS LISTS OF ALL THE SCANDALS IN ALL THE TAMA AREA HIGH SCHOOLS.
WELL...
...THAT'S NEWS TO ME!
MUTTER
MUTTER
TEE-HEE!
YOU'VE GOTTA BE KIDDING. AND HERE WE WENT TO ALL THE TROUBLE OF GETTING THE OTHER SCHOOLS TO HELP US!
AAH, WHAT-EVER.
JUST SO LONG AS WE STOP HAYASHIMIZU FROM GETTING THAT FILE.
ENCHROACHING
HEY! NO FAIR GANGING UP ON ME!
THIS SUCKS!

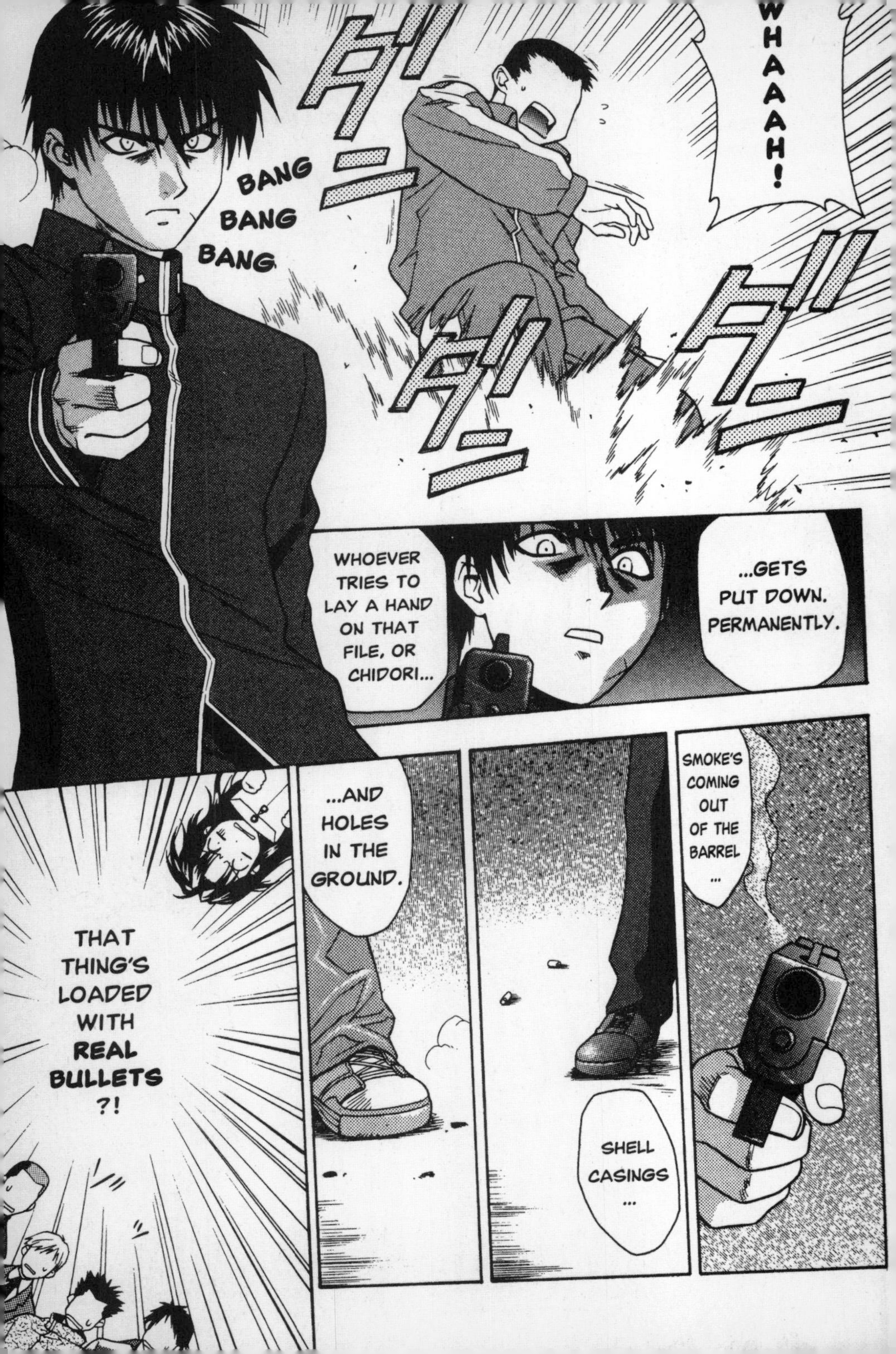
WHAAAAH!
WHOEVER TRIES TO LAY A HAND ON THAT FILE, OR CHIDORI...
...GETS PUT DOWN. PERMANENTLY.
BANG BANG BANG
SMOKE'S COMING OUT OF THE BARREL ...
SHELL CASINGS ...
...AND HOLES IN THE GROUND.
THAT THING'S LOADED WITH REAL BULLETS ?!

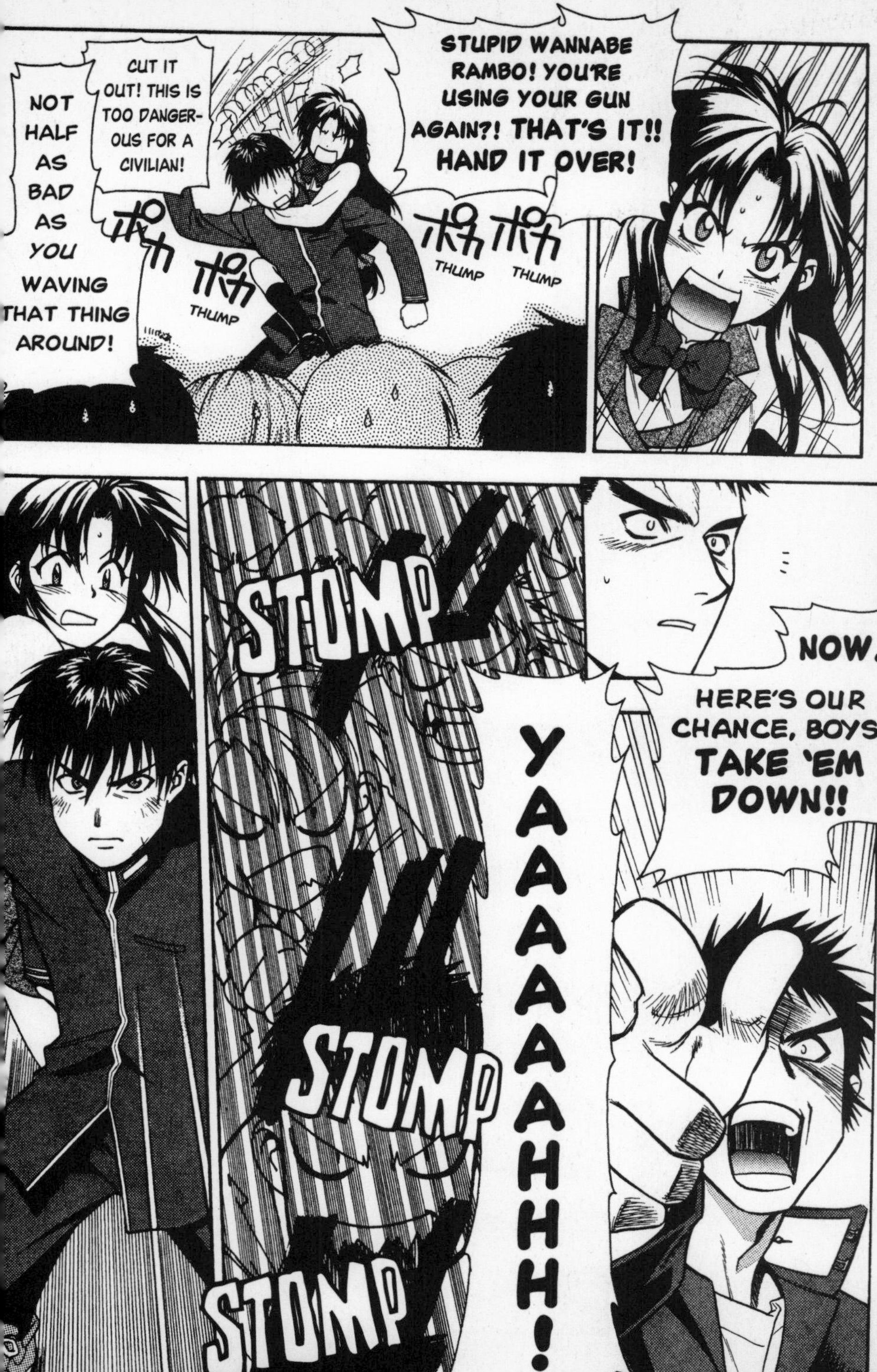
STUPID WANNABE RAMBO! YOU'RE USING YOUR GUN AGAIN?! THAT'S IT!! HAND IT OVER!
THUMP THUMP
CUT IT OUT! THIS IS TOO DANGER-OUS FOR A CIVILIAN!
NOT HALF AS BAD AS YOU WAVING THAT THING AROUND!
THUMP
NOW.
HERE'S OUR CHANCE, BOYS! TAKE 'EM DOWN!!
YAAAAAAHHH!
STOMP
STOMP
STOMP

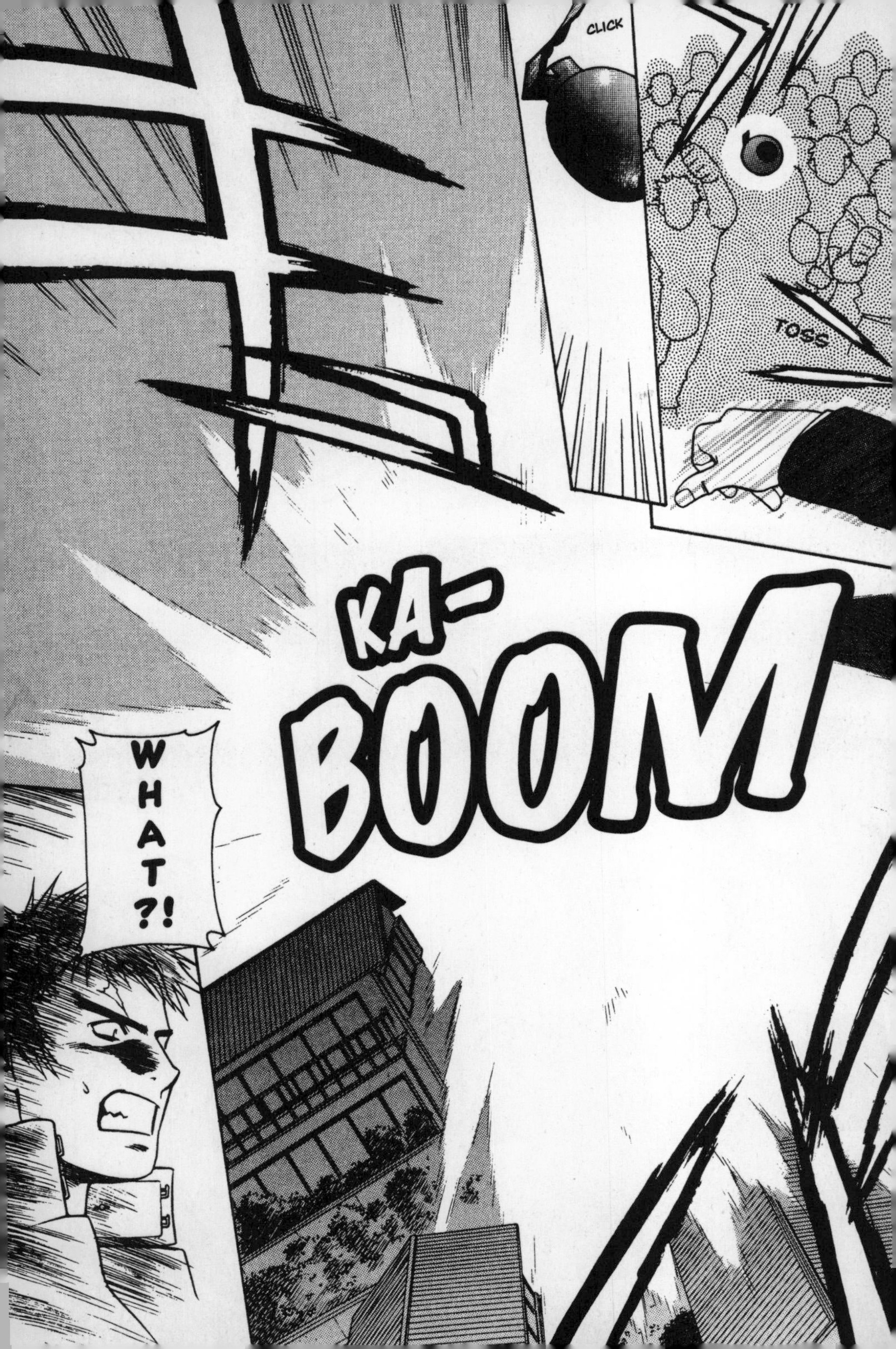
CLICK
TOSS
KA-
BOOM
WHAT?!

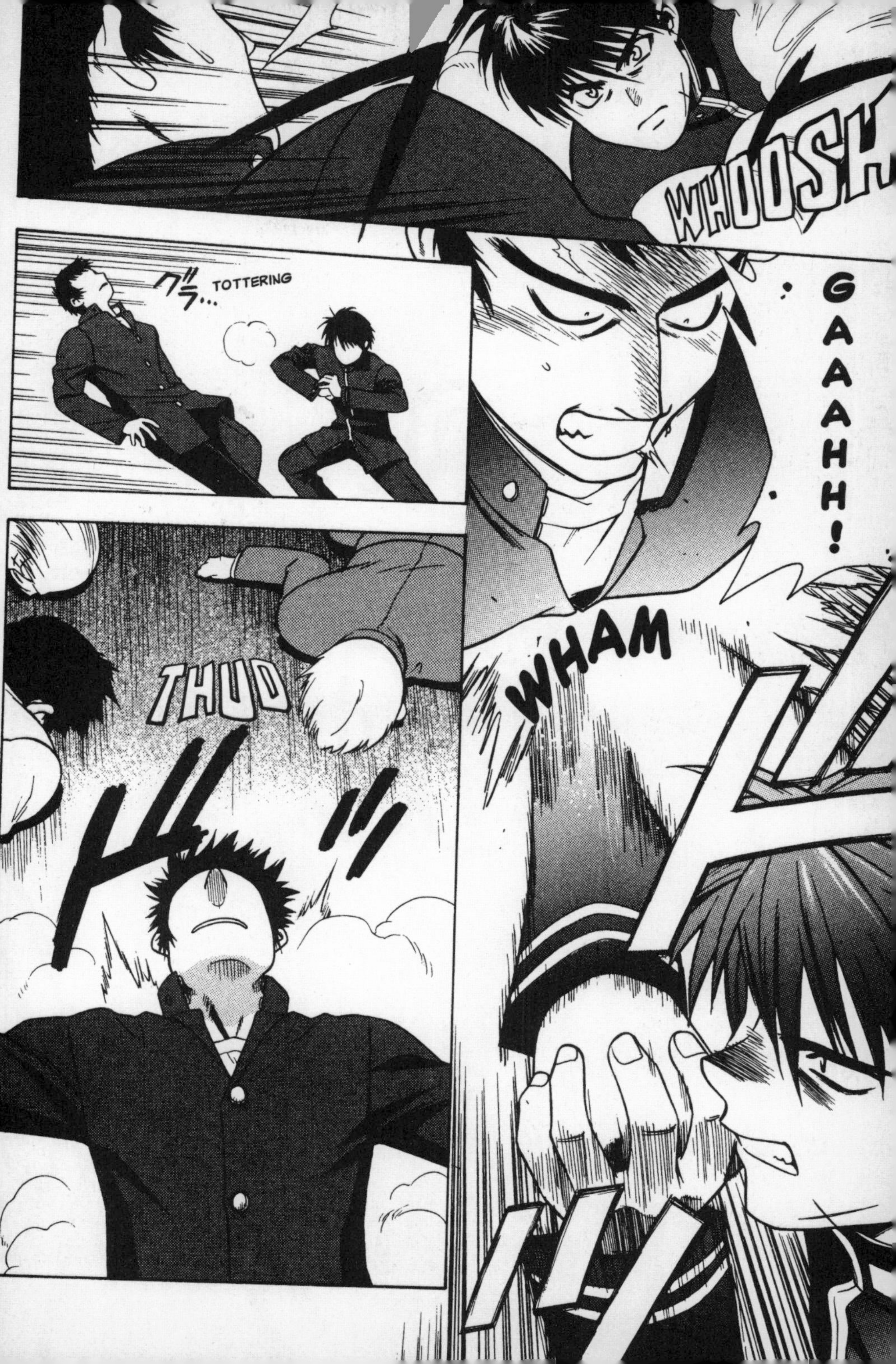
WHOOSH
GAAAHH!
WHAM
グラ... TOTTERING
THUD

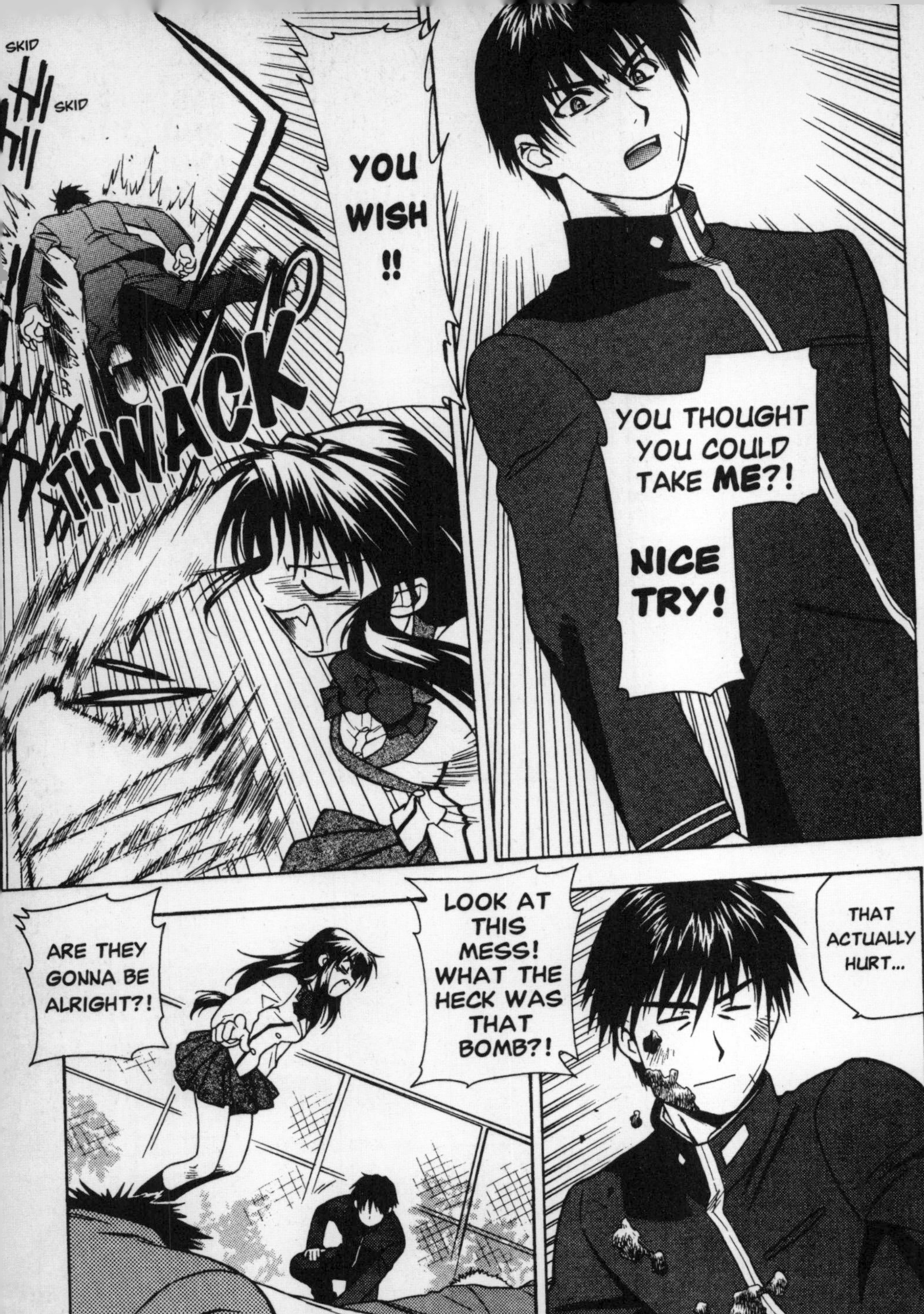

YOU THOUGHT YOU COULD TAKE ME?!
NICE TRY!
YOU WISH !!
THWACK
SKID
SKID
THAT ACTUALLY HURT...
LOOK AT THIS MESS! WHAT THE HECK WAS THAT BOMB?!
ARE THEY GONNA BE ALRIGHT?!

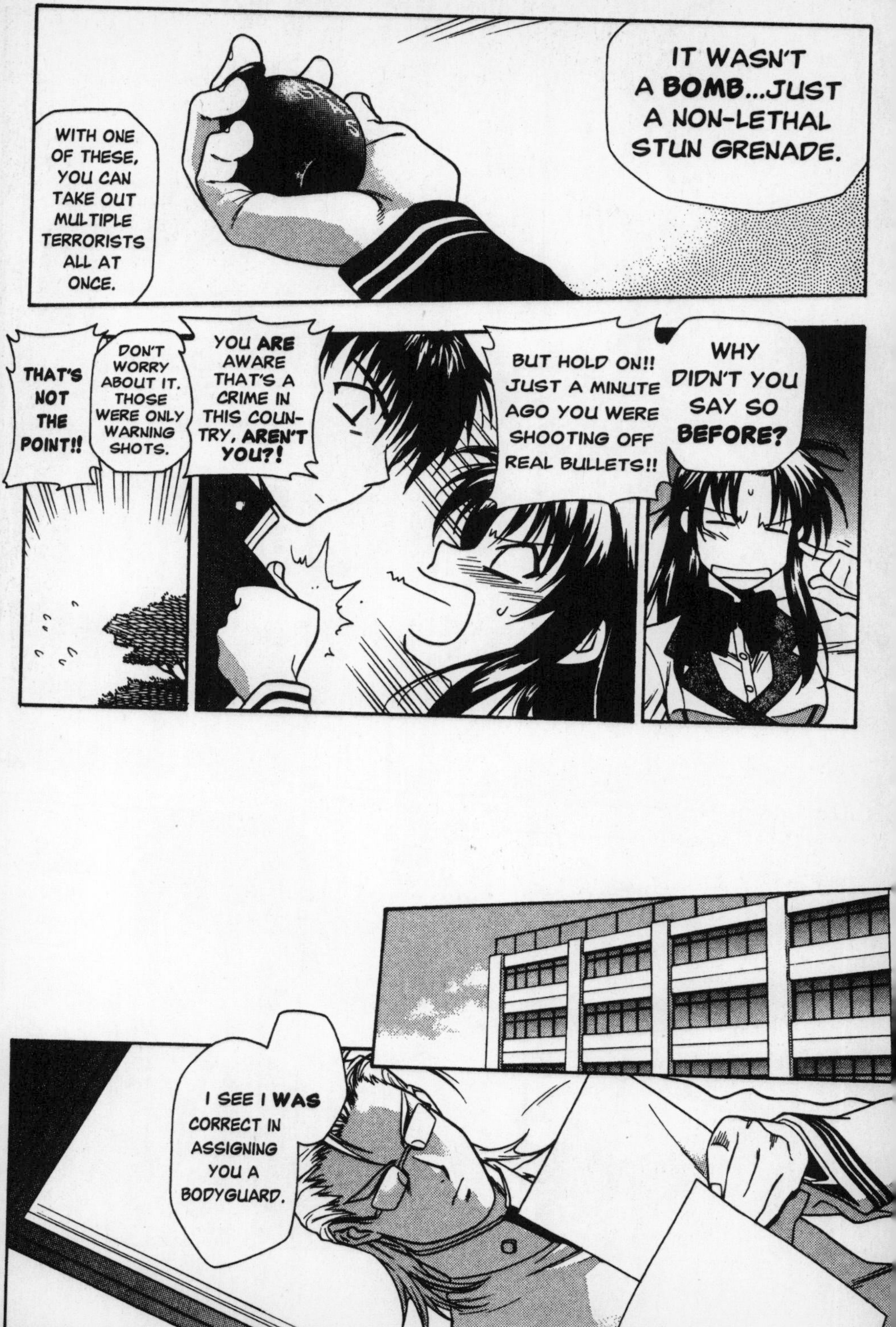
IT WASN'T A BOMB...JUST A NON-LETHAL STUN GRENADE.
WITH ONE OF THESE, YOU CAN TAKE OUT MULTIPLE TERRORISTS ALL AT ONCE.
WHY DIDN'T YOU SAY SO BEFORE?
BUT HOLD ON!! JUST A MINUTE AGO YOU WERE SHOOTING OFF REAL BULLETS!!
YOU ARE AWARE THAT'S A CRIME IN THIS COUN-TRY, AREN'T YOU?!
DON'T WORRY ABOUT IT. THOSE WERE ONLY WARNING SHOTS.
THAT'S NOT THE POINT!!
I SEE I WAS CORRECT IN ASSIGNING YOU A BODYGUARD.

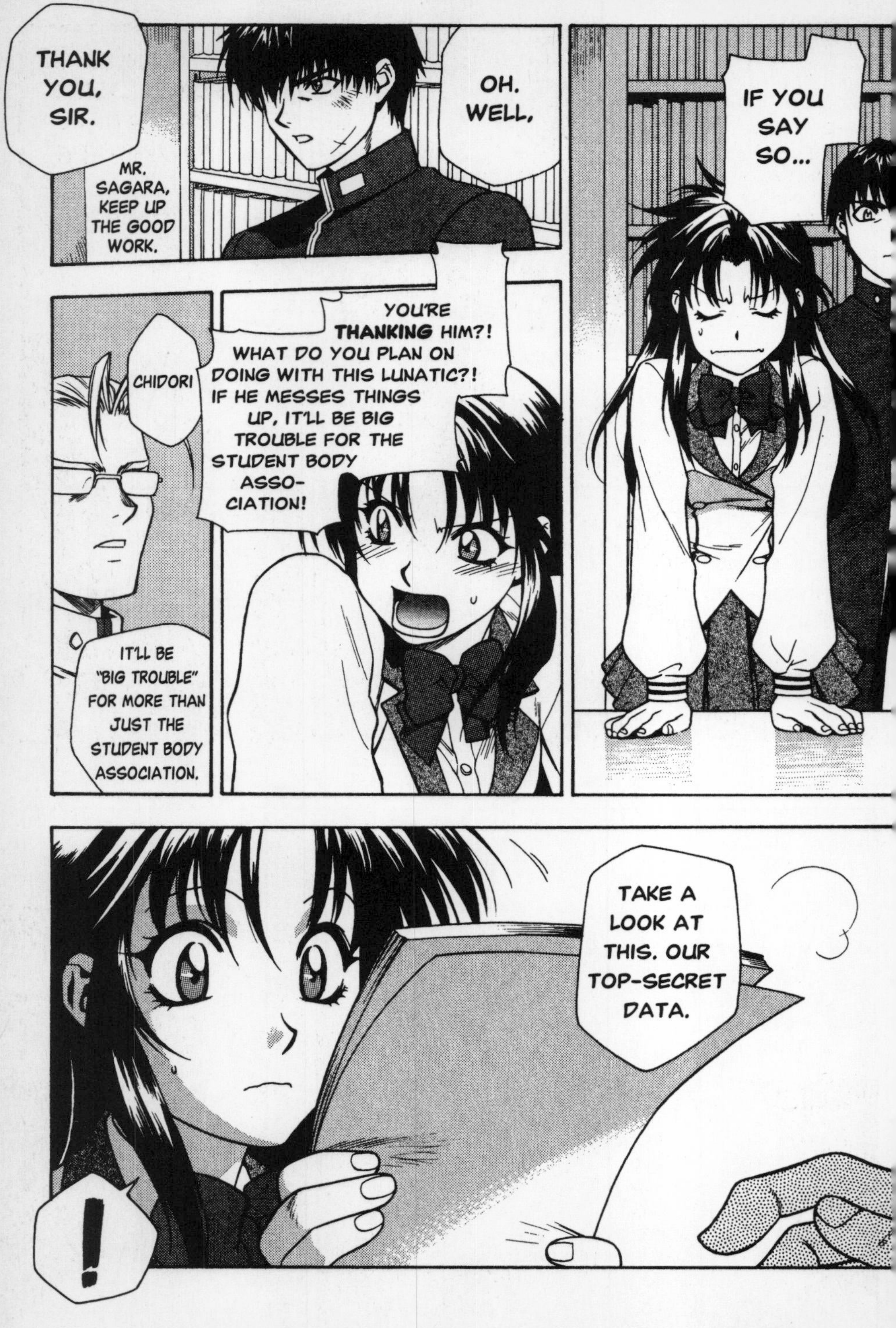
IF YOU SAY SO...
OH. WELL,
THANK YOU, SIR.
MR. SAGARA, KEEP UP THE GOOD WORK.
YOU'RE THANKING HIM?! WHAT DO YOU PLAN ON DOING WITH THIS LUNATIC?! IF HE MESSES THINGS UP, IT'LL BE BIG TROUBLE FOR THE STUDENT BODY ASSO-CIATION!
CHIDORI
IT'LL BE "BIG TROUBLE" FOR MORE THAN JUST THE STUDENT BODY ASSOCIATION.
TAKE A LOOK AT THIS. OUR TOP-SECRET DATA.
!

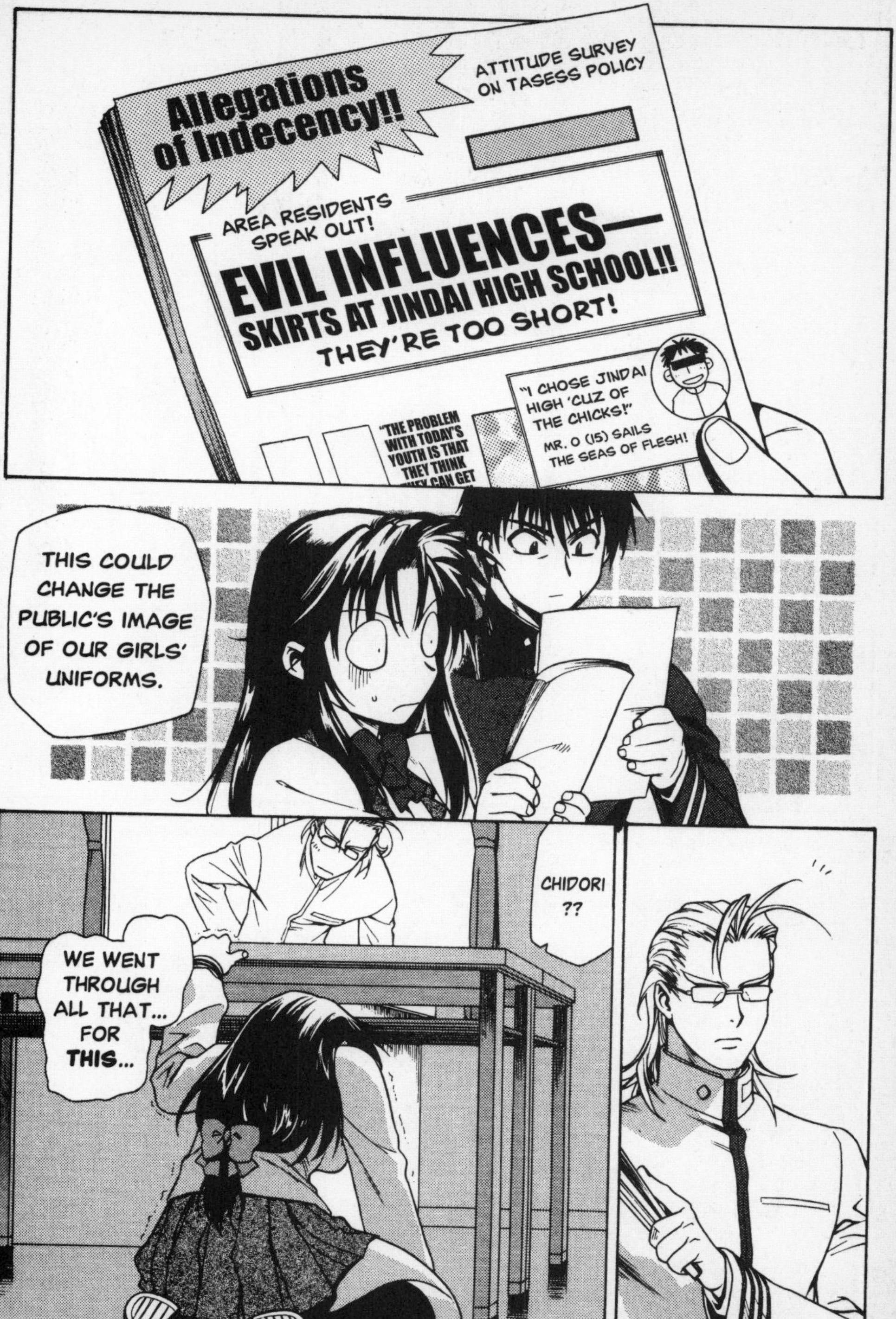
Allegations of Indecency!!
ATTITUDE SURVEY ON TASESS POLICY
AREA RESIDENTS SPEAK OUT!
EVIL INFLUENCES— SKIRTS AT JINDAI HIGH SCHOOL!!
THEY'RE TOO SHORT!
"I CHOSE JINDAI HIGH 'CUZ OF THE CHICKS!"
MR. O (15) SAILS THE SEAS OF FLESH!
"THE PROBLEM WITH TODAY'S YOUTH IS THAT THEY THINK THEY CAN GET
THIS COULD CHANGE THE PUBLIC'S IMAGE OF OUR GIRLS' UNIFORMS.
CHIDORI ??
WE WENT THROUGH ALL THAT... FOR **THIS**...

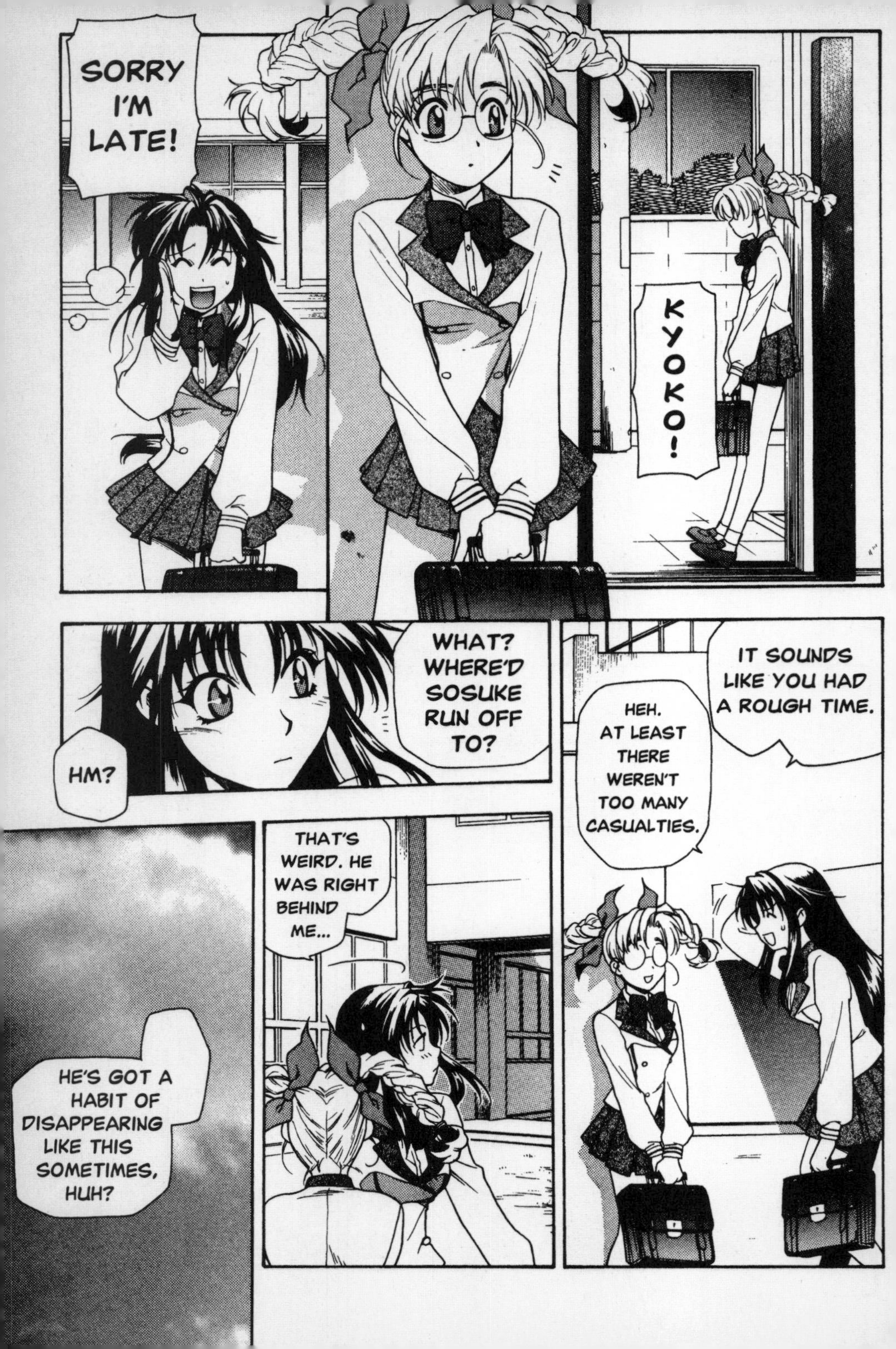
KYOKO!
SORRY I'M LATE!
IT SOUNDS LIKE YOU HAD A ROUGH TIME.
HEH. AT LEAST THERE WEREN'T TOO MANY CASUALTIES.
WHAT? WHERE'D SOSUKE RUN OFF TO?
HM?
THAT'S WEIRD. HE WAS RIGHT BEHIND ME...
HE'S GOT A HABIT OF DISAPPEARING LIKE THIS SOMETIMES, HUH?

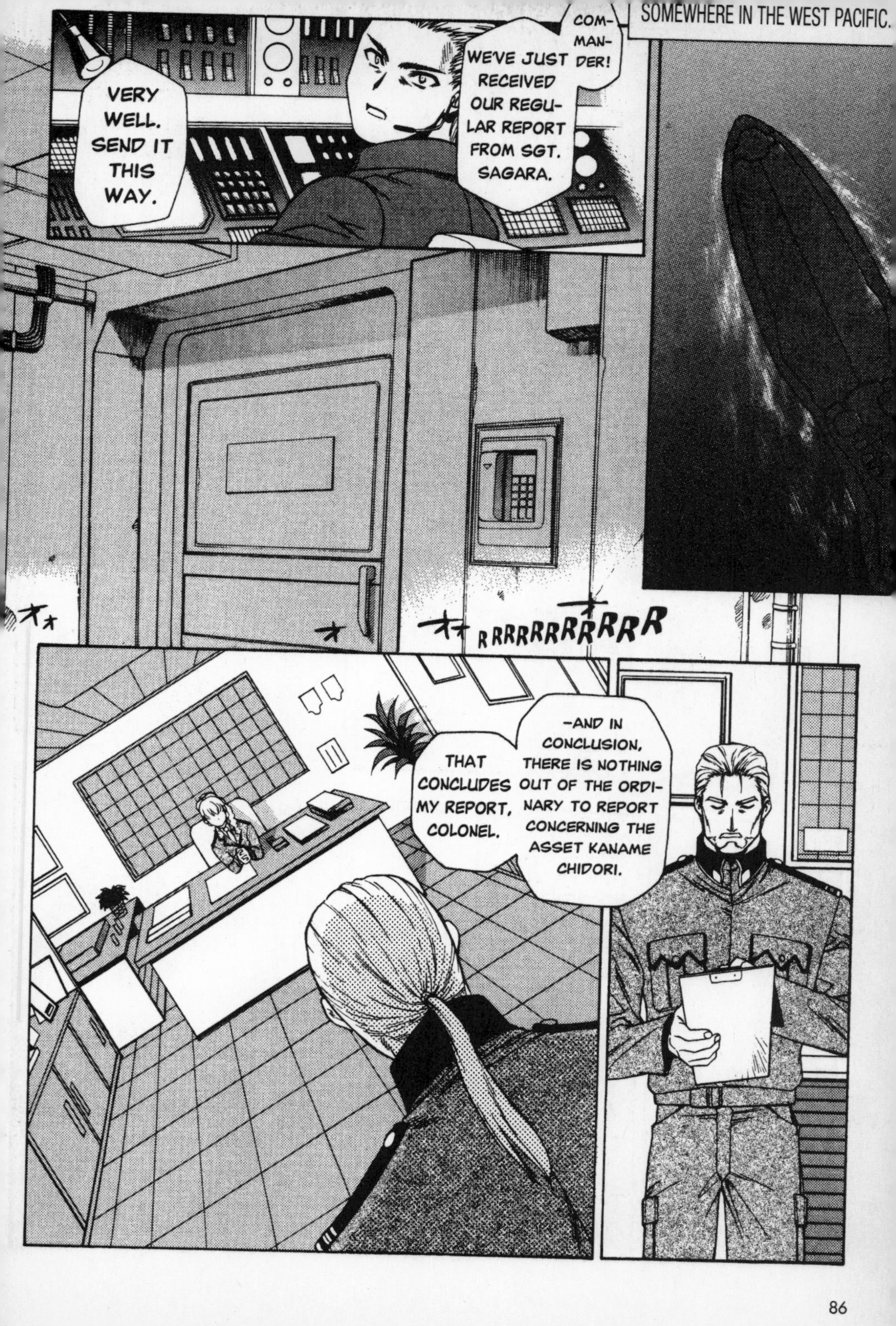
SOMEWHERE IN THE WEST PACIFIC.
COMMANDER!
WE'VE JUST RECEIVED OUR REGULAR REPORT FROM SGT. SAGARA.
VERY WELL. SEND IT THIS WAY.
RRRRRRRRRR
-AND IN CONCLUSION, THERE IS NOTHING OUT OF THE ORDINARY TO REPORT CONCERNING THE ASSET KANAME CHIDORI.
THAT CONCLUDES MY REPORT, COLONEL.

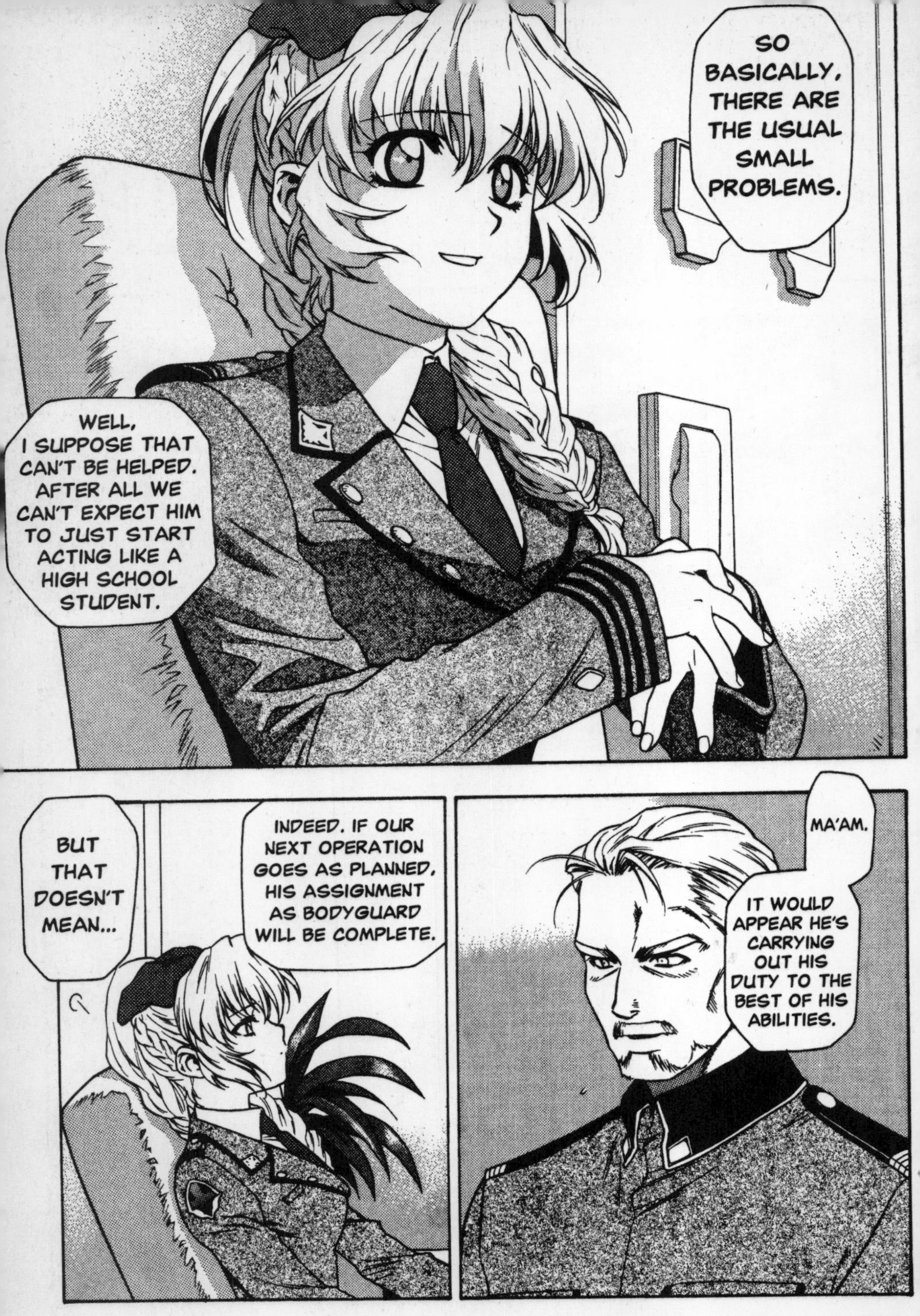
SO BASICALLY, THERE ARE THE USUAL SMALL PROBLEMS.
WELL, I SUPPOSE THAT CAN'T BE HELPED. AFTER ALL WE CAN'T EXPECT HIM TO JUST START ACTING LIKE A HIGH SCHOOL STUDENT.
MA'AM.
IT WOULD APPEAR HE'S CARRYING OUT HIS DUTY TO THE BEST OF HIS ABILITIES.
INDEED. IF OUR NEXT OPERATION GOES AS PLANNED, HIS ASSIGNMENT AS BODYGUARD WILL BE COMPLETE.
BUT THAT DOESN'T MEAN...

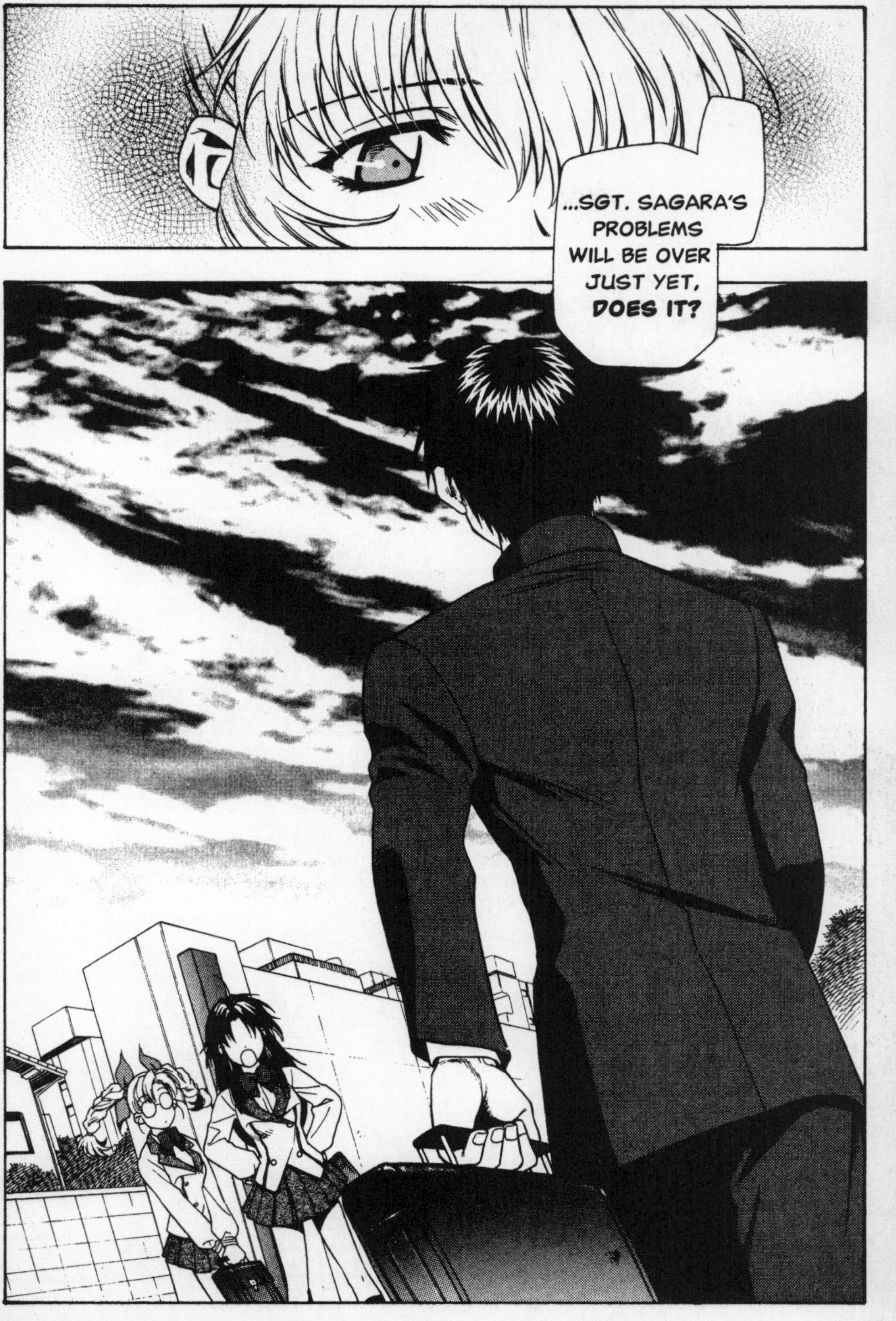
...SGT. SAGARA'S PROBLEMS WILL BE OVER JUST YET, DOES IT?

MISSION:04 [redacted] [Bread and Bullets]

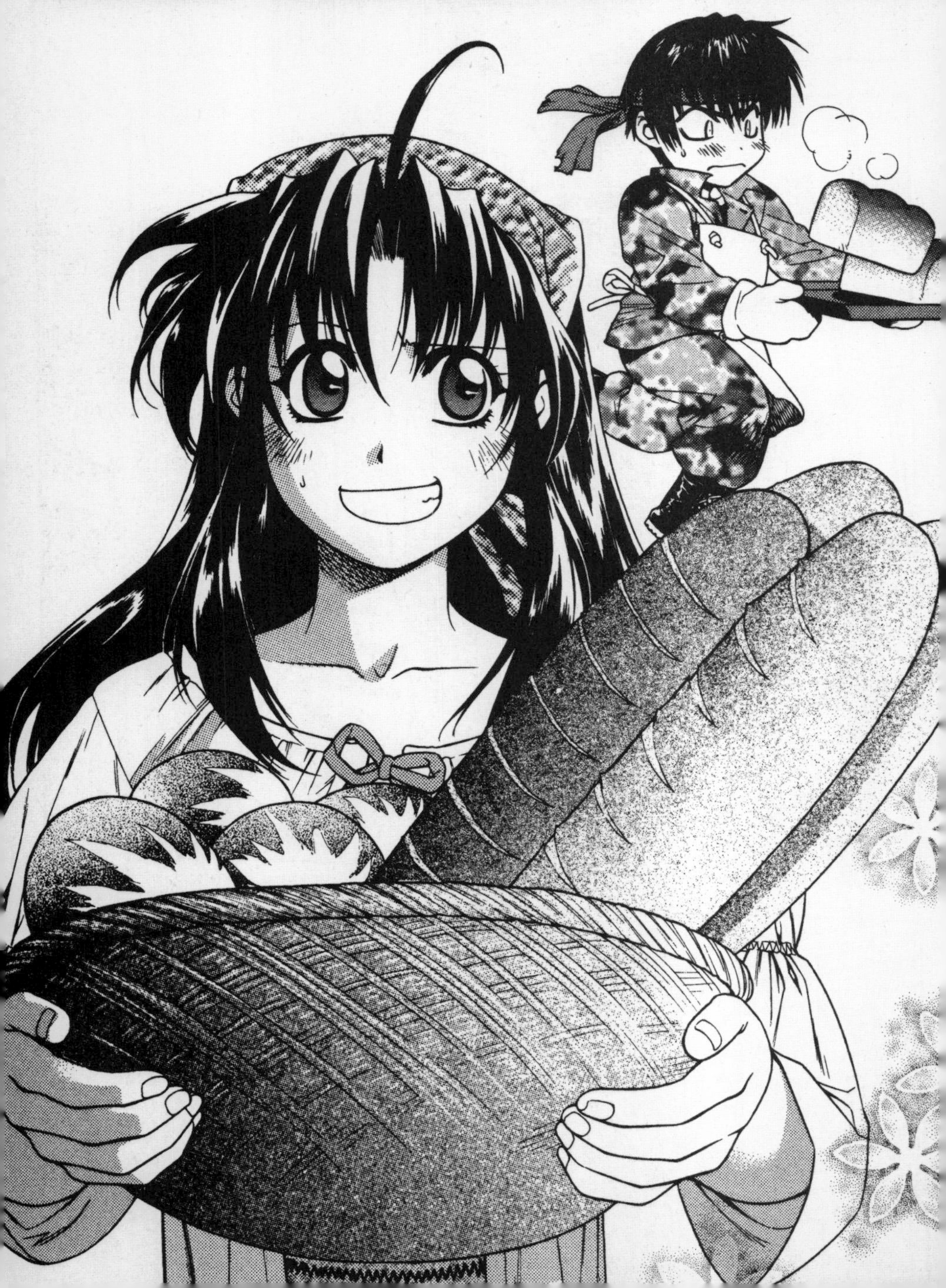

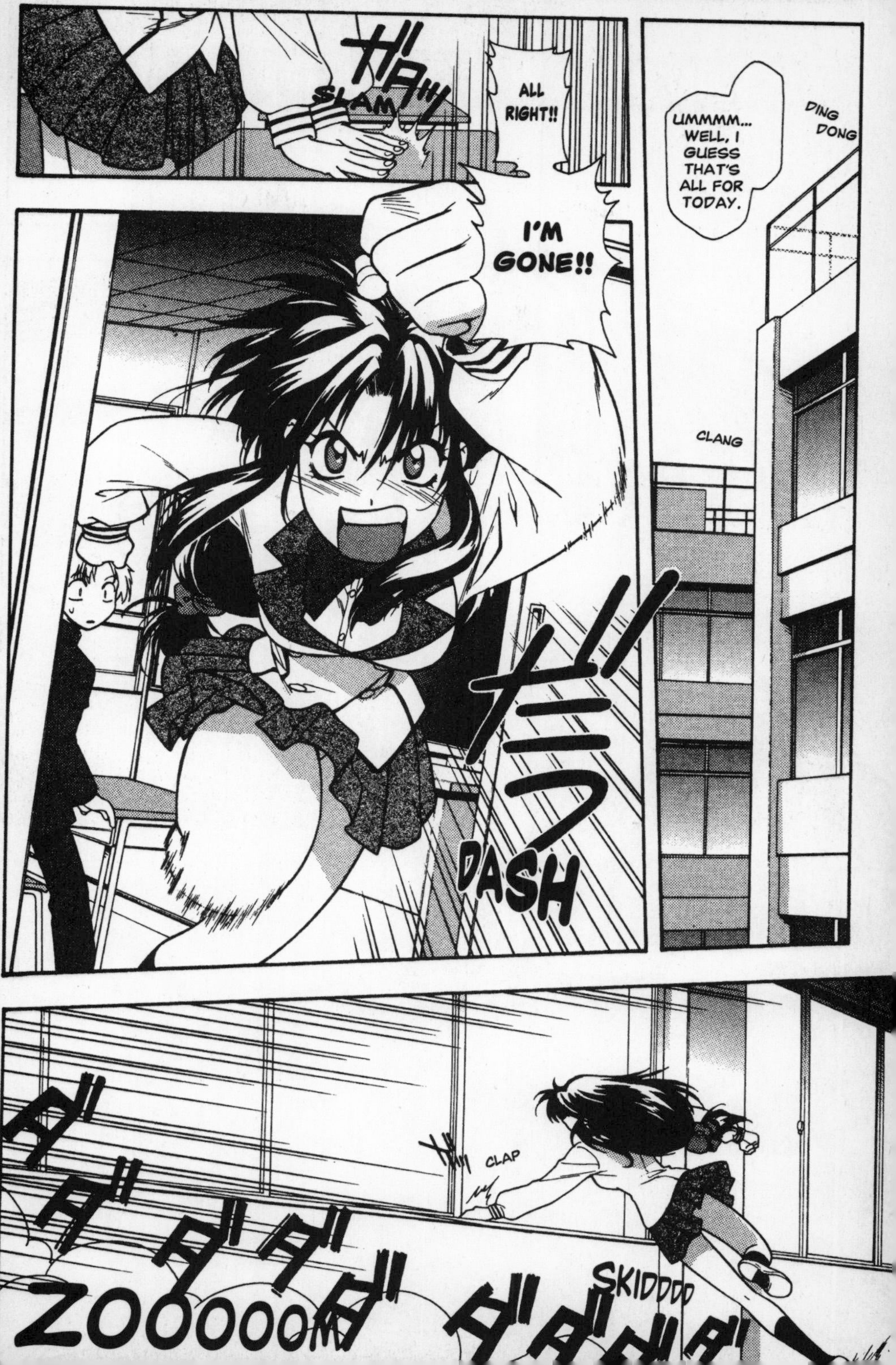

UMMMM... WELL, I GUESS THAT'S ALL FOR TODAY.
DING DONG
CLANG
SLAM
ALL RIGHT!!
I'M GONE!!
DASH
SKIDDDD
CLAP
ZOOOOOM

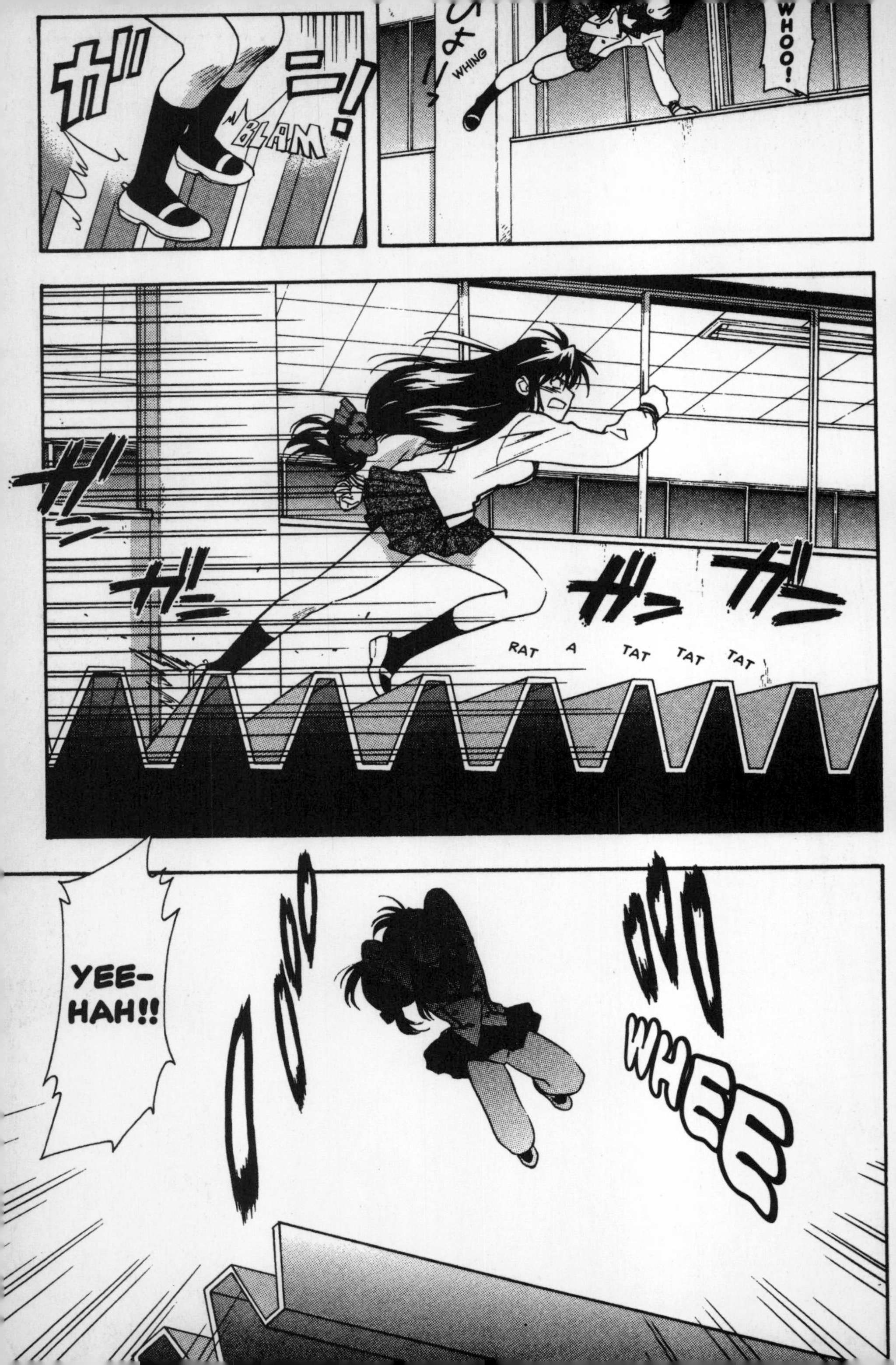
WHING
WHOO!
BLAM
RAT A TAT TAT TAT
YEE-HAH!!
WHEE

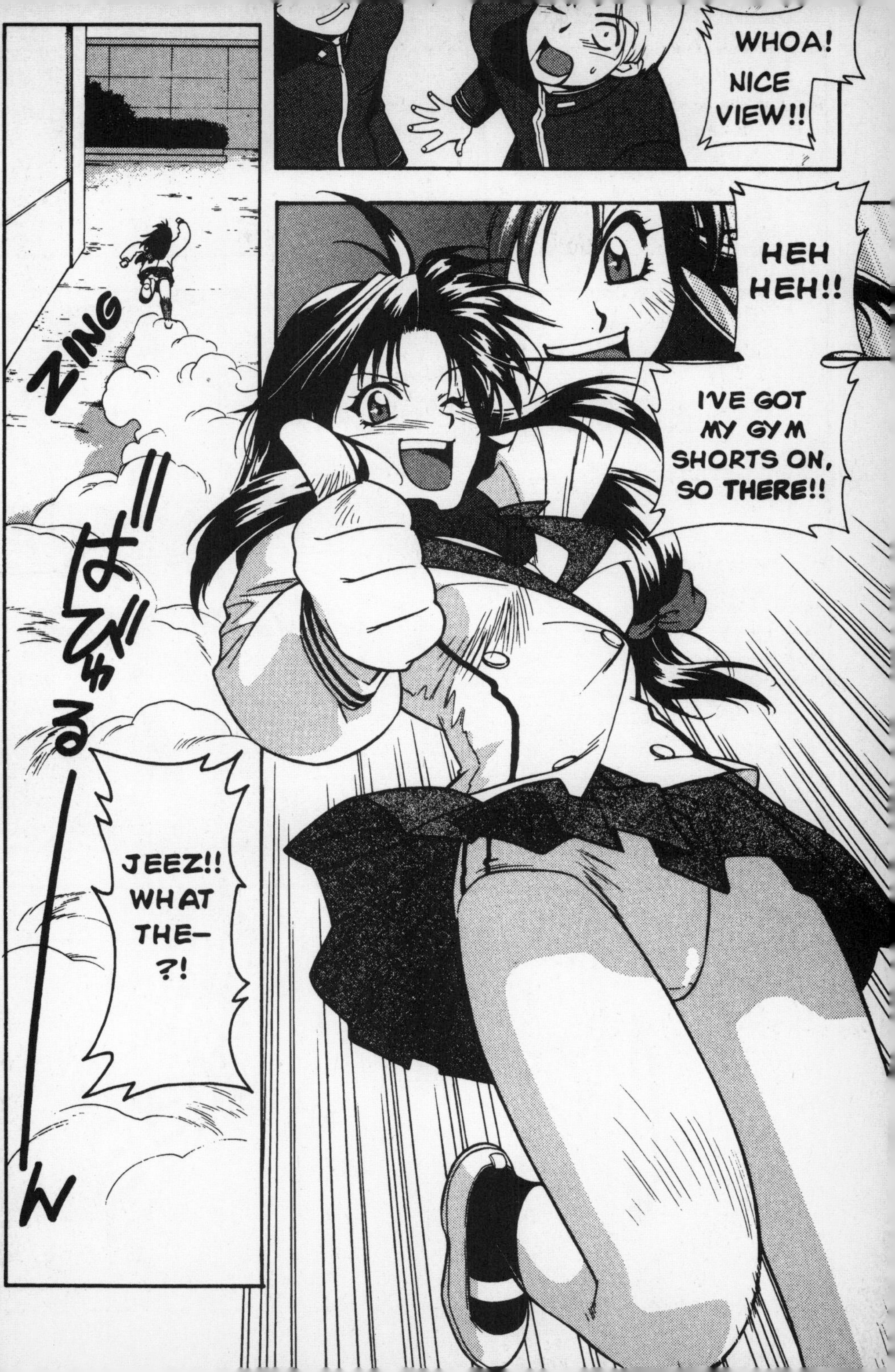
WHOA! NICE VIEW!!
HEH HEH!!
I'VE GOT MY GYM SHORTS ON, SO THERE!!
ZING
ばびゅる
N
JEEZ!! WHAT THE–?!

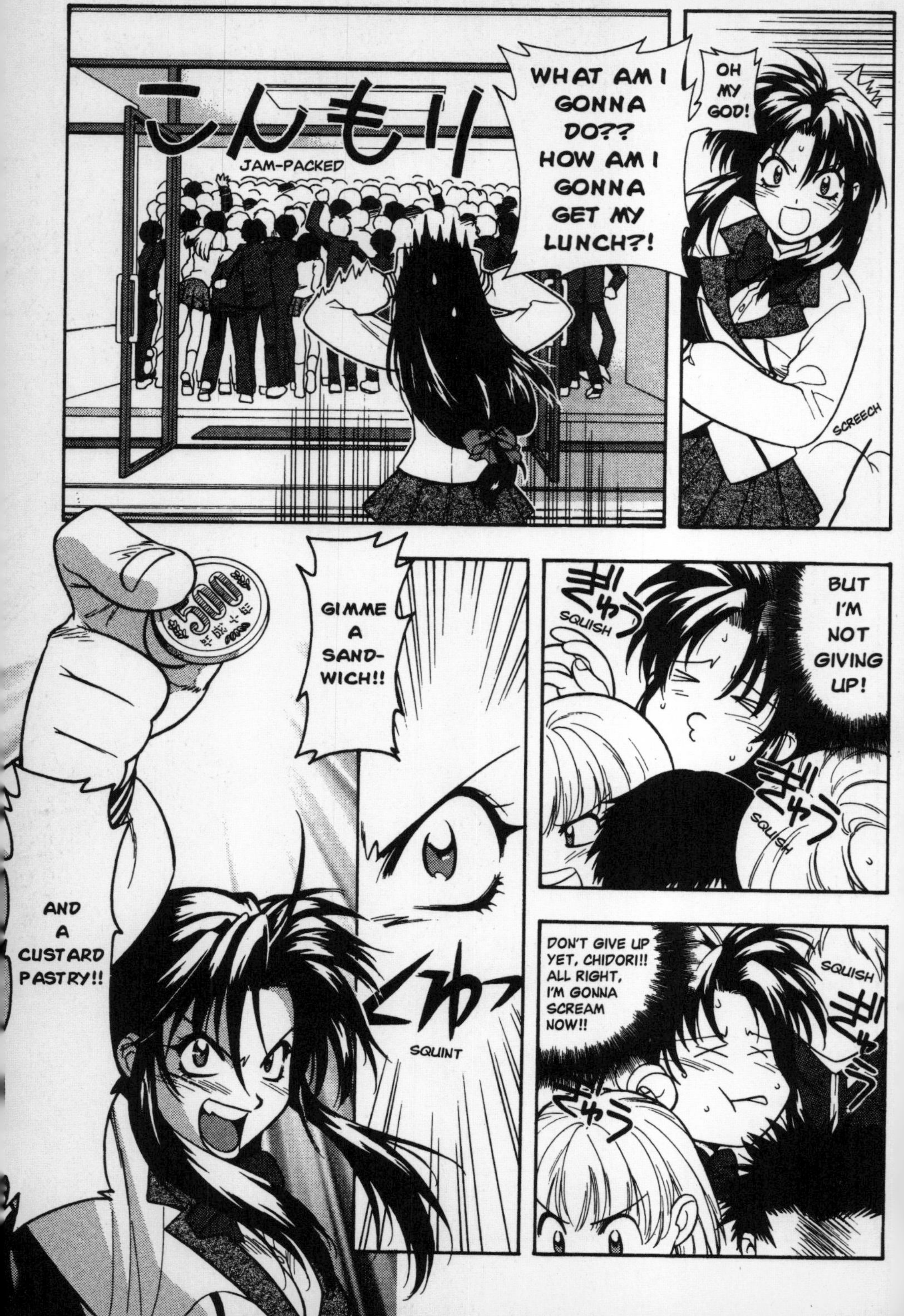
OH MY GOD!
SCREECH
WHAT AM I GONNA DO?? HOW AM I GONNA GET MY LUNCH?!
こんもり
JAM-PACKED
BUT I'M NOT GIVING UP!
ぎゅう
SQUISH
ぎゅう
SQUISH
DON'T GIVE UP YET, CHIDORI!! ALL RIGHT, I'M GONNA SCREAM NOW!!
SQUISH
ぎゅう
GIMME A SANDWICH!!
くわっ
SQUINT
500
AND A CUSTARD PASTRY!!

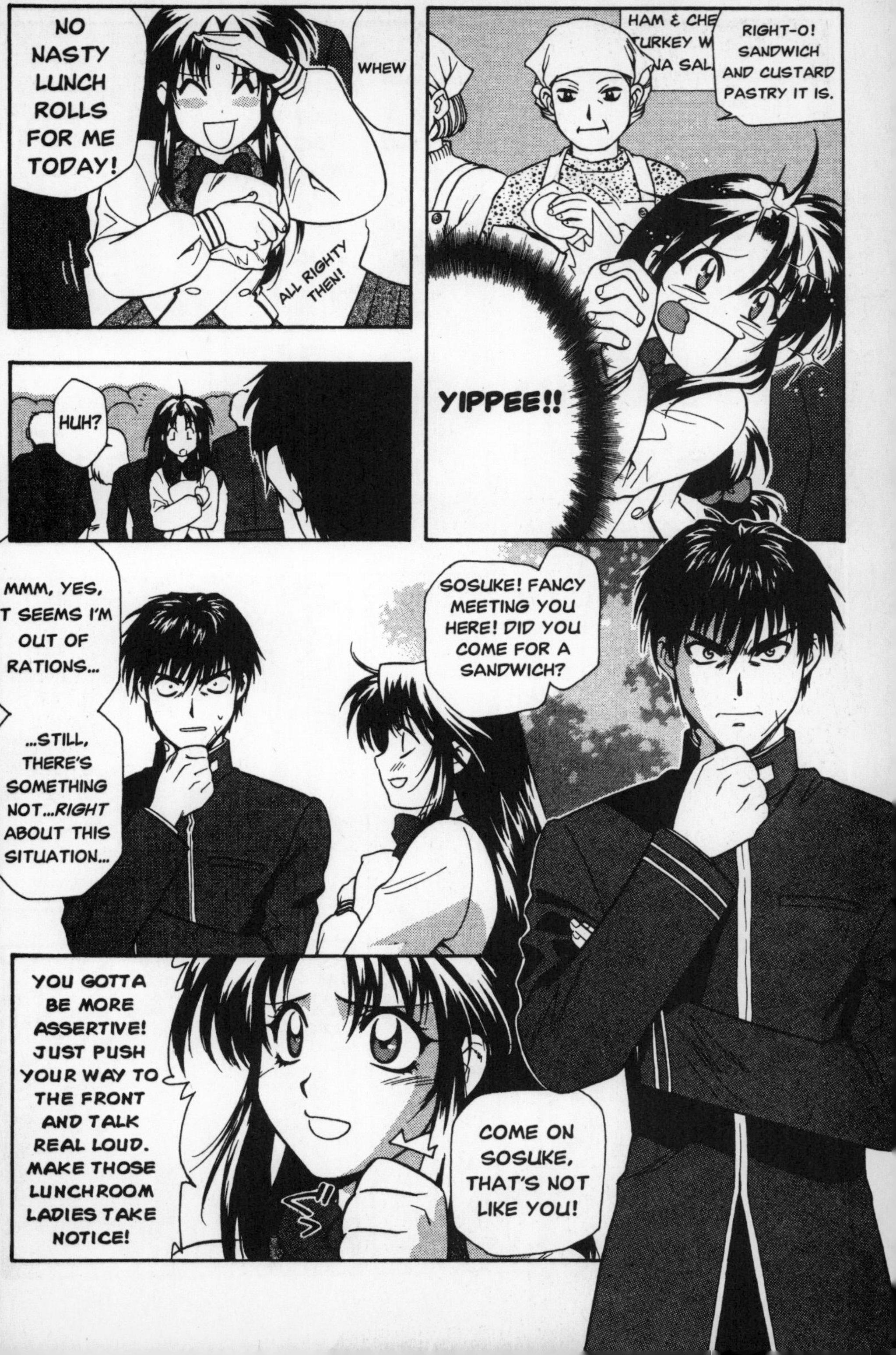
HAM & CHE
TURKEY W
NA SAL
RIGHT-O! SANDWICH AND CUSTARD PASTRY IT IS.
YIPPEE!!
NO NASTY LUNCH ROLLS FOR ME TODAY!
WHEW
ALL RIGHTY THEN!
HUH?
SOSUKE! FANCY MEETING YOU HERE! DID YOU COME FOR A SANDWICH?
MMM, YES, IT SEEMS I'M OUT OF RATIONS...
...STILL, THERE'S SOMETHING NOT...*RIGHT* ABOUT THIS SITUATION...
COME ON SOSUKE, THAT'S NOT LIKE YOU!
YOU GOTTA BE MORE ASSERTIVE! JUST PUSH YOUR WAY TO THE FRONT AND TALK REAL LOUD. MAKE THOSE LUNCHROOM LADIES TAKE NOTICE!

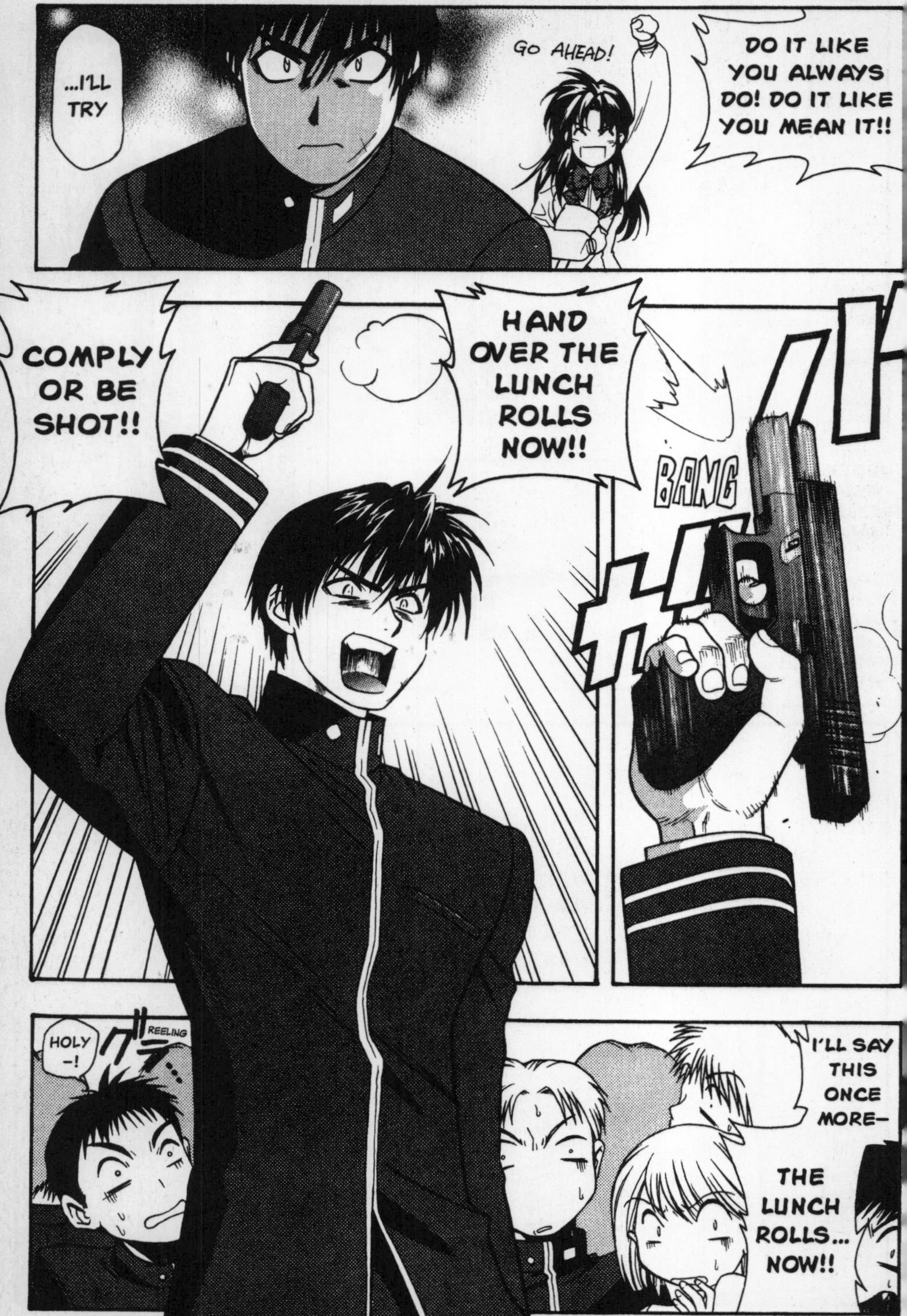

DO IT LIKE YOU ALWAYS DO! DO IT LIKE YOU MEAN IT!!
GO AHEAD!
...I'LL TRY
BANG
HAND OVER THE LUNCH ROLLS NOW!!
COMPLY OR BE SHOT!!
I'LL SAY THIS ONCE MORE—
THE LUNCH ROLLS... NOW!!
REELING
HOLY -!

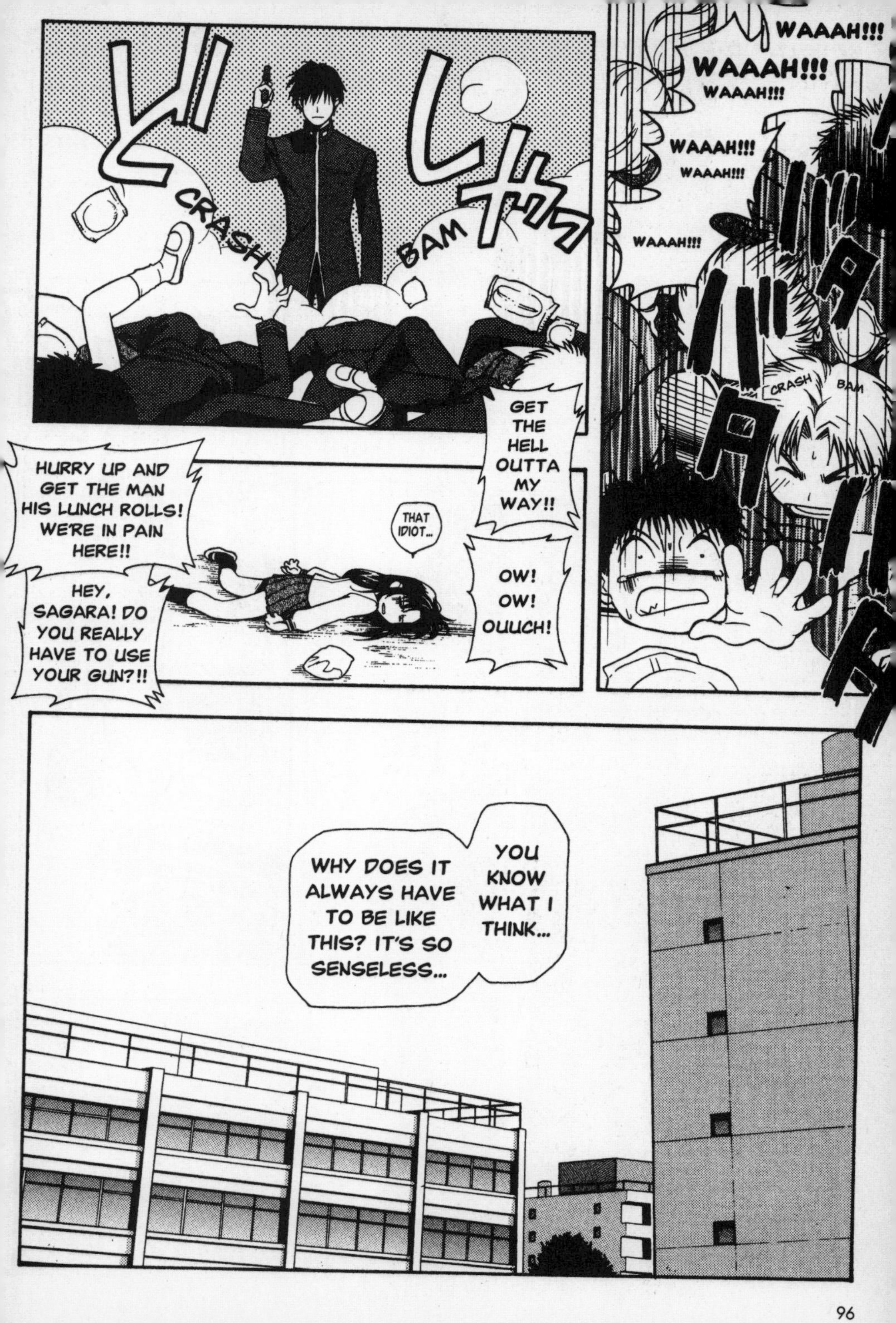
WAAAH!!!
WAAAH!!!
WAAAH!!!
WAAAH!!!
WAAAH!!!
WAAAH!!!
CRASH
BAM
GET THE HELL OUTTA MY WAY!!
OW! OW! OUUCH!
CRASH
BAM
HURRY UP AND GET THE MAN HIS LUNCH ROLLS! WE'RE IN PAIN HERE!!
THAT IDIOT...
HEY, SAGARA! DO YOU REALLY HAVE TO USE YOUR GUN?!!
YOU KNOW WHAT I THINK...
WHY DOES IT ALWAYS HAVE TO BE LIKE THIS? IT'S SO SENSELESS...

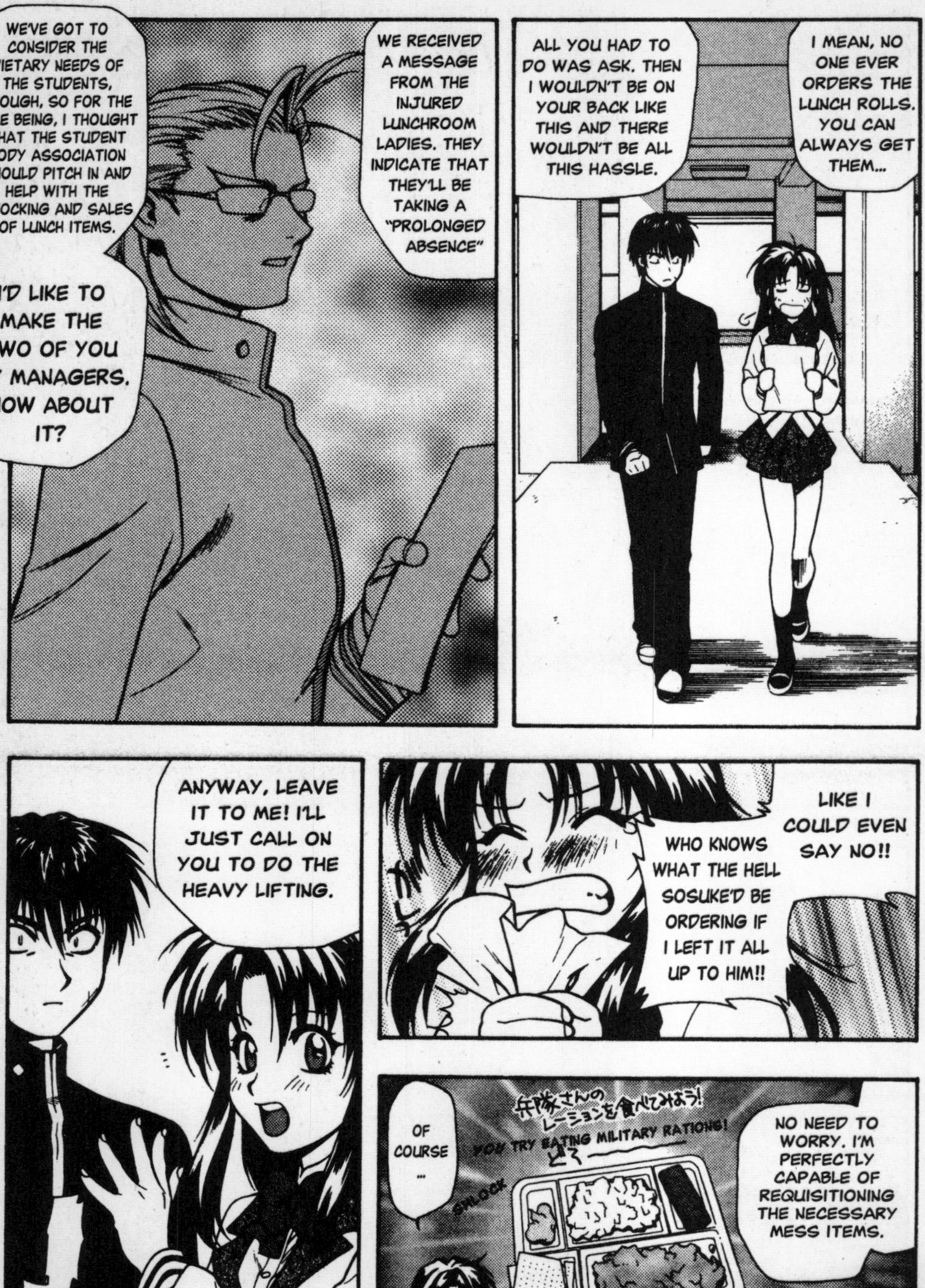
I MEAN, NO ONE EVER ORDERS THE LUNCH ROLLS. YOU CAN ALWAYS GET THEM...
ALL YOU HAD TO DO WAS ASK. THEN I WOULDN'T BE ON YOUR BACK LIKE THIS AND THERE WOULDN'T BE ALL THIS HASSLE.
WE RECEIVED A MESSAGE FROM THE INJURED LUNCHROOM LADIES. THEY INDICATE THAT THEY'LL BE TAKING A "PROLONGED ABSENCE"
WE'VE GOT TO CONSIDER THE DIETARY NEEDS OF THE STUDENTS, THOUGH, SO FOR THE TIME BEING, I THOUGHT THAT THE STUDENT BODY ASSOCIATION SHOULD PITCH IN AND HELP WITH THE STOCKING AND SALES OF LUNCH ITEMS.
I'D LIKE TO MAKE THE TWO OF YOU MY MANAGERS. HOW ABOUT IT?
LIKE I COULD EVEN SAY NO!!
WHO KNOWS WHAT THE HELL SOSUKE'D BE ORDERING IF I LEFT IT ALL UP TO HIM!!
NO NEED TO WORRY. I'M PERFECTLY CAPABLE OF REQUISITIONING THE NECESSARY MESS ITEMS.
兵隊さんのレーションを食べてみよう!
YOU TRY EATING MILITARY RATIONS!
OF COURSE ...
SHLOCK
SLOP
ANYWAY, LEAVE IT TO ME! I'LL JUST CALL ON YOU TO DO THE HEAVY LIFTING.
GRUMBLE GRUMBLE

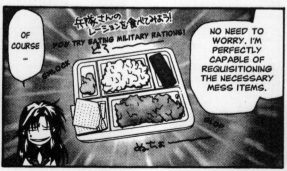

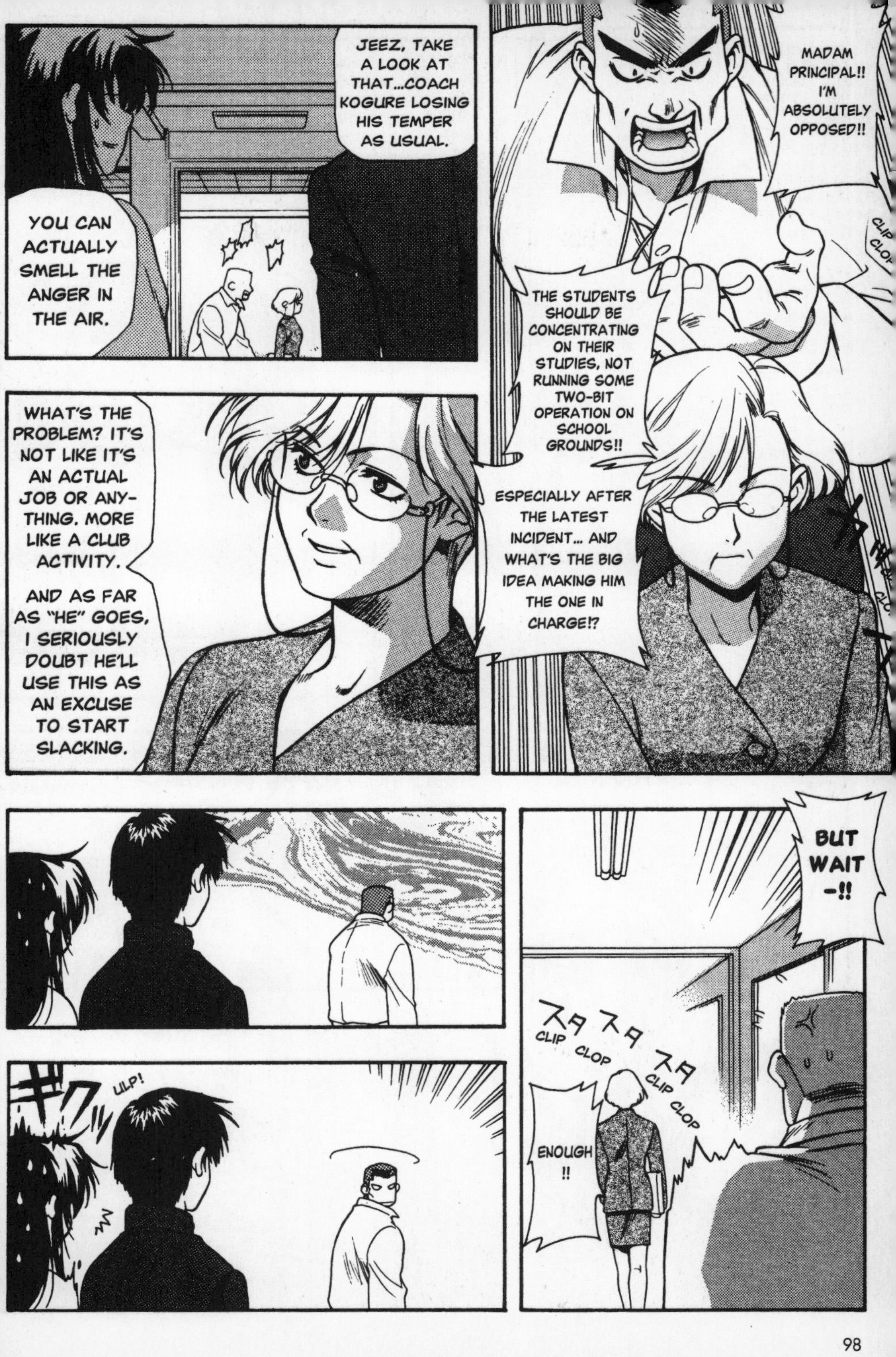
MADAM PRINCIPAL!! I'M ABSOLUTELY OPPOSED!!
CLIP CLOP
THE STUDENTS SHOULD BE CONCENTRATING ON THEIR STUDIES, NOT RUNNING SOME TWO-BIT OPERATION ON SCHOOL GROUNDS!!
ESPECIALLY AFTER THE LATEST INCIDENT... AND WHAT'S THE BIG IDEA MAKING HIM THE ONE IN CHARGE!?
JEEZ, TAKE A LOOK AT THAT...COACH KOGURE LOSING HIS TEMPER AS USUAL.
YOU CAN ACTUALLY SMELL THE ANGER IN THE AIR.
WHAT'S THE PROBLEM? IT'S NOT LIKE IT'S AN ACTUAL JOB OR ANYTHING. MORE LIKE A CLUB ACTIVITY.
AND AS FAR AS "HE" GOES, I SERIOUSLY DOUBT HE'LL USE THIS AS AN EXCUSE TO START SLACKING.
BUT WAIT-!!
スタ スタ スタ
CLIP CLOP CLIP CLOP
ENOUGH!!
ギク
ULP!

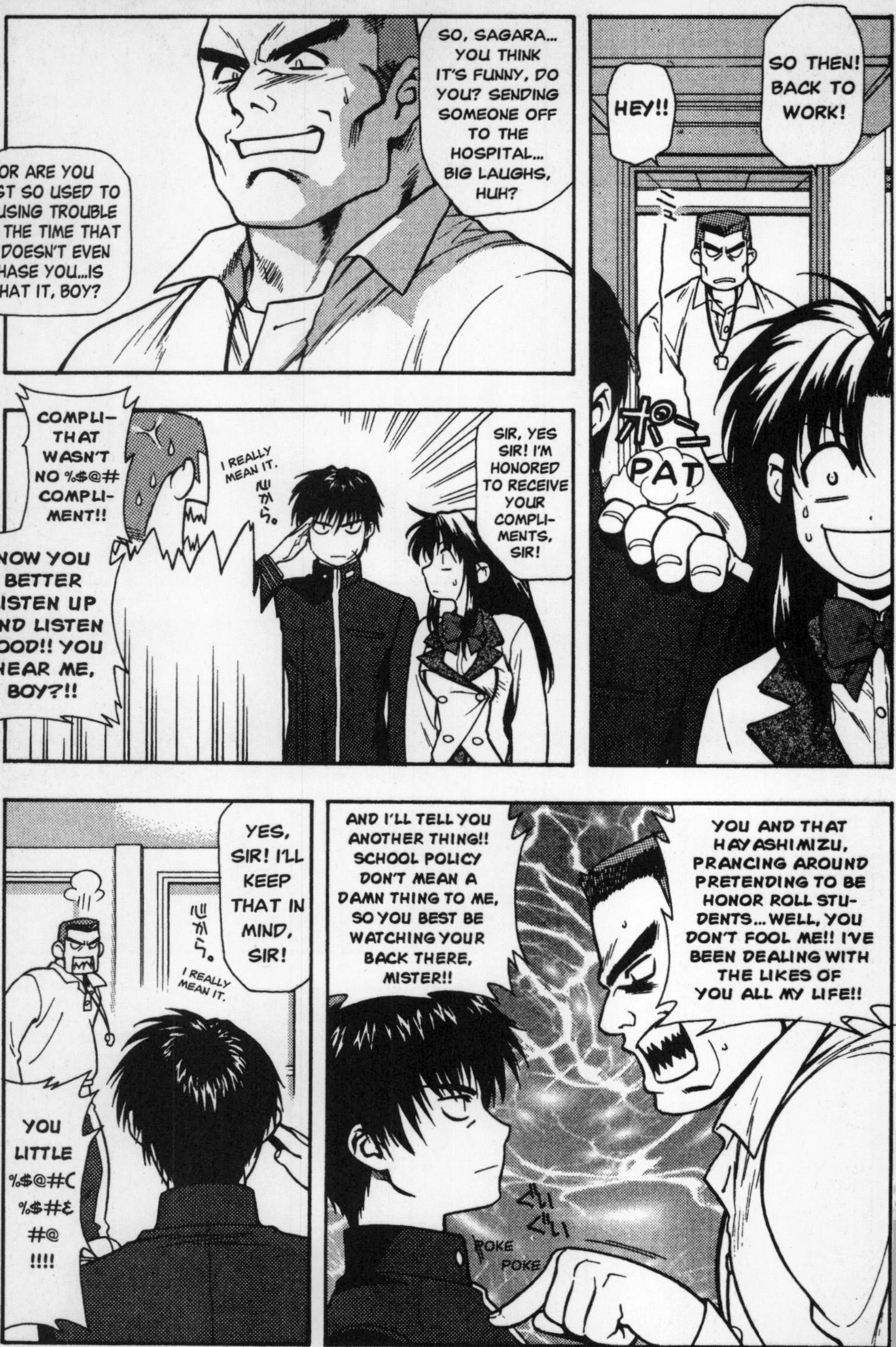

SO THEN! BACK TO WORK!
HEY!!
PAT
SO, SAGARA... YOU THINK IT'S FUNNY, DO YOU? SENDING SOMEONE OFF TO THE HOSPITAL... BIG LAUGHS, HUH?
OR ARE YOU JUST SO USED TO CAUSING TROUBLE ALL THE TIME THAT IT DOESN'T EVEN PHASE YOU...IS THAT IT, BOY?
SIR, YES SIR! I'M HONORED TO RECEIVE YOUR COMPLIMENTS, SIR!
I REALLY MEAN IT.
心から。
COMPLI- THAT WASN'T NO %$@# COMPLIMENT!!
NOW YOU BETTER LISTEN UP AND LISTEN GOOD!! YOU HEAR ME, BOY?!!
YOU AND THAT HAYASHIMIZU, PRANCING AROUND PRETENDING TO BE HONOR ROLL STUDENTS...WELL, YOU DON'T FOOL ME!! I'VE BEEN DEALING WITH THE LIKES OF YOU ALL MY LIFE!!
AND I'LL TELL YOU ANOTHER THING!! SCHOOL POLICY DON'T MEAN A DAMN THING TO ME, SO YOU BEST BE WATCHING YOUR BACK THERE, MISTER!!
POKE
POKE
YES, SIR! I'LL KEEP THAT IN MIND, SIR!
心から。
I REALLY MEAN IT.
YOU LITTLE %$@#(%$#& #@ !!!!

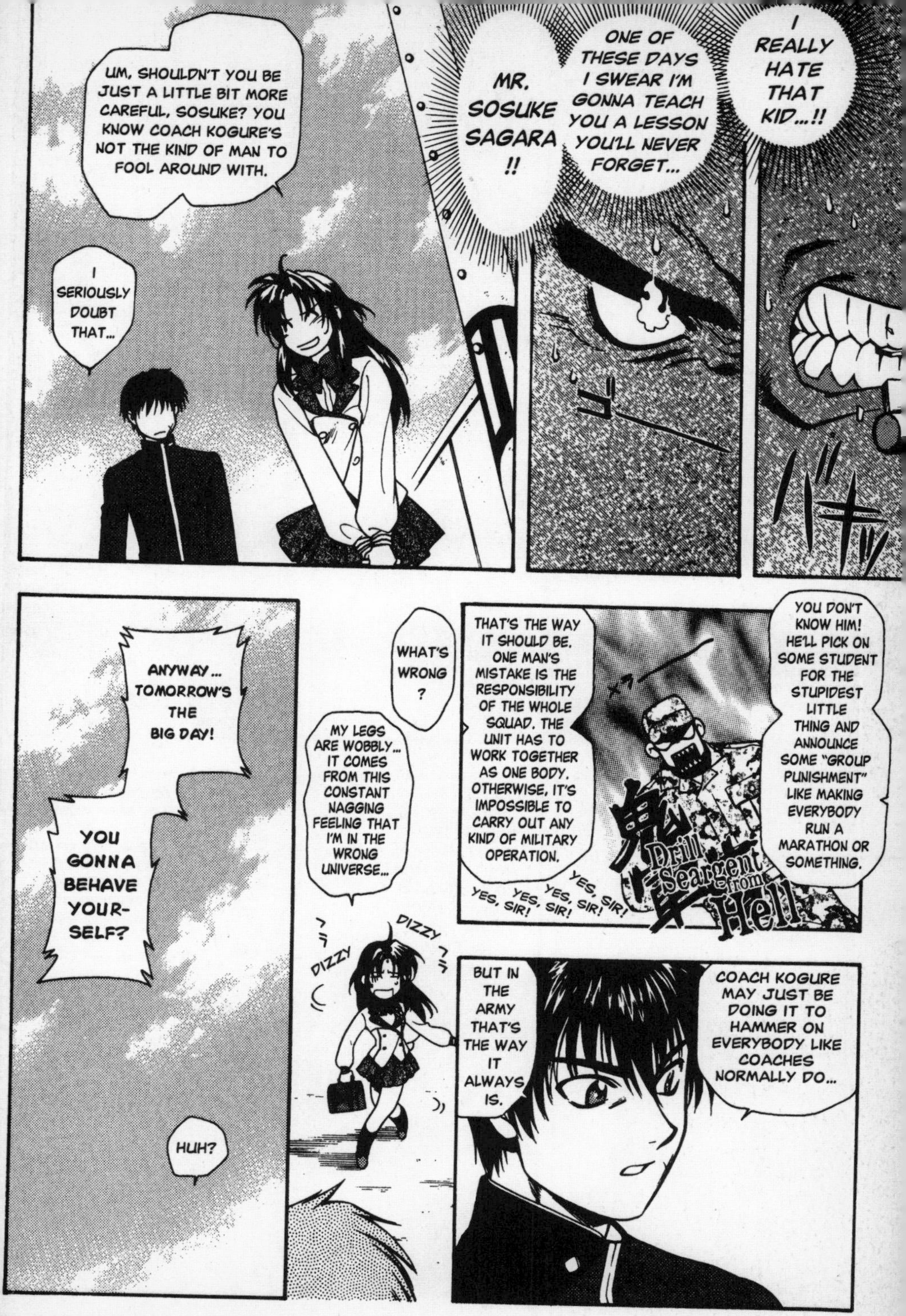
I REALLY HATE THAT KID...!!
ONE OF THESE DAYS I SWEAR I'M GONNA TEACH YOU A LESSON YOU'LL NEVER FORGET...
MR. SOSUKE SAGARA !!
UM, SHOULDN'T YOU BE JUST A LITTLE BIT MORE CAREFUL, SOSUKE? YOU KNOW COACH KOGURE'S NOT THE KIND OF MAN TO FOOL AROUND WITH.
I SERIOUSLY DOUBT THAT...
YOU DON'T KNOW HIM! HE'LL PICK ON SOME STUDENT FOR THE STUPIDEST LITTLE THING AND ANNOUNCE SOME "GROUP PUNISHMENT" LIKE MAKING EVERYBODY RUN A MARATHON OR SOMETHING.
Drill Seargent from Hell
YES, SIR! YES, SIR! YES, SIR!
THAT'S THE WAY IT SHOULD BE. ONE MAN'S MISTAKE IS THE RESPONSIBILITY OF THE WHOLE SQUAD. THE UNIT HAS TO WORK TOGETHER AS ONE BODY. OTHERWISE, IT'S IMPOSSIBLE TO CARRY OUT ANY KIND OF MILITARY OPERATION.
WHAT'S WRONG ?
MY LEGS ARE WOBBLY... IT COMES FROM THIS CONSTANT NAGGING FEELING THAT I'M IN THE WRONG UNIVERSE...
DIZZY
DIZZY
COACH KOGURE MAY JUST BE DOING IT TO HAMMER ON EVERYBODY LIKE COACHES NORMALLY DO...
BUT IN THE ARMY THAT'S THE WAY IT ALWAYS IS.
ANYWAY... TOMORROW'S THE BIG DAY!
YOU GONNA BEHAVE YOUR-SELF?
HUH?

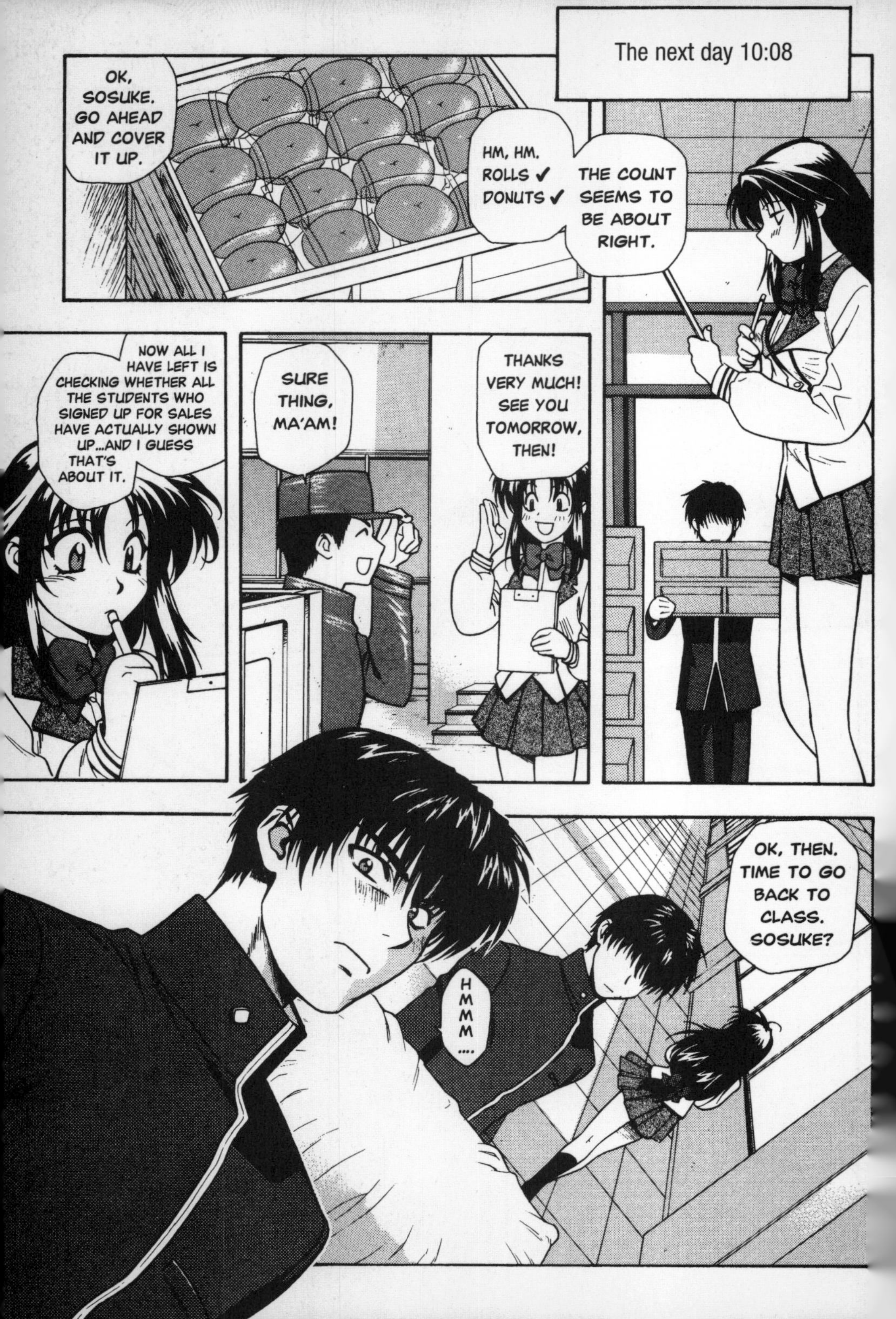
The next day 10:08
HM, HM. ROLLS ✓ DONUTS ✓
THE COUNT SEEMS TO BE ABOUT RIGHT.
OK, SOSUKE. GO AHEAD AND COVER IT UP.
THANKS VERY MUCH! SEE YOU TOMORROW, THEN!
SURE THING, MA'AM!
NOW ALL I HAVE LEFT IS CHECKING WHETHER ALL THE STUDENTS WHO SIGNED UP FOR SALES HAVE ACTUALLY SHOWN UP...AND I GUESS THAT'S ABOUT IT.
OK, THEN. TIME TO GO BACK TO CLASS. SOSUKE?
HMMM....

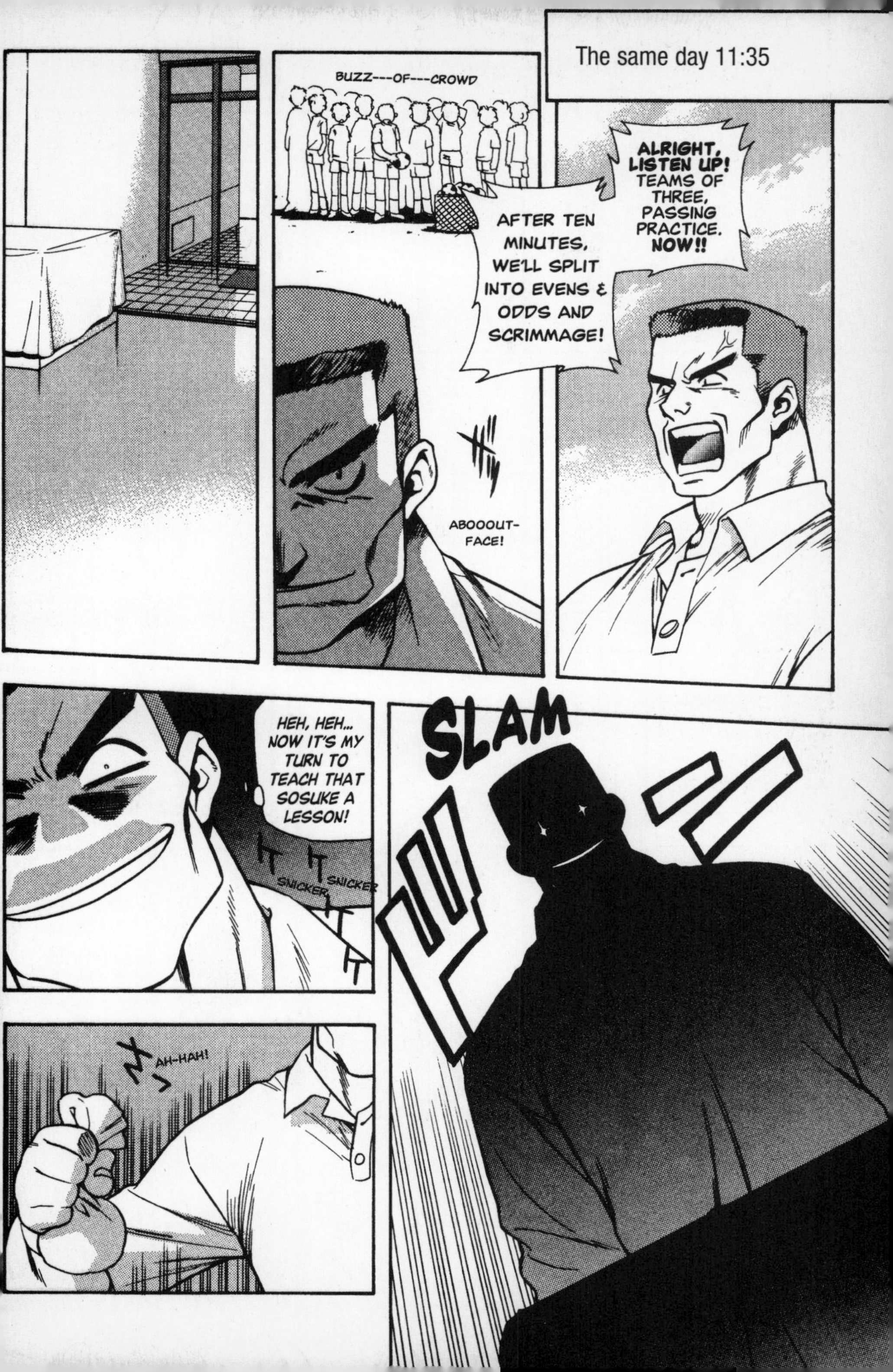
The same day 11:35
ALRIGHT, LISTEN UP! TEAMS OF THREE, PASSING PRACTICE. NOW!!
AFTER TEN MINUTES, WE'LL SPLIT INTO EVENS & ODDS AND SCRIMMAGE!
BUZZ---OF---CROWD
ABOOOUT-FACE!
SLAM
HEH, HEH... NOW IT'S MY TURN TO TEACH THAT SOSUKE A LESSON!
SNICKER
SNICKER
AH-HAH!

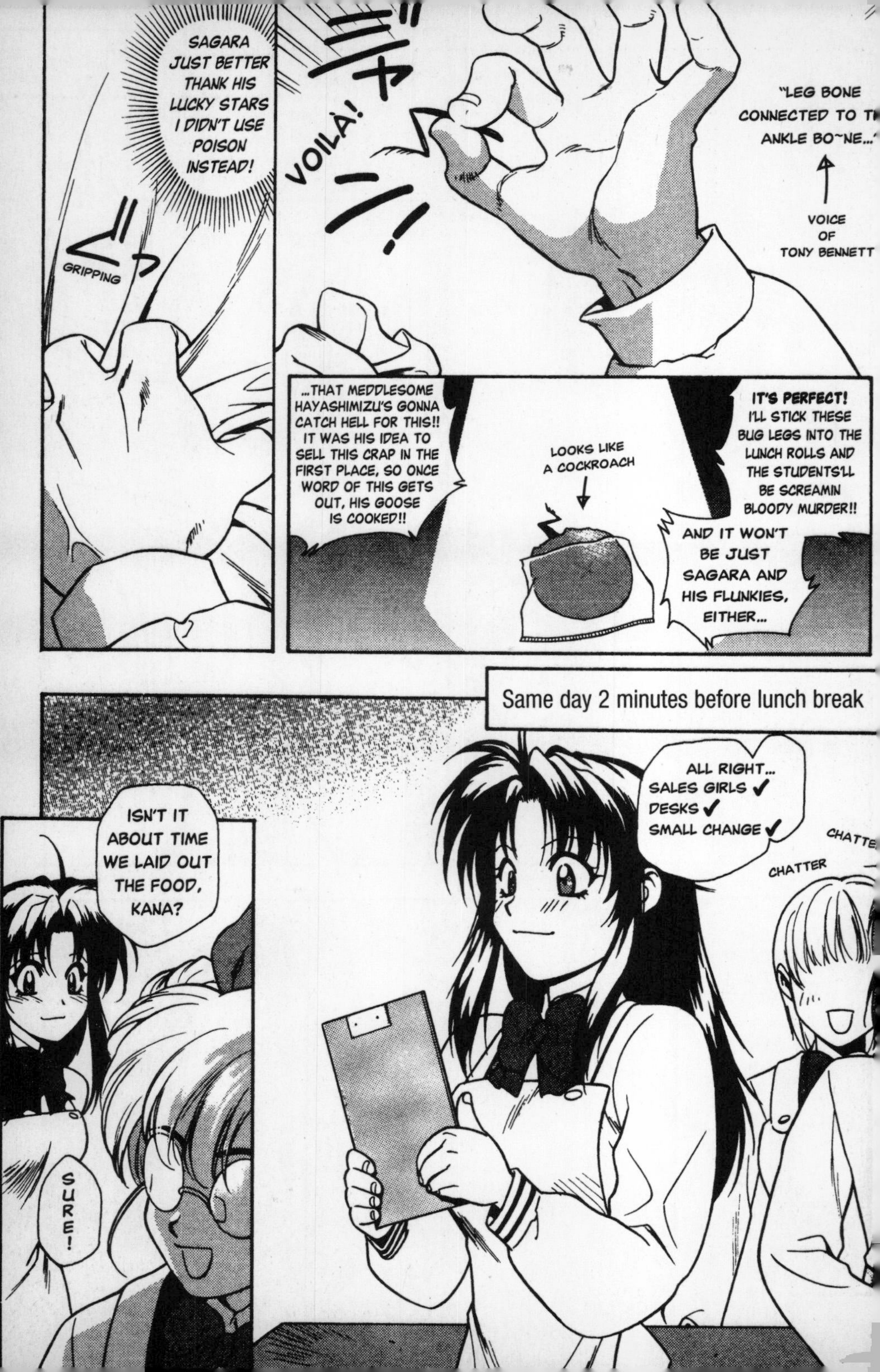

VOILÀ!
“LEG BONE CONNECTED TO T ANKLE BO~NE...”
VOICE OF TONY BENNETT
IT'S PERFECT! I'LL STICK THESE BUG LEGS INTO THE LUNCH ROLLS AND THE STUDENTS'LL BE SCREAMIN BLOODY MURDER!!
AND IT WON'T BE JUST SAGARA AND HIS FLUNKIES, EITHER...
LOOKS LIKE A COCKROACH
...THAT MEDDLESOME HAYASHIMIZU'S GONNA CATCH HELL FOR THIS!! IT WAS HIS IDEA TO SELL THIS CRAP IN THE FIRST PLACE, SO ONCE WORD OF THIS GETS OUT, HIS GOOSE IS COOKED!!
SAGARA JUST BETTER THANK HIS LUCKY STARS I DIDN'T USE POISON INSTEAD!
GRIPPING
Same day 2 minutes before lunch break
ALL RIGHT... SALES GIRLS ✓ DESKS ✓ SMALL CHANGE ✓
CHATTE
CHATTER
ISN'T IT ABOUT TIME WE LAID OUT THE FOOD, KANA?
SURE!

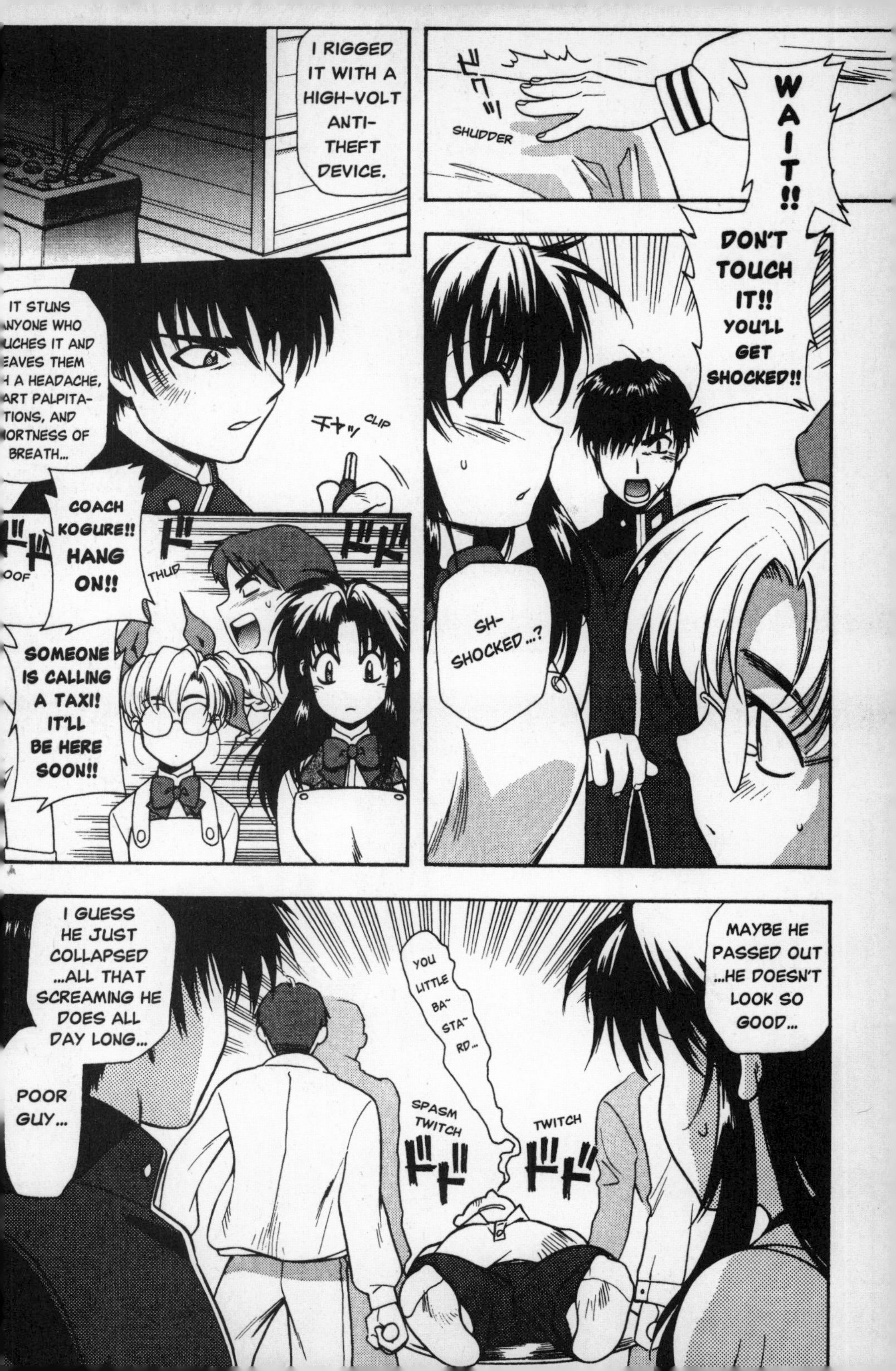

WAIT!!
DON'T TOUCH IT!! YOU'LL GET SHOCKED!!
SHUDDER
I RIGGED IT WITH A HIGH-VOLT ANTI-THEFT DEVICE.
SH-SHOCKED...?
IT STUNS ANYONE WHO UCHES IT AND EAVES THEM H A HEADACHE, ART PALPITATIONS, AND ORTNESS OF BREATH...
CLIP
COACH KOGURE!! HANG ON!!
THUD
OOF
SOMEONE IS CALLING A TAXI! IT'LL BE HERE SOON!!
MAYBE HE PASSED OUT ...HE DOESN'T LOOK SO GOOD...
YOU LITTLE BA~STA~RD...
TWITCH
SPASM TWITCH
I GUESS HE JUST COLLAPSED ...ALL THAT SCREAMING HE DOES ALL DAY LONG...
POOR GUY...

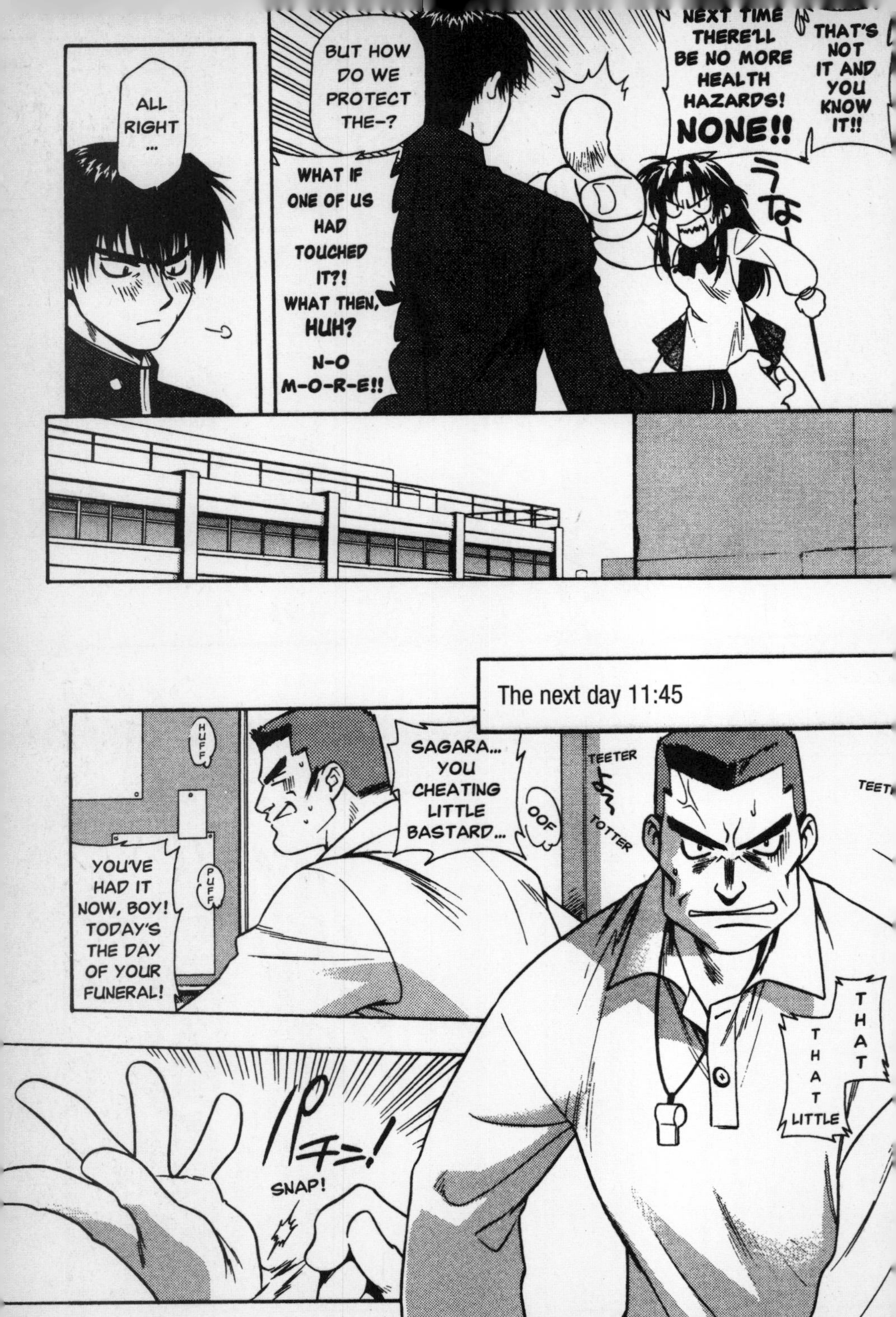
THAT'S NOT IT AND YOU KNOW IT!!
NEXT TIME THERE'LL BE NO MORE HEALTH HAZARDS! NONE!!
うな
BUT HOW DO WE PROTECT THE-?
WHAT IF ONE OF US HAD TOUCHED IT?! WHAT THEN, HUH? N-O M-O-R-E!!
ALL RIGHT ...
The next day 11:45
TEETER
TEETER TOTTER
SAGARA... YOU CHEATING LITTLE BASTARD...
OOF
HUFF
PUFF
YOU'VE HAD IT NOW, BOY! TODAY'S THE DAY OF YOUR FUNERAL!
THAT
THAT LITTLE
パチン!
SNAP!

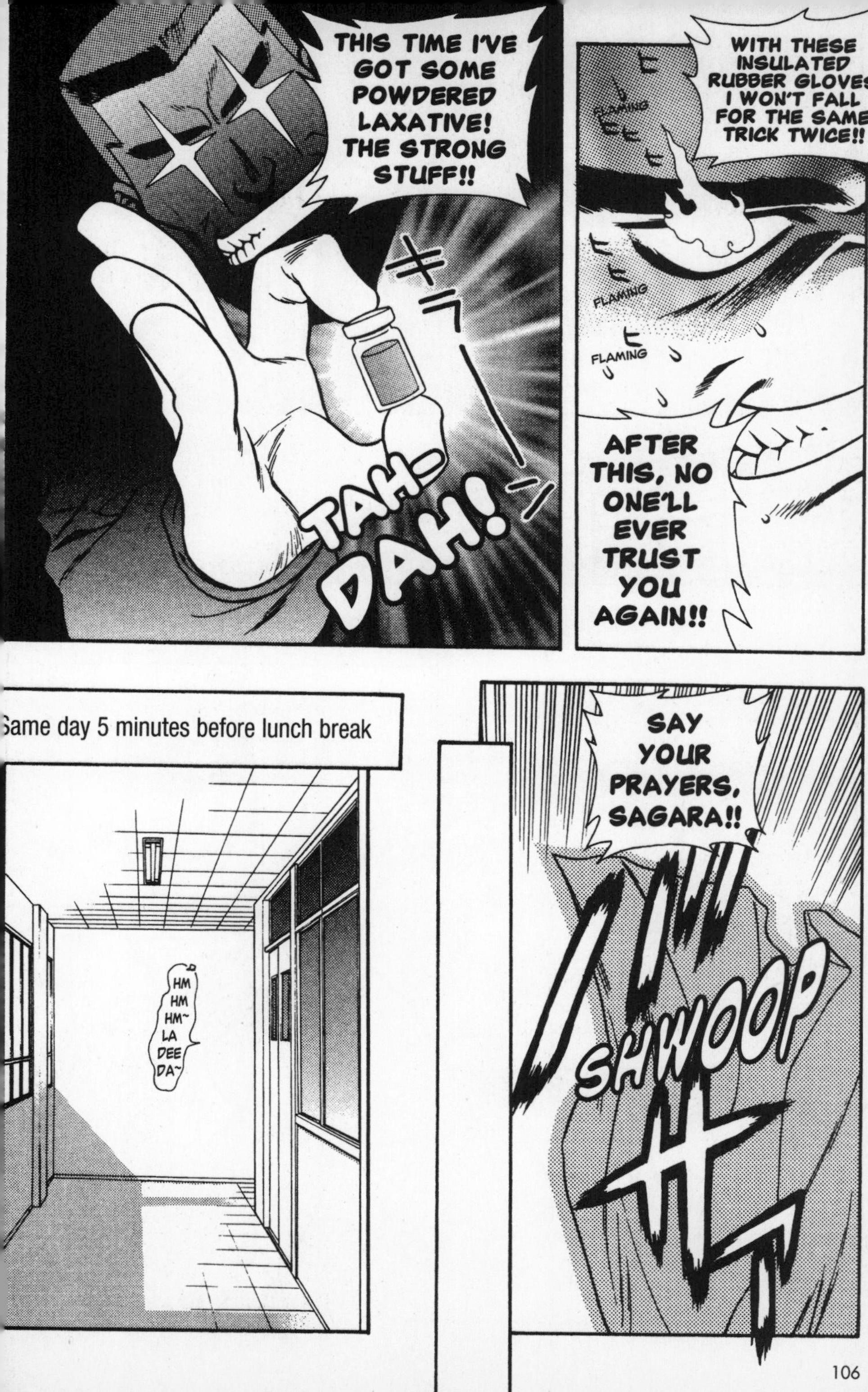
WITH THESE INSULATED RUBBER GLOVES I WON'T FALL FOR THE SAME TRICK TWICE!!
FLAMING
FLAMING
FLAMING
AFTER THIS, NO ONE'LL EVER TRUST YOU AGAIN!!
THIS TIME I'VE GOT SOME POWDERED LAXATIVE! THE STRONG STUFF!!
TAH-DAH!
SAY YOUR PRAYERS, SAGARA!!
SHWOOP
Same day 5 minutes before lunch break
HM HM HM~ LA DEE DA~

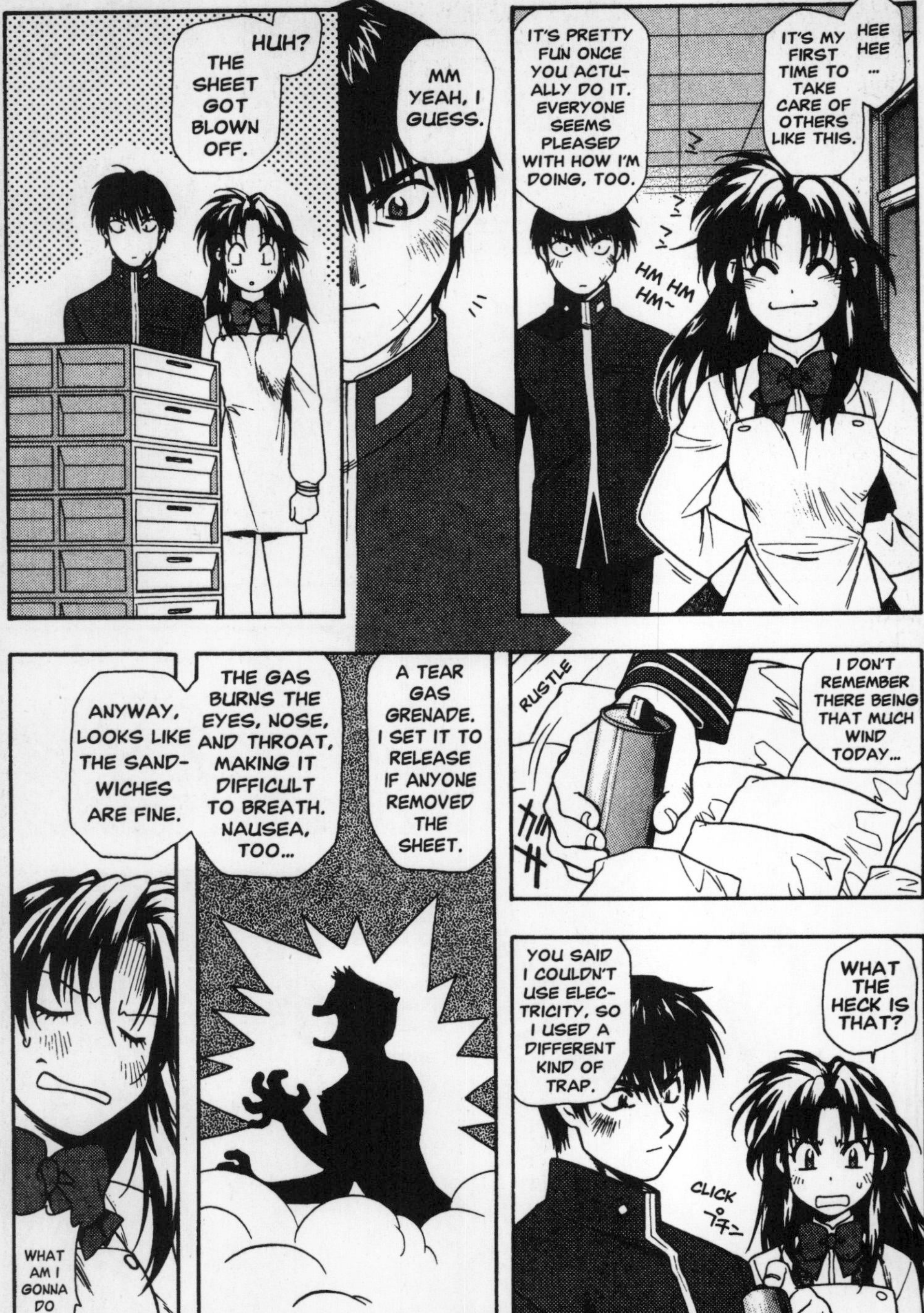
HEE HEE ...
IT'S MY FIRST TIME TO TAKE CARE OF OTHERS LIKE THIS.
HM HM HM~
IT'S PRETTY FUN ONCE YOU ACTUALLY DO IT. EVERYONE SEEMS PLEASED WITH HOW I'M DOING, TOO.
MM YEAH, I GUESS.
HUH? THE SHEET GOT BLOWN OFF.
I DON'T REMEMBER THERE BEING THAT MUCH WIND TODAY...
RUSTLE
WHAT THE HECK IS THAT?
YOU SAID I COULDN'T USE ELECTRICITY, SO I USED A DIFFERENT KIND OF TRAP.
CLICK
A TEAR GAS GRENADE. I SET IT TO RELEASE IF ANYONE REMOVED THE SHEET.
THE GAS BURNS THE EYES, NOSE, AND THROAT, MAKING IT DIFFICULT TO BREATH. NAUSEA, TOO...
ANYWAY, LOOKS LIKE THE SANDWICHES ARE FINE.
WHAT AM I GONNA DO WITH YOU...?

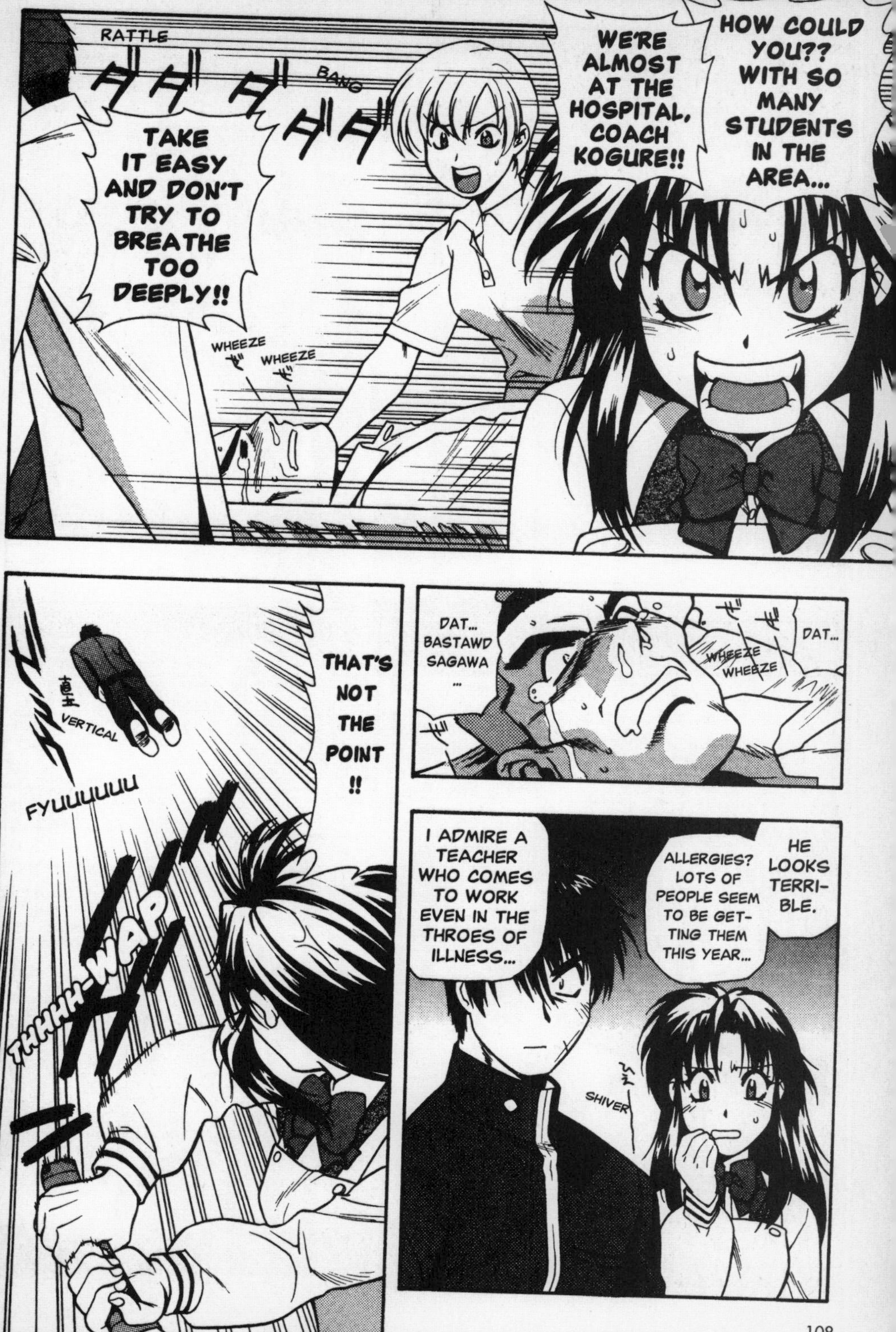
HOW COULD YOU?? WITH SO MANY STUDENTS IN THE AREA...
WE'RE ALMOST AT THE HOSPITAL, COACH KOGURE!!
BANG
RATTLE
TAKE IT EASY AND DON'T TRY TO BREATHE TOO DEEPLY!!
WHEEZE
WHEEZE
DAT...
WHEEZE WHEEZE
DAT... BASTAWD SAGAWA ...
HE LOOKS TERRIBLE.
ALLERGIES? LOTS OF PEOPLE SEEM TO BE GET-TING THEM THIS YEAR...
I ADMIRE A TEACHER WHO COMES TO WORK EVEN IN THE THROES OF ILLNESS...
SHIVER
THAT'S NOT THE POINT !!
VERTICAL
FYUUUUUU
THHHH-WAP

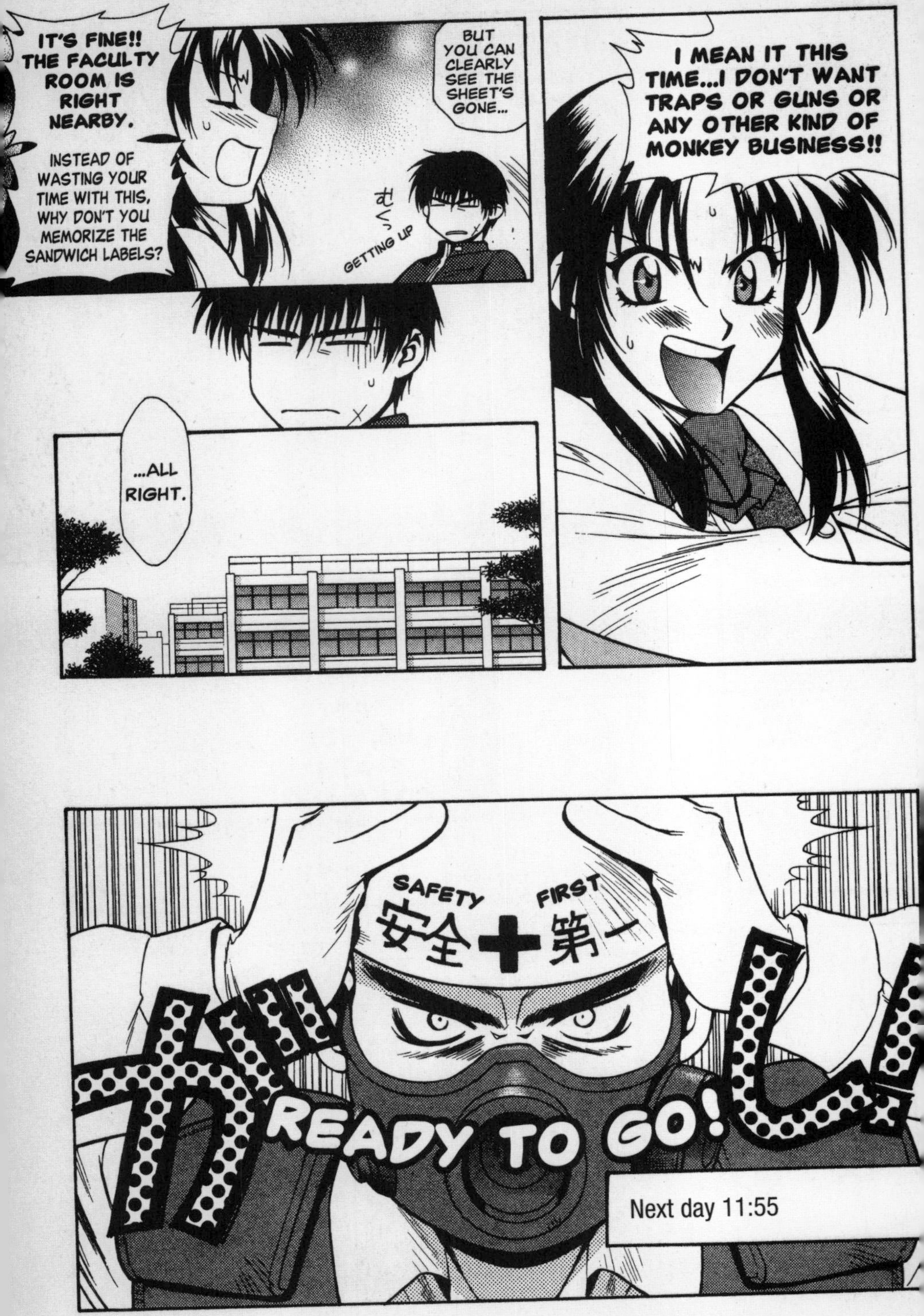
I MEAN IT THIS TIME...I DON'T WANT TRAPS OR GUNS OR ANY OTHER KIND OF MONKEY BUSINESS!!
BUT YOU CAN CLEARLY SEE THE SHEET'S GONE...
IT'S FINE!! THE FACULTY ROOM IS RIGHT NEARBY.
INSTEAD OF WASTING YOUR TIME WITH THIS, WHY DON'T YOU MEMORIZE THE SANDWICH LABELS?
むくっ
GETTING UP
...ALL RIGHT.
SAFETY FIRST
安全第一
READY TO GO!
Next day 11:55

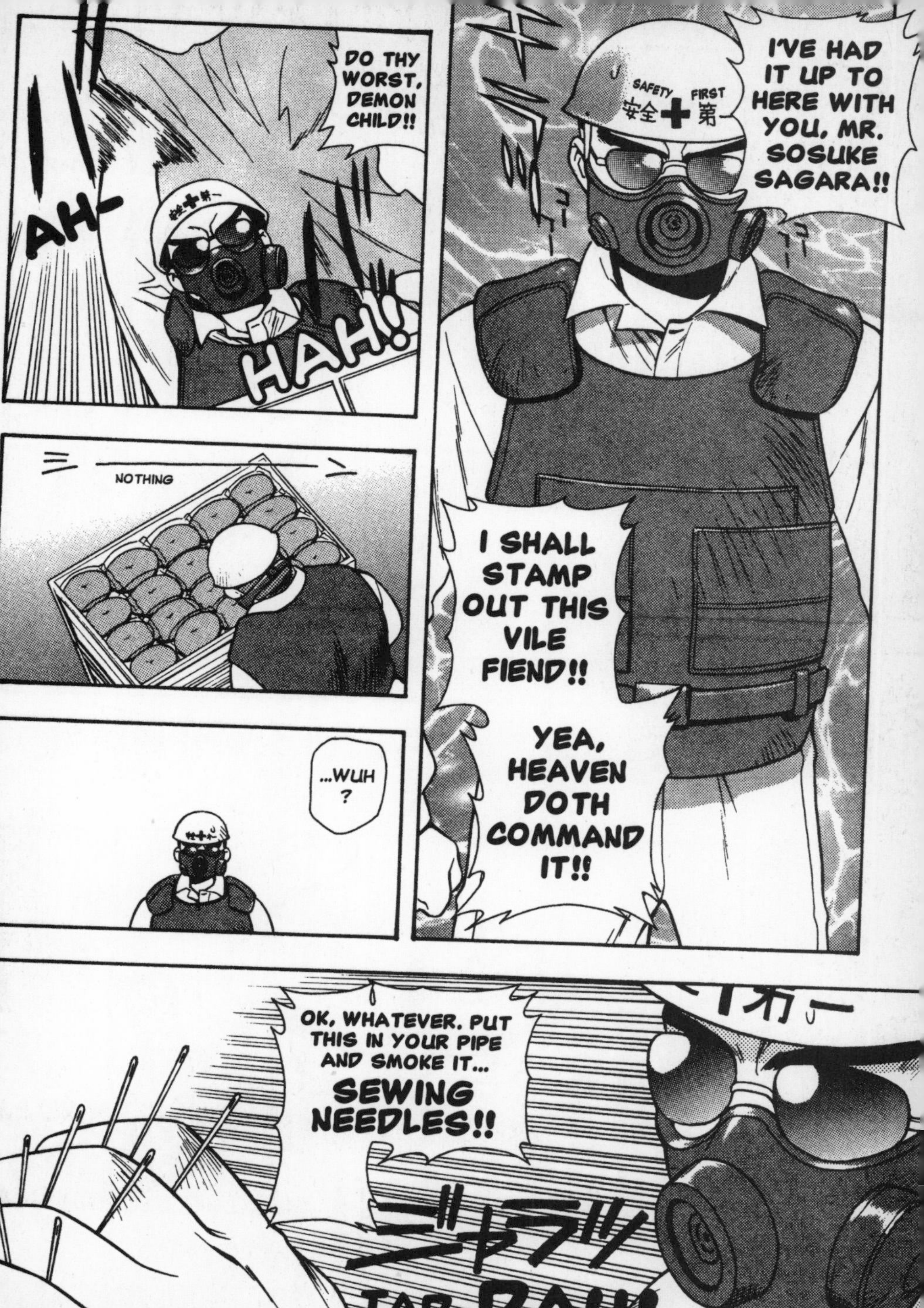
SAFETY FIRST
安全 第
I'VE HAD IT UP TO HERE WITH YOU, MR. SOSUKE SAGARA!!
I SHALL STAMP OUT THIS VILE FIEND!!
YEA, HEAVEN DOTH COMMAND IT!!
DO THY WORST, DEMON CHILD!!
AH-
HAH!!
NOTHING
...WUH ?
OK, WHATEVER. PUT THIS IN YOUR PIPE AND SMOKE IT... SEWING NEEDLES!!
TAD-DAH!

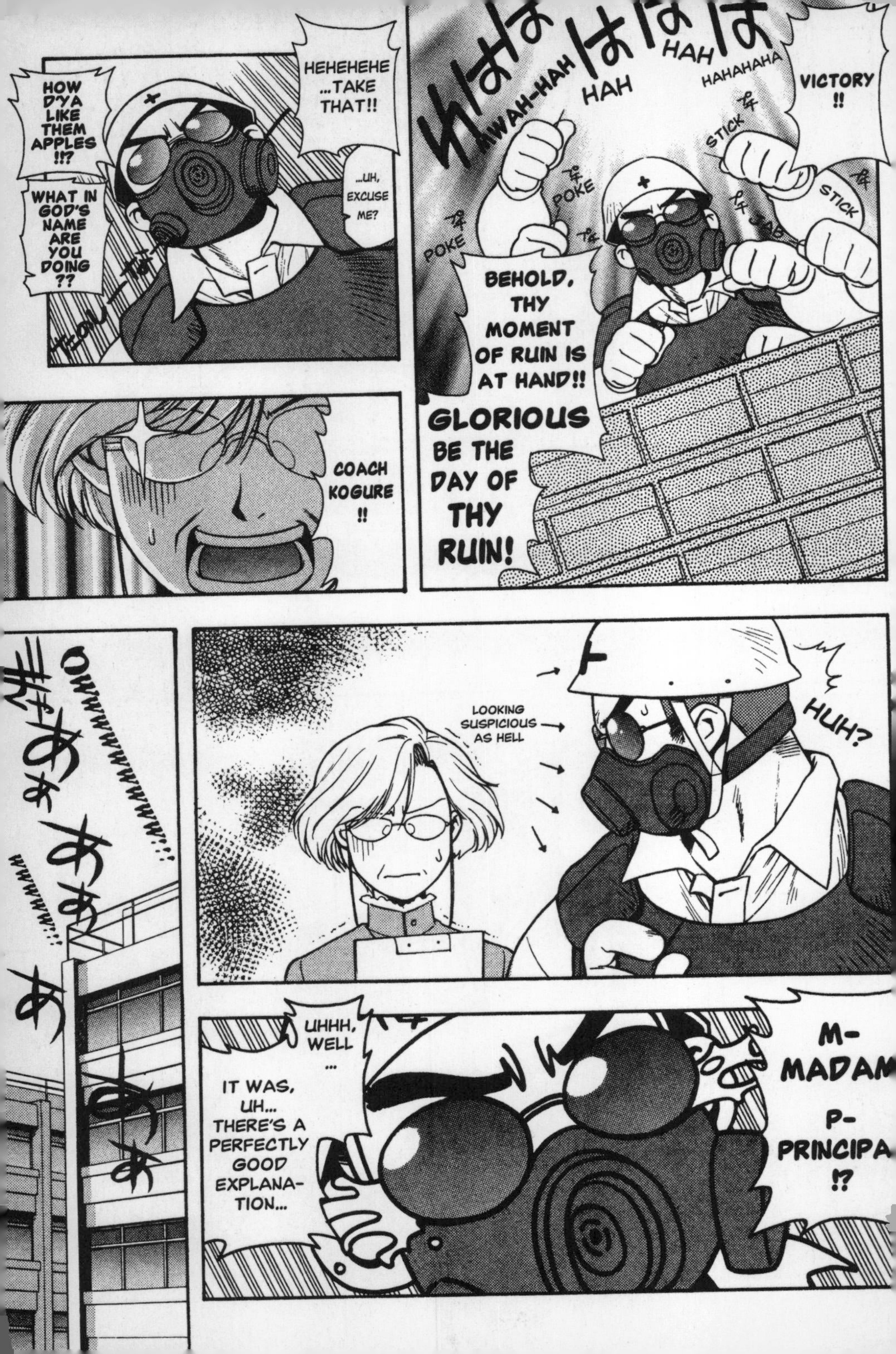
VICTORY!!
HAHAHAHA
HAH
HAH
AWAH-HAH
STICK
STICK
JAB
POKE
POKE
BEHOLD, THY MOMENT OF RUIN IS AT HAND!!
GLORIOUS BE THE DAY OF THY RUIN!
HEHEHEHE ...TAKE THAT!!
...UH, EXCUSE ME?
HOW D'YA LIKE THEM APPLES!!?
WHAT IN GOD'S NAME ARE YOU DOING??
COACH KOGURE!!
HUH?
LOOKING SUSPICIOUS AS HELL
M-MADAM P-PRINCIPA!?
UHHH, WELL...
IT WAS, UH... THERE'S A PERFECTLY GOOD EXPLANATION...
OHMMMMMMMMMMMMMM!!
MMMMMM!!

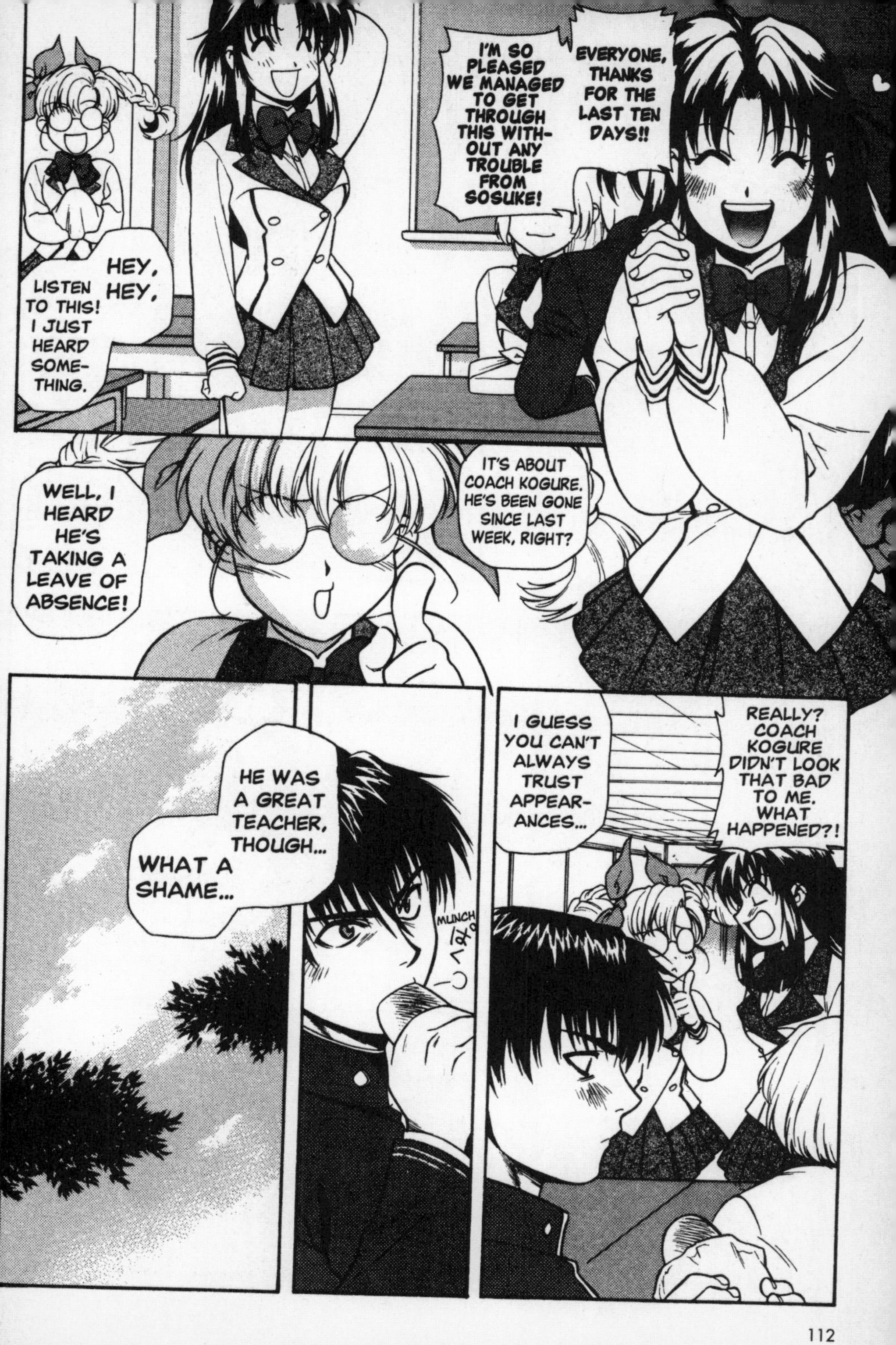
EVERYONE, THANKS FOR THE LAST TEN DAYS!!
I'M SO PLEASED WE MANAGED TO GET THROUGH THIS WITH-OUT ANY TROUBLE FROM SOSUKE!
HEY, HEY, LISTEN TO THIS! I JUST HEARD SOME-THING.
IT'S ABOUT COACH KOGURE. HE'S BEEN GONE SINCE LAST WEEK, RIGHT?
WELL, I HEARD HE'S TAKING A LEAVE OF ABSENCE!
REALLY? COACH KOGURE DIDN'T LOOK THAT BAD TO ME. WHAT HAPPENED?!
I GUESS YOU CAN'T ALWAYS TRUST APPEAR-ANCES...
HE WAS A GREAT TEACHER, THOUGH...
WHAT A SHAME...
MUNCH

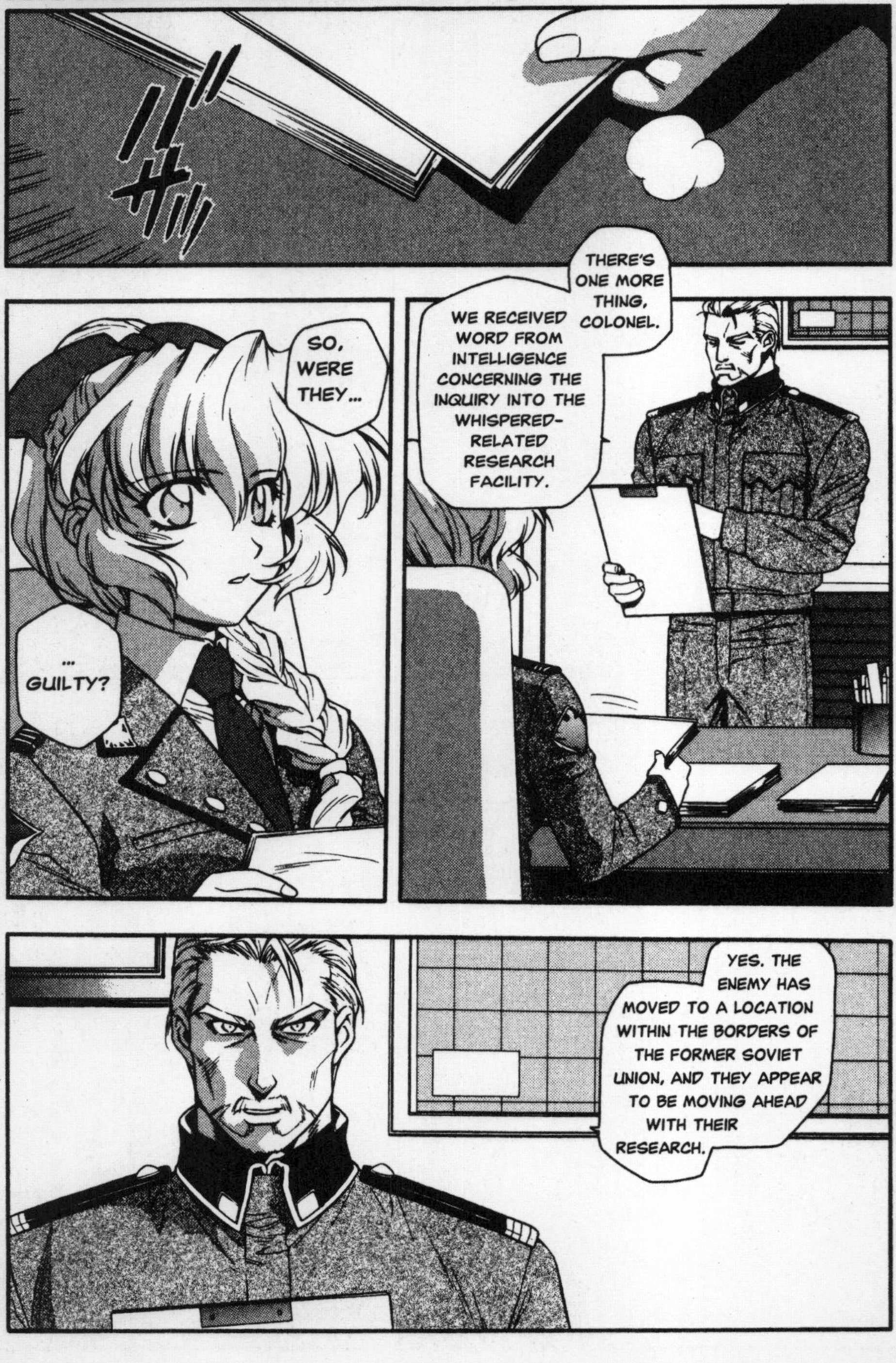
THERE'S ONE MORE THING, COLONEL.
WE RECEIVED WORD FROM INTELLIGENCE CONCERNING THE INQUIRY INTO THE WHISPERED-RELATED RESEARCH FACILITY.
SO, WERE THEY...
... GUILTY?
YES. THE ENEMY HAS MOVED TO A LOCATION WITHIN THE BORDERS OF THE FORMER SOVIET UNION, AND THEY APPEAR TO BE MOVING AHEAD WITH THEIR RESEARCH.

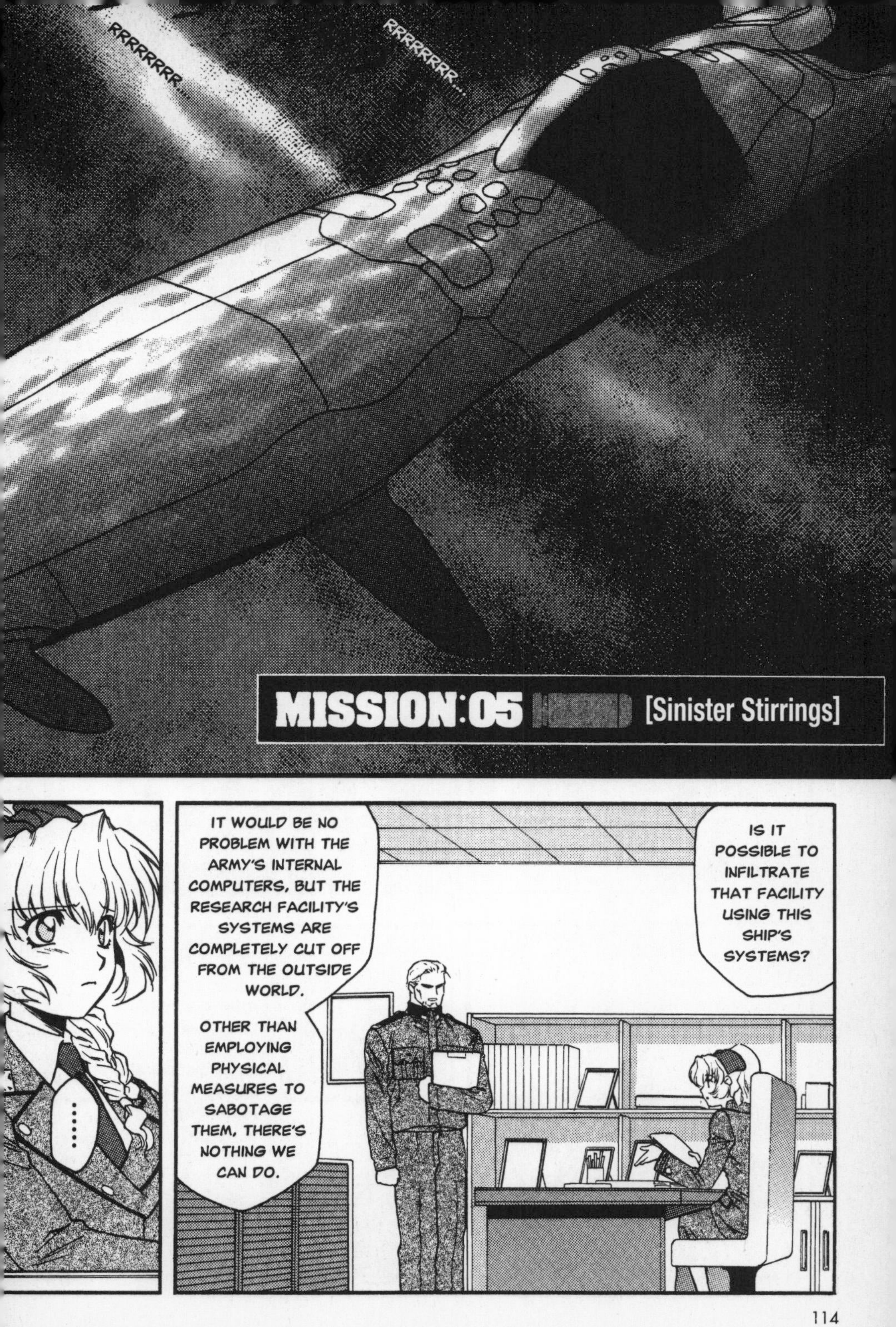
RRRRRRRR...
RRRRRRRRR...
MISSION:05 [Sinister Stirrings]
IS IT POSSIBLE TO INFILTRATE THAT FACILITY USING THIS SHIP'S SYSTEMS?
IT WOULD BE NO PROBLEM WITH THE ARMY'S INTERNAL COMPUTERS, BUT THE RESEARCH FACILITY'S SYSTEMS ARE COMPLETELY CUT OFF FROM THE OUTSIDE WORLD.
OTHER THAN EMPLOYING PHYSICAL MEASURES TO SABOTAGE THEM, THERE'S NOTHING WE CAN DO.
......

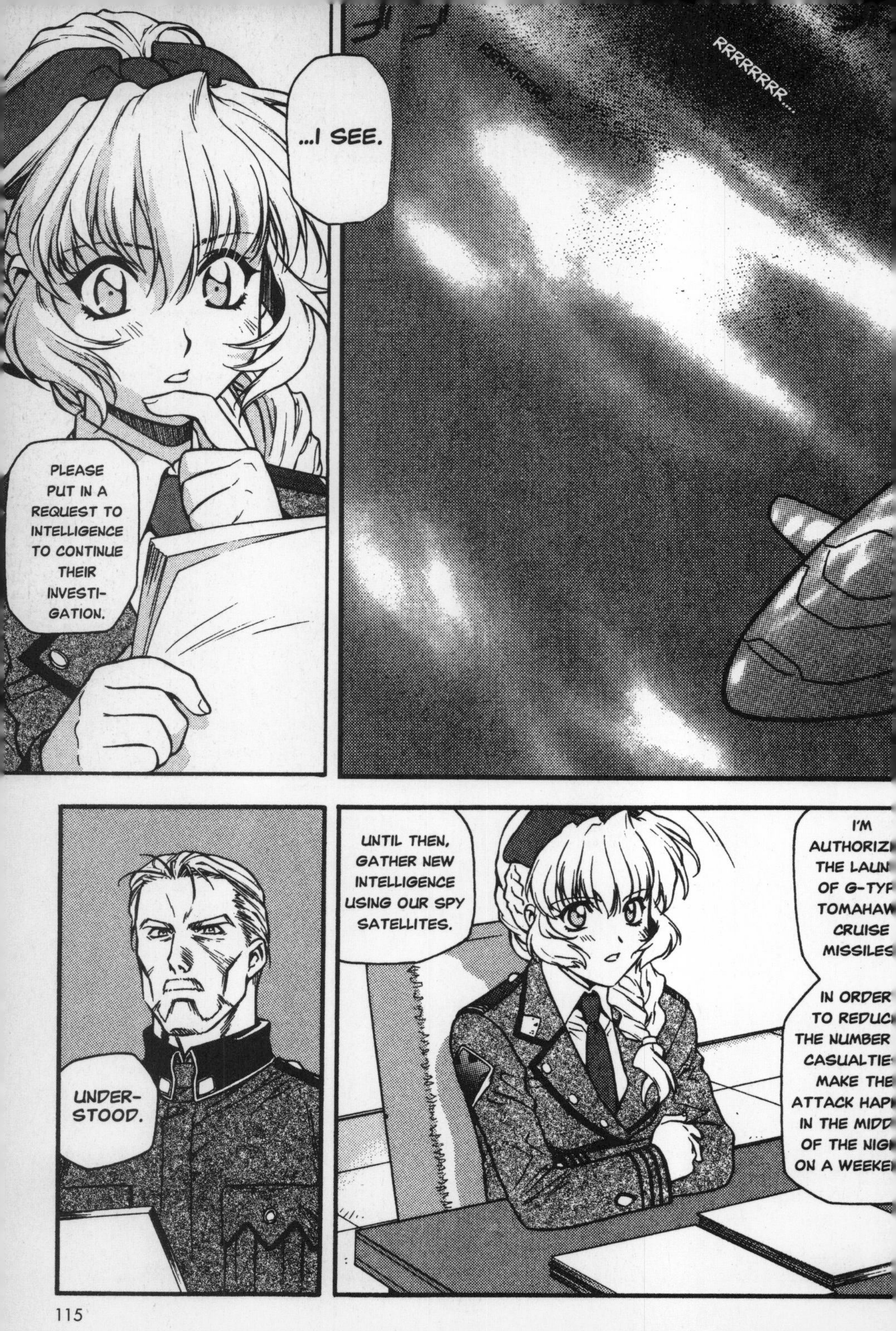
RRRRRRRR....
...I SEE.
PLEASE PUT IN A REQUEST TO INTELLIGENCE TO CONTINUE THEIR INVESTI-GATION.
I'M AUTHORIZ THE LAUN OF G-TYP TOMAHAW CRUISE MISSILES
IN ORDER TO REDUC THE NUMBER CASUALTIE MAKE THE ATTACK HAP IN THE MIDD OF THE NIG ON A WEEKE
UNTIL THEN, GATHER NEW INTELLIGENCE USING OUR SPY SATELLITES.
UNDER-STOOD.

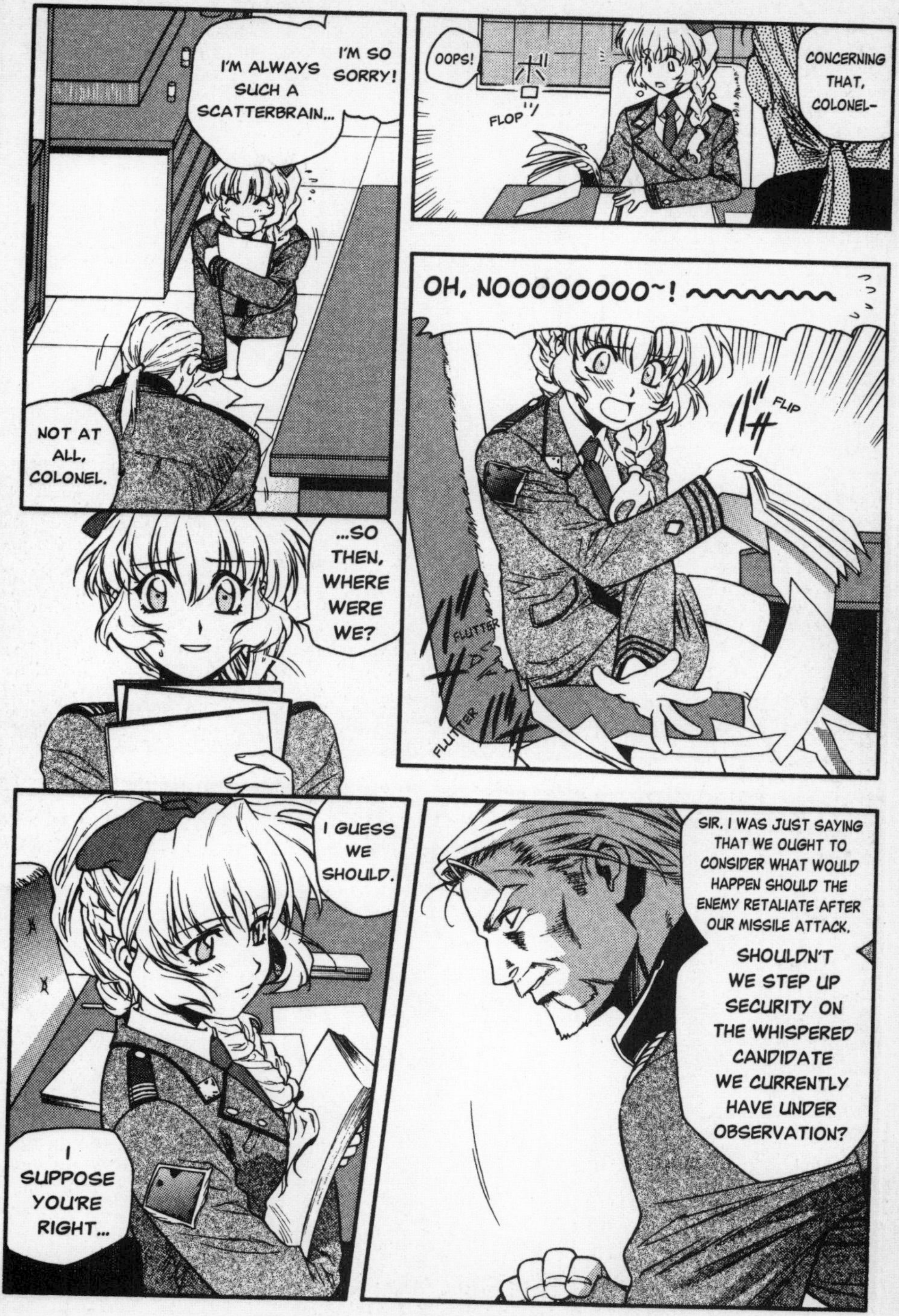
CONCERNING THAT, COLONEL-
OOPS!
ボ
FLOP
OH, NOOOOOOOO~!
FLIP
FLUTTER
FLUTTER
I'M SO SORRY!
I'M ALWAYS SUCH A SCATTERBRAIN...
NOT AT ALL, COLONEL.
...SO THEN, WHERE WERE WE?
SIR, I WAS JUST SAYING THAT WE OUGHT TO CONSIDER WHAT WOULD HAPPEN SHOULD THE ENEMY RETALIATE AFTER OUR MISSILE ATTACK.
SHOULDN'T WE STEP UP SECURITY ON THE WHISPERED CANDIDATE WE CURRENTLY HAVE UNDER OBSERVATION?
I GUESS WE SHOULD.
I SUPPOSE YOU'RE RIGHT...

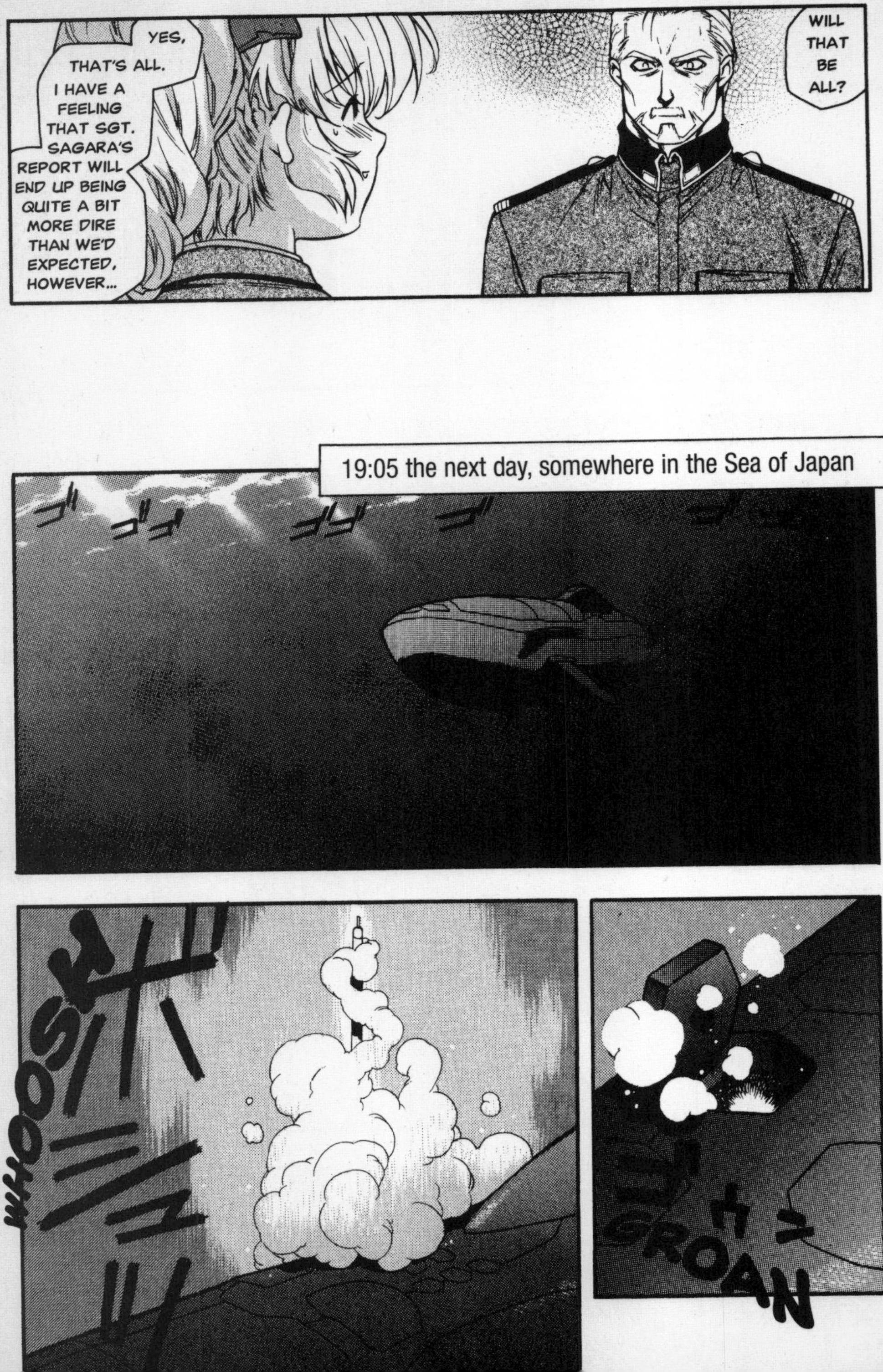
WILL THAT BE ALL?
YES, THAT'S ALL. I HAVE A FEELING THAT SGT. SAGARA'S REPORT WILL END UP BEING QUITE A BIT MORE DIRE THAN WE'D EXPECTED, HOWEVER...
19:05 the next day, somewhere in the Sea of Japan
GROAN
WHOOSH

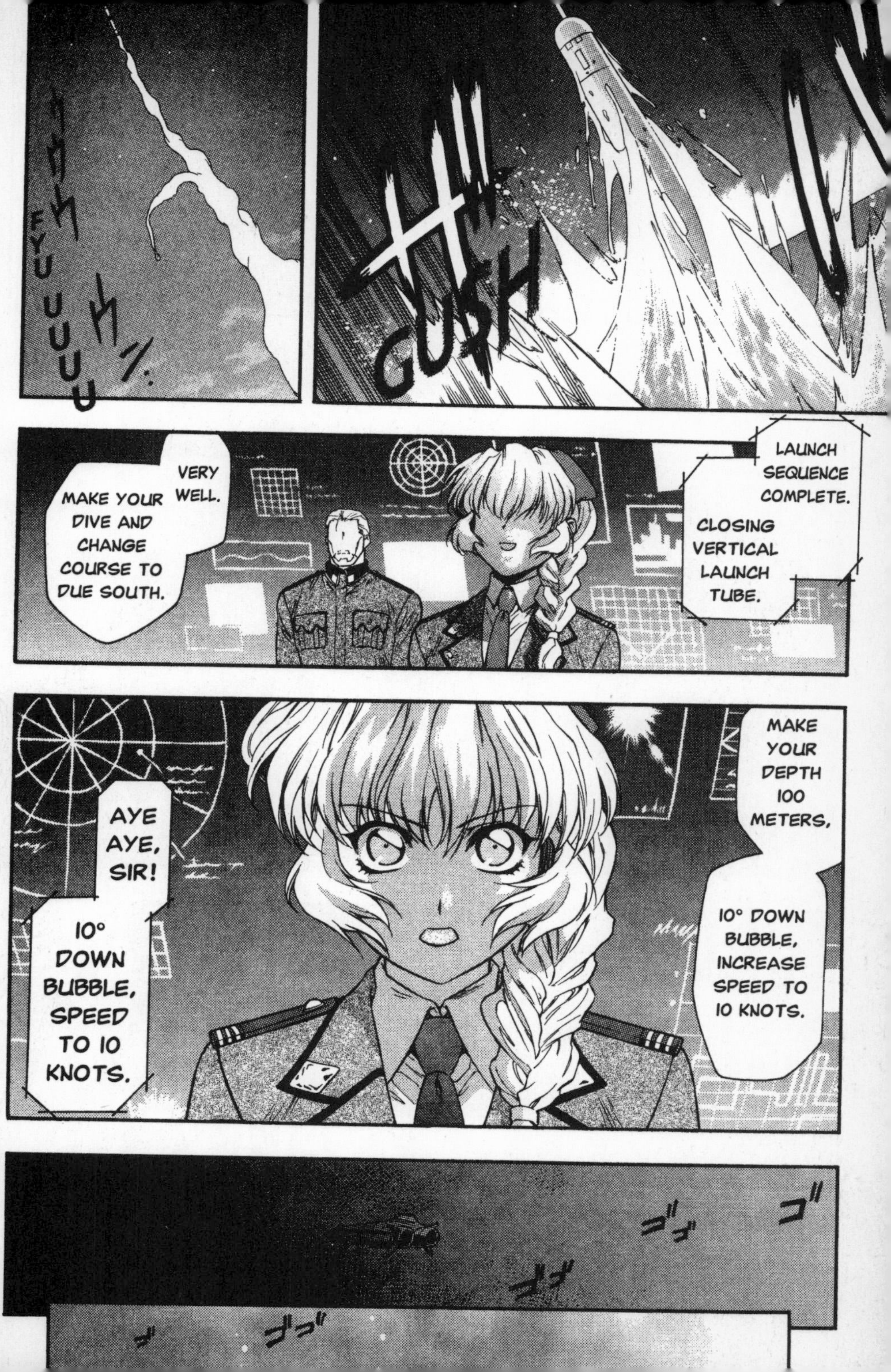
GUSH
FYUUUUUU
LAUNCH SEQUENCE COMPLETE.
CLOSING VERTICAL LAUNCH TUBE.
VERY WELL.
MAKE YOUR DIVE AND CHANGE COURSE TO DUE SOUTH.
MAKE YOUR DEPTH 100 METERS,
10° DOWN BUBBLE, INCREASE SPEED TO 10 KNOTS.
AYE AYE, SIR!
10° DOWN BUBBLE, SPEED TO 10 KNOTS.
ゴ
ゴゴ
ゴゴ
ゴゴ
ゴ

MISSION:06

[Kaname's Cross—Jindai High hanging by a thread!]

PART:01

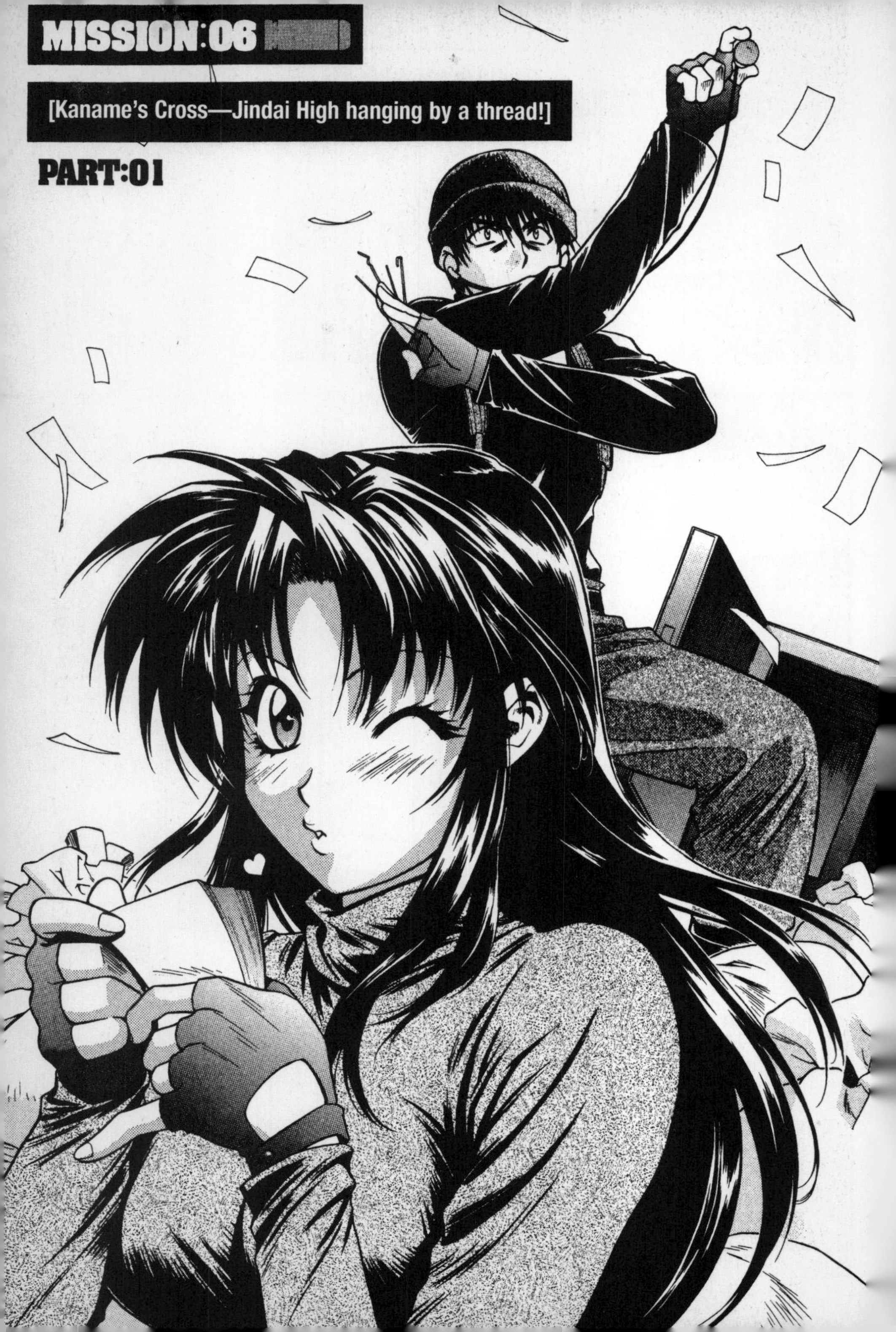

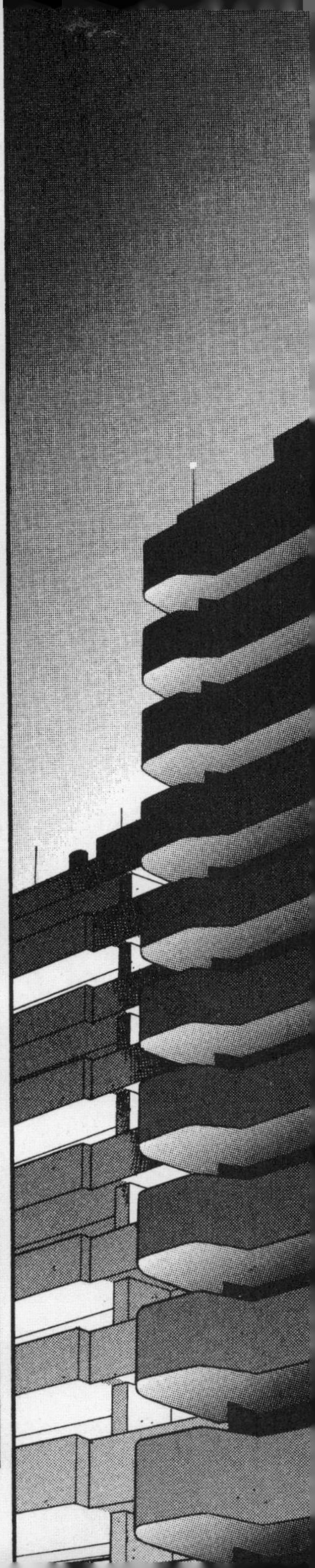

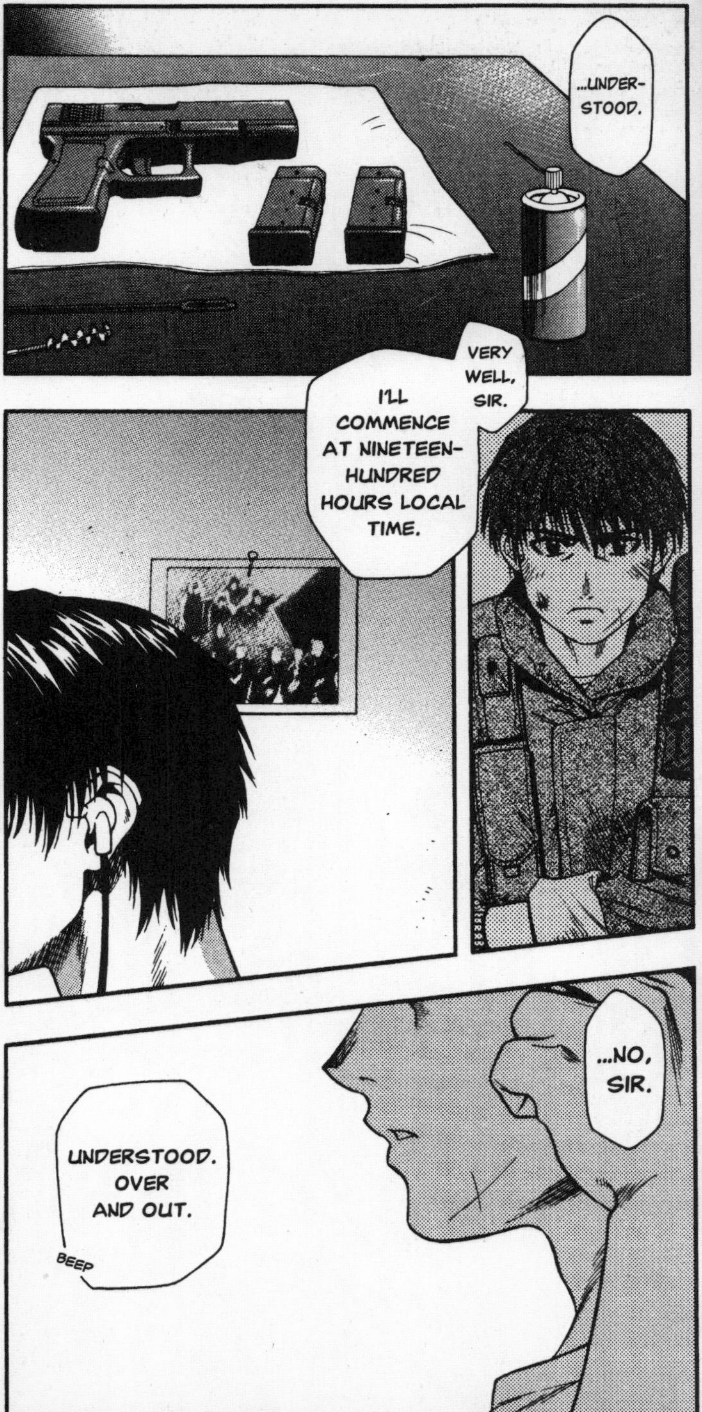
...UNDER-STOOD.
VERY WELL, SIR.
I'LL COMMENCE AT NINETEEN-HUNDRED HOURS LOCAL TIME.
...NO, SIR.
UNDERSTOOD. OVER AND OUT.
BEEP

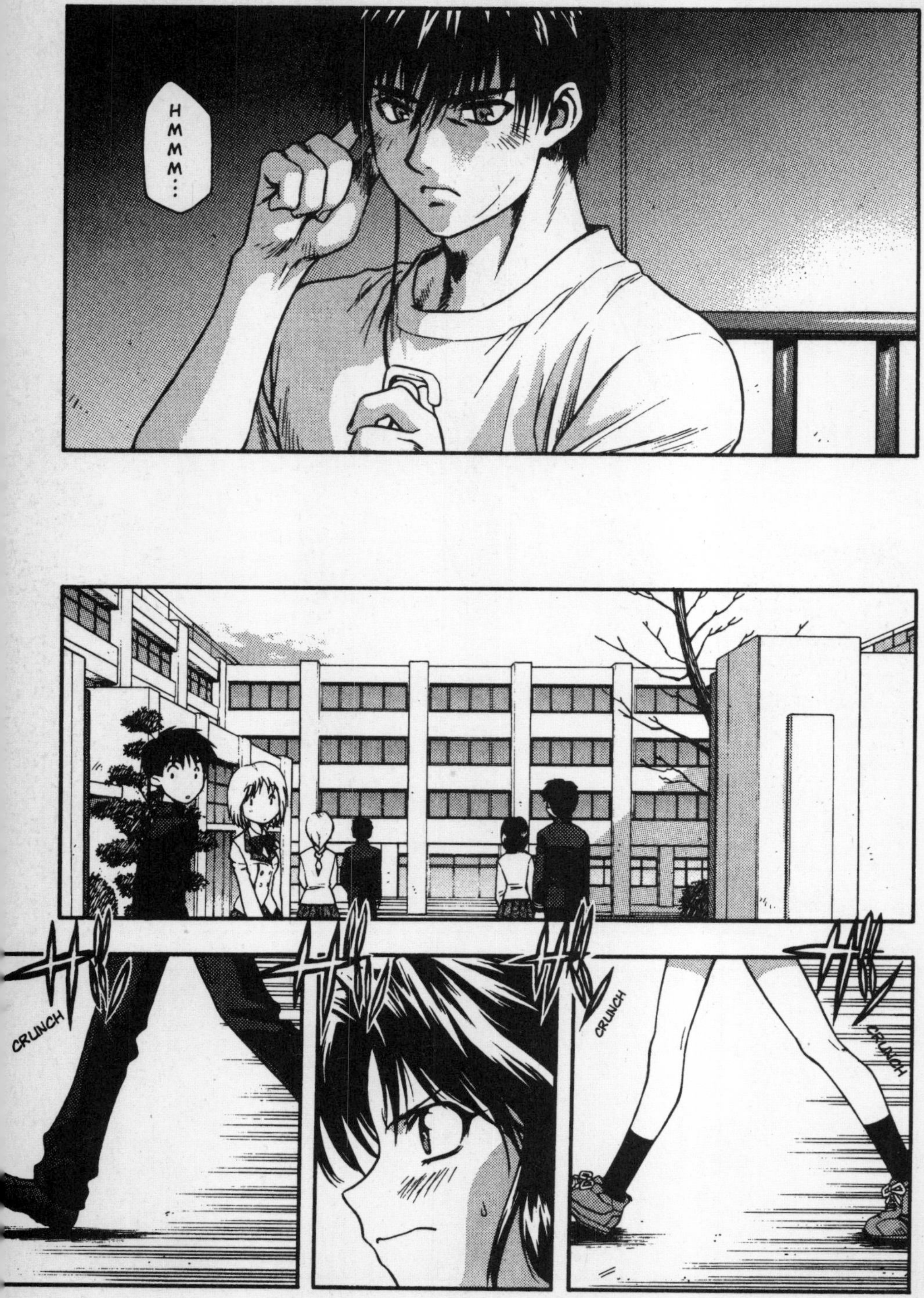
HMMM...
CRUNCH
CRUNCH
CRUNCH

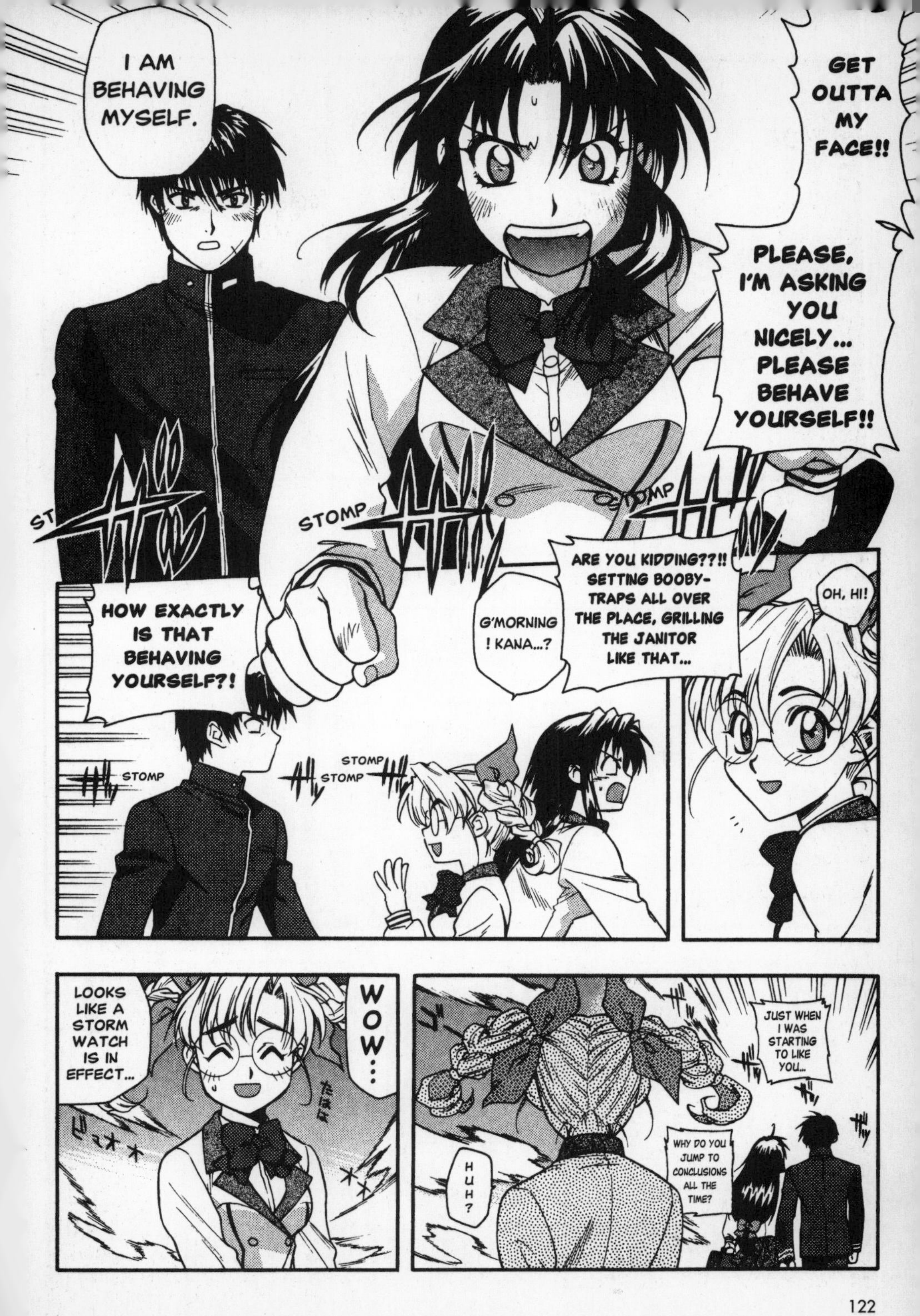

GET OUTTA MY FACE!!
I AM BEHAVING MYSELF.
PLEASE, I'M ASKING YOU NICELY... PLEASE BEHAVE YOURSELF!!
STOMP
STOMP
ST
OH, HI!
ARE YOU KIDDING??!! SETTING BOOBY-TRAPS ALL OVER THE PLACE, GRILLING THE JANITOR LIKE THAT...
G'MORNING ! KANA...?
HOW EXACTLY IS THAT BEHAVING YOURSELF?!
STOMP
STOMP
STOMP
JUST WHEN I WAS STARTING TO LIKE YOU...
HUH?
WHY DO YOU JUMP TO CONCLUSIONS ALL THE TIME?
WOW...
LOOKS LIKE A STORM WATCH IS IN EFFECT...

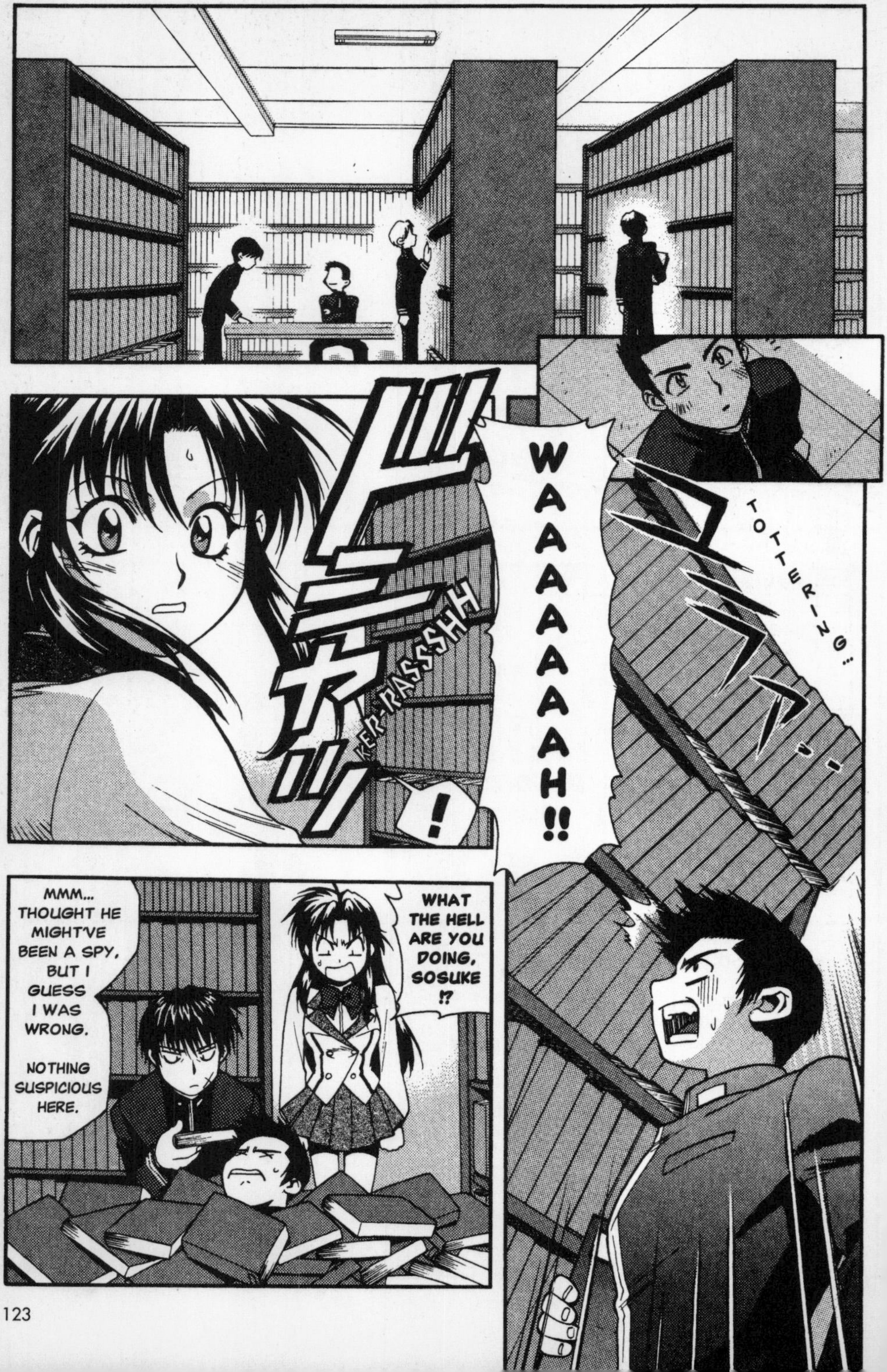
TOTTERING...
WAAAAAAAAAH!!
KER-RASSSHH
!
WHAT THE HELL ARE YOU DOING, SOSUKE!?
MMM... THOUGHT HE MIGHT'VE BEEN A SPY, BUT I GUESS I WAS WRONG.
NOTHING SUSPICIOUS HERE.

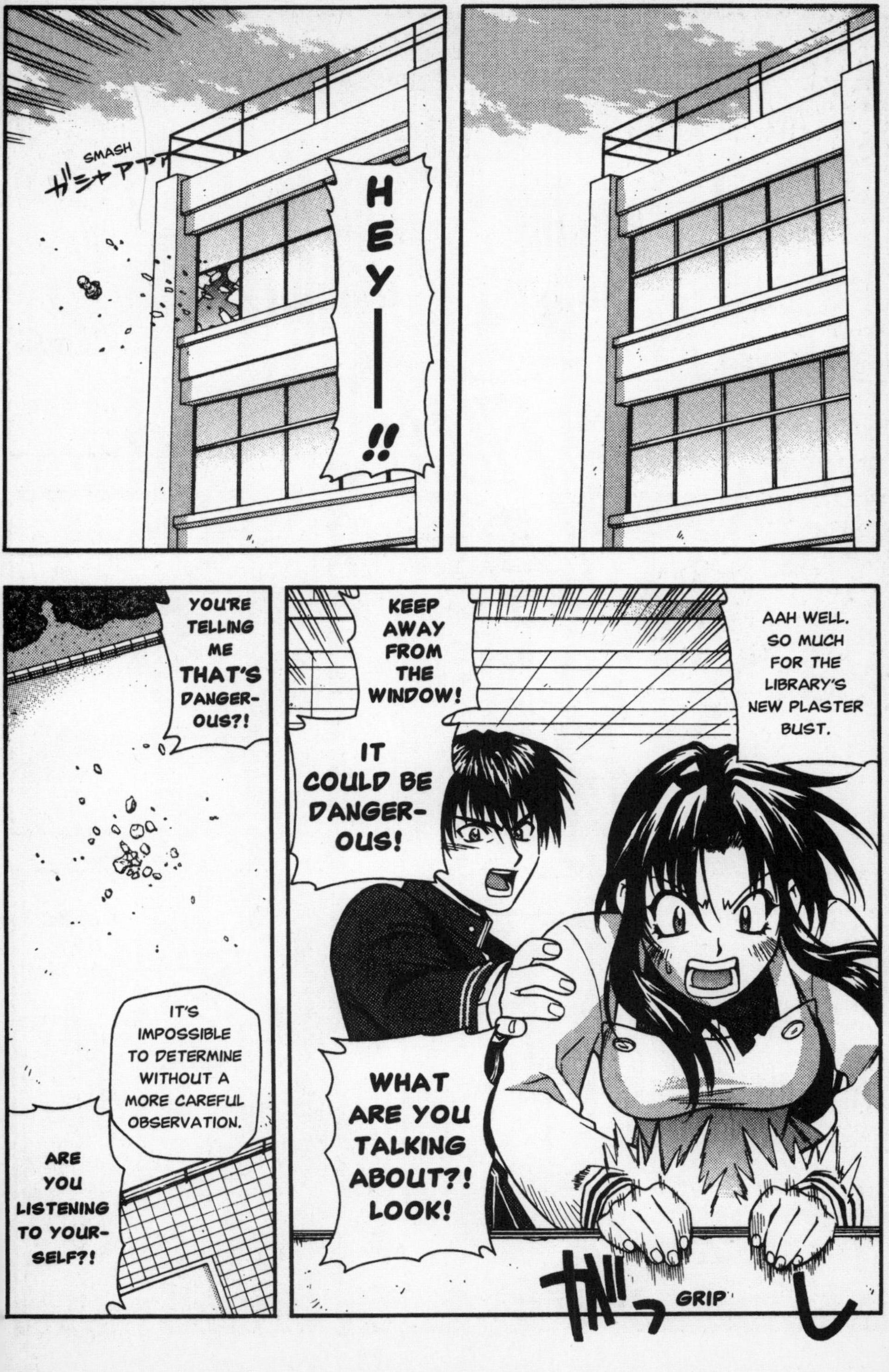
SMASH
ガシャアア
HEY—!!
AAH WELL. SO MUCH FOR THE LIBRARY'S NEW PLASTER BUST.
KEEP AWAY FROM THE WINDOW!
IT COULD BE DANGEROUS!
WHAT ARE YOU TALKING ABOUT?! LOOK!
GRIP
YOU'RE TELLING ME THAT'S DANGEROUS?!
IT'S IMPOSSIBLE TO DETERMINE WITHOUT A MORE CAREFUL OBSERVATION.
ARE YOU LISTENING TO YOURSELF?!

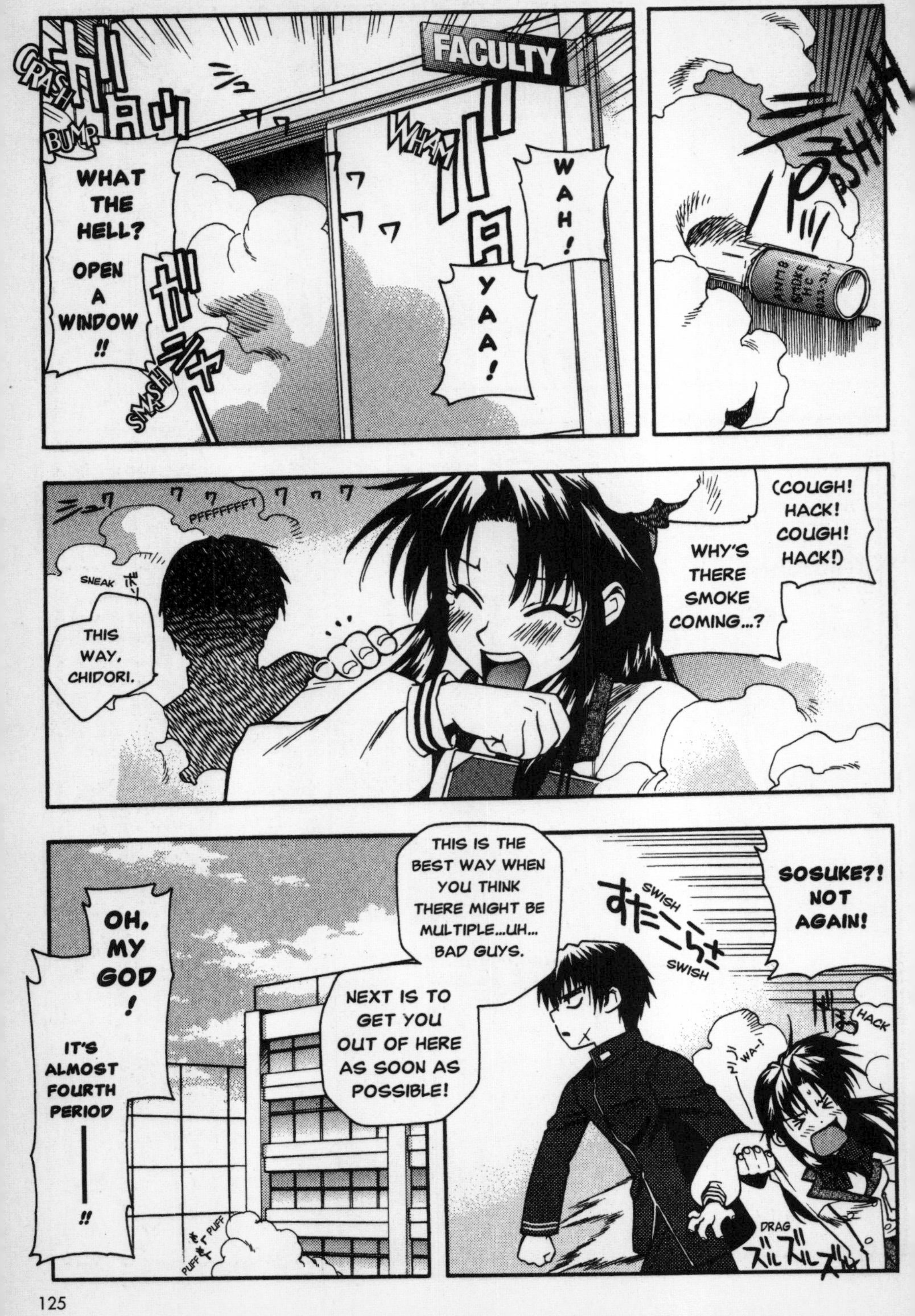

POSHAH
FACULTY
WAH!
YAA!
WHAM
CRASH
BUMP
WHAT THE HELL? OPEN A WINDOW!!
SMASH
(COUGH! HACK! COUGH! HACK!)
WHY'S THERE SMOKE COMING...?
PFFFFFFFFT
SNEAK
THIS WAY, CHIDORI.
SOSUKE?! NOT AGAIN!
SWISH
SWISH
HACK
WA-!
DRAG
THIS IS THE BEST WAY WHEN YOU THINK THERE MIGHT BE MULTIPLE...UH... BAD GUYS.
NEXT IS TO GET YOU OUT OF HERE AS SOON AS POSSIBLE!
OH, MY GOD!
IT'S ALMOST FOURTH PERIOD—!!
PUFF
PUFF

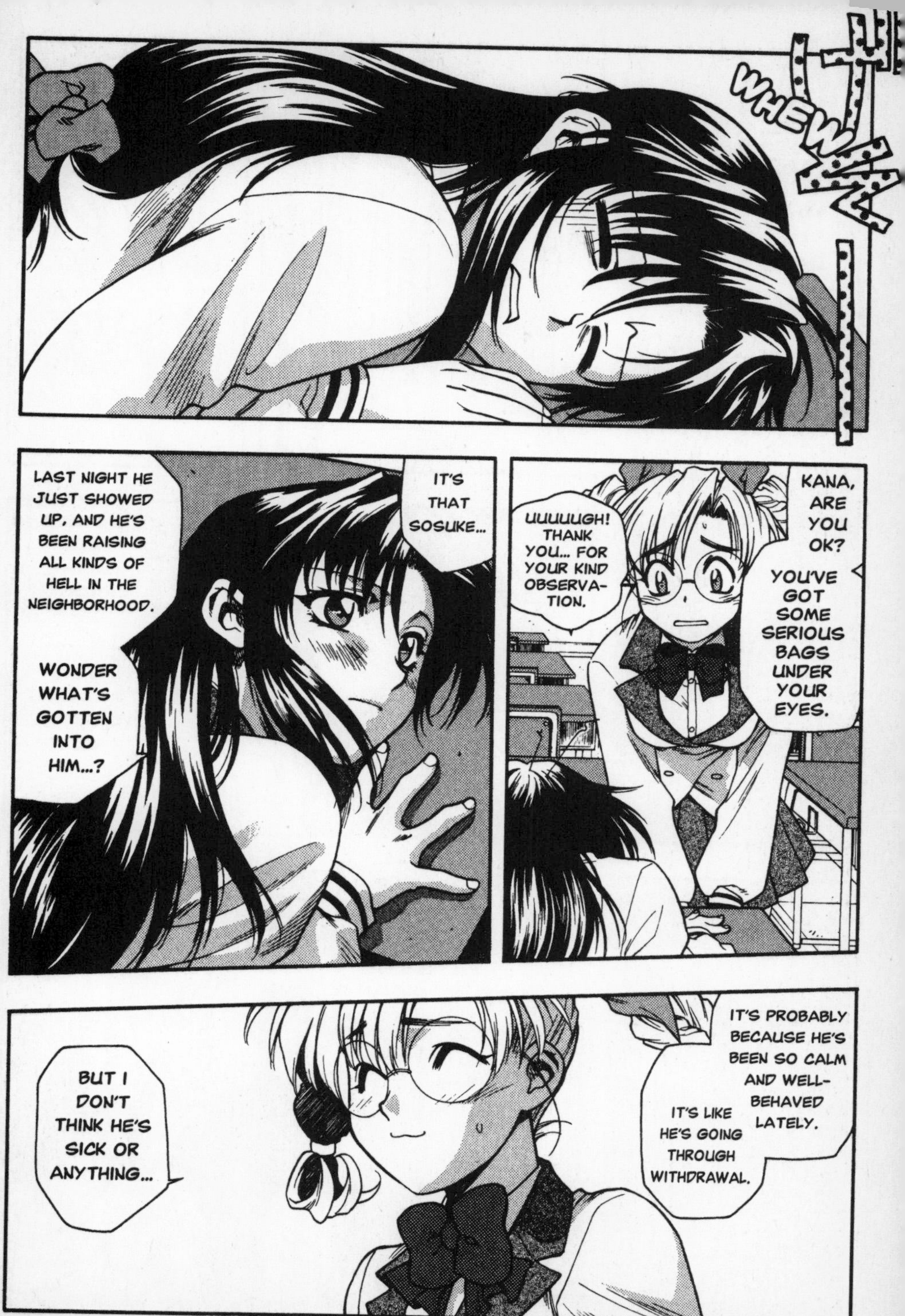
WHEW
KANA, ARE YOU OK?
YOU'VE GOT SOME SERIOUS BAGS UNDER YOUR EYES.
UUUUUGH! THANK YOU... FOR YOUR KIND OBSERVATION.
IT'S THAT SOSUKE...
LAST NIGHT HE JUST SHOWED UP, AND HE'S BEEN RAISING ALL KINDS OF HELL IN THE NEIGHBORHOOD.
WONDER WHAT'S GOTTEN INTO HIM...?
IT'S PROBABLY BECAUSE HE'S BEEN SO CALM AND WELL-BEHAVED LATELY.
IT'S LIKE HE'S GOING THROUGH WITHDRAWAL.
BUT I DON'T THINK HE'S SICK OR ANYTHING...

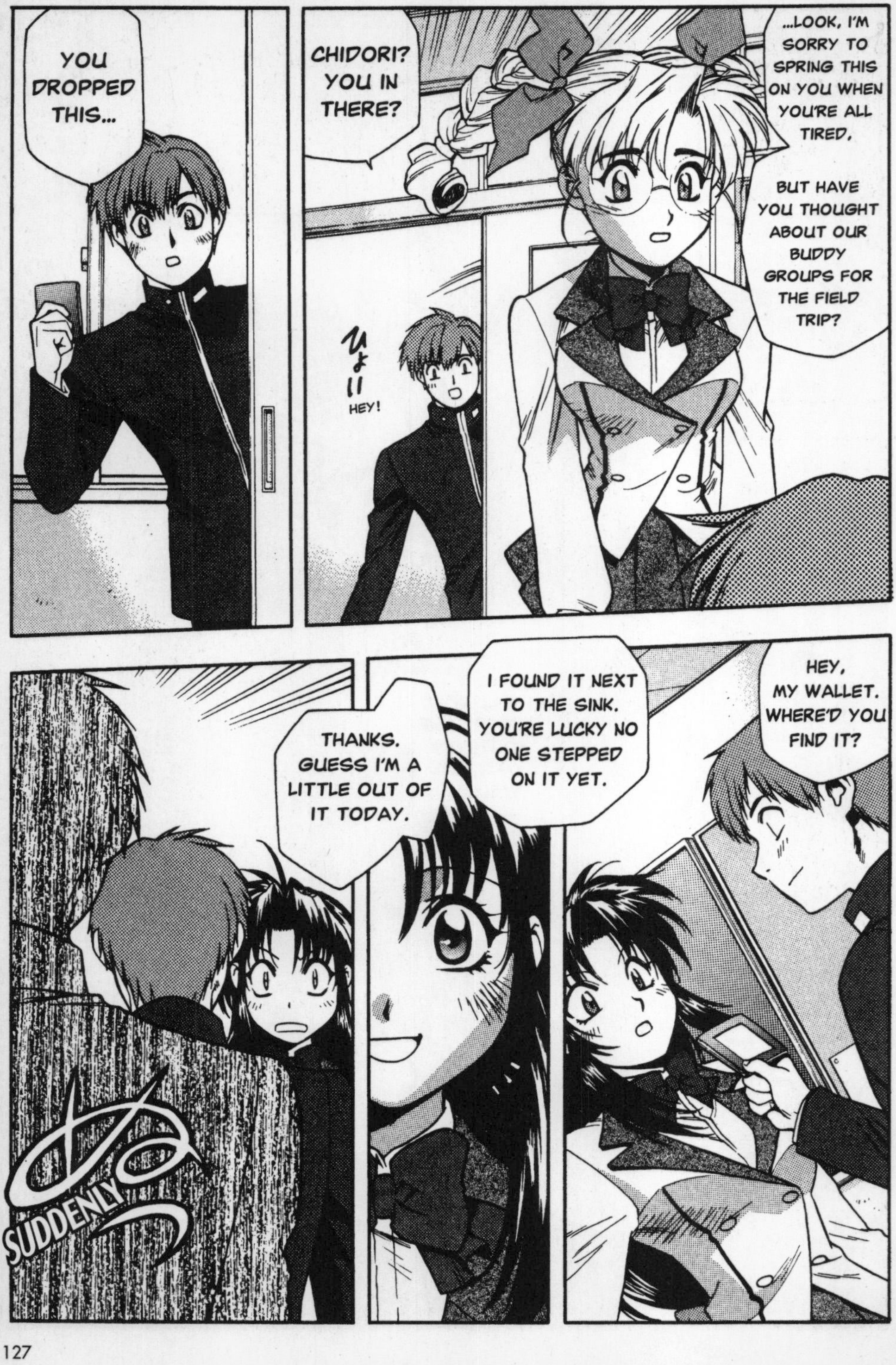
...LOOK, I'M SORRY TO SPRING THIS ON YOU WHEN YOU'RE ALL TIRED,
CHIDORI? YOU IN THERE?
BUT HAVE YOU THOUGHT ABOUT OUR BUDDY GROUPS FOR THE FIELD TRIP?
ひょい
HEY!
YOU DROPPED THIS...
HEY, MY WALLET. WHERE'D YOU FIND IT?
I FOUND IT NEXT TO THE SINK. YOU'RE LUCKY NO ONE STEPPED ON IT YET.
THANKS. GUESS I'M A LITTLE OUT OF IT TODAY.
SUDDENLY

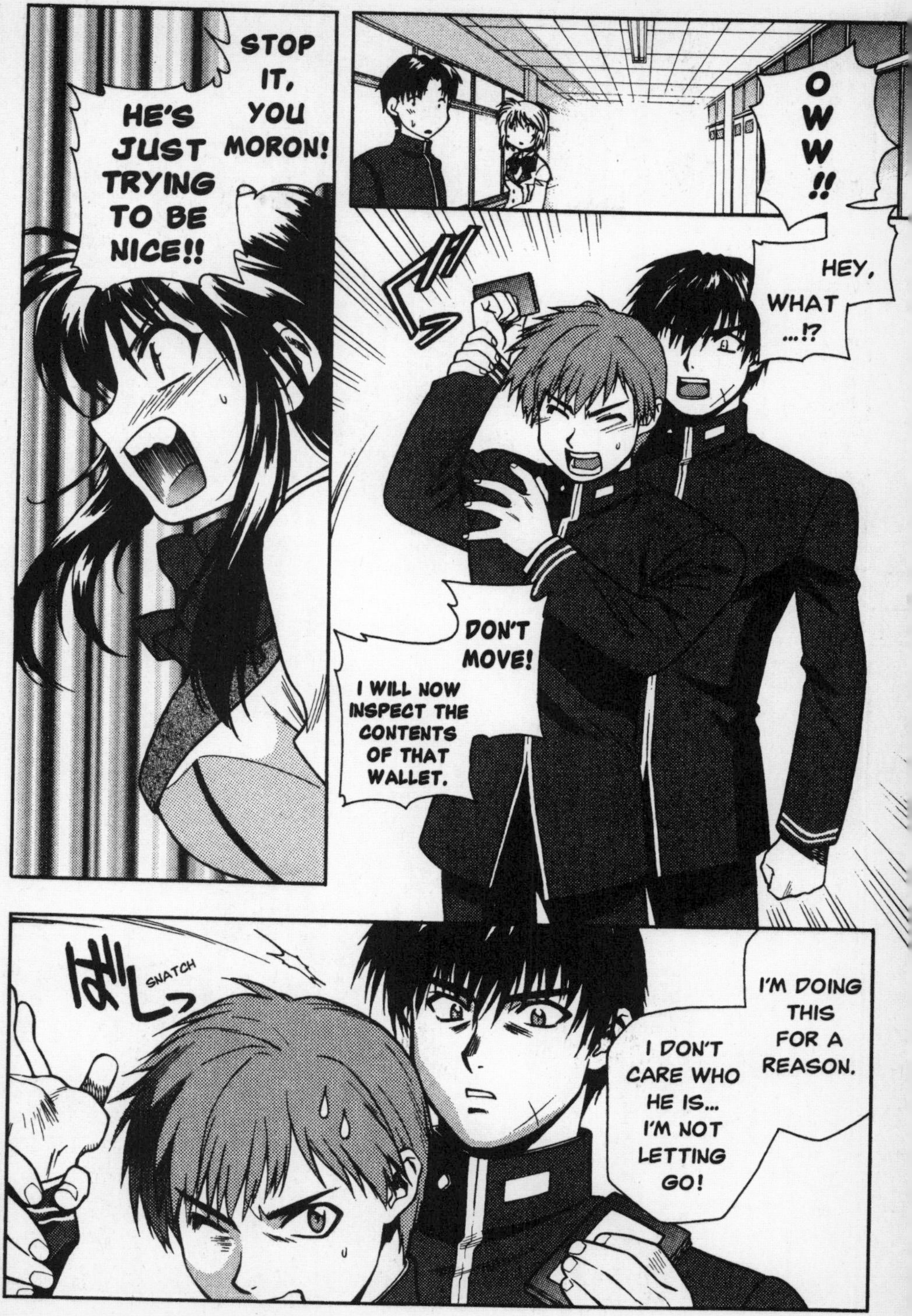
OWW!!
HEY, WHAT ...!?
DON'T MOVE!
I WILL NOW INSPECT THE CONTENTS OF THAT WALLET.
STOP IT, YOU MORON!
HE'S JUST TRYING TO BE NICE!!
I'M DOING THIS FOR A REASON.
I DON'T CARE WHO HE IS... I'M NOT LETTING GO!
ぱしっ SNATCH

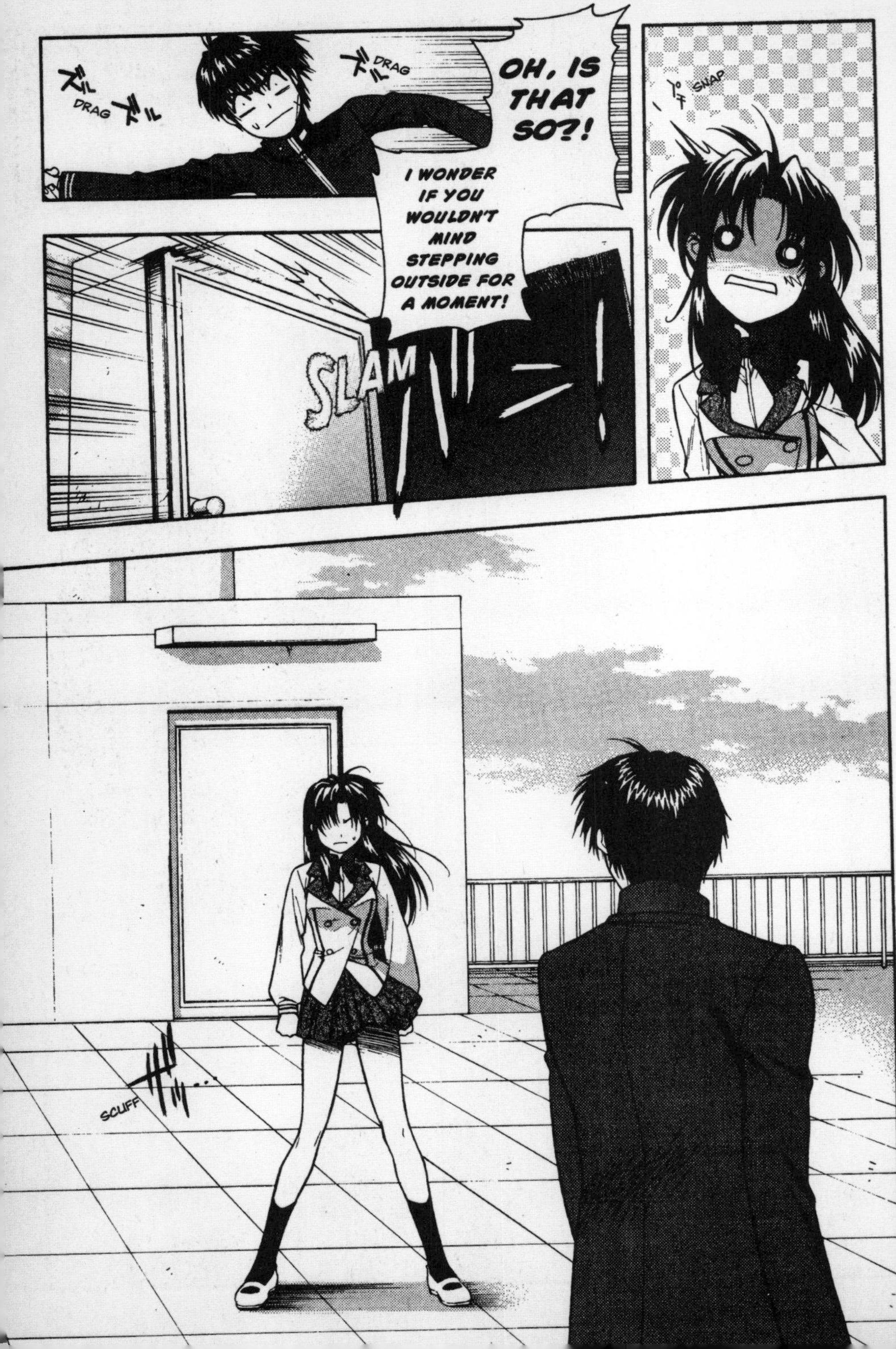
SNAP
DRAG
DRAG
OH, IS THAT SO?!
I WONDER IF YOU WOULDN'T MIND STEPPING OUTSIDE FOR A MOMENT!
SLAM
SCUFF

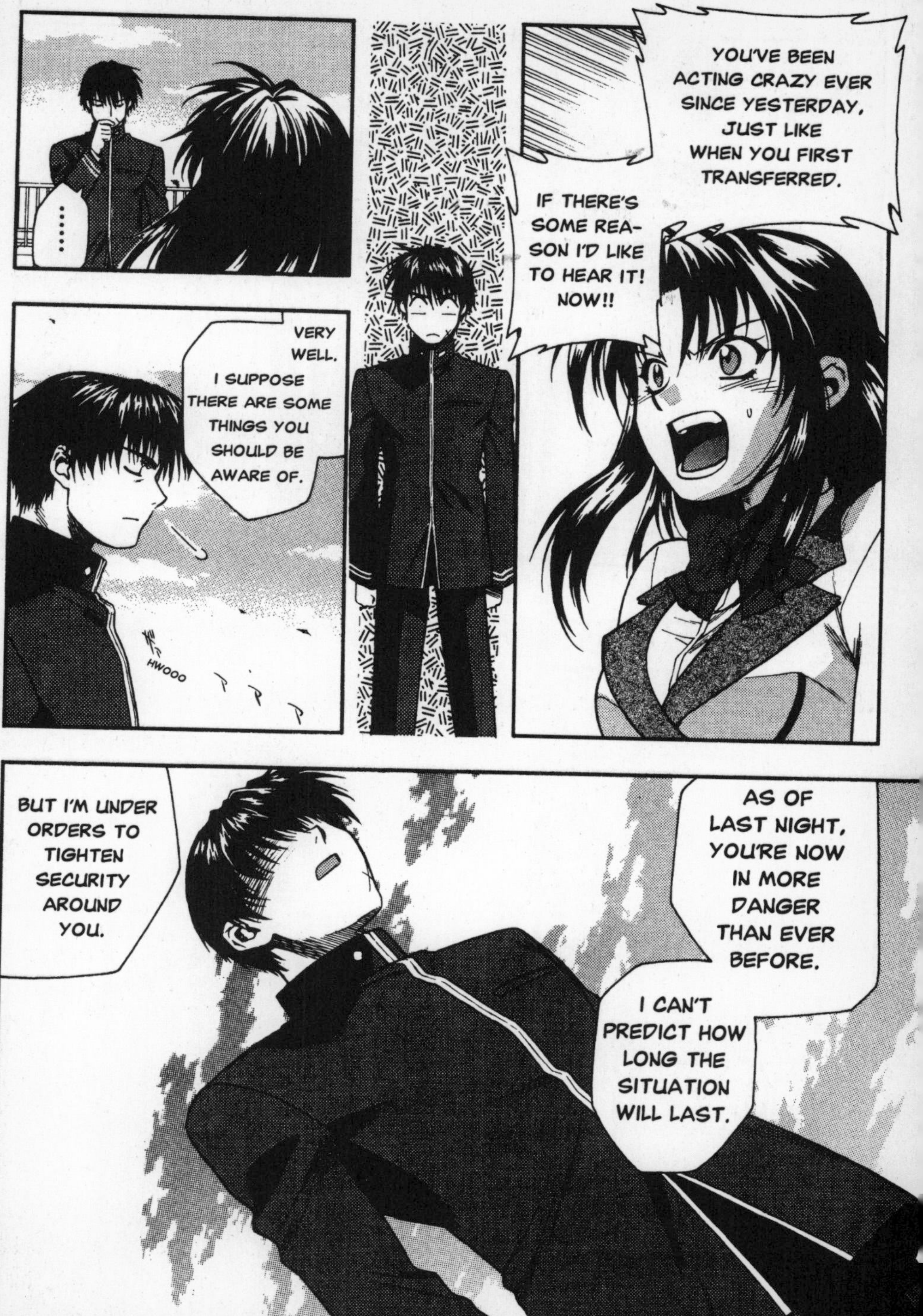
YOU'VE BEEN ACTING CRAZY EVER SINCE YESTERDAY, JUST LIKE WHEN YOU FIRST TRANSFERRED.
IF THERE'S SOME REA-SON I'D LIKE TO HEAR IT! NOW!!
......
VERY WELL. I SUPPOSE THERE ARE SOME THINGS YOU SHOULD BE AWARE OF.
HWOOO
AS OF LAST NIGHT, YOU'RE NOW IN MORE DANGER THAN EVER BEFORE.
I CAN'T PREDICT HOW LONG THE SITUATION WILL LAST.
BUT I'M UNDER ORDERS TO TIGHTEN SECURITY AROUND YOU.

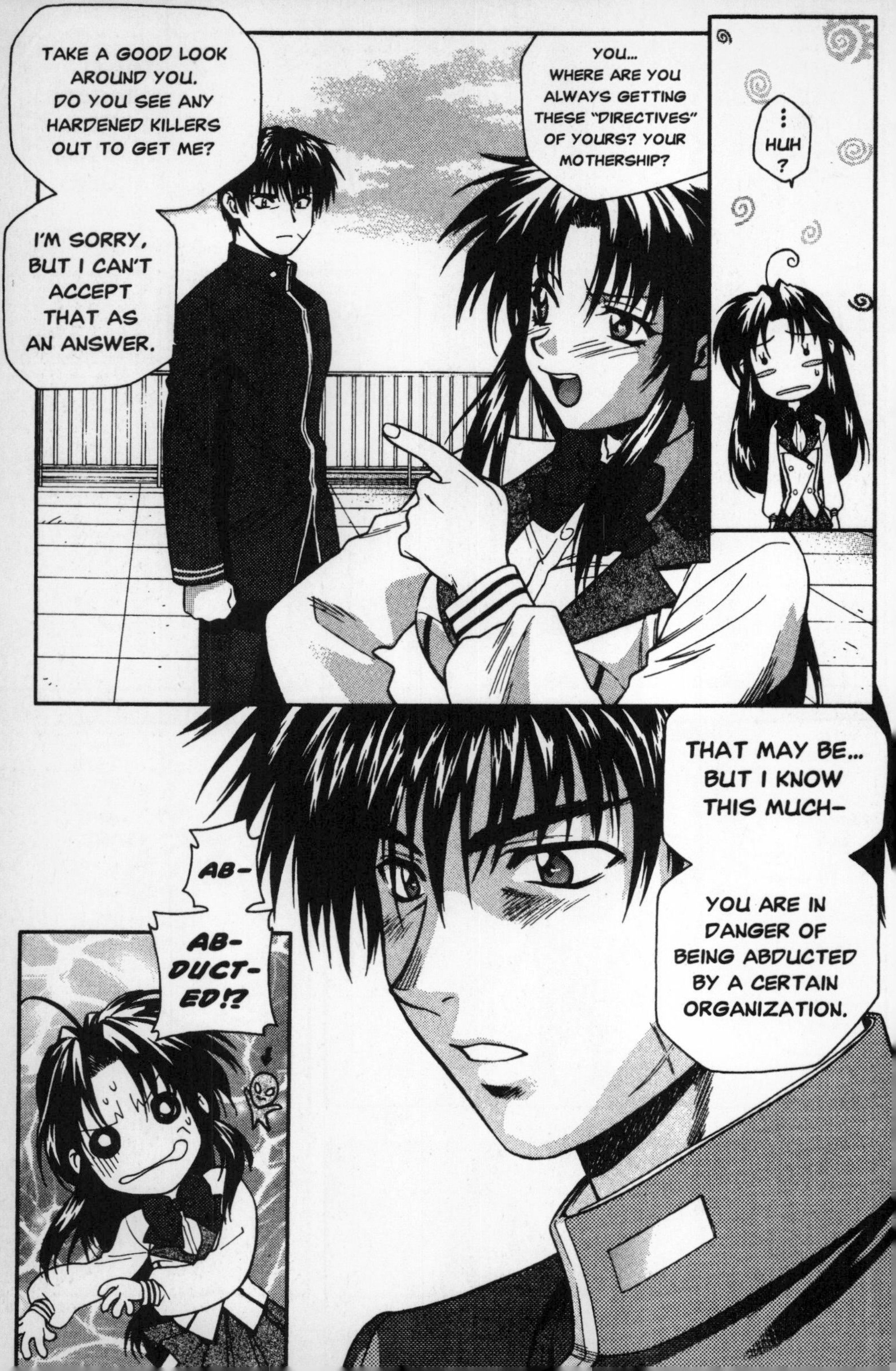

...HUH?
YOU... WHERE ARE YOU ALWAYS GETTING THESE "DIRECTIVES" OF YOURS? YOUR MOTHERSHIP?
TAKE A GOOD LOOK AROUND YOU. DO YOU SEE ANY HARDENED KILLERS OUT TO GET ME?
I'M SORRY, BUT I CAN'T ACCEPT THAT AS AN ANSWER.
THAT MAY BE... BUT I KNOW THIS MUCH-
YOU ARE IN DANGER OF BEING ABDUCTED BY A CERTAIN ORGANIZATION.
AB-
AB-DUCT-ED!?

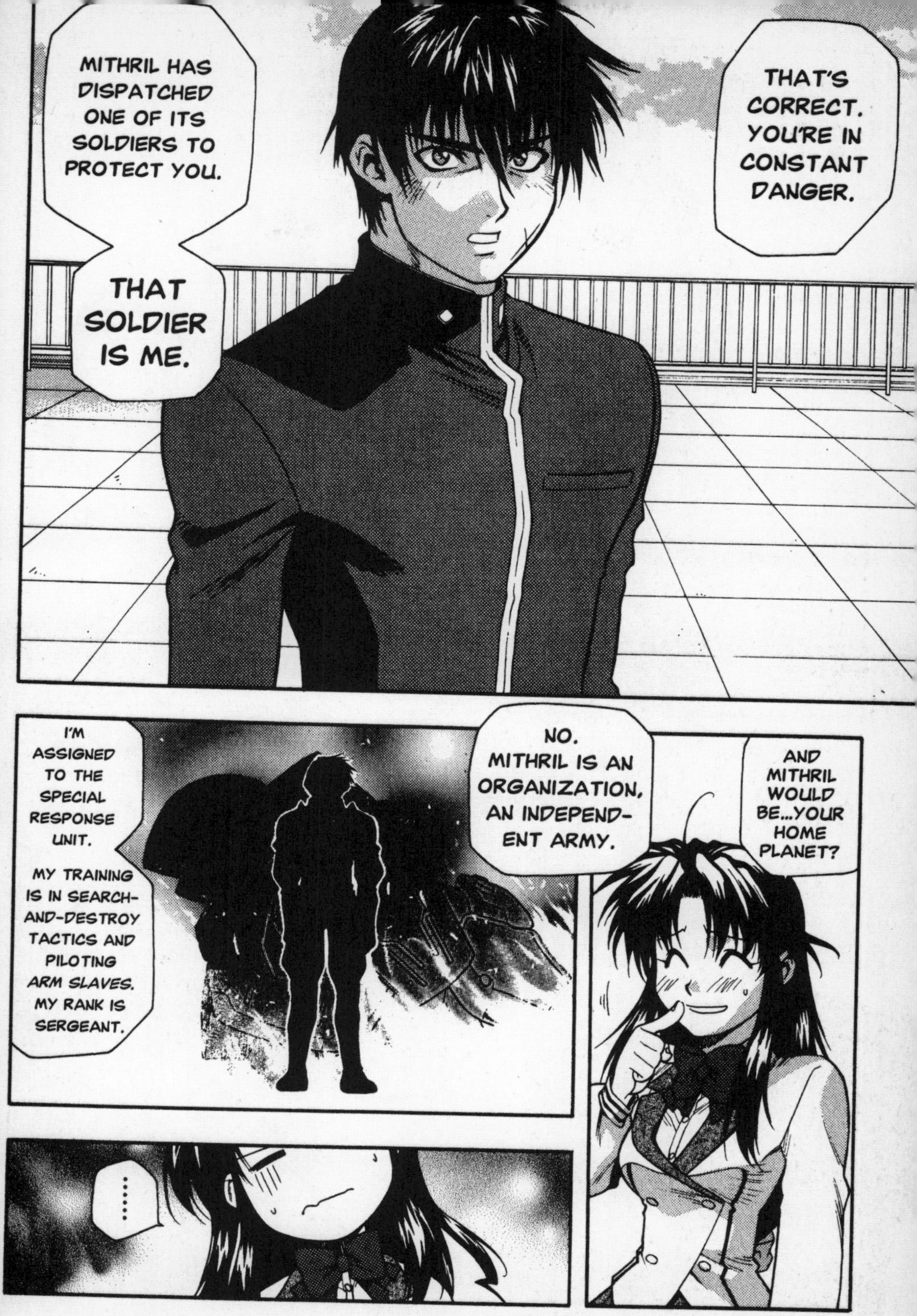
THAT'S CORRECT. YOU'RE IN CONSTANT DANGER.
MITHRIL HAS DISPATCHED ONE OF ITS SOLDIERS TO PROTECT YOU.
THAT SOLDIER IS ME.
AND MITHRIL WOULD BE...YOUR HOME PLANET?
NO. MITHRIL IS AN ORGANIZATION, AN INDEPEND-ENT ARMY.
I'M ASSIGNED TO THE SPECIAL RESPONSE UNIT.
MY TRAINING IS IN SEARCH-AND-DESTROY TACTICS AND PILOTING ARM SLAVES. MY RANK IS SERGEANT.
......

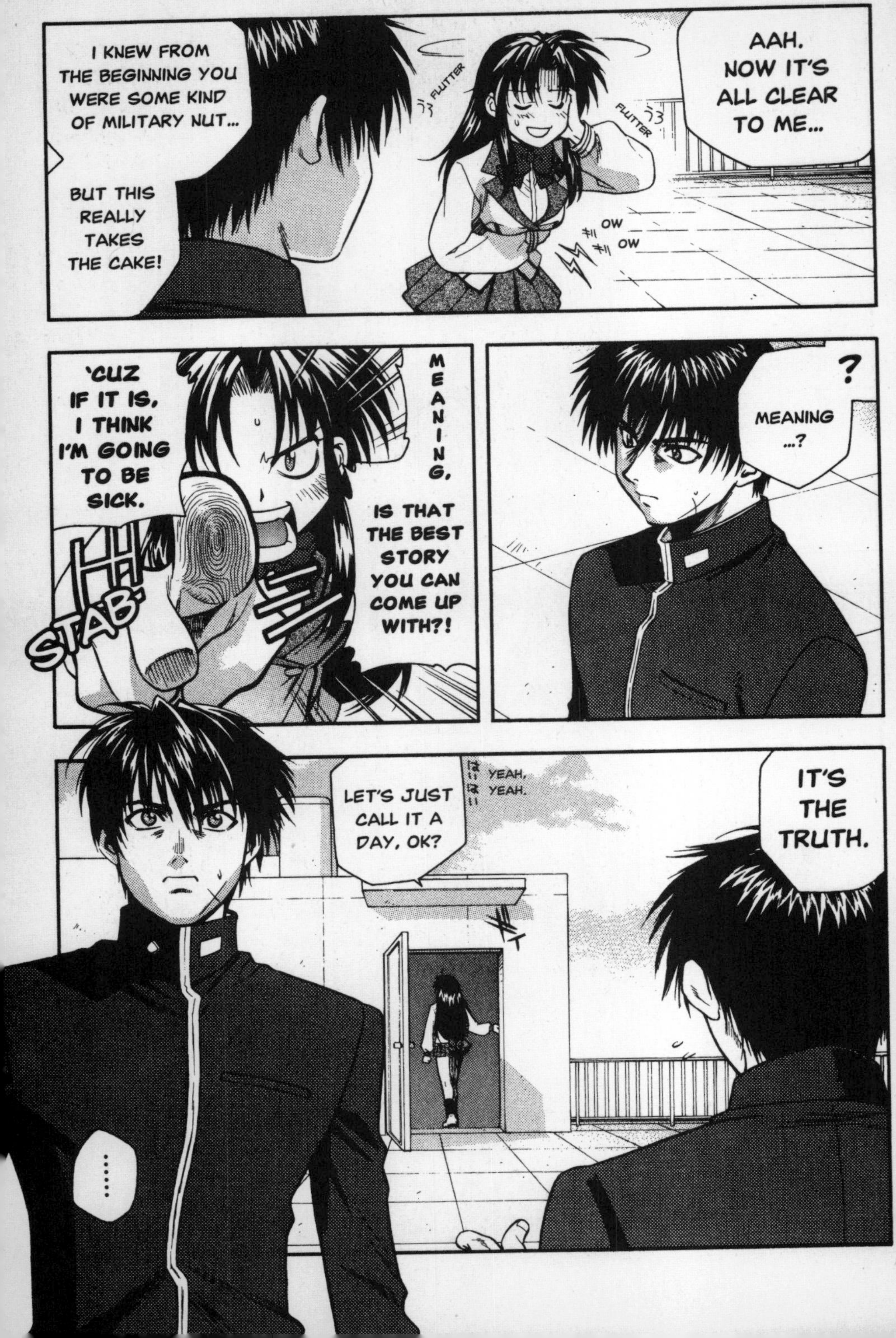

AAH. NOW IT'S ALL CLEAR TO ME...
FLUTTER
FLUTTER
I KNEW FROM THE BEGINNING YOU WERE SOME KIND OF MILITARY NUT...
BUT THIS REALLY TAKES THE CAKE!
OW
OW
?
MEANING ...?
MEANING,
IS THAT THE BEST STORY YOU CAN COME UP WITH?!
'CUZ IF IT IS, I THINK I'M GOING TO BE SICK.
STAB
IT'S THE TRUTH.
YEAH, YEAH.
LET'S JUST CALL IT A DAY, OK?
......

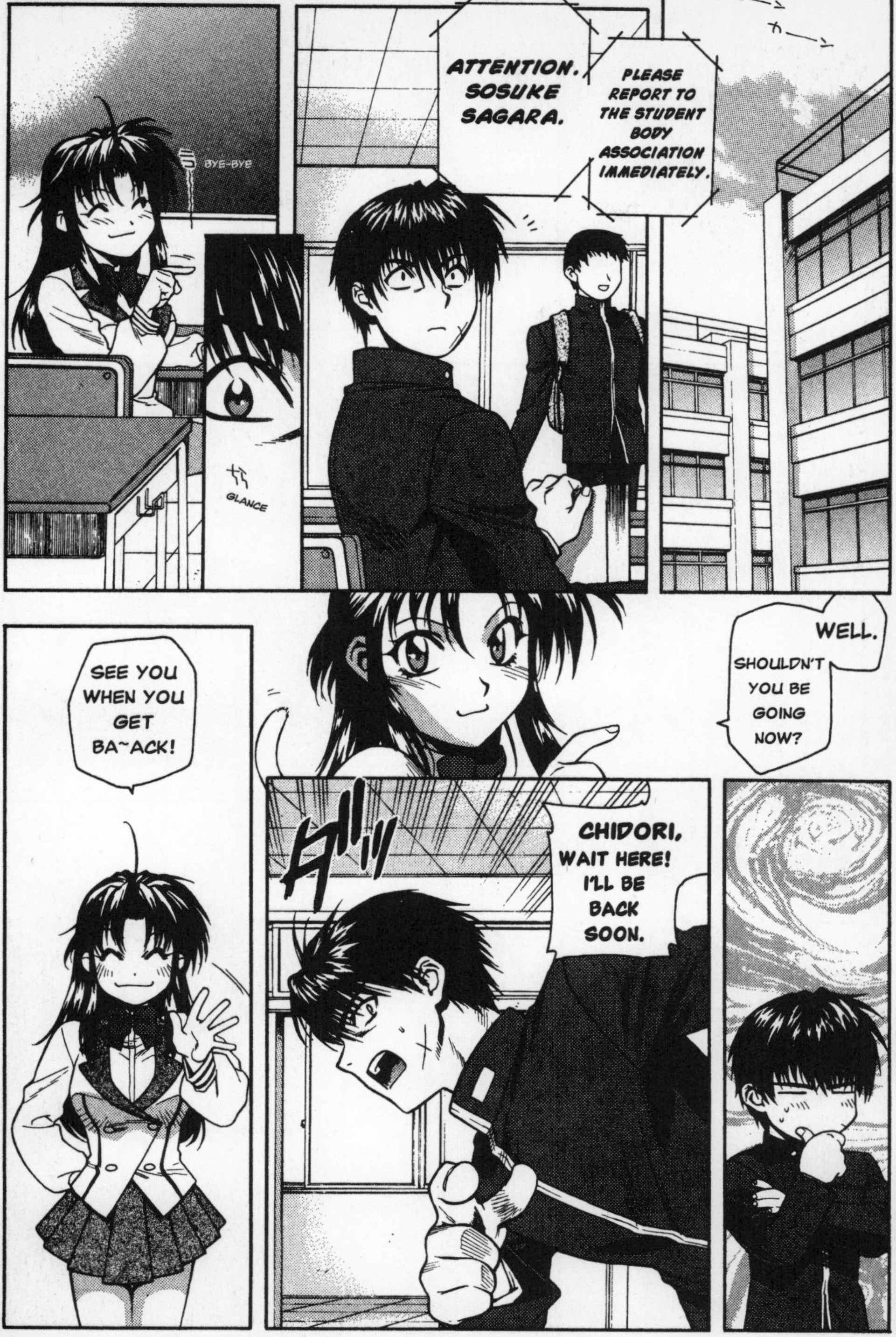
コーン
カーン
ATTENTION. SOSUKE SAGARA.
PLEASE REPORT TO THE STUDENT BODY ASSOCIATION IMMEDIATELY.
GLANCE
BYE-BYE
WELL.
SHOULDN'T YOU BE GOING NOW?
CHIDORI, WAIT HERE! I'LL BE BACK SOON.
SEE YOU WHEN YOU GET BA~ACK!

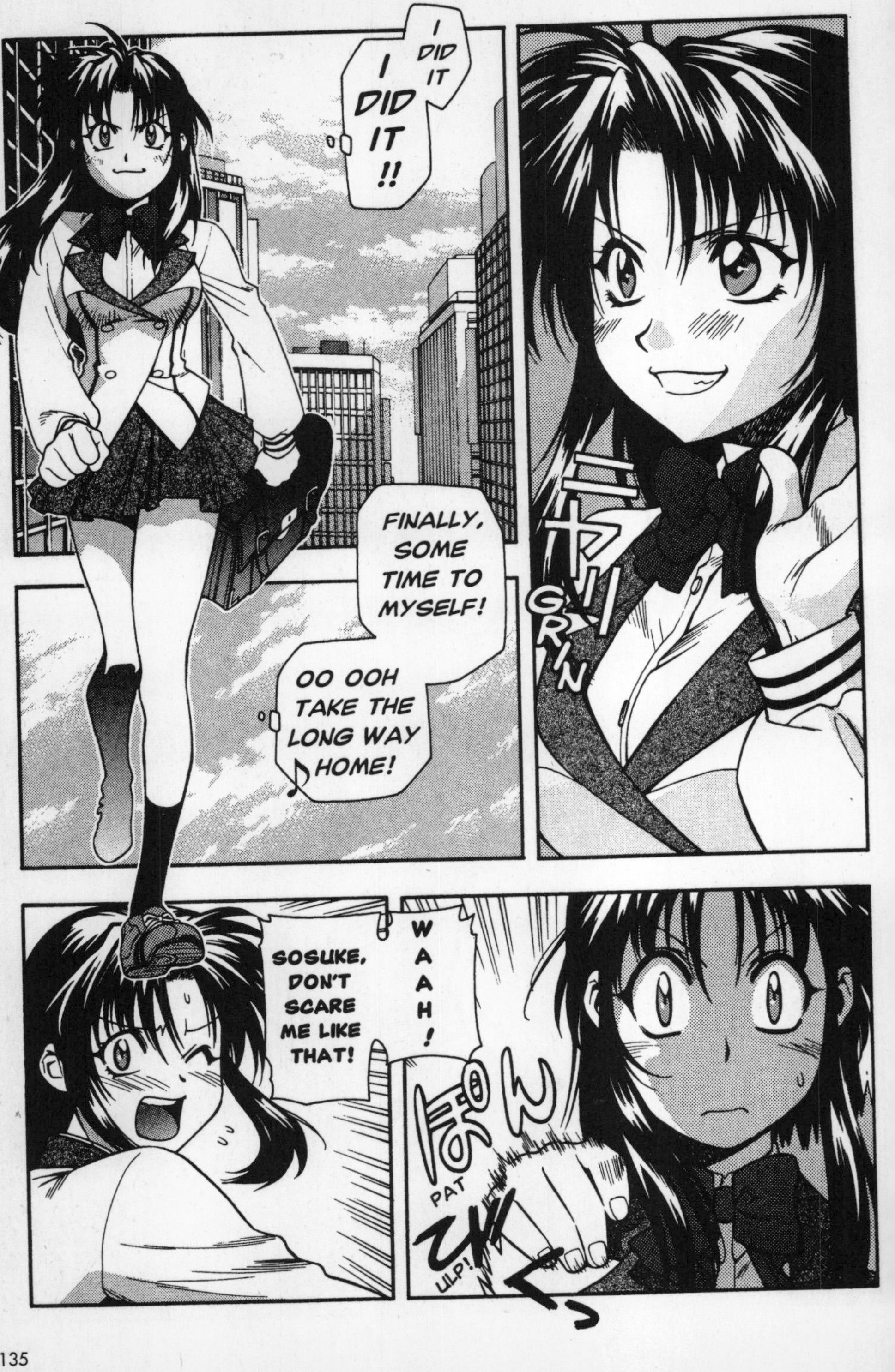
GRIN
I DID IT
I DID IT!!
FINALLY, SOME TIME TO MYSELF!
OO OOH TAKE THE LONG WAY HOME!
WAAH!
PAT
ULP!
SOSUKE, DON'T SCARE ME LIKE THAT!

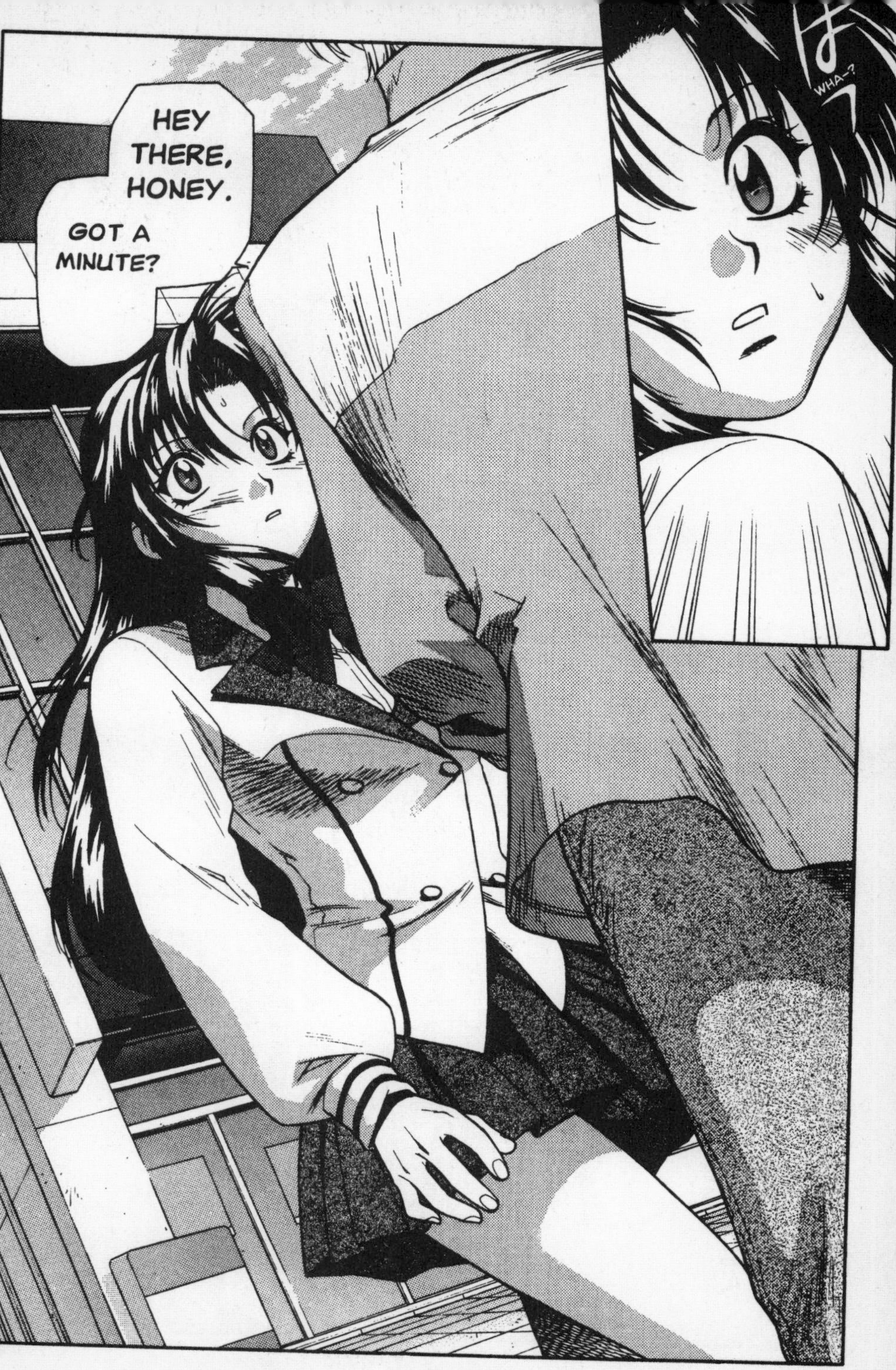
は
WHA-?
HEY THERE, HONEY.
GOT A MINUTE?

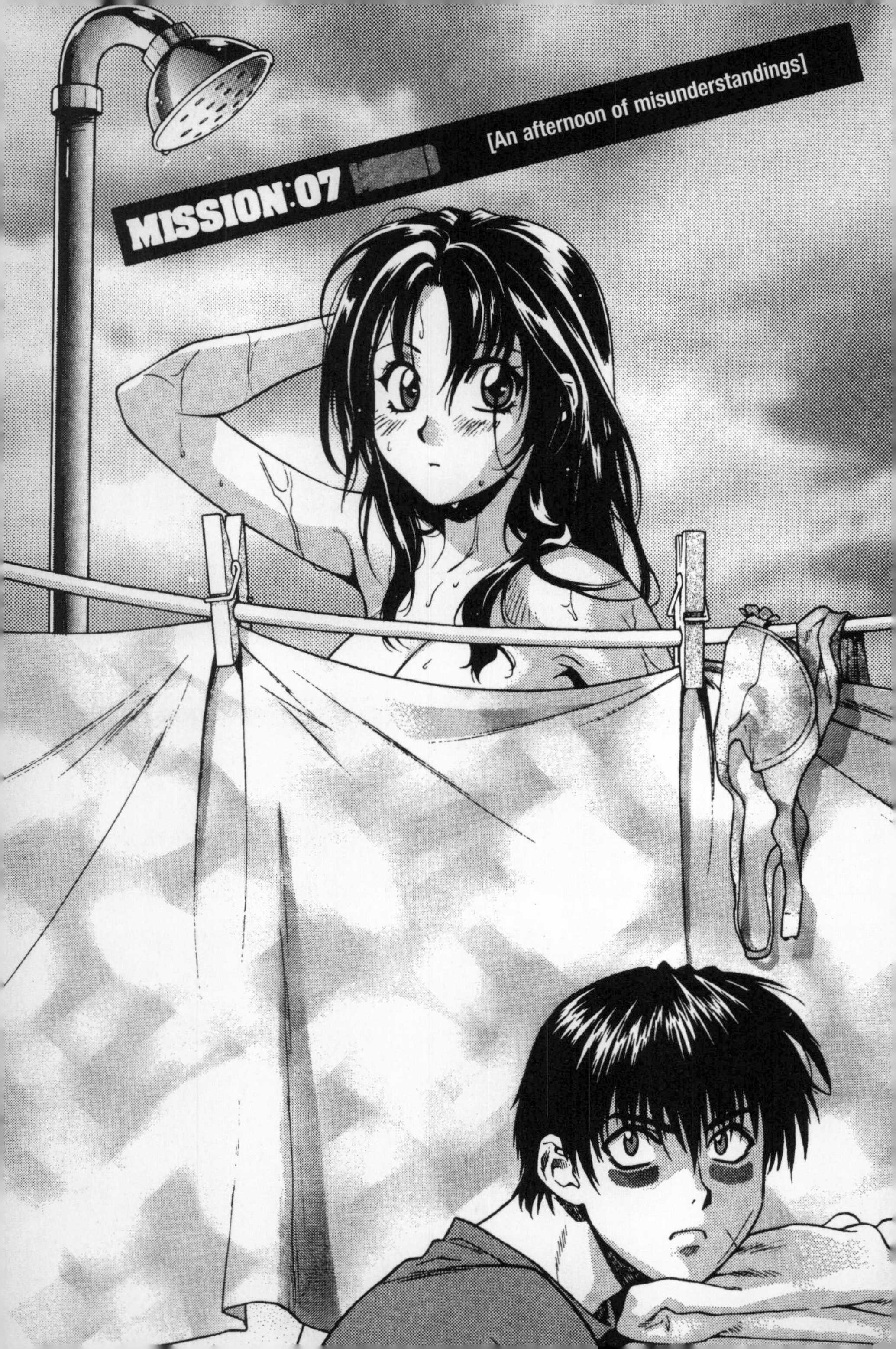
MISSION:07
[An afternoon of misunderstandings]

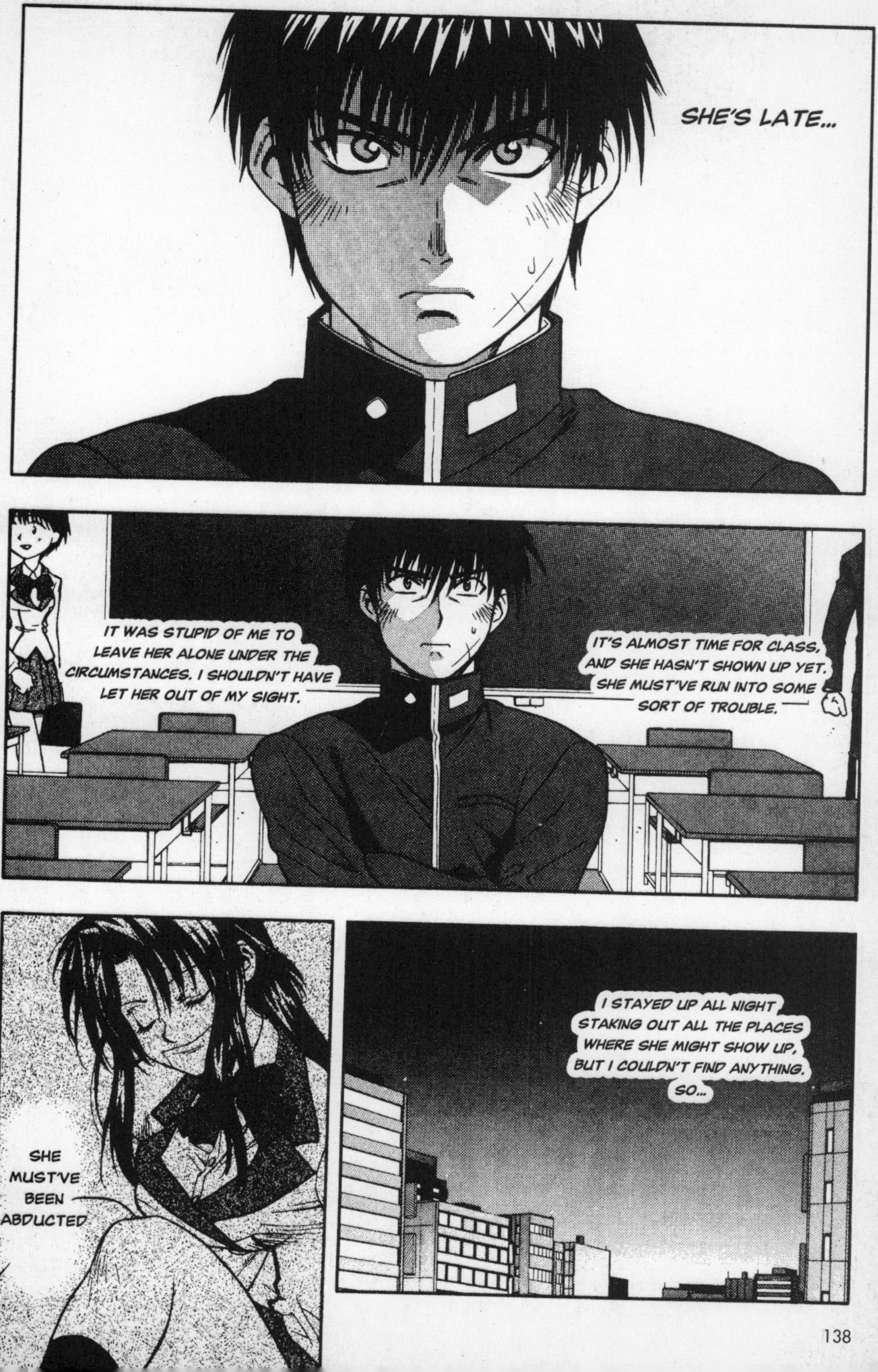
SHE'S LATE...
IT'S ALMOST TIME FOR CLASS, AND SHE HASN'T SHOWN UP YET. SHE MUST'VE RUN INTO SOME SORT OF TROUBLE.
IT WAS STUPID OF ME TO LEAVE HER ALONE UNDER THE CIRCUMSTANCES. I SHOULDN'T HAVE LET HER OUT OF MY SIGHT.
I STAYED UP ALL NIGHT STAKING OUT ALL THE PLACES WHERE SHE MIGHT SHOW UP, BUT I COULDN'T FIND ANYTHING. SO...
SHE MUST'VE BEEN ABDUCTED

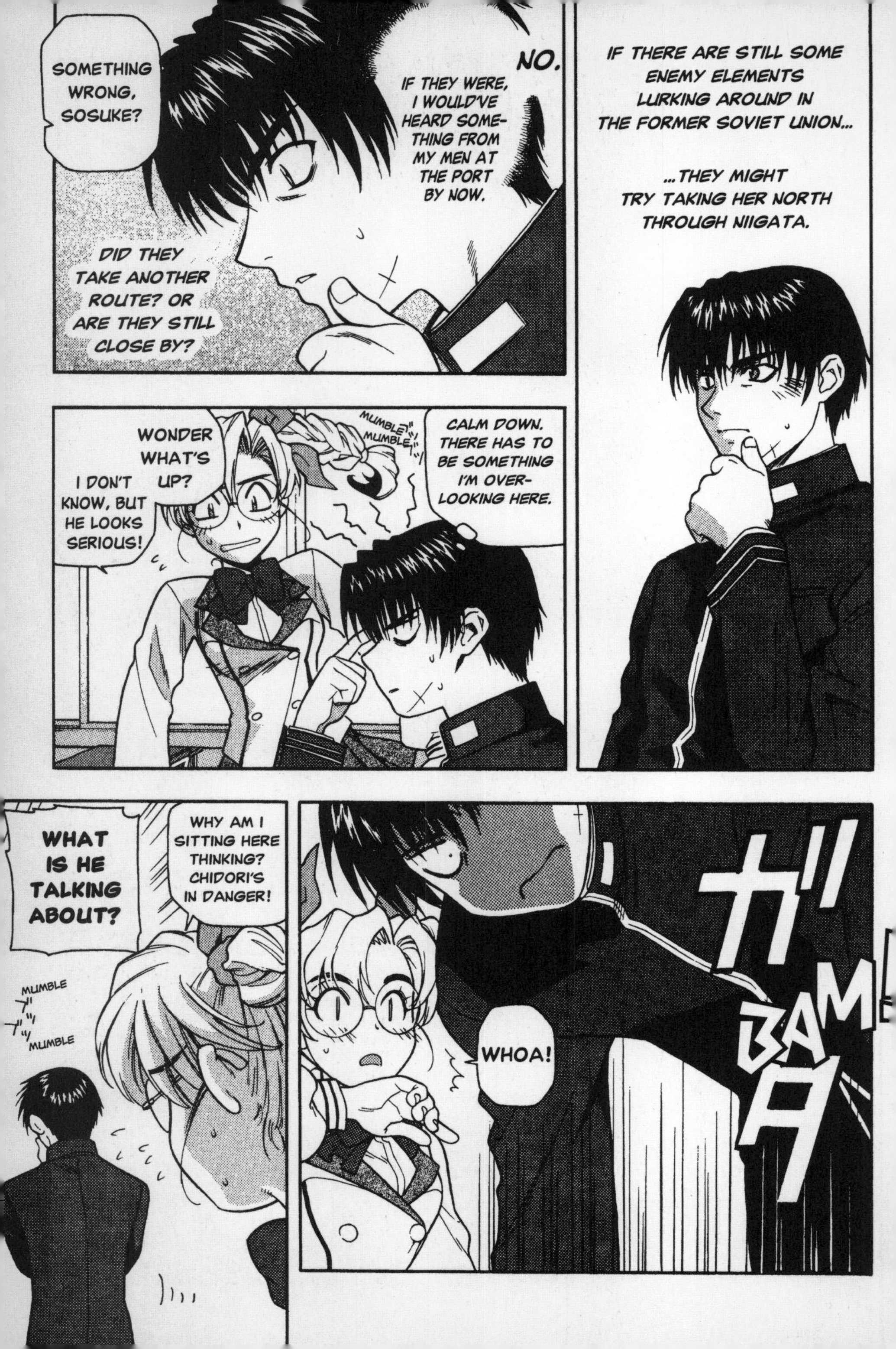
SOMETHING WRONG, SOSUKE?
DID THEY TAKE ANOTHER ROUTE? OR ARE THEY STILL CLOSE BY?
NO.
IF THEY WERE, I WOULD'VE HEARD SOME-THING FROM MY MEN AT THE PORT BY NOW.
IF THERE ARE STILL SOME ENEMY ELEMENTS LURKING AROUND IN THE FORMER SOVIET UNION...
...THEY MIGHT TRY TAKING HER NORTH THROUGH NIIGATA.
WONDER WHAT'S UP?
I DON'T KNOW, BUT HE LOOKS SERIOUS!
MUMBLE MUMBLE
CALM DOWN. THERE HAS TO BE SOMETHING I'M OVER-LOOKING HERE.
WHAT IS HE TALKING ABOUT?
MUMBLE MUMBLE
WHY AM I SITTING HERE THINKING? CHIDORI'S IN DANGER!
ガタ
BAM!
WHOA!

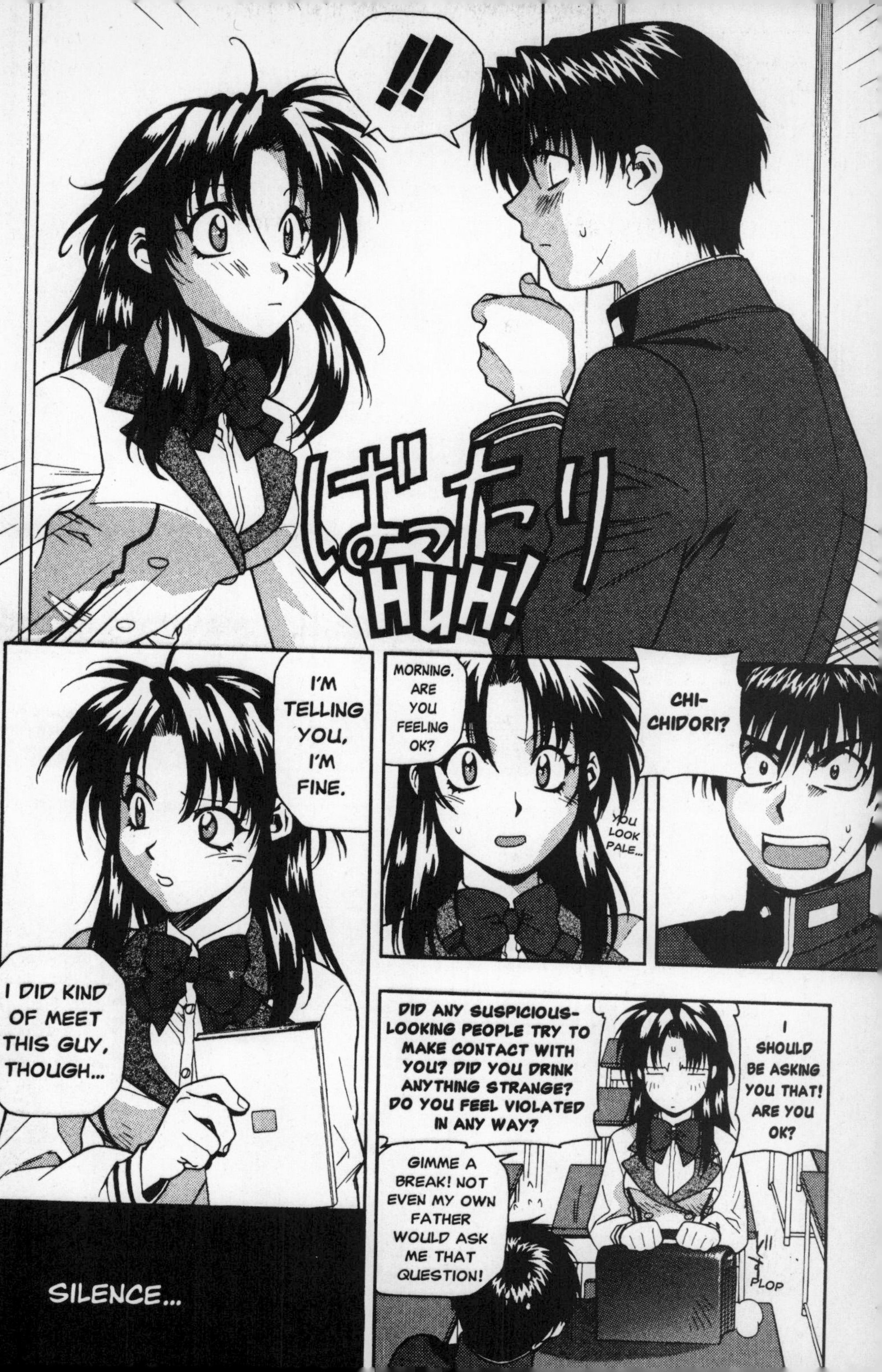
!!
ぱったり
HUH!
CHI-CHIDORI?
MORNING. ARE YOU FEELING OK?
YOU LOOK PALE...
I SHOULD BE ASKING YOU THAT! ARE YOU OK?
DID ANY SUSPICIOUS-LOOKING PEOPLE TRY TO MAKE CONTACT WITH YOU? DID YOU DRINK ANYTHING STRANGE? DO YOU FEEL VIOLATED IN ANY WAY?
GIMME A BREAK! NOT EVEN MY OWN FATHER WOULD ASK ME THAT QUESTION!
PLOP
I'M TELLING YOU, I'M FINE.
I DID KIND OF MEET THIS GUY, THOUGH...
SILENCE...

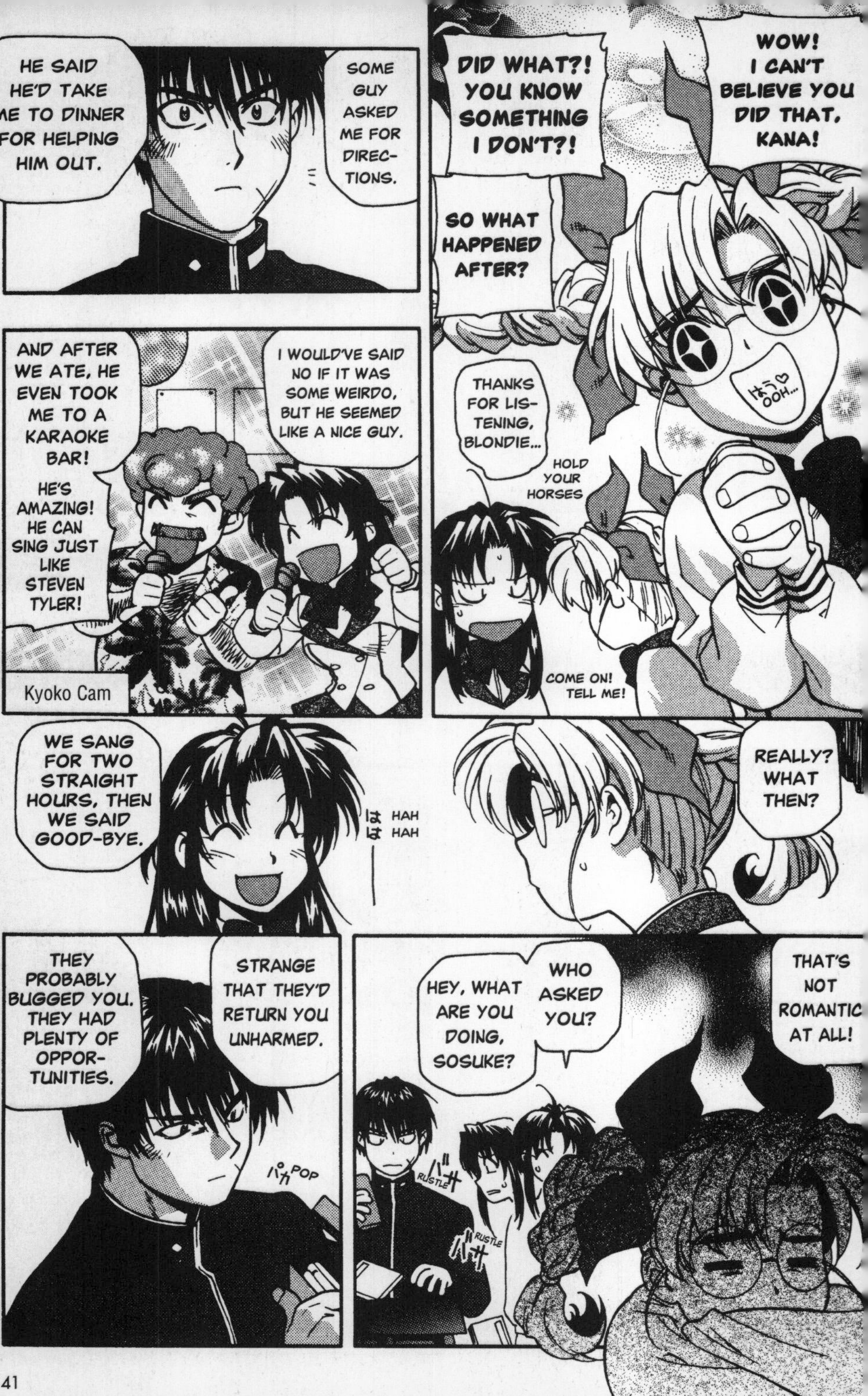
WOW! I CAN'T BELIEVE YOU DID THAT, KANA!
DID WHAT?! YOU KNOW SOMETHING I DON'T?!
OOH...
SO WHAT HAPPENED AFTER?
THANKS FOR LIS-TENING, BLONDIE...
HOLD YOUR HORSES
COME ON! TELL ME!
SOME GUY ASKED ME FOR DIREC-TIONS.
HE SAID HE'D TAKE ME TO DINNER FOR HELPING HIM OUT.
I WOULD'VE SAID NO IF IT WAS SOME WEIRDO, BUT HE SEEMED LIKE A NICE GUY.
AND AFTER WE ATE, HE EVEN TOOK ME TO A KARAOKE BAR!
HE'S AMAZING! HE CAN SING JUST LIKE STEVEN TYLER!
Kyoko Cam
REALLY? WHAT THEN?
WE SANG FOR TWO STRAIGHT HOURS, THEN WE SAID GOOD-BYE.
HAH HAH
THAT'S NOT ROMANTIC AT ALL!
WHO ASKED YOU?
HEY, WHAT ARE YOU DOING, SOSUKE?
RUSTLE
RUSTLE
STRANGE THAT THEY'D RETURN YOU UNHARMED.
THEY PROBABLY BUGGED YOU. THEY HAD PLENTY OF OPPOR-TUNITIES.
POP

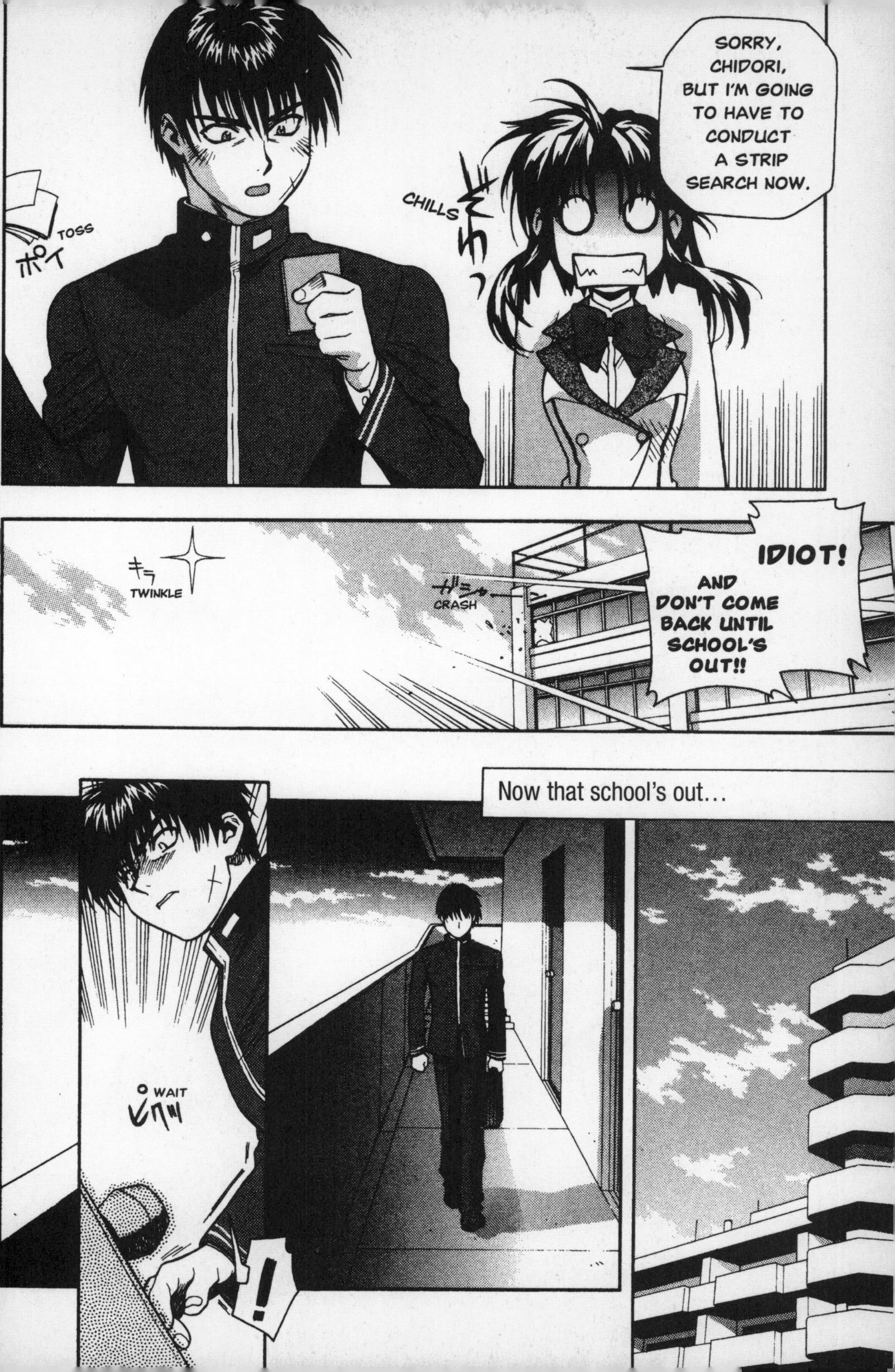
SORRY, CHIDORI, BUT I'M GOING TO HAVE TO CONDUCT A STRIP SEARCH NOW.
CHILLS
TOSS
ポイ
IDIOT!
AND DON'T COME BACK UNTIL SCHOOL'S OUT!!
CRASH
キラ
TWINKLE
Now that school's out…
...
WAIT
!

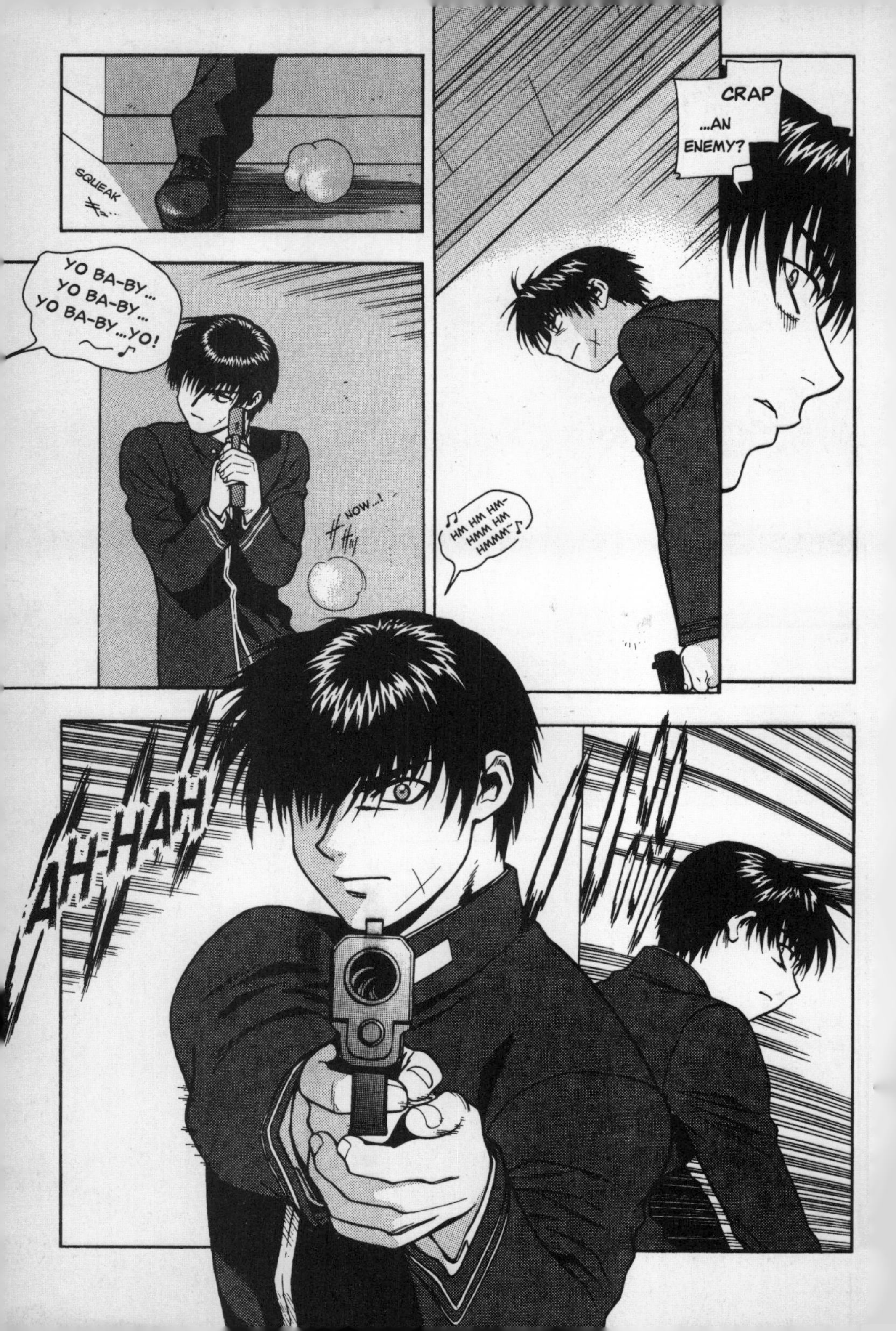
CRAP ...AN ENEMY?
HM HM HM- HMM HM HMMM~
SQUEAK
YO BA-BY... YO BA-BY... YO BA-BY...YO! ~
NOW...!
AH-HAH

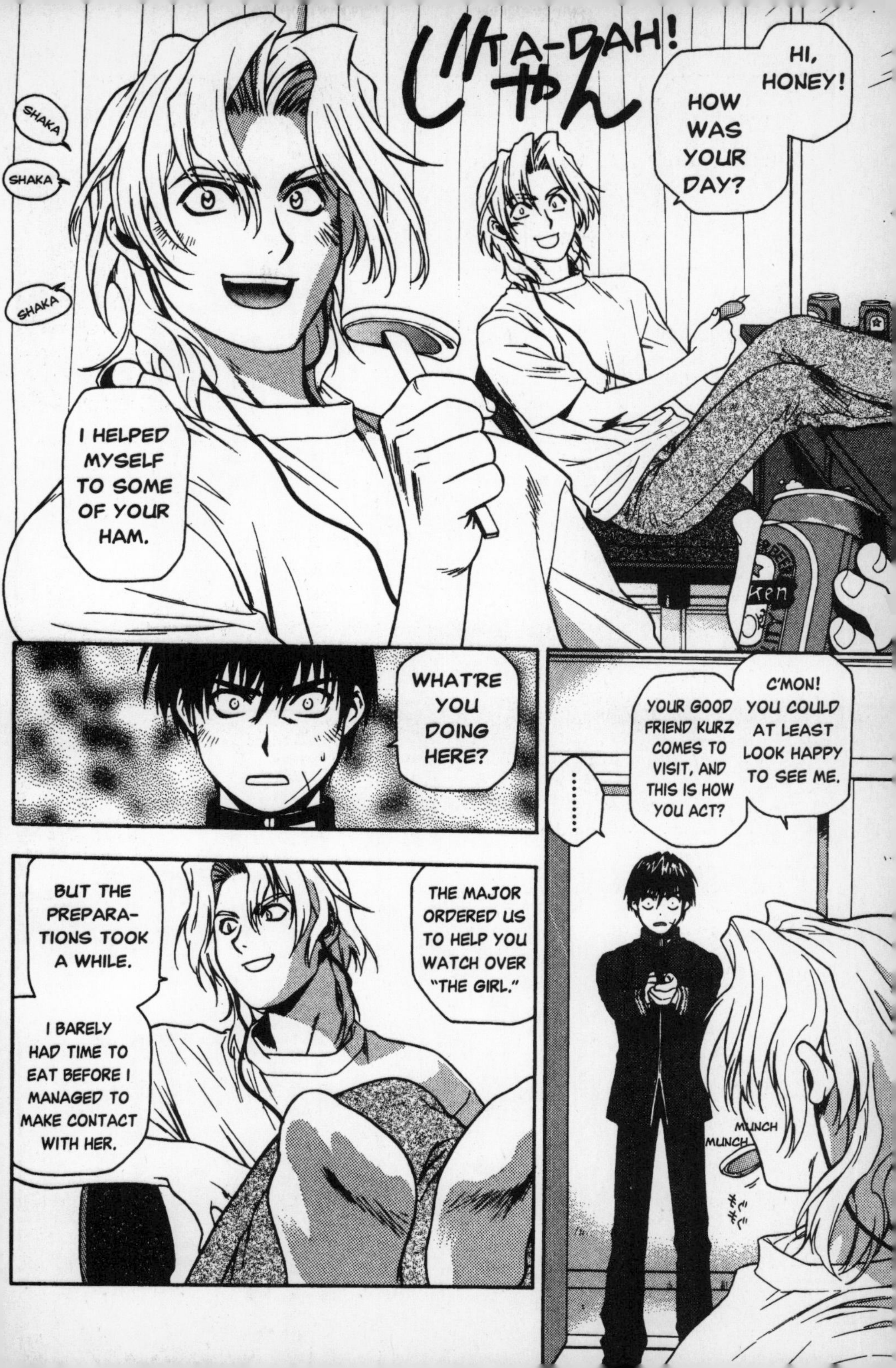
じゃん
KA-DAH!
HI, HONEY!
HOW WAS YOUR DAY?
SHAKA
SHAKA
SHAKA
I HELPED MYSELF TO SOME OF YOUR HAM.
C'MON! YOU COULD AT LEAST LOOK HAPPY TO SEE ME.
YOUR GOOD FRIEND KURZ COMES TO VISIT, AND THIS IS HOW YOU ACT?
......
MUNCH
MUNCH
WHAT'RE YOU DOING HERE?
THE MAJOR ORDERED US TO HELP YOU WATCH OVER "THE GIRL."
BUT THE PREPARA-TIONS TOOK A WHILE.
I BARELY HAD TIME TO EAT BEFORE I MANAGED TO MAKE CONTACT WITH HER.

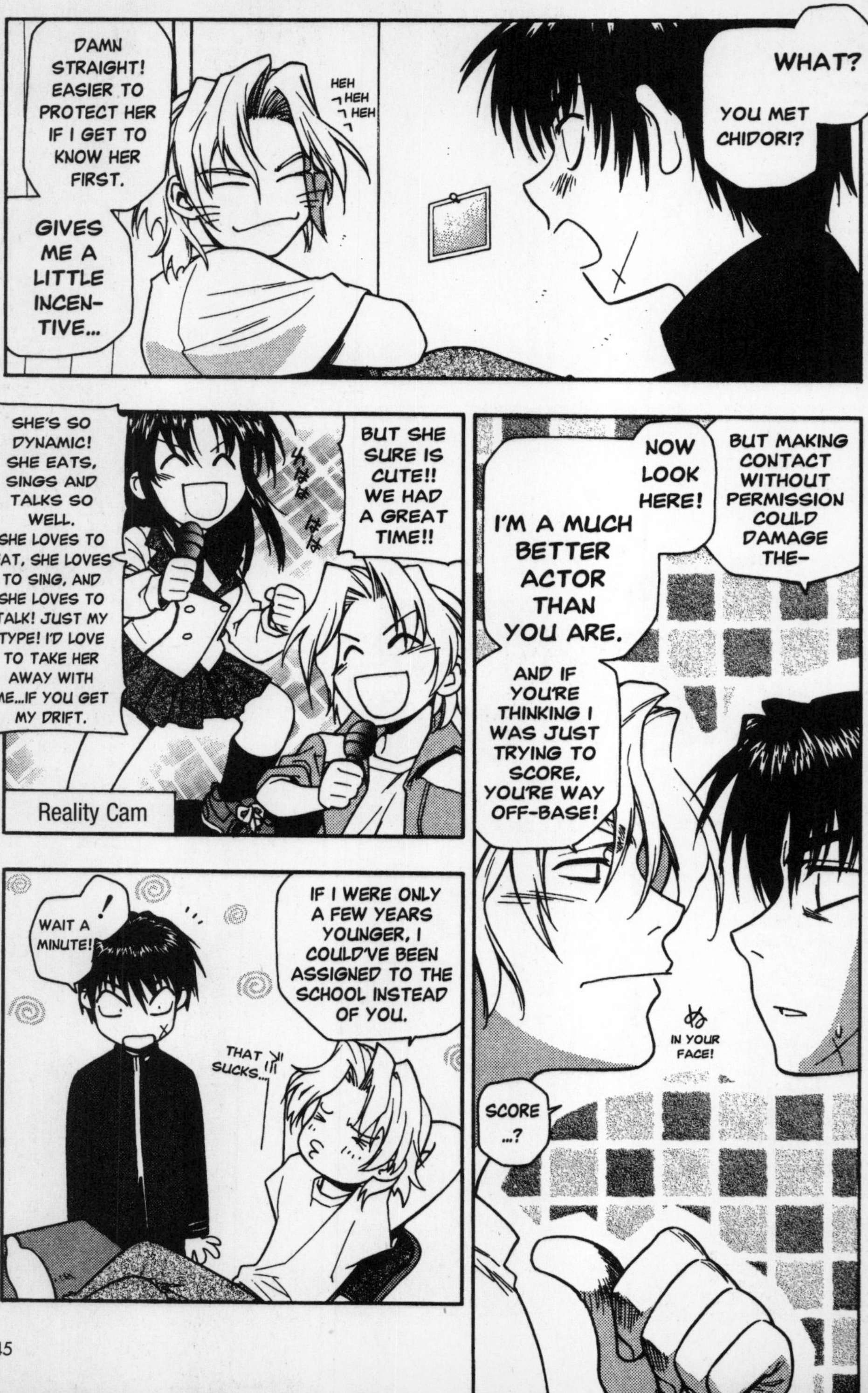
WHAT?
YOU MET CHIDORI?
DAMN STRAIGHT! EASIER TO PROTECT HER IF I GET TO KNOW HER FIRST.
HEH HEH HEH
GIVES ME A LITTLE INCEN-TIVE...
BUT MAKING CONTACT WITHOUT PERMISSION COULD DAMAGE THE-
NOW LOOK HERE!
I'M A MUCH BETTER ACTOR THAN YOU ARE.
AND IF YOU'RE THINKING I WAS JUST TRYING TO SCORE, YOU'RE WAY OFF-BASE!
IN YOUR FACE!
SCORE ...?
BUT SHE SURE IS CUTE!! WE HAD A GREAT TIME!!
SHE'S SO DYNAMIC! SHE EATS, SINGS AND TALKS SO WELL. SHE LOVES TO EAT, SHE LOVES TO SING, AND SHE LOVES TO TALK! JUST MY TYPE! I'D LOVE TO TAKE HER AWAY WITH ME...IF YOU GET MY DRIFT.
Reality Cam
IF I WERE ONLY A FEW YEARS YOUNGER, I COULD'VE BEEN ASSIGNED TO THE SCHOOL INSTEAD OF YOU.
!
WAIT A MINUTE!
THAT SUCKS...

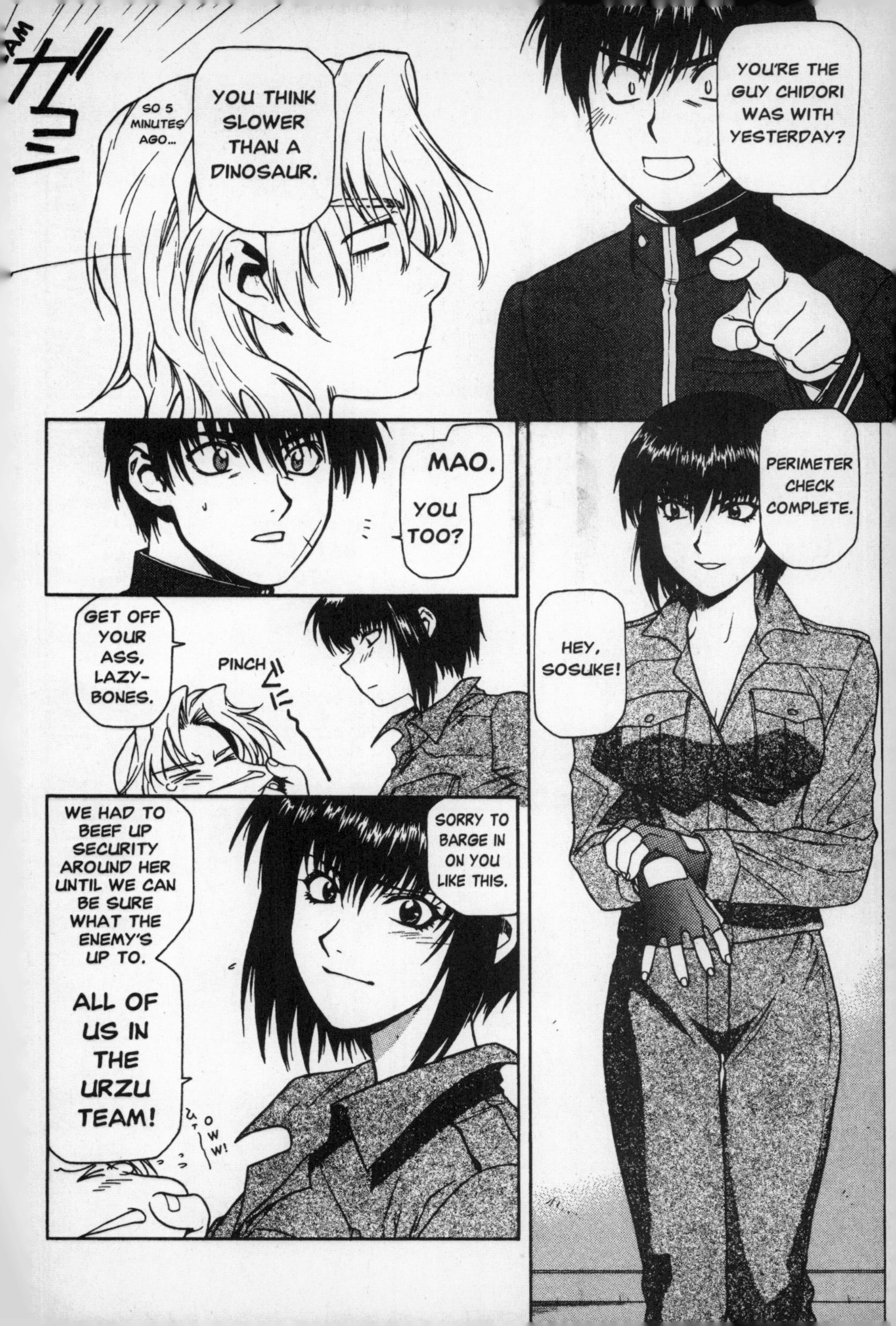

YOU'RE THE GUY CHIDORI WAS WITH YESTERDAY?
SO 5 MINUTES AGO...
YOU THINK SLOWER THAN A DINOSAUR.
PERIMETER CHECK COMPLETE.
HEY, SOSUKE!
MAO.
YOU TOO?
GET OFF YOUR ASS, LAZY-BONES.
PINCH
SORRY TO BARGE IN ON YOU LIKE THIS.
WE HAD TO BEEF UP SECURITY AROUND HER UNTIL WE CAN BE SURE WHAT THE ENEMY'S UP TO.
ALL OF US IN THE URZU TEAM!
OWW!

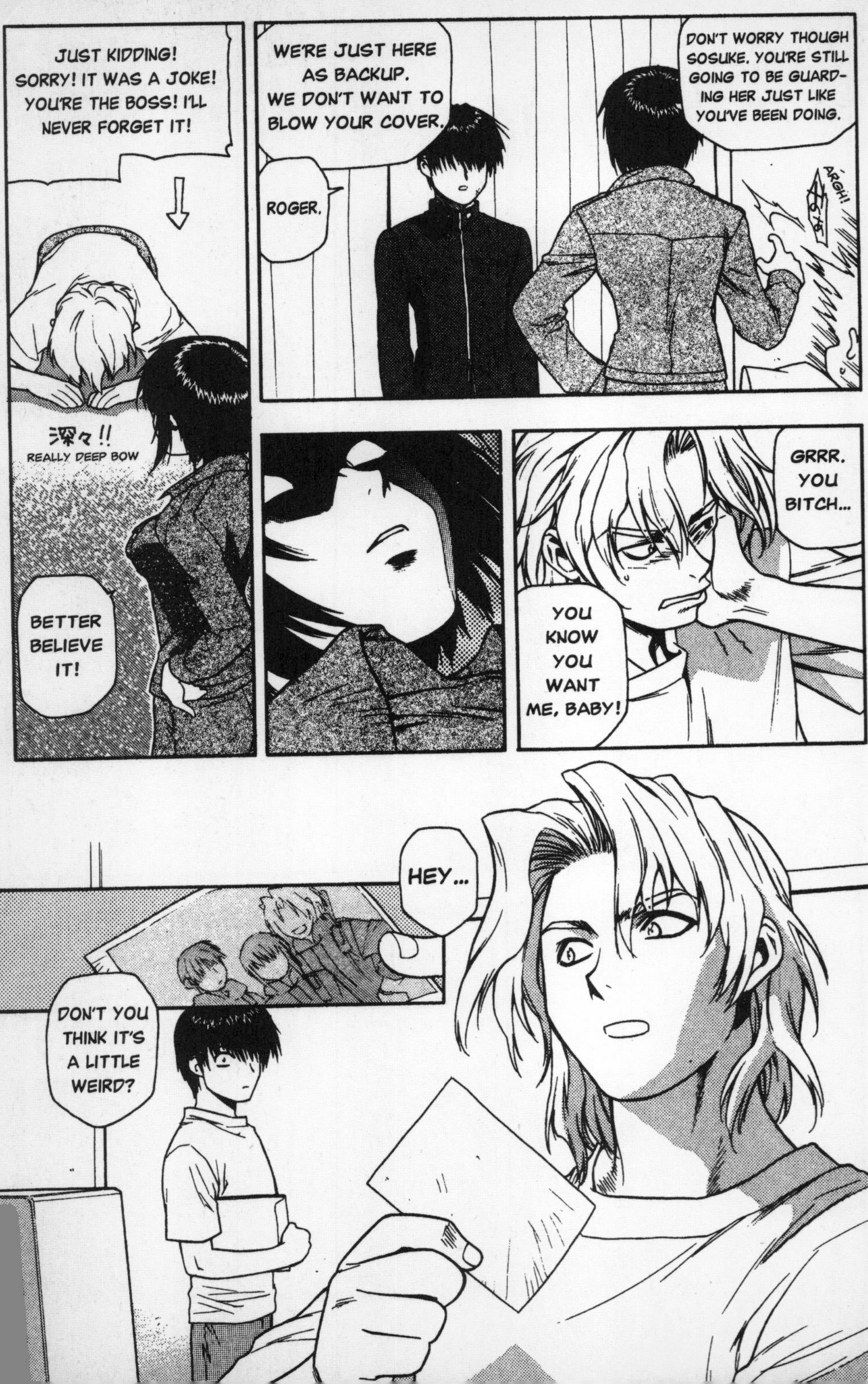
DON'T WORRY THOUGH SOSUKE. YOU'RE STILL GOING TO BE GUARDING HER JUST LIKE YOU'VE BEEN DOING.
WE'RE JUST HERE AS BACKUP. WE DON'T WANT TO BLOW YOUR COVER.
ROGER.
ARGH!
GRRR. YOU BITCH...
YOU KNOW YOU WANT ME, BABY!
JUST KIDDING! SORRY! IT WAS A JOKE! YOU'RE THE BOSS! I'LL NEVER FORGET IT!
深々!!
REALLY DEEP BOW
BETTER BELIEVE IT!
HEY...
DON'T YOU THINK IT'S A LITTLE WEIRD?

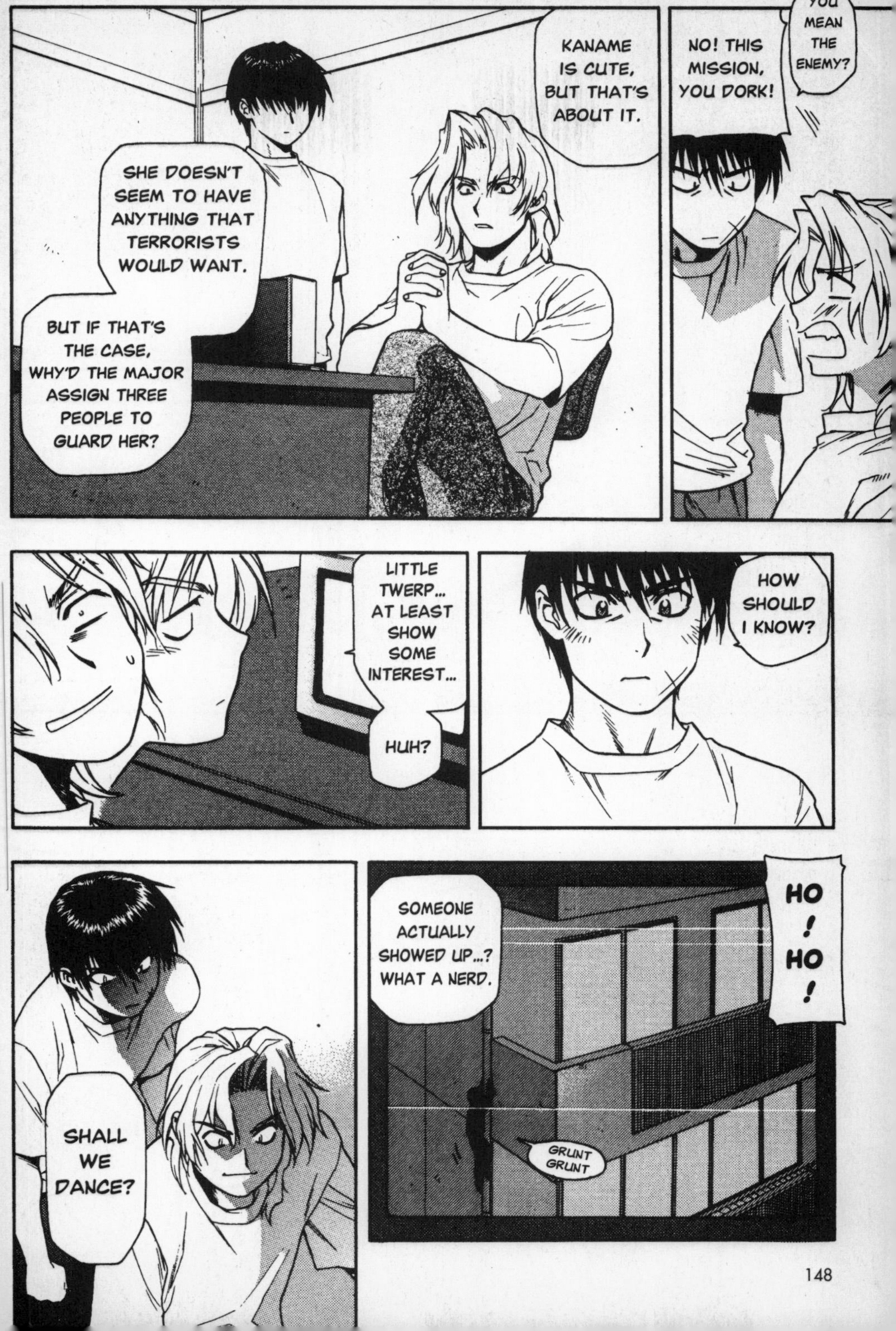
YOU MEAN THE ENEMY?
NO! THIS MISSION, YOU DORK!
KANAME IS CUTE, BUT THAT'S ABOUT IT.
SHE DOESN'T SEEM TO HAVE ANYTHING THAT TERRORISTS WOULD WANT.
BUT IF THAT'S THE CASE, WHY'D THE MAJOR ASSIGN THREE PEOPLE TO GUARD HER?
HOW SHOULD I KNOW?
LITTLE TWERP... AT LEAST SHOW SOME INTEREST...
HUH?
HO! HO!
SOMEONE ACTUALLY SHOWED UP...? WHAT A NERD.
GRUNT GRUNT
SHALL WE DANCE?

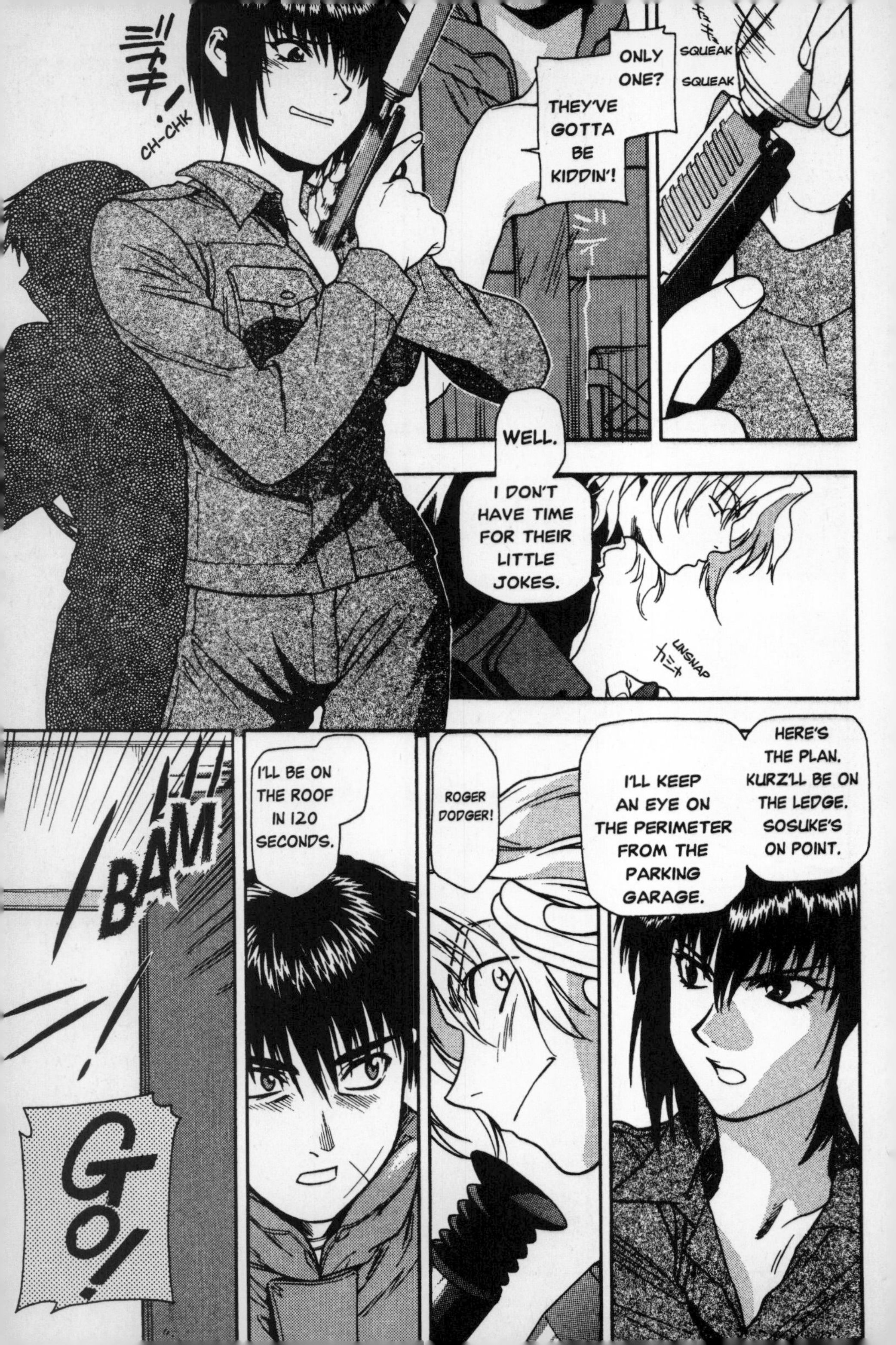
SQUEAK
SQUEAK
ONLY ONE?
THEY'VE GOTTA BE KIDDIN'!
WELL.
I DON'T HAVE TIME FOR THEIR LITTLE JOKES.
UNSNAP
CH-CHK
HERE'S THE PLAN. KURZ'LL BE ON THE LEDGE. SOSUKE'S ON POINT.
I'LL KEEP AN EYE ON THE PERIMETER FROM THE PARKING GARAGE.
ROGER DODGER!
I'LL BE ON THE ROOF IN 120 SECONDS.
BAM
GO!

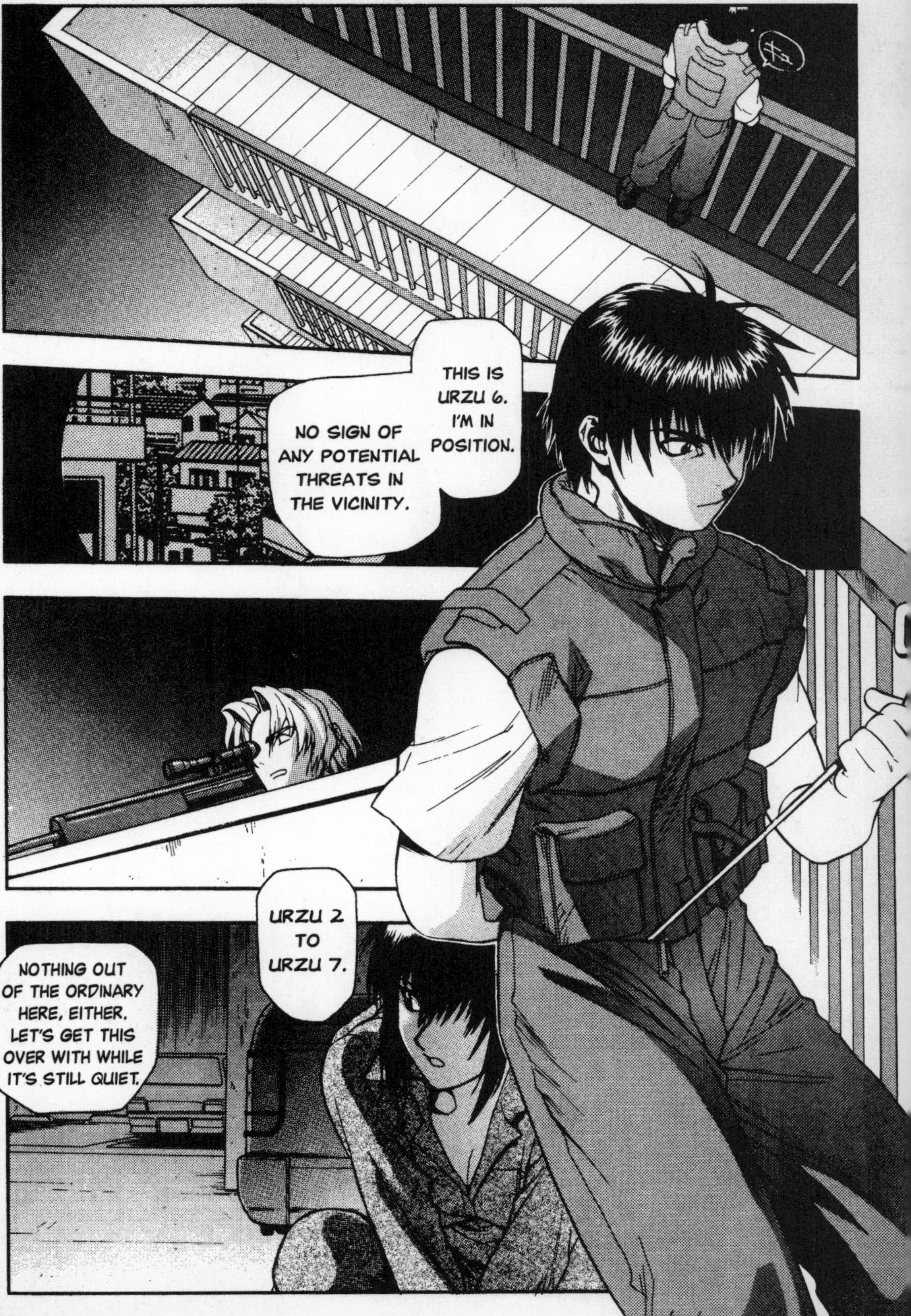
THIS IS URZU 6. I'M IN POSITION.
NO SIGN OF ANY POTENTIAL THREATS IN THE VICINITY.
URZU 2 TO URZU 7.
NOTHING OUT OF THE ORDINARY HERE, EITHER. LET'S GET THIS OVER WITH WHILE IT'S STILL QUIET.

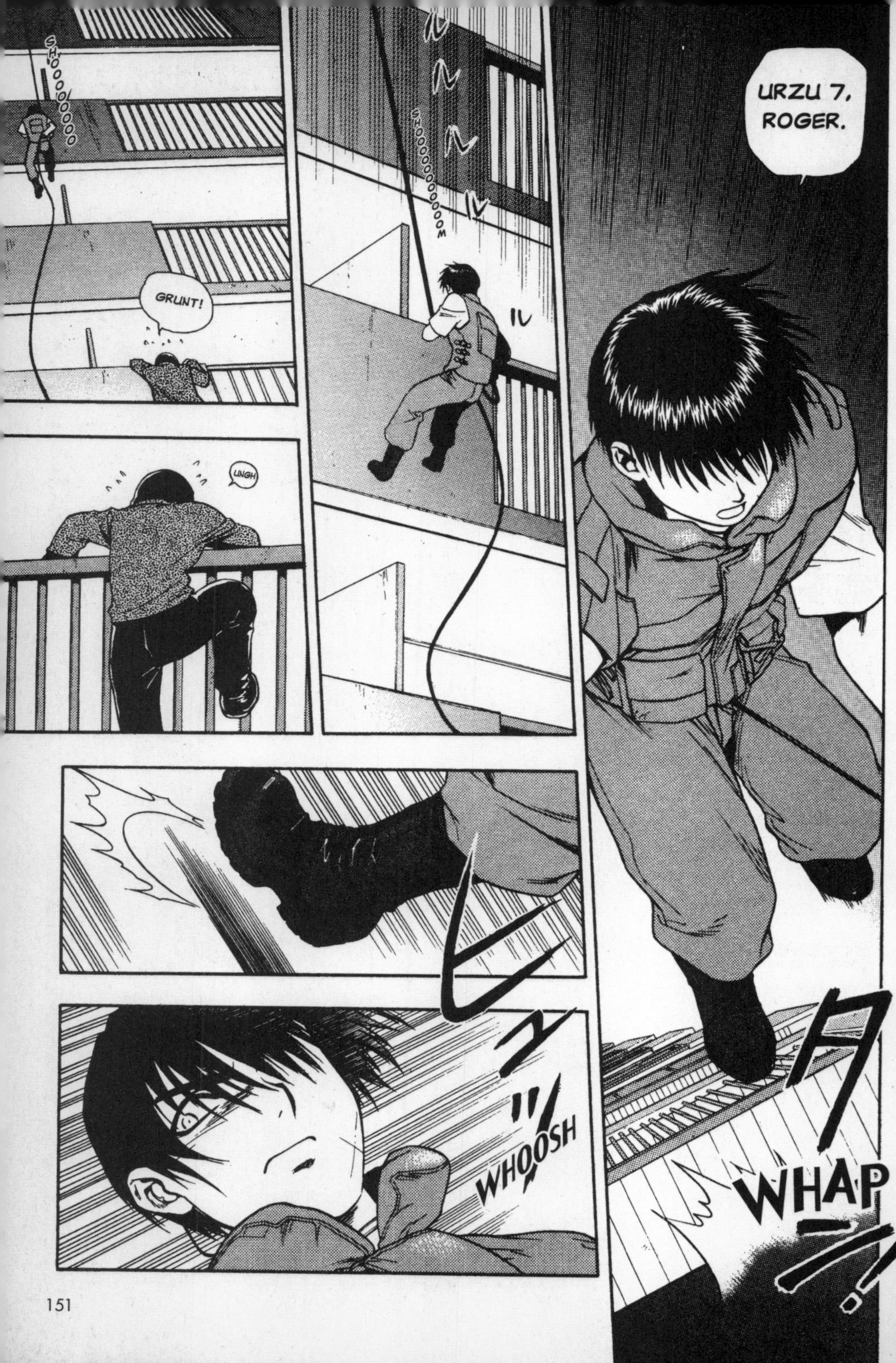

URZU 7, ROGER.
WHAP
SHOOOOOOOOOOOOOM
SHOOOOOOOOOO
GRUNT!
UNGH
WHOOSH

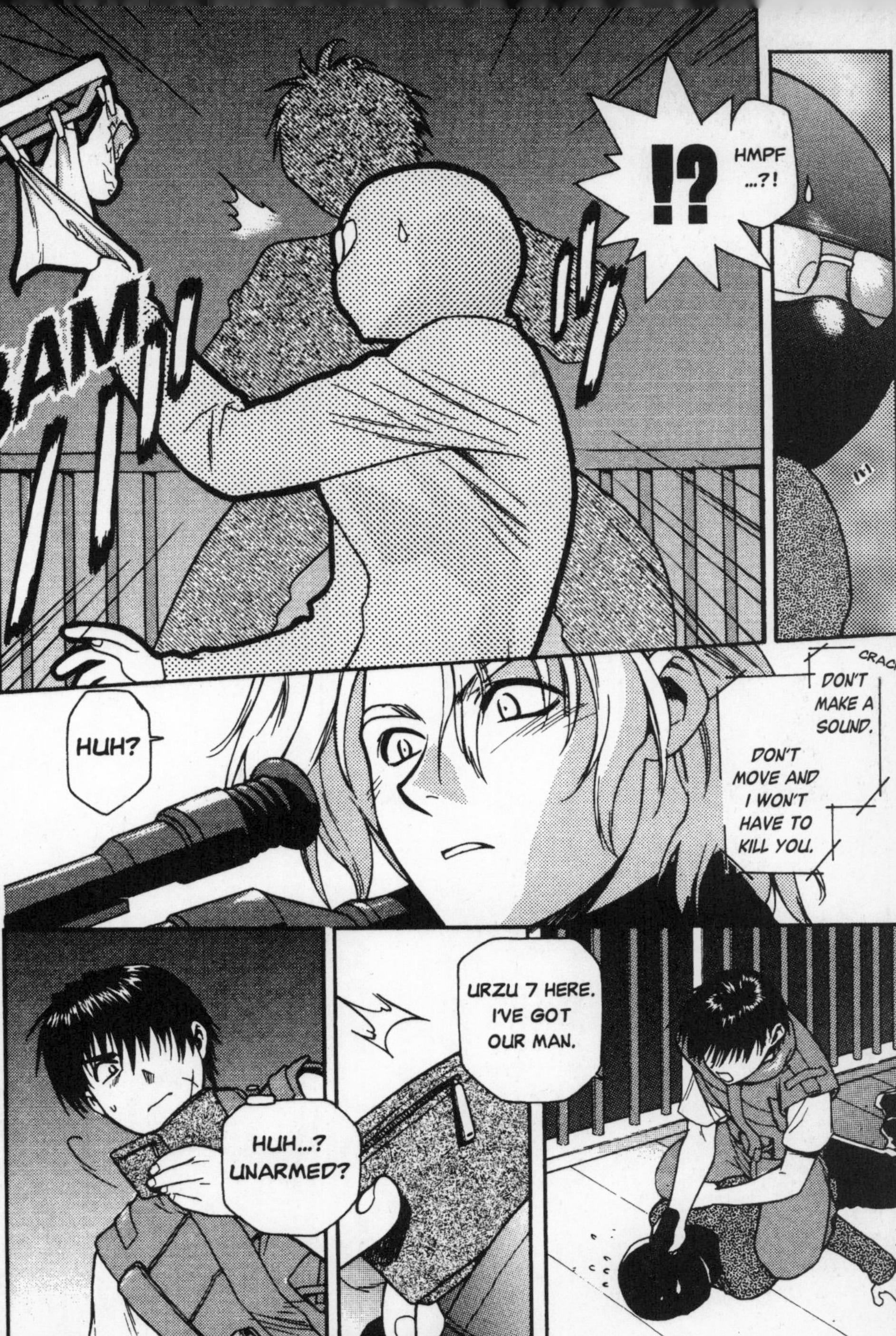
HMPF ...?!
!?
BAM
CRACKLE
DON'T MAKE A SOUND.
DON'T MOVE AND I WON'T HAVE TO KILL YOU.
HUH?
URZU 7 HERE. I'VE GOT OUR MAN.
HUH...? UNARMED?

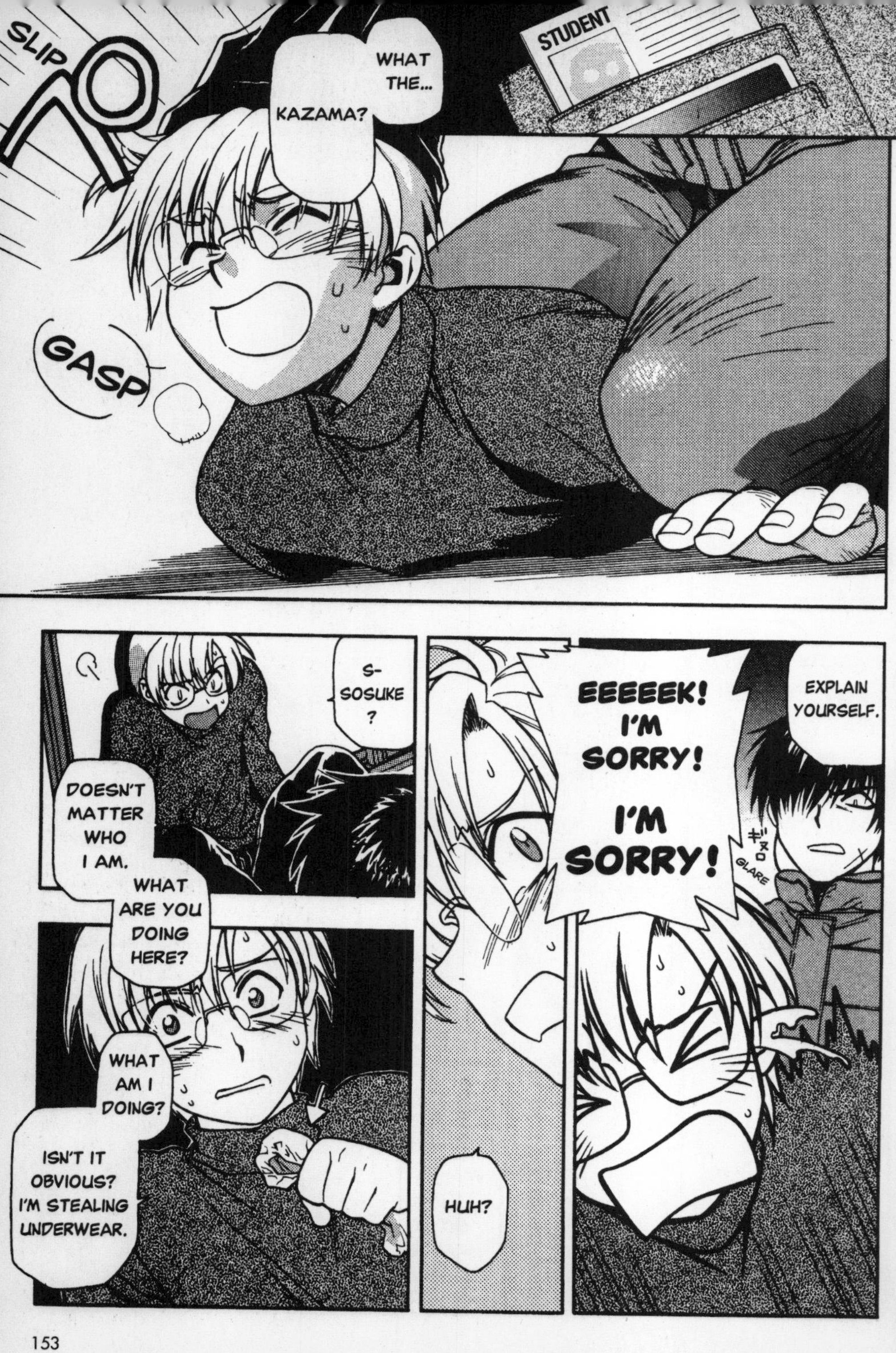
STUDENT
WHAT THE...
KAZAMA?
SLIP
GASP
S-SOSUKE?
DOESN'T MATTER WHO I AM.
WHAT ARE YOU DOING HERE?
WHAT AM I DOING?
ISN'T IT OBVIOUS? I'M STEALING UNDERWEAR.
HUH?
EXPLAIN YOURSELF.
ギヌロ
GLARE
EEEEEK! I'M SORRY!
I'M SORRY!

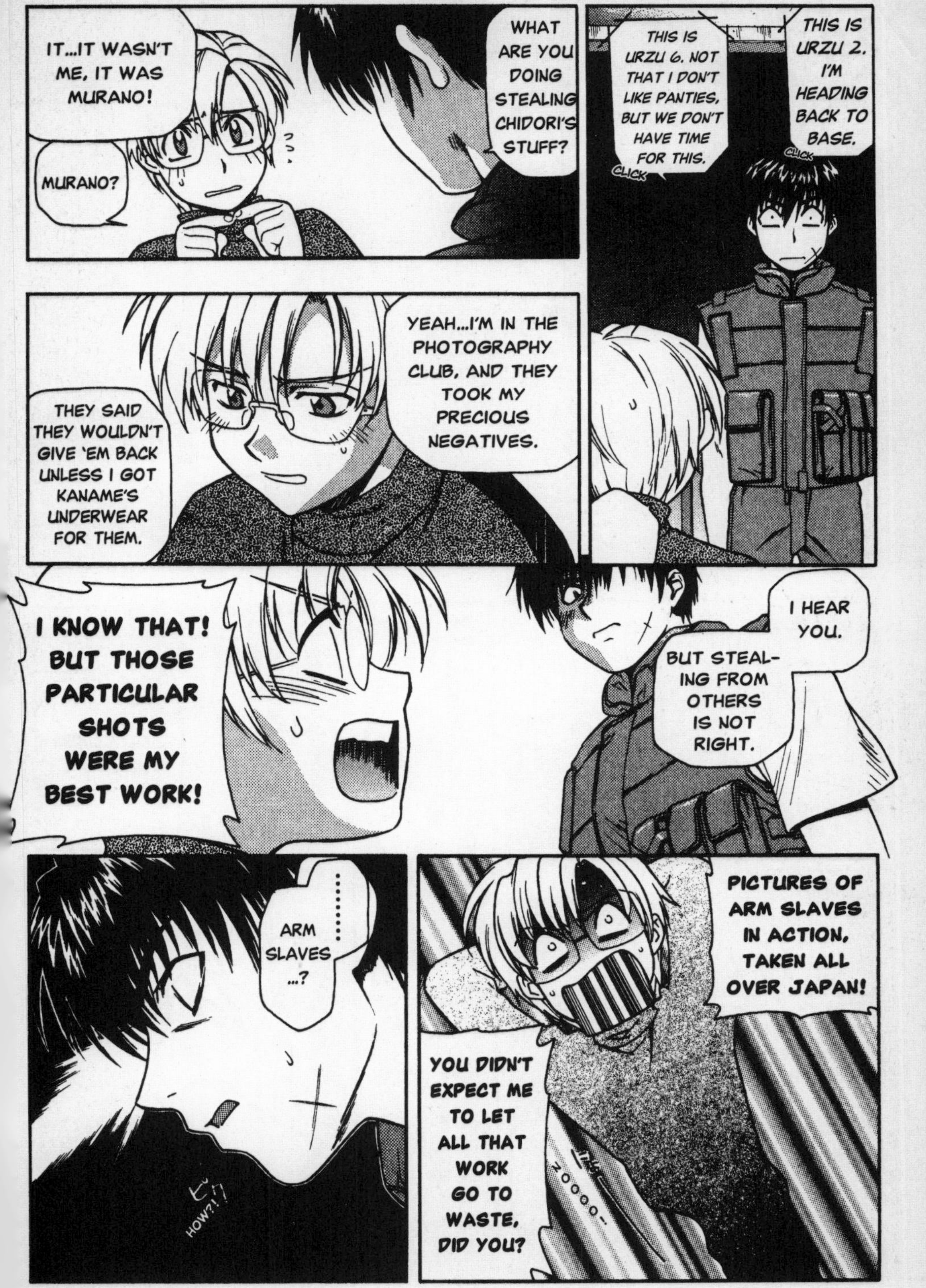
THIS IS URZU 2. I'M HEADING BACK TO BASE.
CLICK
THIS IS URZU 6. NOT THAT I DON'T LIKE PANTIES, BUT WE DON'T HAVE TIME FOR THIS.
CLICK
WHAT ARE YOU DOING STEALING CHIDORI'S STUFF?
IT...IT WASN'T ME, IT WAS MURANO!
MURANO?
YEAH...I'M IN THE PHOTOGRAPHY CLUB, AND THEY TOOK MY PRECIOUS NEGATIVES.
THEY SAID THEY WOULDN'T GIVE 'EM BACK UNLESS I GOT KANAME'S UNDERWEAR FOR THEM.
I HEAR YOU.
BUT STEAL-ING FROM OTHERS IS NOT RIGHT.
I KNOW THAT! BUT THOSE PARTICULAR SHOTS WERE MY BEST WORK!
PICTURES OF ARM SLAVES IN ACTION, TAKEN ALL OVER JAPAN!
YOU DIDN'T EXPECT ME TO LET ALL THAT WORK GO TO WASTE, DID YOU?
......
ARM SLAVES ...?
HOW?!

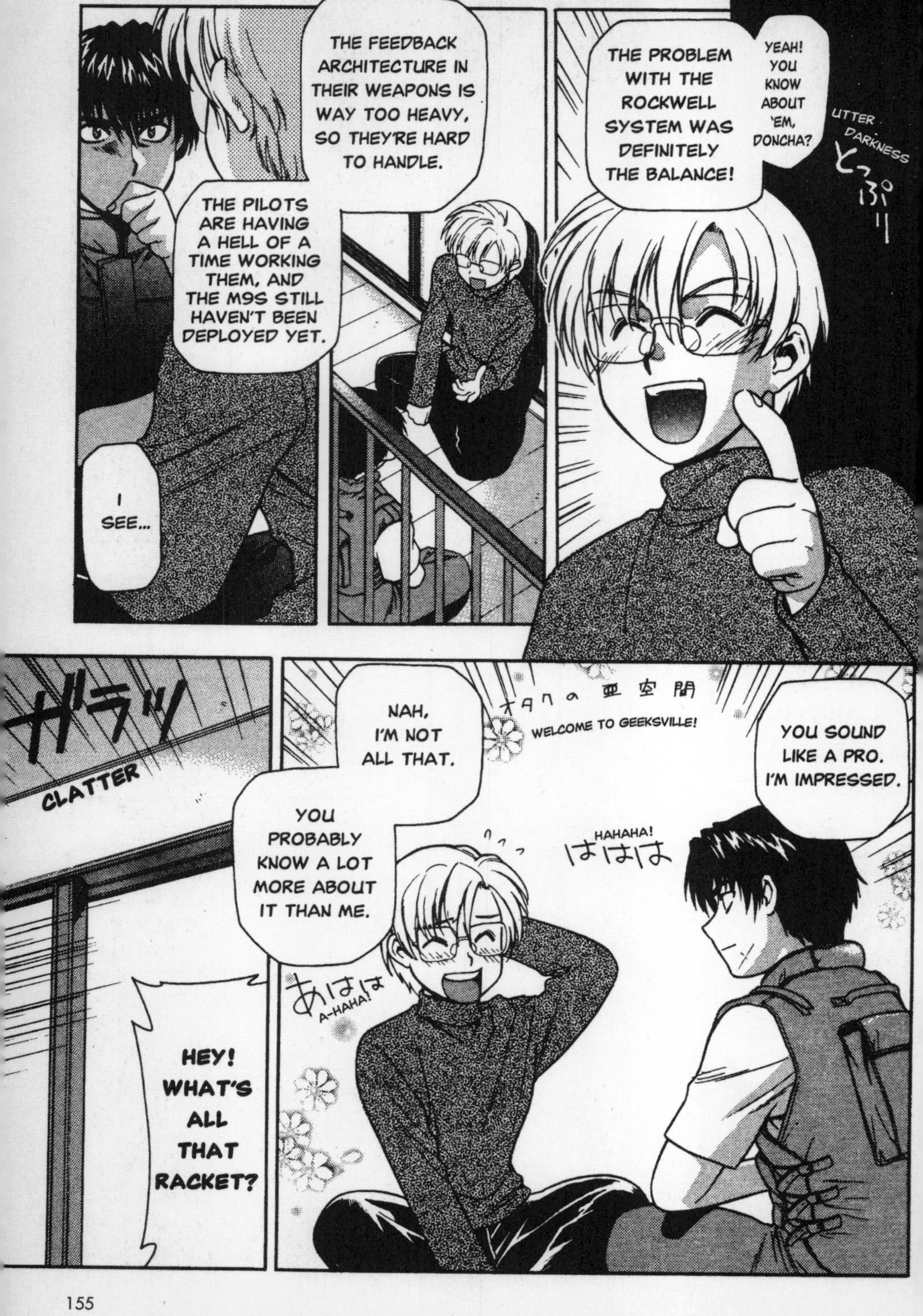
YEAH! YOU KNOW ABOUT 'EM, DONCHA?
THE PROBLEM WITH THE ROCKWELL SYSTEM WAS DEFINITELY THE BALANCE!
とっぷり
UTTER DARKNESS
THE FEEDBACK ARCHITECTURE IN THEIR WEAPONS IS WAY TOO HEAVY, SO THEY'RE HARD TO HANDLE.
THE PILOTS ARE HAVING A HELL OF A TIME WORKING THEM, AND THE M9S STILL HAVEN'T BEEN DEPLOYED YET.
I SEE...
YOU SOUND LIKE A PRO. I'M IMPRESSED.
オタクの亜空間
WELCOME TO GEEKSVILLE!
NAH, I'M NOT ALL THAT.
ははは
HAHAHA!
YOU PROBABLY KNOW A LOT MORE ABOUT IT THAN ME.
あはは
A-HAHA!
ガラッ
CLATTER
HEY! WHAT'S ALL THAT RACKET?

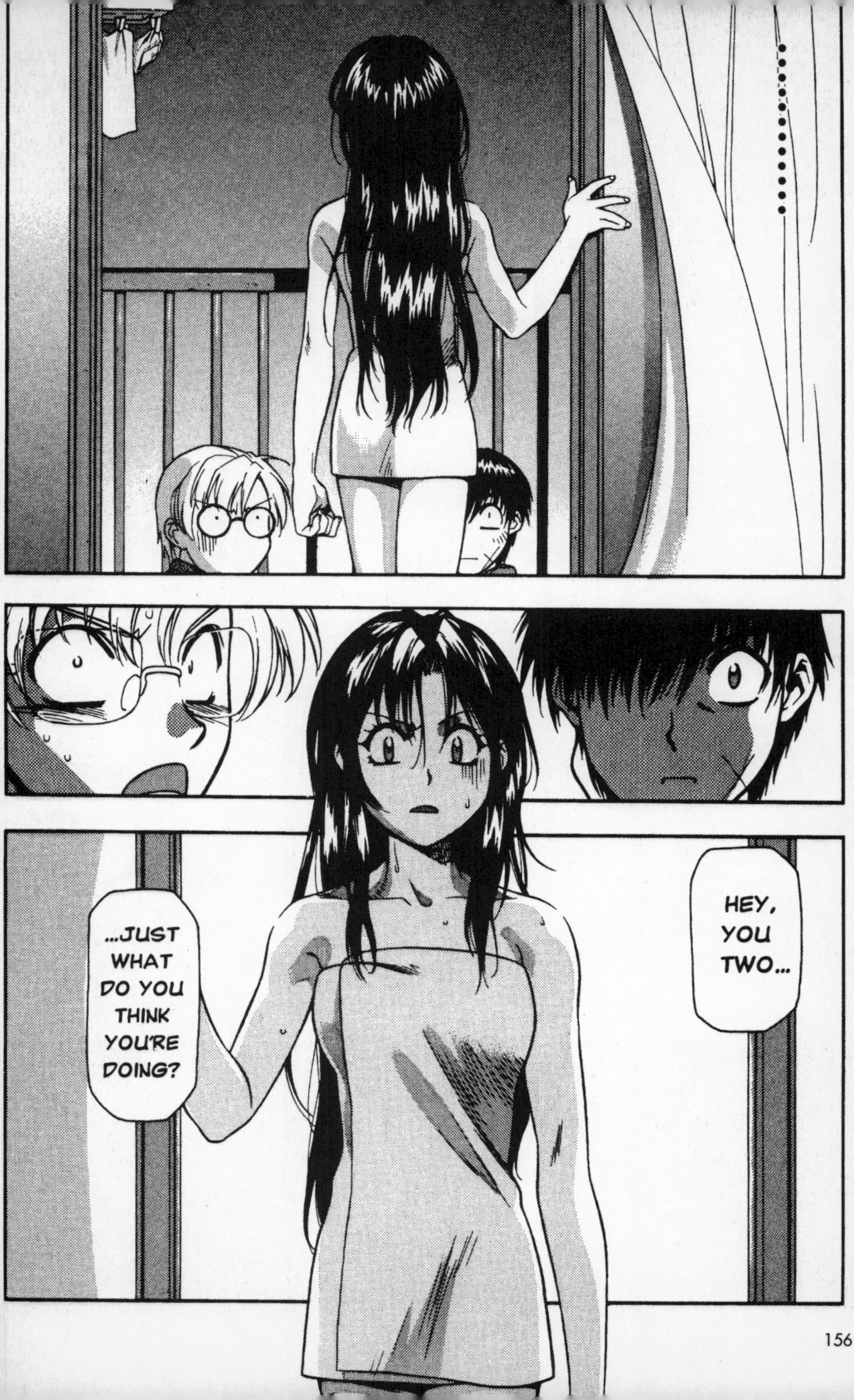
HEY, YOU TWO...
...JUST WHAT DO YOU THINK YOU'RE DOING?

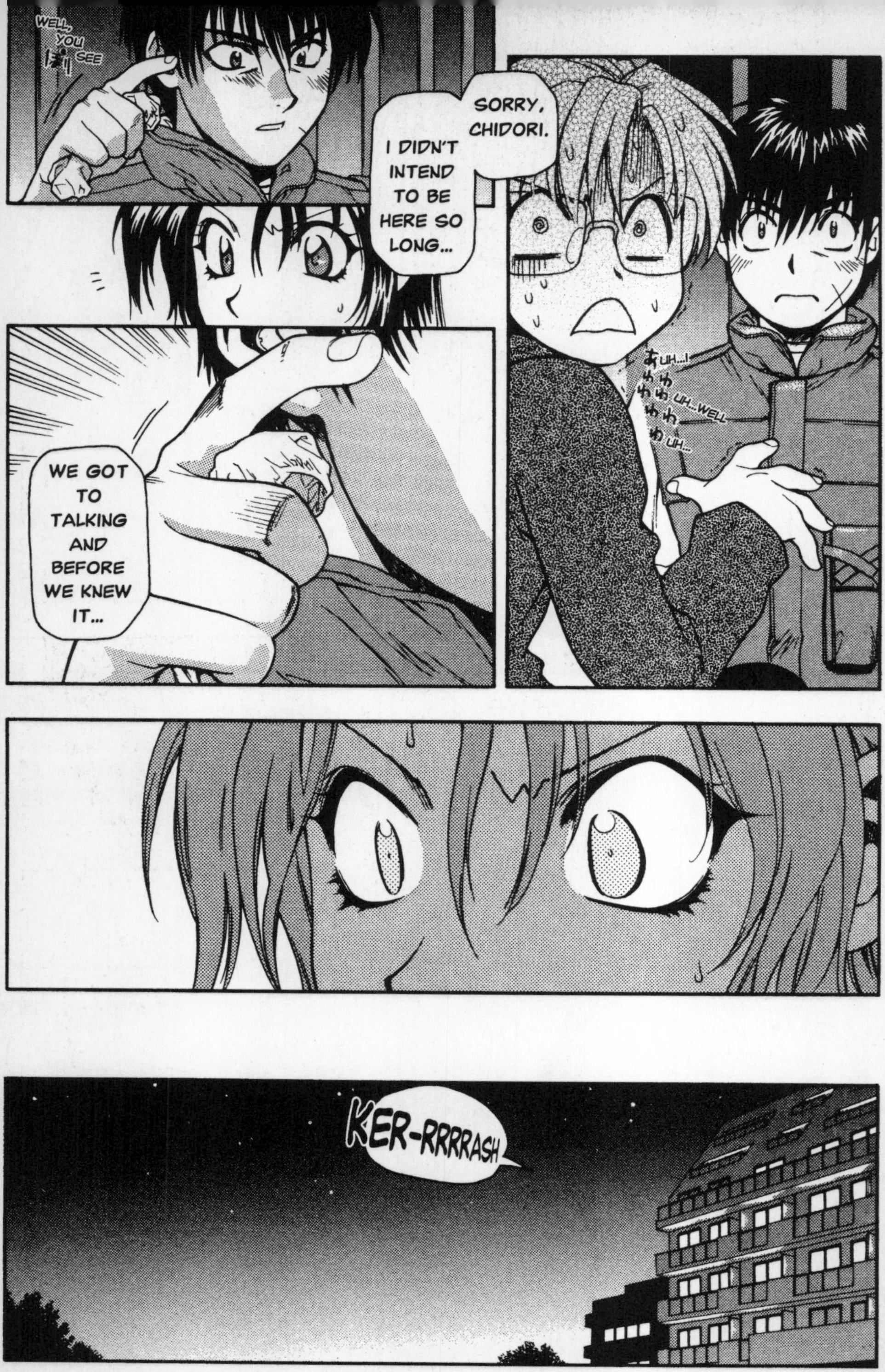
SORRY, CHIDORI. I DIDN'T INTEND TO BE HERE SO LONG...
UH...!
UH...WELL
UH...
WELL, YOU SEE
WE GOT TO TALKING AND BEFORE WE KNEW IT...
KER-RRRRASH

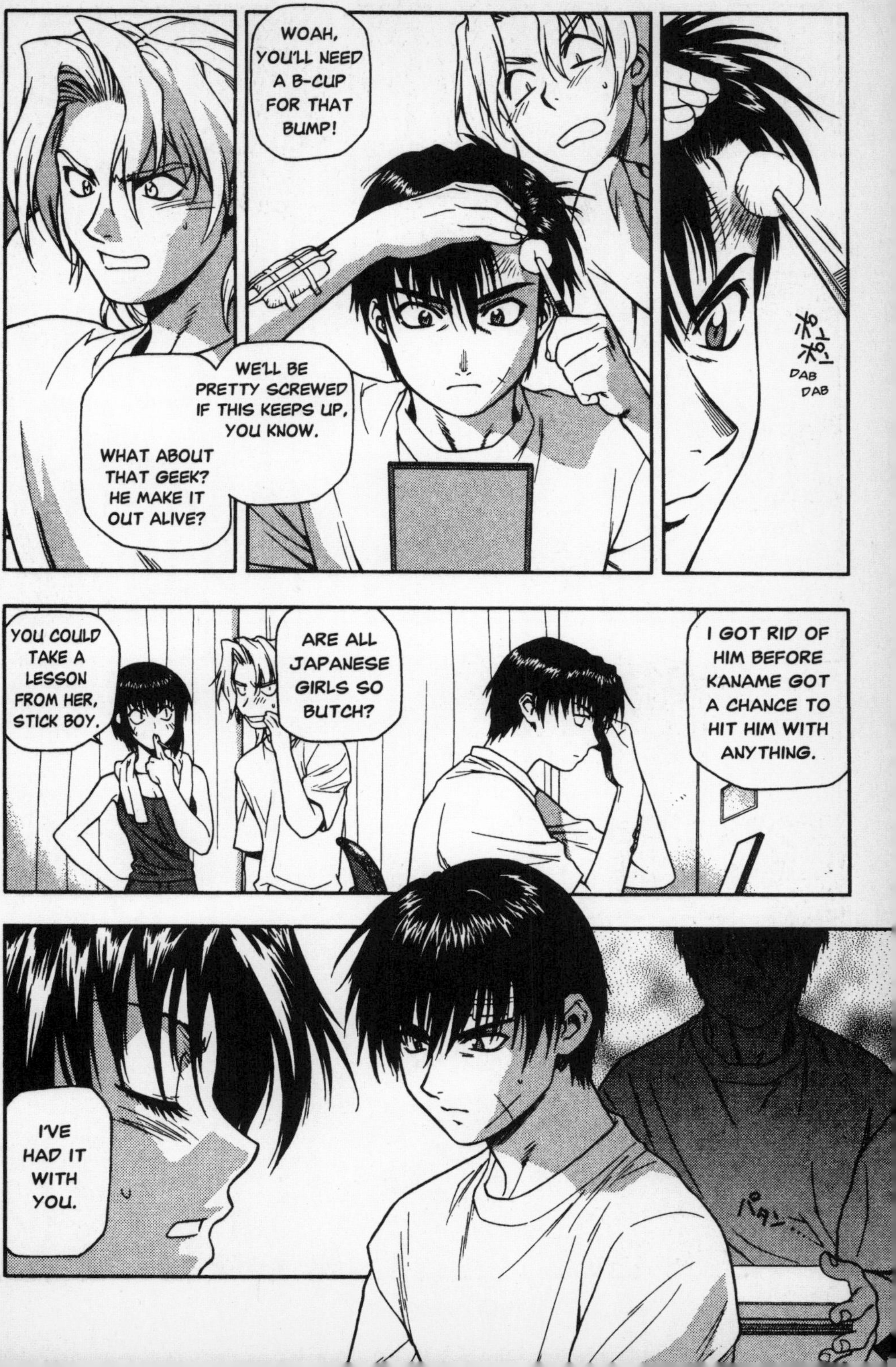
DAB DAB
WOAH, YOU'LL NEED A B-CUP FOR THAT BUMP!
WE'LL BE PRETTY SCREWED IF THIS KEEPS UP, YOU KNOW.
WHAT ABOUT THAT GEEK? HE MAKE IT OUT ALIVE?
I GOT RID OF HIM BEFORE KANAME GOT A CHANCE TO HIT HIM WITH ANYTHING.
ARE ALL JAPANESE GIRLS SO BUTCH?
YOU COULD TAKE A LESSON FROM HER, STICK BOY.
I'VE HAD IT WITH YOU.

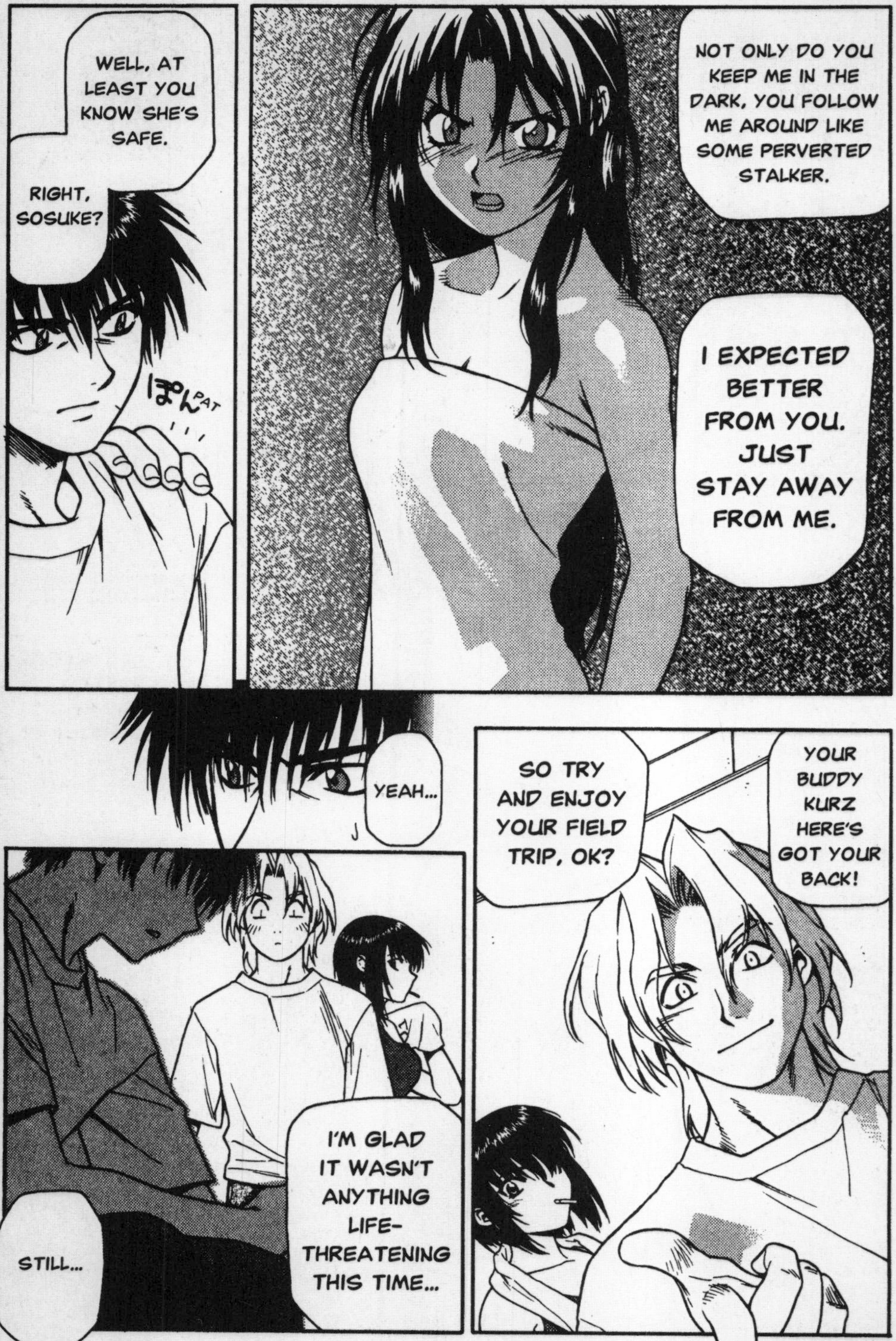
NOT ONLY DO YOU KEEP ME IN THE DARK, YOU FOLLOW ME AROUND LIKE SOME PERVERTED STALKER.
I EXPECTED BETTER FROM YOU. JUST STAY AWAY FROM ME.
WELL, AT LEAST YOU KNOW SHE'S SAFE.
RIGHT, SOSUKE?
ぽん PAT
YOUR BUDDY KURZ HERE'S GOT YOUR BACK!
SO TRY AND ENJOY YOUR FIELD TRIP, OK?
YEAH...
I'M GLAD IT WASN'T ANYTHING LIFE-THREATENING THIS TIME...
STILL...

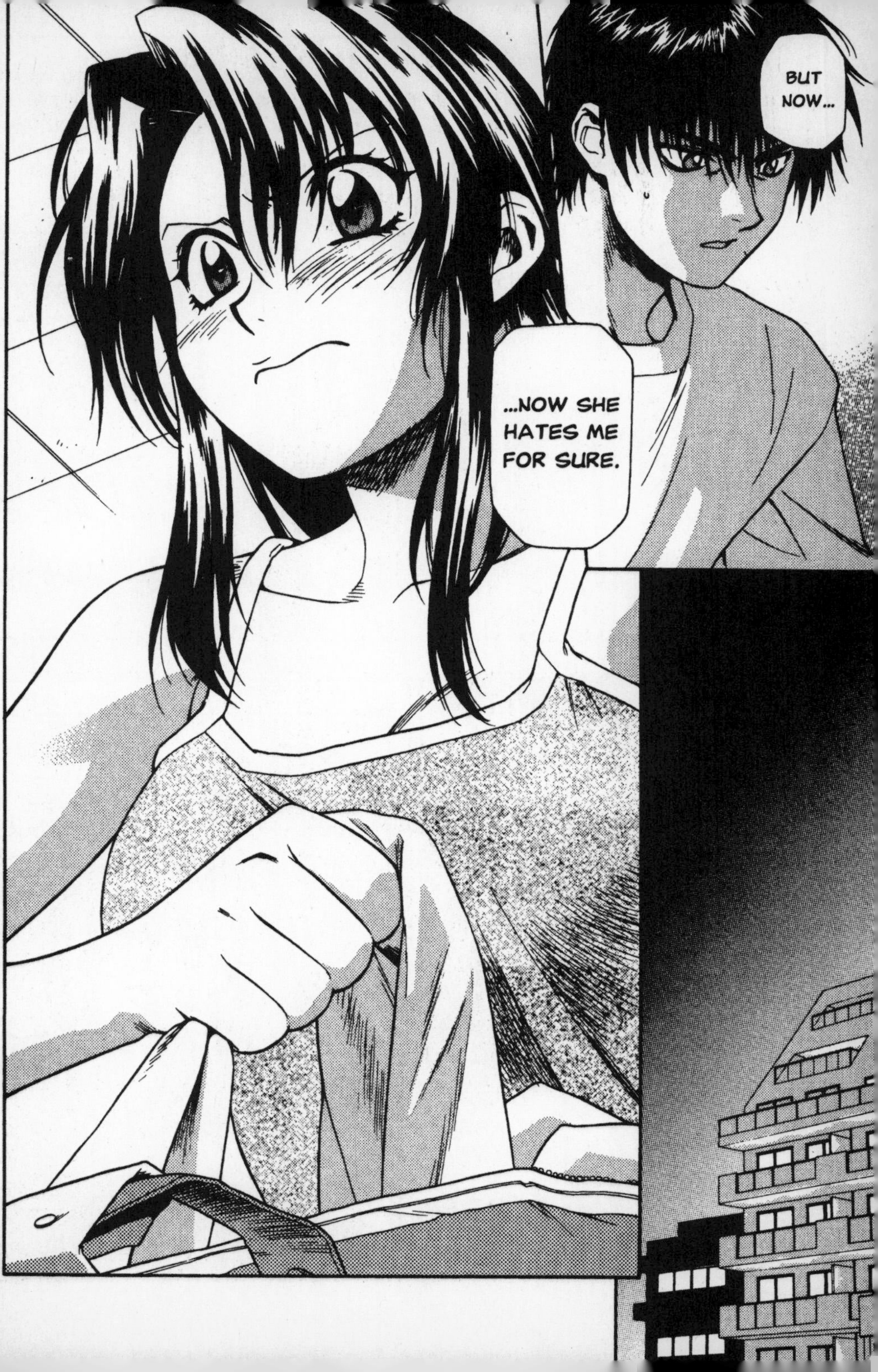
BUT NOW...
...NOW SHE HATES ME FOR SURE.

INCONTINENCE MANGA CHAPTER 56

MATCHING THE FACE

GIB MELSON

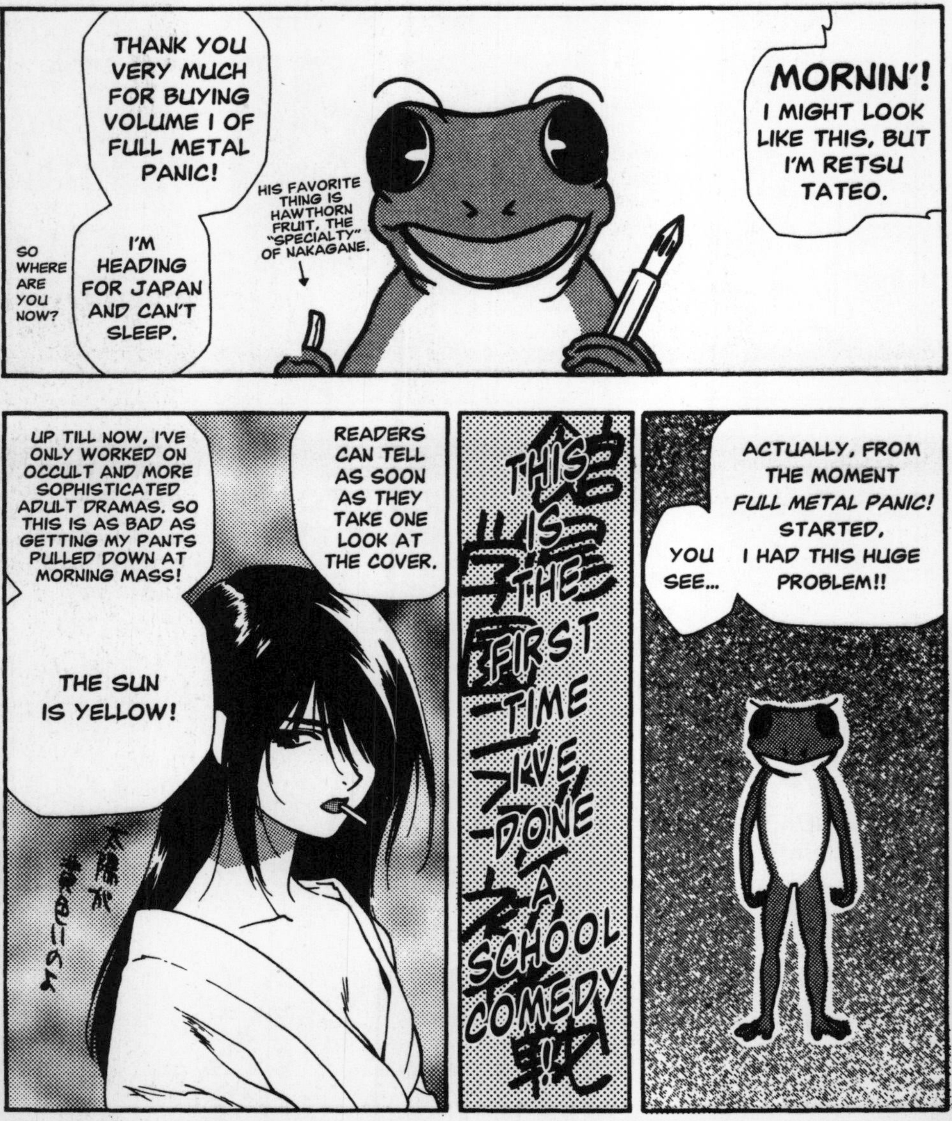
MORNIN'! I MIGHT LOOK LIKE THIS, BUT I'M RETSU TATEO.
THANK YOU VERY MUCH FOR BUYING VOLUME 1 OF FULL METAL PANIC!
HIS FAVORITE THING IS HAWTHORN FRUIT, THE "SPECIALTY" OF NAKAGANE.
I'M HEADING FOR JAPAN AND CAN'T SLEEP.
SO WHERE ARE YOU NOW?
ACTUALLY, FROM THE MOMENT *FULL METAL PANIC!* STARTED, I HAD THIS HUGE PROBLEM!!
YOU SEE...
THIS IS THE FIRST TIME I'VE DONE A SCHOOL COMEDY
READERS CAN TELL AS SOON AS THEY TAKE ONE LOOK AT THE COVER.
UP TILL NOW, I'VE ONLY WORKED ON OCCULT AND MORE SOPHISTICATED ADULT DRAMAS. SO THIS IS AS BAD AS GETTING MY PANTS PULLED DOWN AT MORNING MASS!
THE SUN IS YELLOW!

NEVER HAD THAT HAPPEN BEFORE... ↓

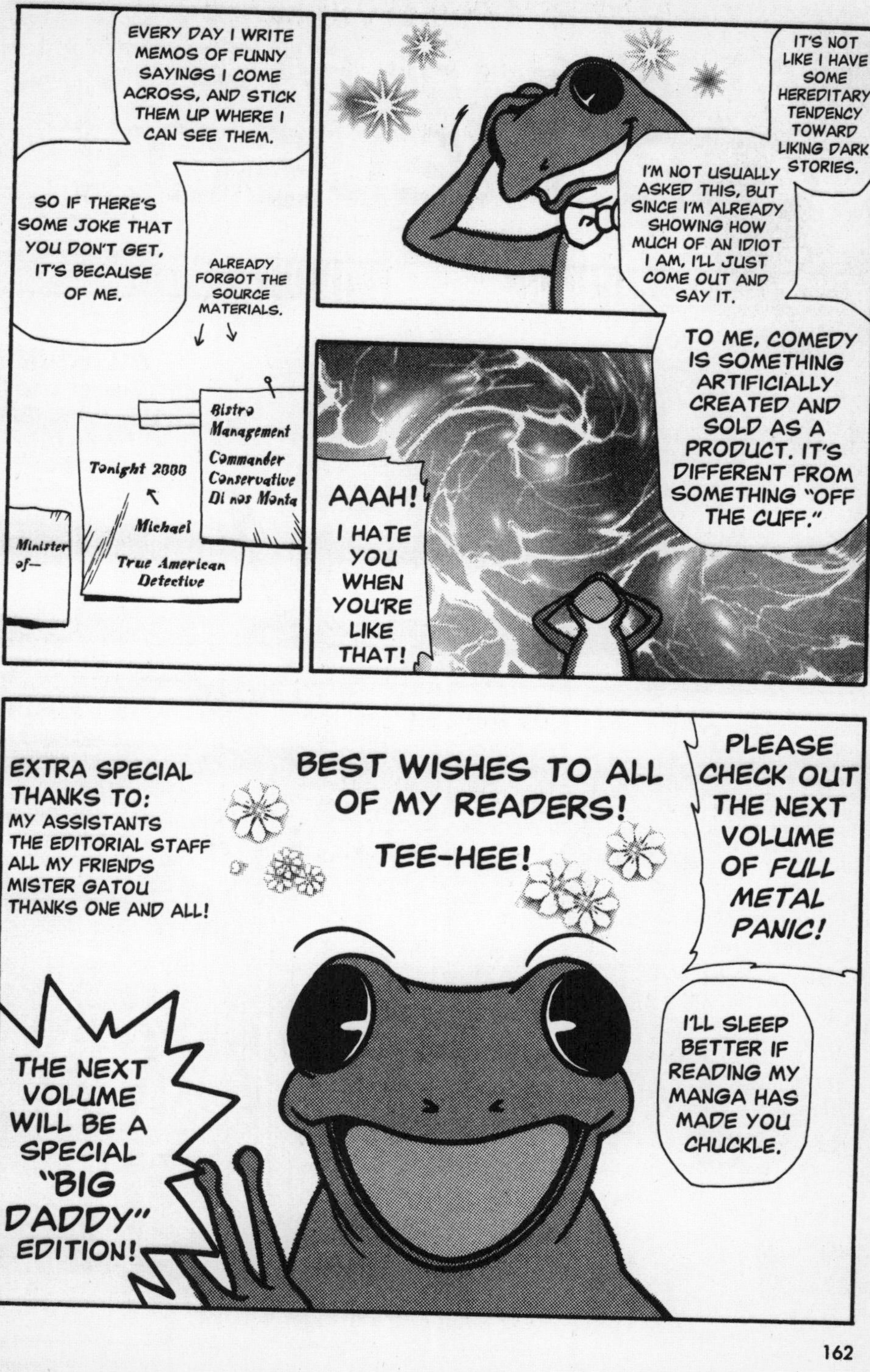
IT'S NOT LIKE I HAVE SOME HEREDITARY TENDENCY TOWARD LIKING DARK STORIES.
I'M NOT USUALLY ASKED THIS, BUT SINCE I'M ALREADY SHOWING HOW MUCH OF AN IDIOT I AM, I'LL JUST COME OUT AND SAY IT.
TO ME, COMEDY IS SOMETHING ARTIFICIALLY CREATED AND SOLD AS A PRODUCT. IT'S DIFFERENT FROM SOMETHING "OFF THE CUFF."
AAAH! I HATE YOU WHEN YOU'RE LIKE THAT!
EVERY DAY I WRITE MEMOS OF FUNNY SAYINGS I COME ACROSS, AND STICK THEM UP WHERE I CAN SEE THEM.
SO IF THERE'S SOME JOKE THAT YOU DON'T GET, IT'S BECAUSE OF ME.
ALREADY FORGOT THE SOURCE MATERIALS.
Bistro Management
Commander Conservative
Di nos Monta
Tonight 2000
Michael
True American Detective
Minister of—
PLEASE CHECK OUT THE NEXT VOLUME OF FULL METAL PANIC!
BEST WISHES TO ALL OF MY READERS!
TEE-HEE!
EXTRA SPECIAL THANKS TO:
MY ASSISTANTS
THE EDITORIAL STAFF
ALL MY FRIENDS
MISTER GATOU
THANKS ONE AND ALL!
I'LL SLEEP BETTER IF READING MY MANGA HAS MADE YOU CHUCKLE.
THE NEXT VOLUME WILL BE A SPECIAL "BIG DADDY" EDITION!

Full Metal Panic! Volume One

Author **SHOUJI GATOU**

Illustrator **RETSU TATEO**

Character Creation **SHIKIDOUJI**

© 2000 RETSU TATEO • SHOUJI GATOU • SHIKIDOUJI

Originally published in Japan in 2000 by KADOKAWA SHOTEN PUBLISHING CO., LTD., Tokyo.

English translation rights arranged with KADOKAWA SHOTEN PUBLISHING CO., LTD., Tokyo.

Translator **JACK WIEDRICK**

Graphic Designer **TAWNA FRANZE**

Graphic Artist **RYAN MASON**

Publishing Editor **SUSAN ITIN**

Executive VP, C.F.O & C.O.O **KEVIN CORCORAN**

President, C.E.O. & Publisher **JOHN LEDFORD**

Email: editor@advfilms.com
www.adv-manga.com
www.advfilms.com

For sales and distribution inquiries please call 1.800.282.7202

ADV MANGA™ is a division of A.D. Vision, Inc.
10114 W. Sam Houston Parkway, Suite 200, Houston, Texas 77099

English Text © 2003 Published by A.D. Vision, Inc. under exclusive license.
ADV MANGA is a trademark of A.D. Vision, Inc.

ISBN: 1-4139-0001-1

First printing, August 2003

10 9 8 7 6 5 4 3 2
Printed in Canada

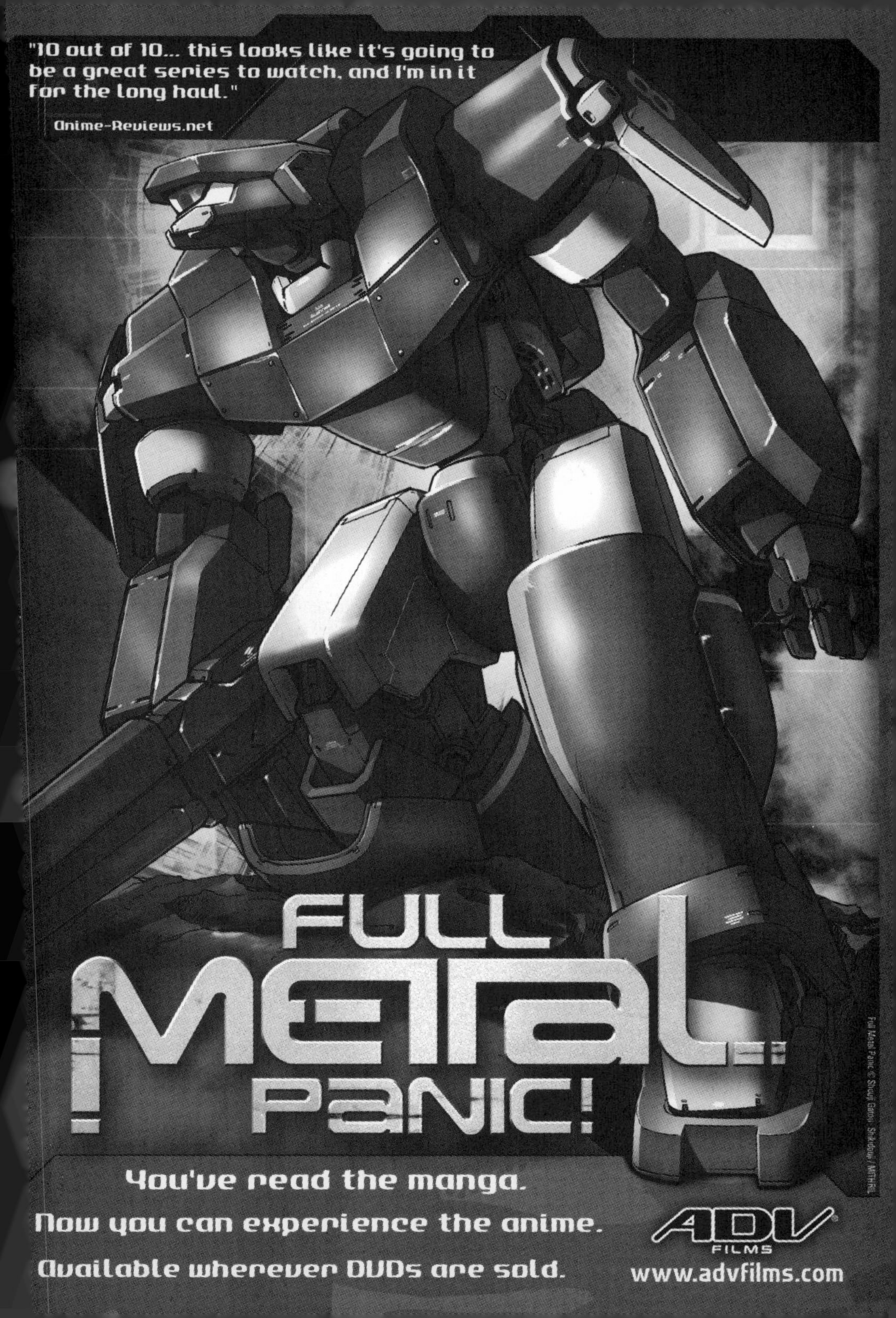
"10 out of 10... this looks like it's going to be a great series to watch, and I'm in it for the long haul."
Anime-Reviews.net
FULL METAL PANIC!
You've read the manga.
Now you can experience the anime.
Available wherever DVDs are sold.
ADV FILMS
www.advfilms.com
Full Metal Panic © Shouji Gatou · Shikidouji / MITHRIL

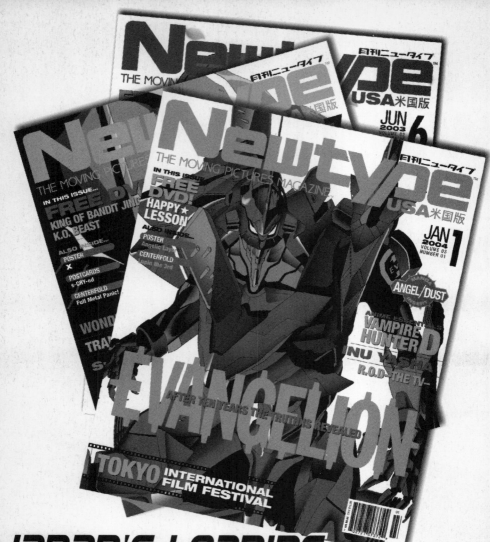
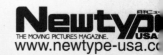

MITHRIL
WANTS YOU

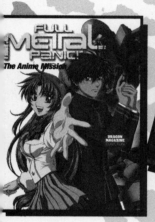

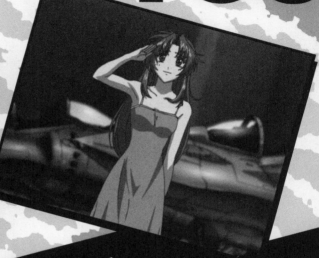

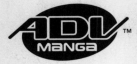

MANGA SURVEY

PLEASE MAIL THE COMPLETED FORM TO: EDITOR – ADV MANGA
c/o A.D. Vision, Inc. 10114 W. Sam Houston Pkwy., Suite 200 Houston, TX 77099

Name:____
Address:____
City, State, Zip:__________________________________

E-Mail:____
Male ☐ Female ☐ Age: ____________________

☐ ***CHECK HERE IF YOU WOULD LIKE TO RECEIVE OTHER INFORMATION OR FUTURE OFFERS FROM ADV.***

All information provided will be used for internal purposes only. We promise not to sell or otherwise divulge your information.

1. Annual Household Income (*Check only one*)
- ☐ Under $25,000
- ☐ $25,000 to $50,000
- ☐ $50,000 to $75,000
- ☐ Over $75,000

2. How do you hear about new Manga releases? (*Check all that apply*)
- ☐ Browsing in Store
- ☐ Internet Reviews
- ☐ Anime News Websites
- ☐ Direct Email Campaigns
- ☐ Magazine Ad
- ☐ Online Advertising
- ☐ Conventions
- ☐ TV Advertising
- ☐ Online forums (message boards and chat rooms)
- ☐ Carrier pigeon
- ☐ Other:____________________

3. Which magazines do you read? (*Check all that apply*)
- ☐ Wizard
- ☐ SPIN
- ☐ Animerica
- ☐ Rolling Stone
- ☐ Maxim
- ☐ DC Comics
- ☐ URB
- ☐ Polygon
- ☐ Original Play Station Magazine
- ☐ Entertainment Weekly
- ☐ YRB
- ☐ EGM
- ☐ Newtype USA
- ☐ SciFi
- ☐ Starlog
- ☐ Wired
- ☐ Vice
- ☐ BPM
- ☐ I hate reading
- ☐ Other:____________

4. Have you visited the ADV Manga website?
- ☐ Yes
- ☐ No

5. Have you made any Manga purchases online from the ADV website?
- ☐ Yes
- ☐ No

6. If you have visited the ADV Manga website, how would you rate your online experience?
- ☐ Excellent
- ☐ Good
- ☐ Average
- ☐ Poor

7. What genre of Manga do you prefer? *(Check all that apply)*
- ☐ adventure
- ☐ romance
- ☐ detective
- ☐ action
- ☐ horror
- ☐ sci-fi/fantasy
- ☐ sports
- ☐ comedy

8. How many manga titles have you purchased in the last 6 months?
- ☐ none
- ☐ 1-4
- ☐ 5-10
- ☐ 11+

9. Where do you make your manga purchases? *(Check all that apply)*
- ☐ comic store
- ☐ bookstore
- ☐ newsstand
- ☐ online
- ☐ other:_____
- ☐ department store
- ☐ grocery store
- ☐ video store
- ☐ video game store

10. Which bookstores do you usually make your manga purchases at?
- ☐ Barnes & Noble
- ☐ Walden Books
- ☐ Suncoast
- ☐ Best Buy
- ☐ Amazon.com
- ☐ Borders
- ☐ Books-A-Million
- ☐ Toys "Я" Us
- ☐ Other bookstore: _____

11. What's your favorite anime/manga website?
- ☐ adv-manga.com
- ☐ advfilms.com
- ☐ rightstuf.com
- ☐ animenewsservice.com
- ☐ animenewsnetwork.com
- ☐ Other:_____
- ☐ animeondvd.com
- ☐ anipike.com
- ☐ animeonline.net
- ☐ planetanime.com
- ☐ animenation.com

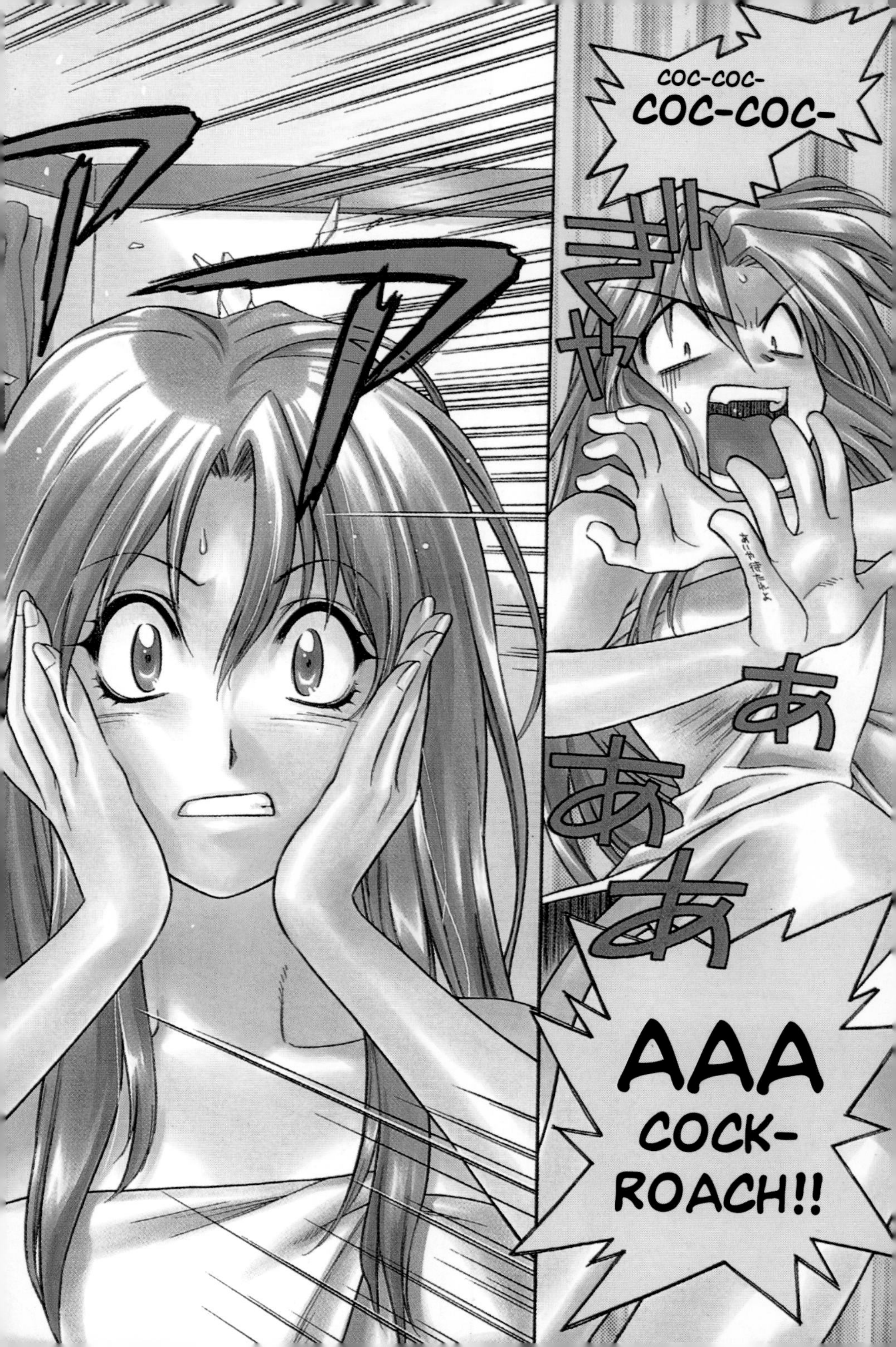
COC-COC-
COC-COC-
ぎゃ
あああ
AAA
COCK-
ROACH!!
アア

MISSION:01

The transfer student is a dangerous soldier!?

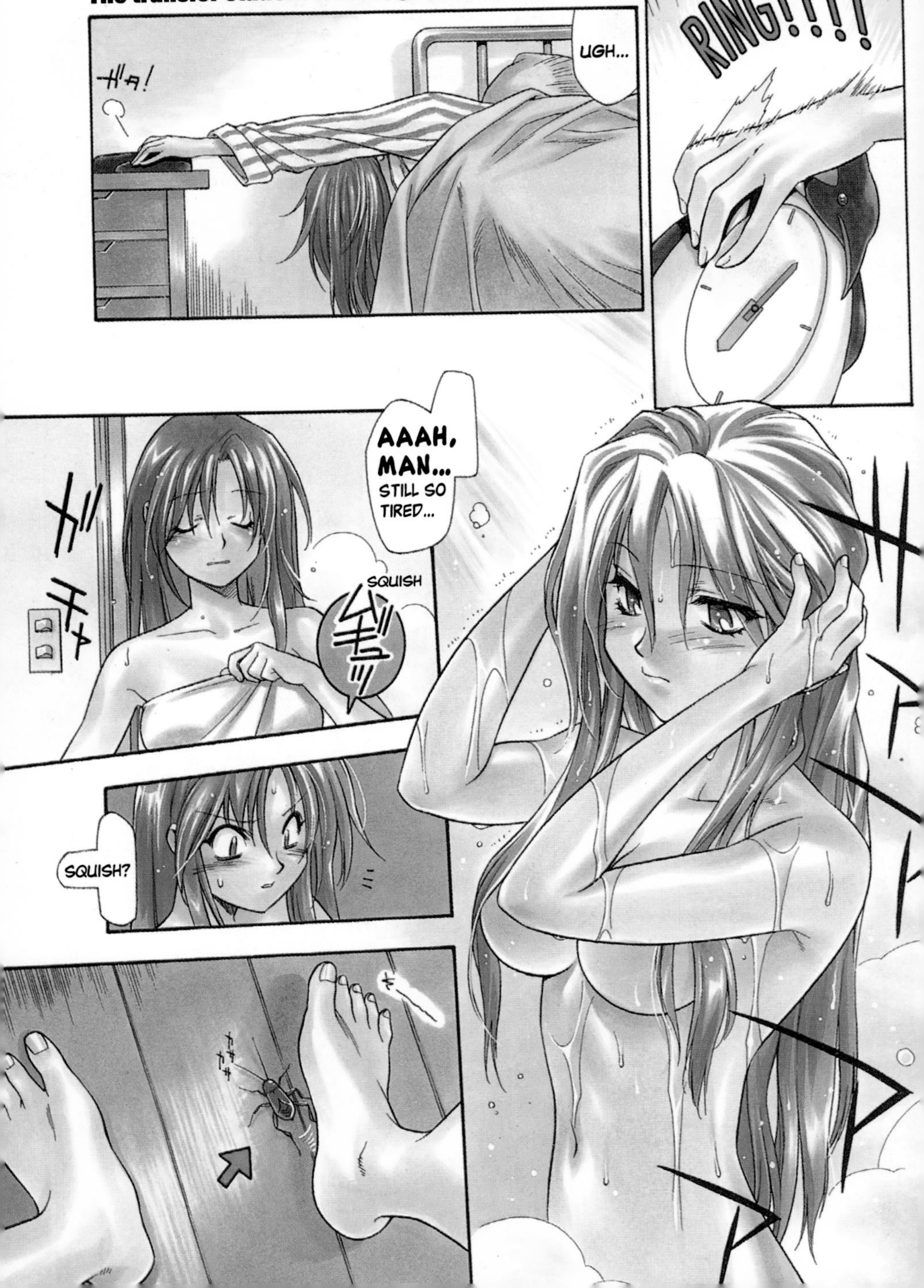
RING!!!!
UGH...
AAAH, MAN... STILL SO TIRED...
SQUISH
SQUISH?